THIS COMPOSITE VOICE
The Role of W. B. Yeats in James Merrill's Poetry

MAJOR LITERARY AUTHORS
VOLUME 24

Studies in Major Literary Authors

Outstanding Dissertations
Volume 24

Edited by
William Cain
Professor of English
Wellesley College

A Routledge Series

Studies in Major Literary Authors
William E. Cain, *General Editor*

1. The Wayward Nun of Amherst
Emily Dickinson in the Medieval Women's Visionary Tradition
Angela Conrad

2. Philip Roth Considered
The Concentrationary Universe of the American Writer
Steven Milowitz

3. The Pusher and the Sufferer
An Unsentimental Reasing of Moby Dick
Suzanne Stein

4. Henry James as a Biographer
A Self among Others
Cathy Moses

5. Joycean Frames
Film and the Fiction of James Joyce
Thomas Burkdall

6. Joseph Conrad and the Art of Sacrifice
The Evolution of the Scpegoat Theme in Joseph Conrad's Fiction
Andrew Mozina

7. Technique and Sensibility in the Fiction and Poetry of Raymond Carver
Arthur F. Bethea

8. Shelley's Textual Seductions
Plotting Utopia in the Erotic and Political Works
Samuel Lyndon Gladden

9. "All the World's a Stage"
Dramatic Sensibility in Mary Shelley's Novels
Charlene E. Bunnell

10. "Thoughts Painfully Intense"
Hawthorne and the Invalid Author
James N. Mancall

11. Sex Theories and the Shaping of Two Moderns
Hemingway and H. D.
Deirdre Anne (McVicker) Pettipiece

12. Word Sightings
Visual Apparatus and Verbal Reality in Stevens, Bishop and O'Hara
Sarah Riggs

13. Delicate Pursuit
Discretion in Henry James and Edith Wharton
Jessica Levine

14. Gertrude Stein and Wallace Stevens
The Performance of Modern Consciousness
Sara J. Ford

15. Lost City
Fitzgerald's New York
Lauraleigh O'Meara

16. Social Dreaming
Dickens and the Fairy Tale
Elaine Ostry

17. Patriarchy and Its Discontents
Sexual Politics in Selected Novels and Stories of Thomas Hardy
Joanna Devereux

18. A New Matrix for Modernism
A Study of the Lives and Poetry of Charlotte Mew and Anna Wickham
Nelljean McConeghey Rice

19. Who Reads *Ulysses*?
The Rhetoric of the Joyce Wars and the Common Reader
Julie Sloan Brannon

20. Naked Liberty and the World of Desire
Elements of Anarchism in the Work of D. H. Lawrence
Simon Casey

21. The Machine that Sings
Modernism, Hart Crane, and the Culture of the Body
Gordon Tapper

22. T. S. Eliot's Civilized Savage
Religious Eroticism and Poetics
Laurie J. MacDiarmid

23. The Carver Chronotope
Inside the Life-World of Raymond Carver's Fiction
G. P. Lainsbury

THIS COMPOSITE VOICE
The Role of W. B. Yeats in James Merrill's Poetry

Mark Bauer

LONDON AND NEW YORK

Published 2003 by Routledge
2 Park Square, Milton Park, Abingdon, Oxon OX14 4RN
52 Vanderbilt Avenue, New York, NY 10017

First issued in paperback 2020

Routledge is an imprint of the Taylor & Francis Group, an informa business

Copyright © 2003 by Taylor & Francis

All rights reserved. No part of this book may be reprinted or reproduced or utilised in any form or by any electronic, mechanical, or other means, now known or hereafter invented, including photocopying and recording, or in any information storage or retrieval system, without permission in writing from the publishers.

Notice:
Product or corporate names may be trademarks or registered trademarks, and are used only for identification and explanation without intent to infringe.

Library of Congress Cataloging-in-Publication Data
Bauer, Mark.
    This composite voice : the role of W. B. Yeats in James Merrill's poetry / by Mark Bauer.
     p. cm. — (Studies in major literary authors ; v. 24)
    Includes bibliographical references and index
    ISBN 0-415-96637-X (hardcover : alk. paper)
    1.Merrill, James Ingram—Criticism and interpretation. 2. Yeats, W. B. (William Butler), 1865–1939—Influence. 3. American poetry—Irish influences.. I. Title. II. Series.
PS3525.E6645 Z57 2003
811'.54—dc21   2003000722

ISBN 13: 978-1-138-99827-8 (pbk)
ISBN 13: 978-0-415-96637-5 (hbk)

WE SPOKE TO U
WITH THIS COMPOSITE VOICE
(ITS FORMULA BASED ON YR OWN)
THAT 1ST YEAR OF YOUR LOVE
  (*Sandover* 265)

Contents

ACKNOWLEDGMENTS	xi
INTRODUCTION	xiii

CHAPTER ONE — 3
Prelude: Merrillian Influence, Kimon Friar, and Yeats — 3
Yeats in Merrill's Early Poems: Moving from Floodedness to Struggle — 32

CHAPTER TWO — 51
Prelude: First Readings of Yeats's *A Vision* — 51
Braving the Fire: Postures of Nonchalance in the Early Ouija Board Poems — 56
Interlude: Returning to Yeats's *A Vision* — 83
Merrill's Dialogues of Self and Soul — 85

CHAPTER THREE — 105
Prelude: Reading Yeats's *Essays and Introductions* — 105
Observing Yeats through Merrill's Changing Lights — 110
   I. Yeats in "Ephraim": The Master's Ghostly Presence — 111
   II. Yeats in *Mirabell*: Parody and Affiliation — 118
   III. Yeats in *Scripts*: Abjection and Apotheosis — 132
   IV. Yeats in "The Higher Keys": Fading into Mastery — 150

CHAPTER FOUR — 155
A Haunted Mastery: Yeats after *Sandover* — 155
Coda: Yeats's Merrill, Merrill's Bloom — 170

APPENDIX A
Merrill's Antithetical Use of "Sailing to Byzantium" in "About the Phoenix"   185

APPENDIX B
Merrill's Early Reading in Metaphysical and Psychological Topics   295

APPENDIX C
Manuscript Variations in *Mirabell* and *Scripts*   197

NOTES   201
WORKS CITED   255
INDEX   263
COPYRIGHT ACKNOWLEDGMENTS   271

Acknowledgments

MANY PEOPLE HAVE HELPED GUIDE AND SUPPORT THIS STUDY, BUT I particularly want to thank J. D. McClatchy, James Merrill's great friend and literary executor, for opening the doors of Merrill's Stonington home to me and for making available invaluable materials from Merrill's libraries and papers. Without his generous cooperation from the beginning to the end of this project, my understanding of the depth of Merrill's poetic engagement with Yeats would have been incalculably diminished. Professor Harold Bloom gave graciously of his time in talking to me about his friendship and conversations with Merrill, and Professors Stephen Yenser (Merrill's other literary executor) and Judith Moffett have also kindly responded to my inquiries, for which I am very grateful. I have also been helped in tracing references and in gaining a sense of Merrill's reading by the catalog Timothy Young, an archival consultant, has compiled of Merrill's libraries at Stonington, Key West, and his apartment in New York. I also want to thank Dr. Jack W. C. Hagstrom for his bibliographic assistance and keen eye. All of Merrill's unpublished writings are copyrighted by The Literary Estate of James Merrill at Washington University and are used with its kind permission.

Of the many people at the University of California at Davis who have assisted and encouraged my work on the original dissertation, I especially want to thank Professors Alan Williamson, Joanne Diehl, and Kari Lokke for their critical support. I am particularly fortunate in having had the deft and sure guidance of Professor Williamson, whose letters and e-mails from Davis to New Haven, Connecticut, kept me on track, even with a continent between us. I also owe heartfelt thanks to my friends Aidan Wasley, Niki Parisier, and Susan Rieger for their stalwart encouragement of my writing and research. And for his countless helps and reassurances, large and small, and for his loving presence in my life, I especially want to thank my partner, Joe Gordon, to whom this book is dedicated.

Introduction

ESPECIALLY SINCE THE PUBLICATION OF *THE CHANGING LIGHT AT SANDOVER*, readers of James Merrill's poetry have noted affinities (and pointed contrasts) between Merrill and Yeats. Yet none has thus far undertaken to uncover the extensive history and particularly vexed nature of this lifelong poetic relationship. To this end, this study draws on little-known biographical material, uncollected poems, manuscript variants, and annotations found in Merrill's copies of Yeats's poems, essays, and *A Vision*, as well as a close examination of Merrill's better-known writing, to establish the many ways in which Merrill contends with the older poet's haunting personality and poetic accomplishment. *THIS COMPOSITE VOICE* also takes up the question of poetic influence in a broader sense by both employing and calling into question Harold Bloom's theories of influence. It shows, for example, how Merrill's homosexuality challenges assumptions of Bloom's Oedipal model and concludes with a discussion of how Merrill seeks to over-master the "master critic" by incorporating Bloom's theories into the subject matter and structure of *The Changing Light at Sandover*, Merrill's most ambitious poem.

Merrill himself first starts to acknowledge the influence of W. B. Yeats in the late 1960s, but in ways that consistently downplay the persuasiveness, endurance, and importance of that influence. When Merrill talks about Yeats it is as a youthful enthusiasm, qualified by other enthusiasms and by his own callowness ("Interview with Brown" 43; *Different* 15). He may hint that Yeats has affected his language in important ways but breaks off before elaborating. Asked, for example, about earlier poets that might be relevant to his work, he tells Donald Sheehan of his passion for Elinor Wylie: ". . . the most magical rhyming we've ever had. There's a glaze of perfection to contend with, but I ate it up; it never put me off—not at least until I went on to Yeats" (35).[1] We are left to speculate about just how and why Merrill "went on to Yeats" after his passion for Wylie's "glaze of perfection."

At least two critics writing before Merrill's "Book of Ephraim" have discussed Yeatsian correspondences in Merrill's work; and, subsequently, many have mentioned similarities or listed poems that show Yeats's influence. Yet only one poem written before "Ephraim" has received extensive examination in light of Yeats's influence.[2] Leslie Brisman's 1985 reading of "Willowware Cup" shows Merrill writing in close response to Yeats's "Lapis Lazuli" and that poem's stance of "earthly transcendence." It also shows how Merrill's poem "covertly describ[es] a relationship to Yeats that involves both great attraction, and great need to represent Yeats as a figure for a past or a rejected self, over and against which Merrill will define what is most his own" (Brisman 198, 191–2). This study takes its cue from Brisman's findings and demonstrates both how pervasive Yeats's influence has been on Merrill and how assiduously Merrill has worked to deflect attention to this relation.

For example, in speaking about strategies of allusion at a 1982 symposium on "Literary Tradition," Merrill chooses to allude to Keats rather than Yeats when referring to "Willowware Cup." As if to signal his interest in controlling the reader's awareness of the direction of his allusions, Merrill remarks, "Whether I wanted to bring it to light or not, to make it explicit or not, was entirely up to me." He continues, "I think of a poem I wrote twenty years ago, a description of a willowware teacup. Luckily I didn't connect my poem, until I had finished it, with a famous poem about a vessel with figures on the outside and images that were both idyllic and violent" ("Literary" 28). Merrill's allusion to "Ode on a Grecian Urn" is apt; but Keats's poem has much less to do with "Willowware Cup" than Yeats's, so that Merrill's remarks about control and his arch deflection of interest onto Keats seem curiously motivated to direct attention away from his relationship with Yeats.[3]

Not until the "Book of Ephraim," and the subsequent books that make up *The Changing Light at Sandover*, does Merrill explicitly acknowledge, in his poetry, that Yeats is a particularly relevant figure. But even here Yeats's role is vexed. In the Sandover books, Merrill abruptly shifts the nature of his poetic project. Now self-consciously following in the line of visionary poets extending from Dante and Milton, through Blake, Shelley, and Yeats, Merrill, for the first time, has to contend more or less explicitly with a host of strong parallels between his own and Yeats's careers and poetic concerns. Like Yeats, Merrill moved from an early aesthetic period to a middle period focusing on thwarted love, to poems informed by visionary experience and a freer, more public, and more directly authoritative voice. Though Yeats worked in the theater more than Merrill, both poets shared similar attitudes about the experience.[4] As poets, Yeats and Merrill returned to the same figures again and again: in Merrill's case, the emblematic bird, mirror, water, fire, and the child of a broken home. Few other poets have made such repeated or consistent use of elements of his own autobiography as Yeats did with Maude Gonne and other contemporaries or Merrill with his parents' divorce and with his lovers, particularly Strato and David Jackson. Merrill's autobiographical stance is also always informed by a very Yeatsian awareness of the Mask, of personality as a contested artifice, and

Introduction

the ongoing project and tension in the desire of perfecting both the life and the work.

Both poets saw theirs as a "myth-starved culture" and wrote their "mythologies" to answer both personal and poetic needs and as contributions to the imaginative lives of their readers.[5] In Merrill's occultism, thematic and situational parallels also abound. Yeats wrote what his "instructors" dictated through his wife; similarly, Merrill transcribed and reworked what had been spelled out on the Ouija board beneath his and DJ's hands.[6] In both cases, contact with the spirit world depends on a marriage relationship. In both systems the spirit world importantly depends on the living, and the self is revealed to be a composite and momentary phenomenon systematically recycling through vales of "soul making." Both poets present spirit communicators that take a determining interest in their work and that authorize progressively more authoritative accounts of human psychology, history, and eschatology; and both poets maintain a pragmatic and shifting blend of skepticism and credulity regarding the nature of their experiences.

Given such parallels, it is not surprising that Merrill's relationship to Yeats becomes more anxious once he starts "Ephraim" and begins to tread so clearly in Yeats's shadow.[7] The chief sign of this anxiety is the way Merrill downplays Yeats's authority throughout *Sandover*, where Merrill's chief tactic is to construct Yeats as a shuffling, mistaken character in the poem's play of otherworldly voices.[8] In "Ephraim," Yeats is "POOR OLD YEATS / STILL SIMPLIFYING," and Yeats's *A Vision* is merely a trying "maze of inner logic, dogma, dates" (S. 14). In *Mirabell*, Yeats and Hugo represent dubious "intellectual machismo" and "doctor everything their voices said" (S. 154); Yeats's occult work is "an immense conceit" given utterance between his wife's snores (S. 178). He is acknowledged as the power that moves DJ's hand on the Ouija board (S. 217), but his relation to DJ, who is called "HAND" by the higher powers, clearly subordinates him to JM, called "SCRIBE." Whereas Merrill accumulates the mountain of transcript that he fashions into his poem, DJ feels a lump forming on his palm and asks, "Is Yeats raising a molehill?" (S. 220). In *Scripts*, the belittling relation between DJ and Yeats continues. DJ wonders: "I fumble / Along, JM finds answers, I feel dumb. / Is that Yeats too, still making the wrong sense?" (S. 424).

When Yeats finally does speak at the end of the trilogy, his voice is tentative. He worries, "WAS I THEN WRONG . . . / TO BUILD MY WINDING STAIR OF MOONSTRUCK-STONE?" (S. 474). "I OFTEN FEAR / [he says about his poetic power] I LEFT IT ALL BACK IN BYZANTIUM" (S. 481). It is only at the end of *Scripts*, after Yeats praises JM (S. 486) and then thanks him for revising his stanza ("I MADE A HASH. YOU'VE MADE IT CLEAR. / THANK YOU.")—that is, only after Merrill fashions himself "*il miglior fabbro*"—that JM replies, "Oh please, Mr Yeats, you who have always / Been such a force in my life!" (S. 492). This assertion, however true, is also highly qualified by the conventions of polite response to praise and pointedly allows ironic reading. Even the volume's "Coda" describes Yeats as a "FOOTNOTE" to the present "TEXT," as if Yeats were now the later and derivative poet. This final section characterizes

Yeats's "WEARY PROUD FORBEARING SMILE / AS OF AN UNREAD VISION ON THE SHELF," so that with this arch, dismissive gesture Merrill completes his overt campaign of diminishing the authority of Yeats and his Vision (S. 527).

This last gesture of making Yeats seem the later and supplementary poet serves as an excellent example of what Harold Bloom terms Apophrades, or a poem's "attempt to make of its belatedness an earliness" with regard to the precursor poet (*Map* 100). As we shall see, Bloom's theory of poetic influence provides particularly apt aesthetic and psychological explanations for what motivates Merrill's campaign of diminishment against Yeats, as well as for a number of his particular strategies and the overall progress of that campaign. Yet it should not be taken as a wholly adequate model for discussing Merrill's relations with past poets more generally.[9]

Edward Said rightly calls Bloom's theory a "radically masculine theory of poetic composition, or poetic interpretation, and more, of poetic existence" in that for Bloom poetry is always both the quest for and struggle against the authority and originality of the True Father and his privileged relationship with the Muse (23). This Oedipal drama is a matter of life and death for the poet, as poet, since for Bloom the precursor's poem has already done what the younger poet would do, namely (in language and in his own reading) "it has survived death" (*Map* 19). His poetry is thus the younger poet's means of rebelling against the potentially overwhelming scandal of "being spoken to by a dead man (the precursor) outrageously more alive than [the poet] himself"; so too, if the younger poet is to have any poetic life of his own, he "must *misinterpret* the father, by the crucial act of misprision, which is the rewriting of the father"(Ibid.).

Thus, for Bloom, Satan's Hell is a misreading of his Father's Heaven; Milton struggles with Spenser, "and this struggle both form[s] and malform[s]" him; Wordsworth's Great Ode is "shadowed" by its anxious rewriting of Milton's *Lycidas,* and Blake writes to "correct" Milton even more thoroughly (*Anxiety* 20–22, 10–11; *Map* 83). Yeats is similarly "formed and malformed" by his struggle with his composite poetic fathers, Shelley and Blake;[10] and as, I will argue in part, Merrill too is shaped by his ongoing quarrel with Yeats.

For Bloom, poetry is "a disciplined perverseness"; it is "misunderstanding, misinterpretation, misalliance" (*Anxiety* 95). As well as this insight about the precursor's reach into the future and the younger poet's anxious and belated efforts to rewrite the past, Bloom's theory offers a progressive anatomy of six ways in which a poet, in the "person" of his poem, imposes his revisionary misinterpretations upon his precursor. These "revisionary ratios," which may characterize aspects of a poem as well as aspects of a poet's career, follow a pattern that derives from Bloom's Kabbalistic account of creation, which moves from what he calls modes of "limitation" to modes of "representation." In this model, the first acts of creation are always characterized by restriction, withdrawal, emptying; and only after the vessel has been broken may the poet build forth, re-present, his contribution to creation (*Map* 5). Thus, the limiting ratio of Clinamen, or swerving away from the precursor, is followed by the rep-

Introduction xvii

resentative ratio of Tessera, in which the poet completes or extends the parent-poem, "as though the precursor had failed to go far enough" (*Anxiety* 14). The cycle then swings back to the limiting ratio of Kenosis, or the emptying-out or deflation of both poet and precursor, followed by the representative ratio of Daemonization, in which the poet opens himself to "a power in the parent-poem" but a power more properly from beyond the precursor himself (Ibid. 15). These ratios are followed in turn by the limiting Askesis, or curtailing a part of the poet's "own human and imaginative endowment," and the representative Apophrades, in which the poet "in his own final phase" holds his poem open to the precursor so that it now seems "as though the later poet himself had written the precursor's characteristic work" (Ibid. 15–16).

This summary of Bloom's theory is meant merely to suggest the basic outlines of its particularly masculine, Oedipal dynamic and the modes of poetic misprision Bloom has identified. As we shall see, Bloom's account of an anxious relation between poet and precursor and his six "revisionary ratios" provide an uncannily accurate description of many important features of Merrill's poetic responses to Yeats, not just in *The Changing Light of Sandover*, but throughout Merrill's career. Initially, in the poems of his first decades, Merrill moves from a period of "flooded apprenticeship" (Bloom *Anxiety* 16) through a period of struggle to assert his mastery and vocation, into a period where struggle with Yeats as precursor poet becomes part of his mastery, and then into a final period mixing assurance and doubt, strength and decline. Merrill's poetry is haunted by the figure and the accomplishment of W. B. Yeats in a relationship that takes on particular vehemence when Merrill assumes the spiritualist, mythopoetic mantle so firmly identified with Yeats. In the Sandover books, Yeats becomes all but explicitly the poetic father Merrill would deny, just as Auden is the benign father he consciously adopts. Yet as much as Merrill's relation with Yeats corresponds to the patterns propounded by Bloom, Merrill is also determined that the critic should not have the last word. In *Sandover*, Merrill's voices mock the critic ["HIDEOUS BLOOMS . . . STIR UP RIVALRY AT HIGH LEVELS" (S. 193)] while Merrill himself endeavors to subsume Bloom's theories into a more comprehensive vision of poetic influence.[11]

In this study, the opening section of Chapter One shows the young Merrill to be profoundly self-divided between maternal and paternal influences, both as a poet and as a person. It argues that Merrill's "maternal muse" and unfailingly benign notions of poetic influence operate as screens allowing him to fend off explicit engagement with the Oedipal struggles characteristic of his ongoing relationship with Yeats. This section further argues that, for both poetic and personal reasons, Yeats becomes Merrill's masculine precursor *par excellence*. It also points to Merrill's erotically charged poetic apprenticeship under Kimon Friar as strongly determinative of the aims and aversions of much of his subsequent career. Turning more closely to the early poetry, the chapter then examines how, in Bloom's terms, Merrill's early poetry moved from a Yeats-saturated period of poetic "floodedness" to the self-quarreling "struggle" with the older poet that characterizes Merrill's more mature work. It argues that Yeats was the presiding poetic figure at the crucial scene Merrill's poetic calling *(Dichterberuf)* in Ravenna in 1952 and that Merrill's ambivalent quarrel with Yeats's "Condition of Fire" and passages from *Per Amica Silentia Lunae* underlies an important group of his early "fire poems."

The second chapter introduces previously unstudied annotations from Merrill's copy of Yeats's *A Vision* to show the ways in which, as a reader, Merrill turned to Yeats to find perspectives on personal questions and on his own occult experiences. The chapter also considers the ways in which Merrill deploys Yeatsian allusion in works that address Merrill's early experiences at the Ouija board and how, in later poems, Merrill continues to mine his productive ambivalence toward Yeats. What we will observe is that Merrill often employs the devices of glancing allusion, deliberate obscurity, irony, and a characteristic lightness of tone to cultivate a posture of nonchalance toward Yeats. Nonetheless, at pivotal moments in the poetry before *Sandover*, Merrill also strongly engages with the older poet as part of his own ongoing dialogue between self and soul.

Chapter Three opens by examining Merrill's notes in Yeats's *Essays and Introductions* as evidence of his returning to Yeats for guidance as he composes *Sandover*, his multi-voiced, occult epic. The chapter then traces Merrill's increasingly explicit engagement with Yeats through each of *Sandover's* major divisions: from first establishing Yeats as a significant but pointedly absent presence in "Ephraim," to the parodic deployments of Yeatsian imagery and aspects of Yeats's *Vision* system in *Mirabell* and the tellingly ambivalent moment of Yeats's "appearance" in *Scripts*, to Yeats's continued ghostly, but authorizing presence in "The Higher Keys." This chapter also draws on manuscript variants and autograph annotations to trace Merrill's deliberate shaping of Yeats's role in the poem.

The fourth chapter begins with a discussion of how Merrill continues, both in his memoir and in poems after *Sandover*, to draw on Yeats, now with considerably less ambivalence but with no loss of authority. This chapter argues that the later poetry increasingly shows Merrill's mastery of the internal divisions that have colored his earlier poetic relation with Yeats. The chapter concludes with a section that examines how Yeats operates as a "voice of power" in Merrill's poetry and how Merrill's poetic practice reclaims what Yeats considers the False Mask of poetic Dispersal. This final section of the chapter also returns to questions of influence, arguing that however much Bloomian theory may be particularly relevant to the relationship between Merrill and Yeats, that same relationship suggests the limitations of Bloom's agonistic approaches.

THIS COMPOSITE VOICE

Chapter One

PRELUDE: MERRILLIAN INFLUENCE, KIMON FRIAR, AND YEATS

IN HIS 1995 APPRECIATION, WRITTEN SHORTLY AFTER MERRILL'S DEATH, AND again in a recent article on the figure of Merrill's mother in his poetry, J. D. McClatchy characterizes what he terms Merrill's "split personality" and how it was represented in and thrown into "stronger relief" by his parents' divorce:

> As much his father's son as his mother's boy, he had a temperament that by turns revealed what we may as well call paternal and maternal sides. He was drawn equally to the rational and the fanciful, the passionate and the ironic, America and Europe. And, from the very beginning, his ambition as a poet was—like the child attempting to reconcile his warring parents—to harmonize those two sides of his life. ("Braving" 50)

> [Merrill was] as much heir to Father Time as to Mother Nature. Mind vs. style, reason vs. sensation, idea and fact, . . . German and French, verse and language, legend and realism—the list could be extended through nearly every impulse or setting in the poems, which tingle with such oppositions, such divided loyalties. ("Inner Room" 5)

Both as poet and as a person, Merrill is animated by the division between what McClatchy calls "paternal and maternal characteristics" (Ibid.) In his efforts to construct double-minded harmonies that would reconcile his divided loyalties, Merrill vacillates in his allegiance not just between maternal beauties and paternal power, but between a whole range of moral and aesthetic constructions or introjections of both the Good Mother/Bad Mother and the Good Father/Bad Father. Early in *The Changing Light at Sandover*, Merrill affirms that "my own mother . . . [is] the breath drawn after every line, / Essential to its making as to mine" (S. 84). Yet as well as this sustaining maternal breath, she is also "my dragon" (Ibid.). She is identified in *Sandover* with Joanna ("Smoke pouring from her nostrils"), the "abhorred" character distilled from Merrill's "destructive / Anima," whom the "symbolic apparatus" of the lost novel requires to be "'routed'" before Leo, a Merrill-character, can be healed and his spiritual child (the poem) be born (S. 33, 67,35, 71). Likewise, Merrill's father both attracts and repels. He is represented as the predatory sexual shadow that "afflicts" both child and mother ("Scenes of Childhood"); his "soul eclipsed by twin black pupils, sex / And business" ("The Broken Home"). But he is also depicted as the worldly and "very kind" Ali Pasha ("Yánnina"), who, in the recuperative vision of Merrill's memoir, "remains an almost perversely mild and undemanding presence in my thoughts, triggering none of the imaginary confrontations I have with my mother. . . . [In his company] I didn't care if I ever wrote another poem; I lay back, contented, in the very arms of Time" (*Different* 42).

In these lines we begin to see what is at stake for Merrill in these parental representations. His mother and father both threaten and sustain him. Both guarantee that the divisions in Merrill's life and the work are never simple. It is, after all, Joanna, the dragon mother, who carries with her the emblem of Merrill's later poetry, "the gift-wrapped Ouija board" (S. 35), and it is Merrill's idealized father whose generous contentment turns out to "cost more than it was worth" in terms of poetic disengagement ("I didn't care if I ever wrote another poem.") and "an almost limitless boredom" (*Different* 42). Parental figures and impulses proliferate in Merrill's work, creating a poetics of surrogacy, as well as surrogacy's inherent themes of love and loss. Out of the divisions of his Broken Home, and out of his own self-divisions, maternal and paternal, Merrill again and again strives both to be and to make the metrical child that mends life's "scissorings" ("Up and Down, 2/ The Emerald," "Yánnina"). He counts it "Barbarity / To serve uncooked one's bloody tranche de vie" and, instead, insists on "style. / Poetic justice," that recuperative "spell / Which in mid sentence, turn[s] iron to sunlight"—while managing to give his readers both the cold, dividing iron and the healing sunlight (S. 496).

In Merrill's work, questions of maternal and paternal ambitions, characteristics, and influence soon raise the question of poetic influence itself. Many besides Merrill have noted the "parental" role played by Proust and Elizabeth Bishop in his poetry, and by "Maria [Mitsotáki] and Auden in the Sandover books" (*Recitative* 7), and Helen Vendler pointedly asks why the poem needs "a ghostly father and a ghostly mother" ("Interview with Vendler" 51). In keeping with Merrill's recuperative ambitions, Merrill's remarks about poetic influence characterize the process as invariably benign, sociable, "amenable." As we shall see, he suggests a model of poetic influence that is more or less maternal and gay-inflected in its positive overtones. But, as we shall also see, particularly with regard to Merrill's relationship with Yeats, quite another model of poetic influence—one characterized by Oedipal rivalry with the father—also clearly obtains. Although Merrill's anxious relations with Yeats's poetry and personality continue until at least the last decade of his life, Merrill disavows any sense of rivalry or competition toward Yeats or any other poet.

Instead, Merrill's discussions of poetic influence emphasize two strands (which, of course, intermingle): one, a free and deliberate appropriation of congenial styles and material (the image here is that of the "good student") and the other, a passive receptivity toward the shaping power of other voices, other intelligences (where the poet becomes the "malleable vessel" or "modest Scribe"). Whether active or passive, mimetic craftsman or Sensitive Plant, discerning shopper or "docile taker[]-in of seed" (S. 154), the poet reveals attitudes of adult wish fulfillment stemming from a child's enduring needs and desires.

In the "congenial" account, Merrill celebrates what attracts him to a particular writer: Wylie's "magical" rhymes and intricate stanzas ("Interview with Sheehan" 35), the "gaudy" diversity of Stevens' diction (Ibid., "James Merrill at Home" 23), Pope's lightness of manner ("James Merrill: Education" 3), Rilke's thematic "emphasis on the *acceptance* of pain and loneliness" ("Interview with Brown" 43, emphasis in original), Mallarmé's hermeticism ("Interview with Boatwright" 39; "James Merrill at Home" 23), Auden's captivating facility and range ("James Merrill at Home" 24), Cavafy's "desert-dry tone, his mirage-like technical effects" ("James Merrill" Bolt 40). In this regard, Merrill depicts his reading as a scene of active poetic instruction: "Joyce teaches us to immerse the mythical elements in a well-known setting; Cocteau teaches us to immerse them in a contemporary spoken idiom" ("Interview with Sheehan" 31); "I remember reading *The Sea and the Mirror* when I was in the army (just the place for that) and being dazzled by the range of forms, which meant most to me at that time. Certainly I was inspired to try some of those things myself" ("Interview with Brown" 42);

> [With Stevens' *Notes Toward a Supreme Fiction*] I found myself basking in a climate that Proust might have called one of 'involuntary philosophy.' A world of painterly particulars . . . charged with novel meanings; or potentially charged with them; or alternately charged with thought and (by the enchantment of language) absolved from thought as well. I at once set about writing poems in which colorful scenery gave rise to questions about the nature of reality. (*Recitative* 117)1

Merrill also names two writers, Proust and Dante, who "have remained emblematic, throughout my life, of what a writer can achieve" ("James Merrill on Poetry" 5): Proust as "a writer of sentences and a viewer of society . . . showed us there was nothing too commonplace or too trivial which once seen as a phenomenon either of light or of social behavior couldn't be dwelt on in perfect seriousness" ("James Merrill at Home" 22); and Dante's *Commedia*, because its "energy and splendor," "sustaining divinatory intelligence," "great concision," and "wealth of diction and detail," excited Merrill's enduring interest in similar achievements (*Recitative* 88, 89, 93). This seemingly un-anxious poetic modeling is manifestly not what Harold Bloom characterizes as that "happy" relation, "causing no anxieties, where a stronger poet appropriates from a weaker one" (*Figures* 12). No one would argue that either Proust or Dante is the "weaker" artist; nonetheless, both provide Merrill with important means for coming to terms with Yeats's more problematic achievements. Proust sponsors Merrill's commitment to various forms of human temporality and various modes and objects of attention against Yeats's more apocalyptic notions of time and subject matter; likewise, Dante sponsors Merrill's range of diction, his rising and falling "middle flight" in the service of an alternate (and prior) sublimity.

Merrill places Proust and Dante "beyond anxiety," not because they are weaker, but because each seems safely beyond compare: Proust by being supremely an artist of prose, that "mildly nightmarish medium, to which," Merrill anxiously asserts, "*there is no end*"(*Recitative* xiii, Merrill's emphasis); and Dante by being supremely an artist of "passionate faith," rather than of "our intrepid doubts" (Ibid. 87). By adopting the role of the "good student" toward both these lofty and other lesser writers (Elinor Wylie is the principal example), Merrill not only adopts the stance of earlier modernists who famously "chose their influences where it suited them," seeming to make up or recreate traditions at will, and for whom "the past was a museum, and tradition a chest of souvenirs" (Stade 499); but he also makes of such a stance an "exemplary" screen-narrative, behind which more problematic poets exert their influence unacknowledged.

I do not want to argue that Merrill's "good student" is perfectly successful in insulating him from the anxieties attendant on making Proust and Dante emblematic of what a writer can achieve. Proust's prose, as prose, that is in its very "endlessness," raises the specter of mortality for Merrill. It is, as Merrill remarks, "coterminous with one's very life" (*Recitative* xiii). Similarly, Dante's faith awakens fears that undermine pragmatic complacencies of judgment and one's sense of self: "To believe, however, that Dante had in any real sense seen God threatened both the poem and us. Who wanted song to curdle overnight into mere scripture, or himself to be trivialized in the glare of too much truth?" (*Recitative* 87). Rather, what I would like to suggest here is that Merrill's image of himself as the active "good student" of poetic influence allows him to appropriate from both greater and lesser lights in his campaign against Yeats. Bloom notes the "happy" posture in which a stronger appropriates from weaker poets to defend against the "influx" of the precursor (*Figures* 12). What Merrill lets us see is that a younger poet may also appropriate from stronger writers in his quest to avoid another strong poet's influence, so long as he marks these writers as sufficiently distant, sufficiently different, or sufficiently "amenable."

In the other, "receptive," strand of his thinking about influence, Merrill emphasizes his own passivity before the independent powers of music, language, and story. This is the strand that Merrill acknowledges when he characterizes himself (and his lover, DJ) as "more the docile [intellectual] takers-in of seed" (S. 154). This is the strand Merrill elaborates into the theory of "cloning" developed in *Mirabell* and that he again draws upon when he compares "we the living" to Japanese puppets in "Prose of Departure":

> Seldom do we the living, for that matter, feel more "ourselves" than when spoken through, or motivated, by "invisible" forces such as these ["the overruling passions, the social or genetic imperatives, that propel a given character"]. It is especially true if, like a puppet overcome by woe, we also appear to be struggling free of them.
>
> <div align="right">(<i>The Inner Room</i> 67)</div>

The freeing hyperbole of puppetry aside, it is in this last sentence that Merrill comes closest to a Bloomian conception of influence. The poet appears to be most fully himself, most "original," when struggling to be free of his precursors, who have already determined the "overruling passions" and imperatives of his consciousness as a poet. And yet this struggle to be free of influence is itself part, and perhaps the greatest part, of how influence operates in shaping an original performance. This remark, perhaps because it does not directly address matters of poetic influence, is also one of Merrill's very few explicit acknowledgments of the ambiguous but central role of struggle in a poet's engagement with the forces that want to speak through and motivate him.

We first see this "shaping" power of seemingly "external" circumstance in Merrill's reminiscences of being read to or told stories as a child. After recalling a risible story told by his governess, "Mademoiselle," Merrill comments, "I too was being imprinted there and then" (*Recitative* 4). Later, Merrill's own reading attains such shaping force: "I've often felt something like that 'cloning' in my own life. What if somebody had not told me to read Proust? The act of sitting there reading; I mean it was as if my mind was being permanently changed and tampered with" ("Exploring" 424).

Here "tampered with" recalls the transformative effect of opera in "Matinees" ["'My father having tampered with your mouth, / From now on, metal, music, myth / Will seem to taint its words.'"] and, by all accounts, the opera, too, is an early influence of just this shaping sort:

> Thus opera was from the start an education less musical than sentimental. . . . We were the puppets! . . . Surrendering to adult voices in the darkened house or singing along in my room to a drinking-song whose flip side was a prayer, I found myself trying on emotions till then inconceivable, against the day when I should be old enough to wear them in public." (*Different* 113–14)

Merrill's metaphor in this passage is drawn from the externalizing conceit of emotions as clothes (as is Yeats's "A Coat"); but the sense persists that in providing an emotional wardrobe, opera or song also instills (or installs) particular emotions, thus "tampering" with what is "inside" ["what Thaïs inwardly suffered, what mad Lucia, what even her heartless brother and nitwit husband 'felt'" (*Different* 114)].

Merrill's advice to prospective poets reflects both the active and receptive strands of his thought: "Learn if possible from reading—and imitating—the poets that enchant you.... Travel if you can, cultivate 'alienation' if you like. There's no need to wallow in the assumptions of your time and place, since your work will reflect them, whatever you do" ("James Merrill on Poetry" 7, 22). Merrill seems at pains in these remarks to portray a poetic apprenticeship as an "empowering" mix of personal will and fatalism (one works hard to "imitate" what already "enchants"). Such a stance suggests a sensibility improbably untainted by melancholia or modern subjectivity, since in none of Merrill's remarks about poetic influence or education does he suggest that conflict or anxiety regarding previous poets plays any significant role in the making of a poet.[2] The most we hear about any such struggle is of some early "sibling rivalry," usually with Freddy Buechner at Lawrenceville.[3]

To a question from Ashley Brown ("By the time you started publishing, back in the 1940s, some young poets were almost painfully aware of the achievement of their predecessors—Eliot and Stevens and Auden and the rest—two generations of modernists. Did you feel their presence was something to resist?") Merrill responds:

> No, I don't think I ever felt that. They seemed very much their own men. They represented the immediate past. I felt no sense of competition, if you could call it that. If I had any sense of competition, it was with people at most five years older than I was. My reaction to Stevens, for instance, was merely that it was wonderful to mention strange colors along with big abstract words. (41–42)

In a later appreciation, Merrill praises Stevens' influential achievements saying, "all this was accomplished affably, without undue intimidation, so that the young practitioner could seek out his own faith, in his own time, and arrive (with any luck) at his own humanity" (*Recitative* 120).

In Merrill's emphasis on the "affability" of Stevens' example it is easy to overlook what, for Merrill, is at stake in matters of poetic influence: control over one's own beliefs, the progress of one's career, and, ultimately, the shape or content of one's character and relations to others. These are precisely the concerns that most often inform the struggles and anxieties between parent and child. They are also the concerns that that deeply inform Merrill's ambivalent relations with Kimon Friar and W. B. Yeats, as well as such Oedipally charged works as "Variations: White Stag, Black Bear," "Midas among the Goldenrods," *The Seraglio*, "Scenes of Childhood," *The (Diblos) Notebook*, and "The Broken Home."

Nevertheless, Merrill avoids any suggestion of Oedipal struggle in his accounts of poetic influence. Instead, he prefers to construct "the *unities* of home and world, and world and page" in terms of "surrogate parents" and prefers, too, the "safe ease and mystery of their influence: Proust and Elizabeth Bishop; Maria and Auden in the Sandover books" (*Recitative* 7, emphasis added). We notice at once that these literary and fictive "surrogates" are given and chosen in ways that real parents never are—Bloom argues that "no strong poet ... can choose his precursor, any more than any person can choose his father" (*Map* 12)—hence, perhaps, these figure's reassuring "safe ease" for Merrill and even, perhaps, their "mystery."[4]

In his 1993 memoir, *A Different Person*, Merrill goes so far as to offer Kimon Friar and Mina Diamantopoulos as "a benign revision of my own family romance: a father who read Yeats, a mother without prejudice—parents whose primary interests were cultural and whose mutual attraction, bewildering to a youngster, had burned off like fog in morning sunlight" (23). Here the fantasy seems, in part, to be that had Merrill had a "father who read Yeats," he would have been spared his ambivalent relations toward both father and Yeats (just as a "mother without prejudice" would have spared him his ambivalence about his own homosexuality).

Especially in *Sandover*, Merrill places himself (or "JM") in a child's idealizing position of both benefiting from and seeming to choose or create his parents. Maria Mitsotáki (MM) is "matter-of-fact mother" (S. 135), "Maman" to JM's "ENFANT"; a loving, amusing, solicitous companion, she is of the highest lineage [the daughter "at once" of a Prime Minister of Greece (S. 102) and of Nature (S. 467)], she sacrifices her life for the sake of "HER CHILD'S FURIOUS WORK" (S. 465). But she is also Plato and the child of Merrill's own "mother wit" (S. 464, 327).[5] WHA, on the other hand, is coach and advisor, colleague and guide, JM's older, other self. He is "father of forms" (S. 135) with the rough edges of Auden's own faith [THE CHURCH / MY DEARS THE DREARY DREARY DEAD BANG WRONG / CHURCH" (S. 128)], his own time, his own humanity, smoothed away by Merrill's posthumous revisions. Both surrogates are, have been, or want to be gay (S. 190). Each is a mirror self, a mirror which the child must shatter to release himself into his full power, but whose destruction (again, fancifully) leaves "undestroyed [the] heartscape" he rises from (S. 517).[6]

These are a child's enduring fantasies, shaped or censored to mask anxiety, in which the wished-for influence of the "good mother" dominates. [Even WHA is figured as a strict but self-reproachful "nurse" in Merrill's elegy (S. 306).] In remarks before the Academy of American Poets, Merrill speaks of his "maternal muse" and recounts: "My earliest writings, at nine or ten, owed nothing to Tennyson or Shakespeare. Rather, I imitated the doggerel my mother sometimes produced on family occasions" ("James Merrill: Education" 1). About his mother's needlepoint, Merrill elsewhere reports: "Once in a while my mother would let me complete a stitch. It fascinated me. It had nothing really to do with the world, yet somehow. . . . Was it the world becoming art?" ("Interview with McClatchy" 73).[7]

This is the benign, maternal model of influence that Merrill argues has been most significant in his life: art as collaborative, sociable stitchery, in which the young poet both actively chooses to imitate what fascinates him and receptively follows the practice of a beloved parental figure. The governing impulse is transformative and compensatory: one writes poems because they remake the world (which is itself apt to overwhelm or disappoint)—remaking it into something enchanting, finished, presentable, and often into something hypothetical [like the "trying on" of "inconceivable" emotions (*Different* 114)] or ideal [at once "charged with thought and . . . absolved from thought"(*Recitative* 117)]. The characteristic emotional tone of

Merrillian poetic influence is affability. Very little erotic charge (let alone aggression) enters any of Merrill's "official" accounts of poetic influence. At most his language projects a wryly camp or gay inflection: those "docile takers-in of seed" in *Sandover*, or the way he rises each morning to write "like Kundry in Parsifal with a shriek and a shudder to do my Klingsor's bidding . . . here slubbing an image, there inverting a hypothesis—I set about clothing the blindingly nude mind of my latest master" (*Different* 202).

Eros, aggression, and anxiety do, however, inform Merrill's remarks when the subject of poetic influence is not so explicit. In response to Helen Vendler's question about whether *Sandover* "needed a ghostly father and ghostly mother," Merrill reveals considerably more about the charged and overlapping realms of parent and precursor:

> Strange about parents. We have such easy access to them and such daunting problems of communication. Over the Ouija board it was just the other way. A certain apparatus was needed to get in touch—but then! Affection, understanding, tact, surprises, laughter, tears. Why the *poem* needed Wystan and Maria I'm not sure. Without being Dante, can I think of them as Virgil and Beatrice? . . . In life, there are no perfect affections. Estrangements among the living reek of unfinished business. Poems get written *to* the person no longer reachable. . . . Your question looks down into smoking chasms and up into innocent blankness. Given the power—without being Orpheus, either—would I bring any of these figures back to earth?
> ("Interview with Vendler" 51–2, emphasis in original)

Merrill leaves this question hanging, having brought himself and us to the very brink of the pit of anxiety concerning parents and precursors. The Ouija board with its ghostly parent/precursors seems to offer the poet a middle-flight between the smoking chasms, in which "Oedipus became Empedocles" ("Santorini: Stopping the Leak"), and the innocent blankness of no speech. But the figures of Dante and Orpheus (whose identities Merrill clearly adopts by refusing) suggest that the seeming ease and ready access Merrill finds with his ghostly parents is purchased at the price of descents and ascents much more strenuous than he is ready to acknowledge (except by the glancing power of allusion).

Merrill suggests that *he* needs Wystan and Maria in compensation for the difficulties and frustrations of communicating with his actual parents. This notion of compensation across categories (real parents versus parent figures) seems only partially satisfying. As we shall see in *Sandover*, Wystan and Maria compensate (and cover) even more for the anxieties raised by Merrill's relation to Yeats. It is not just "estrangements among the living" that reek of unfinished business; so do the estrangements entailed by a demanding precursor, since it is also out of *this* "unfinished business" that new poems come. Merrill's poems do "get written" [note the sense of passive fatedness here] "*to* the person no longer reachable." It is precisely by creating, in himself, that distance across which he would reach, that enabling ambivalence which both draws him toward and insulates him from the precursor, that many of his strongest poems are made.

In contrast to his explicit and determinedly benign characterizations of poetic influence and his "maternal muse," Merrill makes only rare and oblique connections between poetry and his father's influence—or his father's money, for that matter, surely a ready metonymy for "influence." Even though no less an authority than the archangel Michael declares, "ALL CHILDREN WANT . . . TO IMITATE THE FATHER (S. 476), Merrill does not discuss how this rule applies to him or his work. And even though, in college, when his writing and academic honors have provided him a sense of enhanced stature *vis-à-vis* his formidable father and Merrill recalls feeling, "One day I might even be his equal" (*Different* 150), rarely does he suggest any sense of rivalry with either his father or his poetic "fathers."

Merrill does however tell a story of "the primal ballroom—in Southampton" which he identifies very strongly with his father. It is a room, Merrill says, "that must have answered beautifully to my father's Gatsby side," a room that tells of vast wealth and power:

> Four families could have lived in it. Two pianos *did*, and an organ, with pipes that covered the whole upper half of a wall, and a huge spiral column of gilded wood in each corner. And a monster stone fireplace with a buffalo head above it. At night it was often dark. . . . So that, after being sent to bed, I'd have to make my way through the ballroom in order to get upstairs. Once I didn't—I sat clutching my knees on one of the window seats, hidden by the twenty-foot-high red damask curtains, for hours it seemed, listening to my name being called throughout the house. . . . It's a room I remember *him* in, not my mother. He took me aside there, one evening, to warn me—with tears in his eyes—against the drink in his hand. We didn't *call* it the ballroom—it was the music room. . . . Looking back, even going back to visit while my father still had that house, I could see how much grander the room was than any of the uses we'd put it to, so maybe the ghostly presences appeared in order to make up for a thousand unrealized possibilities.
>
> ("Interview with McClatchy" 74–75, emphasis in original)

I want to emphasize two aspects of this remarkable story told, in writing, to J. D. McClatchy for his 1982 *Paris Review* interview. As well as the overwhelming grandeur of the room, we sense in its dark vastness, a scene of emptiness in which the father is an overwhelming, but also hauntingly absent, presence, who memorably accosts his child with his own failing. Part of the disturbing emptiness of this paternal relation comes through in Merrill's sense of the room's "thousand unrealized possibilities." It is here we get the first intimations that Merrill writes to "make up for" a paternal emptiness, and that his "ghostly presences" call him to compensatory acts of poetry which involve precisely the repeated realization of possibilities.

Merrill presents another version of how he was impelled to answer for the aching monumental emptiness of his father's room in a Class Day talk, delivered at Amherst College in 1980. In thinking about the poets of this century "whose work means the most to us," Merrill remarks:

> When we look at the men we notice a drift toward the more or less monumental. Sometimes a highly compressed monument, a sketch for a monument—I'm thinking of *The Waste Land* or *Notes Toward a Supreme Fiction*; sometimes, as with Pound or Lowell or Dr. Williams, a huge, unruly text that grapples ravenously with everything under the sun. Now these men began by writing small, controllable, we might say from our present vantage "unisex" poems. As time went on, though, through their ambitious reading, their thinking, their critical pronouncements, *a kind of vacuum charged with expectation, if not with dread, took shape around them, asking to be filled with grander stuff.* . . . I speak, alas, from experience, having felt a similar pressure at work in my own case, and seen also, though fighting it every step of the way, how little choice I had in the matter. (*Recitative* 161, emphasis added).

In light of the vast glooms of his father's ballroom, this "vacuum charged with expectation, if not with dread" takes on particular resonance, as does Merrill's insistence on his active resistance in the face of what amounts to the compulsion of natural law: "THE VACUUM MOTHER N ABHORS" (S. 453).

We see more of what this "asking to be filled with grander stuff" entails (as well as another instance of Merrill's "carefully" marshaled volition) when we return to his account of "the original, the primal ballroom":

> That same sense probably accounts for my "redecoration" in the Epilogue [of *Sandover*]—making the room conform to an ideal much sunnier, much more silvery, that I began to trust only as an adult, while keeping carefully out of my mind (until that passage had been written) the story of how Cronus cuts off the scrotum, or "ballroom," of his father Uranus and throws it into the sea, where it begins to foam and shine, and the goddess of Love and Beauty is born.
> ("Interview with McClatchy" 75)

Merrill's task as a poet is not simply to take over and recast his father's room. To preside at the birth of his own maternal muse requires the violent displacement of the father and the appropriation of his influential "seed." In Merrill's account, the "primal ballroom" is in every sense a "primal scene." Merrill is clearly Cronus in this telling—"Time . . . a child, playing a board game" (S. 60); his father is Uranus or Money. The victory we know goes to the younger; the father after all "was 'in his prime' / At three score ten. But money was not time" ("Broken Home"). And though we may wonder at the rigors of his self-deceptive "double mindedness," Merrill prefers to keep such scenes of violence "carefully out of my mind," displacing both violence and threat back onto the figure of the father: "Father Time" ("The

Broken Home"), "Time the destroyer" (S. 440), "Time! The forbidden, the forgotten theme—" (S. 438).

Bloom, writing "against Freud," argues that the Primal Scene is always already a Scene of Interpretation or Instruction (*Map* 55). Rather than an event "given" by circumstances, the Primal Scene always entails "a self-knowing founded on a self-making"; that is, the "viewer" literally "makes sense" of a scene out of what he already knows: "a young Wordsworth had to know a possibility of sublimity in the self before he could know it in Milton" (Ibid.). In this sense, the Primal Scene is always "staged" [Bloom says it is "necessarily a stage performance or fantastic fiction" (*Map* 47)] in that the Scene of Instruction is "necessarily a place cleared by the newcomer in himself, cleared by an initial contraction or withdrawal that makes possible all further self-limitations, and all restituting modes of self-representation" (Ibid.).[8]

Merrill's description of the vastness of his father's music room gives a vivid sense of just the sort of interior space that Merrill created through his own self-withdrawal (behind the red damask curtains, hearing his name being called). In this tableau, we sense Merrill's early self-knowledge of the rich and demanding lack the room would come to represent: the "Empty perfection" of The Ballroom at Sandover, that "great room" he would reimagine and populate with all the grand company of his poem (S. 556–57).

Bloom also argues that the Primal Scene depends on an even more primal fixation on either a person or an image (Merrill gives both) and that this fixation, in its repetition, constitutes the Primal repression behind the scene (*Map* 56–9). Bloom continues: "Poetic repetition [which "repeats a Primal repression"] quests, despite itself, for the mediated vision of the fathers, since such mediation holds open the perpetual possibility of one's own sublimity, one's election to the realm of true Instructors" (Ibid. 59). This "mediated vision of the fathers" is precisely the vision of grandeur that the music room offers the young Merrill: the "perpetual possibility" of "ghostly presences" in himself with which to fulfill the "thousand unrealized possibilities," seen in himself but authorized by his father and this room, of his own sublimity, his own calling as a maker of lyric stanzas or "music rooms."

As we have noted, Merrill schools himself to avoid the anxiety of these primal scenes. He prefers to think of repaying his debt to his father's authority and money, for example, "in currency / Plentiful and precious as the free / Heart-high chamiso's windswept gold that frost / Hurts into blossom at no further cost" (S. 49). That is, he prefers to imagine a return which is innocent as nature in its productive, necessary "Hurts"—a repayment that concludes the cycle of injury and "cost" and thus also steps "out of nature" into the realm of art. He prefers to think of the poet as "the eater of time"—and himself, as we have seen, as one of "the docile takers-in of seed" ("Interview with Sheehan" 26; S. 154). He prefers the "sunnier, more silvery" image of his inheritance to the scene of violent overthrow and prefers to see the immortality conferred by art as time's banishment (S. 438). In his earlier poems,

Merrill struggles with the "monster stone fireplace," often conferring the burden of each element of this father-identified phrase onto his own manikin or monumental Yeats. In writing *Sandover*, these terms are displaced into the cosmos and other world and finally claimed as elements of God B.

But these attempts at banishment, displacement, and denial are never complete. As we shall see, "Monsters," "stony" faces, "rocky" voices, and paternal "fires" inform Merrill's poetry from the start and persist into his last collection, *A Scattering of Salts* (in poems such as "Arabian Night" and "My Father's Irish Setters"). About his father, Merrill writes:

> He was a powerful and unpredictable man, never more so, in my young eyes, than when, pretending to want for his scrapbook the poems and stories I'd written up to then, he had a small edition of them handsomely produced during *my senior year at Lawrenceville*. Jim's Book, as he titled it, thrilled me for days, then mortified me for a quarter-century. I wouldn't put it past my father to have foreseen the furthest consequences of his brilliant, unsettling gesture, which . . . looked like approbation but was aimed at waking me up. (*Recitative* 6)

In this passage, we sense in Merrill's double reading of his father's gesture his own ambivalent response. The same wake-up "pat" that "opened my eyes enough to see how much remained to be learned about writing" (Ibid.) also challenged Merrill's attachment to the maternal practice of occasional language stitchery: "For her as for me, poems already in books were off limits" ("James Merrill: Education" 1). Seeing his work already in a book pointed out the direction of an ambitious career, but not so much by what he had achieved as by what he lacked, "how much remained to be learned." Here again we note the self-limiting economy of a primal Scene of Instruction. In the young Merrill's "reception" of this gesture, we sense again Merrill's ambivalent reading of his father's connection to a compelling lack, the "vacuum charged with expectation, if not with dread" that would ask "to be filled with grander stuff."

If Merrill's father opens a psychic space that Merrill would seek to fill with the power of poetry, it is Merrill's mother who gradually becomes identified with all the ambivalent attractions and threats of the world and life itself. She is "Mother Earth" in "The Broken Home." She is "the ancient, ageless woman of the world" in *Sandover* (92), and although hers becomes "the breath drawn after every line" (S. 84), it is a breath that sounds with "that faintest hiss / And slither, as of life / Escaping into space" ("Scenes of Childhood"). In contrast, Merrill comes to identify his father with both the grandeur of the "heavens" and the demanding lack that is "the abyss // of night" ("Scenes of Childhood). J. D. McClatchy is surely right in concluding his essay on the figure of the Mother in Merrill's poetry that she is "the image of the world itself: muse and model, scold and siren, security and danger and love" ("Inner Room" 22). He argues too that she is "vessel of all desires" and "priestess . . . of all the mysteries of formation, nourishment, preservation and transformation. Which is why, finally she is to be identified with the art of poetry itself" (19). But it is a paternal influence (out of a "broad / Path of vague stars"), whether figured as heavenly or as a great abyss, that impels Merrill to his poetic calling.

However "vague," these paternal stars are nonetheless potent. They shine with the same light as those "whose fine cold eyes / First told us, locked on ours: / You are the heroes without name / Or origin" ("Scenes of Childhood"). In these lines, we see Merrill's "Scenes of Childhood" culminating in a Bloomian primal Scene of Instruction. Out of the vague influence of the stars, a commanding glance initiates the young poet into the heroism of the poet's quest—that of moving imaginatively from being something created, with a given name and origin, to a being that creates, god-like because it is beyond both name and origin.[9]

But Merrill's initiation into a masculine-identified poetic is neither immediate nor direct. His parents' divorce and his own homosexuality establish in Merrill a profound ambivalence for all things imaginatively identified with his father. On the one hand, the powerful father is always an object of suspicion, the path to be avoided: "At first I wanted nothing to do with him—hadn't he Destroyed Our Home?" (*Different* 150). On the other hand, his father is the embodiment of an ambivalent "contentment" (*Different* 42) and allied to the frightening, seductive grandeur of the music room, that realm of "unrealized possibilities" ("Interview with McClatchy" 75). As we have seen, Merrill disavows any interest in or experience with typical male poetic rivalries ("Interview with Brown" 41–2). He also draws on women's perspective in voicing his suspicions of typically male monumental ambitions:

> When we look at the men we notice a drift toward the more or less monumental. . . . And [I] wistfully thought how while men have built monuments to themselves—as well as to women: look at the Taj Mahal—no woman has ever gone on record as wanting one" (*Recitative* 161).

Yet, as we have seen, the father is also the locus of a powerful mix of resentment, rivalry, and an appropriative desire: figured most strongly in the story "of how Cronus cuts off the scrotum, or 'ballroom,' of his father Uranus and throws it into the sea, where it begins to foam and shine, and the goddess of Love and Beauty is born" ("Interview with McClatchy" 75).

The process whereby Yeats becomes the chief exemplar of the masculine poet for Merrill, and the object of these highly charged Oedipal relations, begins at least by Merrill's freshman year at Amherst. By his own accounts, Merrill had been reading a good deal of Rilke and Yeats at the end of high school ("Interview with Sheehan" 35, "Interview with Brown" 43). Merrill does not say what first attracted him to Yeats, but it is telling that he holds up Yeats in contrast to Wylie's feminine "glaze of perfection" ("Interview with Sheehan" 35). This "shaped and polished and begemmed" language would later characterize the kind of poetry Merrill wanted to move away from (*Different* 5–6). Rather than the "verbal artifacts . . . set on the page with never a thought of being uttered by a living voice," Merrill would hope to write the kind of poem that owed something to the male world of the Greek café, a poetry that "engaged in dialogue, in fluent speech and vehement gesture. . . . [that would] set eyes flashing and smoke pouring from lips" (*Different* 6, 18).[10]

But the poems Merrill wrote at Amherst had not yet taken him this far. The second semester of his freshman year, Merrill took advantage of a "tête-à-tête" with Robert Frost to show him several short poems and remarks that, despite Frost's kind remarks about "touches of 'seeing' he found original, . . . I knew secretly how much they owed, that year, to Rilke and Yeats" (*Different* 15). Rilke, who seemed by far "more poetic to me than Yeats," had an appeal that was "more than literary" and almost maternal: "Rilke helps you with suffering, especially in your adolescence" ("Interview with Brown" 43). Yeats, on the other hand, offered a certain distance from the immediately personal, seeming "by comparison somewhat external to one's situation" (Ibid.). Yeats took one "out of nature," whether into the dreamy balladry of the Celtic Twilight or the visionary glamour of Byzantium, and Merrill particularly mentions having read "Sailing to Byzantium" while he was in the army at the very end of World War II. He remarks: "It got through to me because of the circumstances. I couldn't wait to get "out of nature" myself" (Ibid.).

Both Rilke and Yeats, of course, also wrote famously of the distances and separations of love—their work acting as a kind of homeopathic or sympathetic balm for the young poet who felt "lonely" that year "in the vast chamber full of voices" that was his early poetry (*Different* 15). But "relief [for this loneliness] was at hand," as Merrill makes clear, in the shape of the intimate personal and literary relationship he developed with Kimon Friar shortly after returning to Amherst from the army (Ibid.). Merrill had very likely already begun his ambivalent fascination with the strength of Yeats's poetic personality: his assertiveness and austere sensuality; his heroic and visionary claims; his strategies of vacillation, technical range and mastery; and the range of worlds he brings into his poetry. But the evidence of memoirs and poems all point to the catalyzing and enduring effect of his friendship with Friar in making Yeats Merrill's most problematic poetic father.

We need to understand the terms of this early relationship if we are to understand why, of the several grand and paternal models for poetry that Friar and Merrill's Amherst reading presented him, Yeats's becomes the most important and most vexing throughout his career. As we shall see, Merrill is "chosen" by Yeats in no small part because he was first chosen by Friar. Merrill's movement from "floodedness" to "struggle," to repeat Bloom's terms, in his poetic relation with Yeats is first established by similarly Oedipal entanglements with Friar, who was at once Merrill's mentor, lover, and surrogate father.

Merrill gives a glancing account of Friar's considerable influence in his memoir, *A Different Person*, and Friar provides further details in his much briefer reminiscence, "Amherst Days."[11] I give passages from both sources at length to establish the necessary background.

Prelude: Merrillian Influence, Kimon Friar, and Yeats

FROM *A DIFFERENT PERSON*:

> Early in 1945, when I returned to Amherst as a veteran of nineteen, Kimon was teaching world literature to the would-be army officers still on campus. . . . Soon he was regularly criticizing my poems and I was attending his weekly workshop and lectures at the YMHA in New York, for he had a career quite apart from his duties at college. . . . After the lecture we would stop by the Gotham Book Mart and stock up on poets I'd never heard of. Then? Why not tea with Anaïs Nin, a drink with W. H. Auden, a late party at Maya Deren's? Any thing was possible. In a matter of months my existing sense of how to write, who to take seriously, what to feel, and where to go from there had undergone lightening revisions. Not all of it stuck, but when the smoke cleared, the schoolboy imitator of Elinor Wylie had turned into this new person who read Hart Crane and Robert Lowell with an air of total comprehension and whose own poems—designed, after Stevens' dictum, to "resist the intelligence / Almost successfully"—now began appearing in magazines. By then, too, Kimon and I were lovers. The double goal of numberless adolescent daydreams was being realized.
>
> And yet this first love, so largely the intoxication of *being* loved by such a man, failed to surmount the three obstacles in its path: my own callowness, my mother's horrified opposition, and a year away from each other. On his return from that year, in 1947—I was twenty-one then, able to do as I pleased—I nonetheless told Kimon that I couldn't cope; the break left us both numb, confused, guilty. . . . (18–19)
>
> My friendship with Kimon, however smoothed over by these reunions, kept deteriorating. . . . The day came when we agreed not to see each other or communicate for a while, and twenty-five years passed. Out of sight wasn't, however, out of mind.
>
> Kimon believed that myth was indispensable to poetry. In times like ours, when religion played no vital imaginative role and the political myths were turning to radioactive ash in the hands of the superpowers, the poet had no choice but to live by some personal mythology of his own construction. One day when the time was ripe, Kimon planned to write a long poem based on Yeats's system: spiritualism, the phases of the moon, the gyres of history. A long poem was the test of any poet's powers. He cited Dante, Milton, Rilke, Pound. What would their shorter works amount to without the great achievements that crowned them? The notion struck me at twenty—at forty, too, for that matter—as a dangerous form of megalomania, and I wasn't buying any of it. But at fifty? Longer than Dante, dottier than Pound, and full of spirits more talkative than Yeats himself might have wished, the Sandover project held me captive. It was Kimon's dream, only I was realizing it in his stead. In his copy of the poem I wrote: "Dear Kimon, who'd have thought? You would!" (27)

FROM "AMHERST DAYS":

> "Look here," I told the young poet (Merrill was 19, I was 33), "you are already a splendid poet. I should like to teach you whatever I know, talk to you about

my enthusiasms and theories and listen to yours, and try to give you here, and at The Poetry Center on weekends, a creative environment to supplement technique. We shall have only this academic year together.... If you would like to work with me, you must place yourself completely under my direction in a crash course. I shall give you private lessons every day in technique and aesthetics, and commission poems from you as though you were a cabinet maker and I was ordering furniture. I shall set you the theme of each poem, the meter ..., the stanza form, the rhyme scheme ..., the symbols, the imagery, the orchestration in family groups of vowels and consonants. I intend to drive you hard. What do you say?"

"Try me!" Merrill answered.

I have never before or since worked with a poet with so much excitement and profound satisfaction. I would ask Merrill, for instance, to write a poem about the swan, using the imagery of the lake, in a seven-line stanza form intermingling pentameters, tetrameters, and trimeters, using approximate rhyme. He brought me "The Black Swan." Or the subject matter might be "Medusa" (my personal symbol of the art form), to be written in a favorite stanza form of mine.... Merrill would return, often the next day, with a poem precise to the last detail, often surpassing expectation....

I sought to be sensitive to his own inclinations that he might more fully mine his own proclivities. I saw similarities in style and temperament to Wallace Stevens, and introduced him more fully to that poet's work, and to poets for whom I had an especial fondness: Keats, Crane, Hopkins, and in particular Yeats, for in 1939 I had written my master's thesis on *A Vision* when that book was scorned by critics as theosophic nonsense.... Merrill attended many of my lectures and the readings, including my course on "The Writing of Poetry" ... [and] many lectures in my two other courses ["Aspects of Duality in Literature and Art," in which Friar developed his "aesthetic theory of a tension and not a harmony between opposites," and "Contemporary Epics in Prose and Poetry," this course focusing "in particular" on Yeats's later poems and *A Vision*].... I was particularly fond of saying that all poets in our day must strive to become a Dante, and that if Yeats had written *A Vision* in poetic form instead of prose it would have been one of the great epic poems of modern times. I had envisaged rewriting "The Phases of the Moon" and the "Historical Phases," in a pastiche of Yeatsian and original phrases and characters, but ignoring what Merrill was later to use as his central theme in *Sandover*, the Realm of the Dead.

The only time Merrill would not follow my direction was when I wanted him to write a long narrative poem, for he kept insisting that long poems were an impossibility, an anomaly in our times. I told him it would not matter whether or not the poem turned out to be good or bad: he would be forced to use his creativity in structuring such a poem, and it would challenge and widen the range of his imagination.... But Merrill adamantly refused.... Only after he had written *Sandover* did he read the *Odyssey* through [Friar's translation of Kazantzakis's monumental *Odyssey: A Modern Sequel*], writing me two lovely letters of praise, apologizing for having taken "twenty years to mature" [an echo of JM's compliant to WHA about the originality of *Mirabell*: "I want it mine, but cannot spare the twenty / Years in a cool dark place that *Ephraim* took / In order to be palatable wine" (S. 261)] .... When he sent me a copy of *Sandover*, he wrote the inscription: "Dear Kimon—who'd have thought? *You* would. With love always— Jimmy."

What emerges from these two accounts is something of the intense rigor of Friar's tuition, the vigorous "shaping hand" he employed in working to refashion Merrill's poetic sensibility and in making him a "different person" after his own aesthetic desires. As Merrill says, "Not all of it stuck," but a lot did: the breadth of Merrill's reading, his confident place socializing with the likes of Anaïs Nin, W. H. Auden, and Maya Deren; even remarks about Dante and Thomas Aquinas in *Sandover* seem to reflect Friar's enduring legacy.[12] These passages also provide an understanding of why breaking with Friar would have been both difficult and necessary for Merrill to forge an independent poetic identity.[13] Indeed, one way of reading *A Different Person* is as an account of just this effort to achieve emotional and poetic independence from Friar's instruction (this as much as from his mother's "horrified opposition" to his homosexuality and from all the expectations that followed from his father's considerable wealth). We also gain an understanding of why Yeats would remain so closely associated with Friar in Merrill's mind, and why his influence and the paired figure of Friar/Yeats should remain so fraught with ambivalence for Merrill for many years to come.

Yet, as we shall see, even during Merrill's particularly Yeats-saturated apprenticeship under Friar, Merrill always maintained a thread of implicit criticism of both Yeats and his mentor. After breaking up with Friar, Merrill's sojourn in Europe (1950–52) only began his work of attaining poetic independence. In *The (Diblos) Notebook* (1965), Merrill revisits his relationship with Friar and employs Yeats as a kind of cudgel to mete out a rough "poetic justice" against his former mentor (and the Yeats-haunted aspects of himself Leslie Brisman identified in "Willowware Cup").[14]

Merrill's engagement with Friar seems to fade by the end of the 1960s. Yet, as Merrill puts it, "Out of sight wasn't, however, out of mind," and during the years from 1965 to 1980, Merrill's Friar-inflected quarrel with Yeats persists and deepens. Because of Merrill's ambivalence toward his former mentor, it was not until well after he has completed *Sandover* that is he willing to take up Friar's version of Kazantzakis' *Odyssey* and not until considerably later that he acknowledges his own visionary epic as a realization of "Kimon's dream" of "a long poem based on Yeats's system" (*Different* 27). *Sandover* itself fairly crackles with the express anxiety that it might in fact be someone else's poem and loudly protests its status as *dictée* ["it's all by someone else! . . . I want it mine"(S. 261)]. Throughout the long poem, Merrill fetishizes the pose of his own passivity before the dictating voices, while at the same time making sure that his poem belittles and punishes the two figures most closely associated with Friar and similar "dictations": Yeats and, ironically, his partner David Jackson, who for over thirty years replaced Friar as Merrill's lover and most constant companion.

Before turning to the evidence of poems written most fully under Friar's influence, I would like to examine *The (Diblos) Notebook* to see how thoroughly Merrill mixes Yeats and Friar and how "rough" his justice is toward the latter. The novel is an experimental *roman à clef*, based on the characters of Kimon Friar and Friar's wife, Mina Diamantopoulos. Merrill's 1994 "Afterword" describes the novel as "perilously drenched with real life," a "little fiction, written to conceal how little of a fiction it is" (149). Certainly none of Merrill's work reveals as graphically (or typographically) the animating tensions between desire and denial, vision and revision, process and product, experience and artifice, and, in Yeats's terms, the tensions between Will and Mask, Daimon and Poet, as does this novel. It concludes with the nameless, young author insisting: "Tomorrow I'll make peace with Orson [the Friar character]. I've got to, I want to, before sailing home" (145). Thus, the novel is, in part, Merrill's effort to make his peace with Friar at a time when Merrill's annual visits to Greece created proximity, when his experiences at the Ouija board created pressure to reassess Friar's interest in Yeats, and when experiments in narrative prose might help him overcome the "impossibility" of the long narrative poem that Friar had so insisted he attempt—Friar's version of Yeats's "of all things not impossible the most difficult" (*Per Amica* 332).

From its outset, the novel gives an accurate if gently mocking picture of Friar's intellectual interests and manner; and in each instance Yeats colors Merrill's portrait of Orestes/Orson/Friar like a pervasive thematic wash. At one point, Orestes limns in something of Friar's early relation with Mina Diamantopoulos, the woman who was to become his wife: "She recites Sophocles, I reply with Keats & Yeats. . . . I am not in love with her, nor she with me, though we have slept together 3 or 4 times out of tenderness" (50). As in Yeats's "Meditations in Time of Civil War," Friar/Orestes takes pride in *his* "Platonic table," as in "*His* cottage. *His* rock-garden. *His* private cove" (59, 37 emphasis in the original). He has his indispensable "vision," as well as his "'tragic' view" (113, 143) and lectures on one of Yeats's favorite themes, "The Tragic Dualism of Man" (57). In a description compounded almost wholly of Yeatsian elements, we learn that "O. wore myth day & night like an unbecoming color . . . ~~Myth~~ Metaphor formed like ice between him & the world. Backwards, forwards, sideways he glided, spiraling, curvetting . . . " (62).[15] This gyring Yeatsian dance becomes more explicit in the merging of dance and dancer by which the writer characterizes Orestes' talk: "his instances leapt forth in their classic leotards. Body & Soul, Eros & Death, Time & Eternity, the Mayfly & the Abyss" (57). The talk itself is figured as a kind of intoxication, the manic incarnation of a god; he finishes "breathing heavily like a dancer" and receives his "homage" from his listeners (58). Orestes/Friar talks like "those dancers for whom the dance had been, more than play, a meditation the body itself thinking, choosing, rejoicing" (59). Language is Orestes/Friar's Unity of Being, his Condition of Fire: "Orestes talk popped with allusion and paradox. It was like sitting by a fire" (101).

Yet Merrill also signals his early distrust as well as his attraction to such Yeatsian discourse: "Words like 'antithesis' or 'metaphysical,' or sentences beginning 'The poet in his lonely search for belief . . . ' made his eyes shift nervously, but he enjoyed the relish with which Orestes could utter them" (100). An entry in one of Merrill's notebooks makes a similar point about Friar's talk:

> "His subject is Man, his tragic fate and heroic defiance in the face of extinction"—Bruce Chatwin on Malraux. Why do I so loathe this kind of talk? I heard it first, I think, from Kimon and took it even then with distrust. (Kuusisto 192)[16]

Merrill's unnamed young writer also entertains the possibility that the Friar character might be gay: "Perhaps he was in love with me—he said he found me beautiful in every way. For all I know he was (is) queer . . . " But, given this "disturbing" possibility, the narrator is careful to deflect attention away from bodies onto minds, in order to maintain his own, archly linguistic (and untutored), pose of heterosexuality. If Orson is queer, the writer continues:

> then only on a level at which pederast & pedagogue merge into one dignified eminence. He loved anyone who was willing to learn from him. Instead of making a pass and teaching my body something new (it had mastered little but a few active verbs, all quite regular) he taught me that the mind, that my mind, was a holy & frightening thing. Who wouldn't have believed him? I know who. The person I am today. (56)[17]

This passage shows Merrill adopting the mask of what he is not—not straight, not active, not untutored—but in a way that serves to emphasize the compelling pedagogical force of Friar's character (even as it also suggests the instability of the author's heterosexual persona—as if all that a homosexual "identity" might require is another kind of "teaching").[18] The erotic undercurrent in the relationship between the Friar character, Orestes/Orson, and Sandy, Merrill's doubly fictive double, does surface, albeit momentarily, in the euphoria of their dance at the Panegyri; but this coded homosocial/homosexual encounter is largely overwritten by the writer's masks of fiction and heterosexuality.[19]

Merrill's relationship with Friar in the pivotal year 1945–46 also literalizes Yeats's sexual wrestling between Daimon and poet.[20] As in Yeats, such coital "Unity of Being" is fleeting and issues only in loss and disappointment, which in turn becomes the material and stance of the poet (Bloom *Yeats* 230–34). As the poet who will largely make his poetic career out of his "chronicles of love and loss" (S. 176), Merrill seems to follow Yeats in affirming: "The poet finds and makes his mask in disappointment" (*Per Amica* 337). Yet part of Merrill also wants to affirm a recuperative aesthetic credo: "Art. It cures affliction" ("Farewell Performance"); "Form's what affirms" ("The Thousand and Second Night"). By projecting this ambivalence outward, by making Friar and Yeats bear the burden of his own aestheticism, Merrill creates the daimonic role for these two figures. They become his Yeatsian "anti-self," who set him "to the hardest work among those not impossible," and with whom he stages the struggle that is his art (*Per Amica* 336).[21] Both in this early period and subsequently, Merrill continues to resist (even as he evokes) a Yeats-and-Friar-inspired aesthetic credo that sees art as the answer to or redemption of such Yeatsian disappointment. As the *Diblos* writer puts it, "Love hasn't worked, not this year, & art isn't the answer" (133). For Merrill (as for the Yeats he gives less credence to), the golden bird and plummet-measured face undoubtedly enrich and charm, but their alchemy is fleeting. Aesthetic fixity ultimately appalls and fails to serve the needs of life or the needs of Merrill's art, his "chronicles of love and loss" (S. 176).

To see better how this interplay of Oedipal attractions and resistance plays out under Friar's Yeats-saturated instruction we need only turn to Merrill's treatment of the Gorgon, Medusa. For Friar, Medusa represents his "personal symbol of the art form" ("Amherst"). She is "perfection in its absolute form; pattern devoid of subject: death. She is that final touch of form of which Walter Pater wrote: the rarefaction of all arts even beyond the abstraction of music . . . that impossible perfection . . . that element in all creation which we call pattern, and in the pursuit of which our living often becomes tenuous and withers away" ("Medusa-Mask" 2).[22] Friar gives his account of the "pursuit of Medusa by Perseus" in a brief essay reprinted from "Poetry" that heads the only number of "The Medusa," the Amherst journal, which Merrill co-edited in 1946 with William Burford. It was here that Merrill first published "The Black Swan" and "The Broken Bowl," as well as his Friar-directed exercise on the theme, "Medusa." In the Perseus/Medusa story Friar sees "the artist's search for an art form with which he might attempt to control those forces forever attempting his disintegration and that of the world" (1).

Thus, from the start, for Friar the issue is control; like Yeats, Friar sees the self and the world so inclined to disintegration that it takes a heroic effort on the part of the artist simply to resist this constant threat.[23] But Friar, again following Yeats, recognizes that there is danger too in this "impossible dream" of control:

> The idea is soon loved better than the relative accident which conceived it,[24] and we search for that Nirvana where everything moves serenely in a celestial equation.[25] . . . If we feed too deeply upon [Medusa's] peerless eyes and seek to pierce beneath her vision, we become lost forever in a living dereliction.[26] We are stone to flame. (2)

Perfection petrifies. Trickery and violence are the only cures "where the stone face revolves like a sick eye" (Merrill, "Medusa"). Thus, the death-dealing Gorgon calls forth her death-dealing nemesis, so that Perseus's victory is a victory over the deadly temptations of formal perfection, the Yeatsian impulse to step "out of nature" and be made an "artifice of eternity." It is a victory won by submission and foolhardy daring, indirection (a mirror-vision), intellectual acuity, and by Hermetic obscurity and lightness (4–5). At the climax of his mirror-vision, the poet will be assailed by deathless beauty. Only a hardening of the heart, only being "flooded" by his own powers, enables the poet's decisive, murderous act. Only thus, Friar asserts, may poetry "take wing from the blood of death, and the poet be unburdened of his vision" (6).

In this light, it is interesting to note that Friar's essay broaches the topic of poetic influence in implicitly agonistic and Oedipal terms: "Psychology has much to say of the son's antagonism for the father . . . , and have not poets always opposed the traditions of their immediate progenitors, generation against generation, school against school?" (1). Friar's essay builds to a climax in which the poet "flooded in the moment of decapitation when wrought to artistry, must strike and strike quickly; then, in that posture made immortal by Cellini, raise the Mask aloft with reverence and averted eyes" (6). More than a murder "wrought to artistry," Friar also makes Perseus's swordplay an act of punishment by emphasizing the blasphemy of Medusa's coupling with Poseidon in the temple of Athena—the moment in which (oceanic) life and (the Gorgon's) formal perfection lose themselves "in the brutality of lust: passion spawning on the floor of wisdom" (3).

Merrill takes up this reading of the Medusa-myth and turns its lessons against both Friar and against himself, adopting a note of sexually anxious "justice" at the conclusion of both his early poem and the later novel. The poem, written directly under Friar's influence, suggests a regime of mutual "disciplinary" violence ["so we / Watch . . . the dry serpent horror / Of days reflected in a doubtful mirror / . . . until / We raise our quivering swords and think to kill."]. In contrast, the novel and the 1968 revision of the poem make it clear that only "only one of us" will "raise his quivering sword" and only the Friar figure will suffer.[27] In this way, in both his early poem "Medusa" and *The (Diblos) Notebook*, Merrill involves Friar in the violence of his own myth, just as he uses Yeatsian figures to critique a Yeatsian position (to which he is also attracted).

Merrill's 1946 poem takes up a number of themes from Friar's essay, but from its opening lines it also revises Friar's account of the Medusa/Perseus myth. Where Friar's Medusa is a figure bespeaking at once timeless perfection and the absolute fixity of death, Merrill immediately subjects the image to the depredations of time: "The head, of course, had fallen to disrepair / If not to disrepute." What Friar casts as abstract archetype, Merrill personalizes, alluding to both the tenor and subject matter of his love affair with Friar: "The snake-haired head with overturned eyeballs, / Being all our summer's pleasure, has become / Our mouldering autumn." The summer spell of Friar's talk of beauty, art, and myth proves inadequate; its emblematic "makeshift waterfalls, / Birds and their songs [prove] false / As all imperishables." Where Friar emphasizes the Persean victory of poetry, Merrill lingers over the allure of the imagination ("like godhead in a world of sense . . . / Whose scope allows perfection to be conceived"). Likewise, Merrill evokes the ambivalent forces of dreaming and time, which keep the allure of Medusan perfection alive: "For, to believe this face [the Medusa mask], it must be dreamed. // As birds assault a blind eye it must be dreamed . . . for still in the still heart / Of time the snakes will writhe, the stone lips part." Against what he takes as Friar's petrifying (and Yeatsian) aestheticism, Merrill opposes "the dry serpent horror / Of days reflected in a doubtful mirror."[28] And finally, where Friar concludes with "that posture made immortal by Cellini," Perseus holding "the Mask aloft with reverent and averted eyes," Merrill finishes with Perseus (in this case doubled as "we") caught in the crisis of preparing to strike: "We raise our quivering swords and think to kill."

Merrill makes sure that we are free to read this posture in two antithetical modes, one heroic and the other deeply ironic, both of which challenge Friar's original. On the one hand, the posture recalls Michelangelo's Moses, who in Freud's view is presented heroically contending with a similar moment of psychological crisis.[29] On the other hand, the posture also seems to comment on Friar's essay by representing Friar's heroic model as the very figure that Friar warns against, the poet as a doomed Narcissus, "fascinated by that inverted image" he holds (5). Thus, even in this early poem, Merrill shows himself the master of the vacillating image, built of both attraction and resistance, "the toy spyglass [that] teaches / That anything worth having's had both ways" (S. 174). In this and many of the poems of this period, we sense the productive tension that informs Merrill's relation with Friar: a desire both to gain by Friar's favor and to assert his poetic independence. It is the same productive ambivalence that characterizes Merrill's relation with Yeats.

Although Friar and Merrill were certainly familiar with Freudian ideas in some detail, it is unlikely that either, writing in 1946, would have been known Freud's posthumous essay "Medusa's Head," which first became widely available in English with the publication of Freud's *Complete Psychological Works* in 1950.[30] Nonetheless there are a number of telling convergences. All three focus on the already severed head or "mask" of the Gorgon. Friar's is the only account to give any attention to Medusa as a woman, "yet virginal in beauty," before her encounter with Perseus ("Medusa-Mask" 3). Yet even here, she is always already Death—not the proud beauty who freely consorts with Poseidon in a meadow, let alone the queen whom the sea-god rapes ("medusa" being Greek for "queen") (Siebers 14), nor the laughing, uncastrated, life- and love-affirming woman Hélène Cixous evokes in her essay "The Laugh of the Medusa."[31] Friar acknowledges that Medusa rivals Athena in beauty but interprets "the passion of Poseidon for Medusa in the Temple of Athena [as] the common lust of life for death," where Poseidon, as "god of all spawning waters, is the symbol of continuous and abundant life" and thus, in Friar's masculinizing reading, the symbol of "the original womb" (3).

In similar fashion, Freud famously employs an equation to reduce the fascination of the Gorgoneion to a particularly male anxiety: "To decapitate = to castrate" (18: 273), and Merrill's poem makes much of another Freudian image of castration, the blind and blinding gaze of the Medusa-mask. Freud's and Friar's accounts also emphasize how the emblem of this beheaded woman works to support particularly male defensive and creative powers. For Freud, the sight of Medusa's severed head excites in the presumptively male spectator a horror that also consoles: "For becoming stiff means an erection. . . . he is still in possession of a penis, and the stiffening reassures him of the fact" (18: 273). For Friar, Medusa's is a "sacrificial death," hers the "Beauty that must die" so that "poetry [Pegasus] should now take wing from the blood of death" ("Medusa-Mask" 6). For both, her head is apotropaic, at once an emblem of and protection against "that portion of Evil [always figured as female] before which every artist shudders in temptation" (Ibid. 2); the Medusa-mask is both prize and token of male power, worn as Freud says "rightly" by Athena, the male-born goddess of rational cunning and culture (18: 273–74). Only Merrill underscores the self-serving, self-reflexive murderousness of the myth's appropriative and sacrificial economy as itself a kind of ineluctable sickness ("maladies of dream / Where the stone face revolves like a sick eye"); for him, the Medusa story becomes a "guileful melody" luring his male lovers to their killing climax, each one ultimately "seeing" the other as Medusa to his Perseus: "We raise our quivering swords and think to kill."

Although Merrill had not read Freud's interpretation of the Medusa-mask, the whole occasion for the poem—that it was written at Friar's bidding and on the theme of Friar's own most personal mythology—sanctions a Freudian reading. For Merrill such an assignment was bound to raise the question of how to use the occasion and dynamic of his relation to Friar to assert his own poetic identity. Given Friar's masculinizing perspective and the murderous economy of the Medusa story, one approach seems plausible: Merrill's Perseus-figure must kill a Friar-identified Medusa. But so strongly does Merrill identify Friar as an older, more authoritative instance of his same "kind," with whom he is bound by passionate ties of desire and distrust, that such an act is already an imaginative patricide. As in Freud's *Group Psychology*, the emergent individuality Merrill seeks to achieve with this poem is an aftereffect of an (imaginary) murder of the father (18:136). According to Freud, the first individual is the epic poet who creates himself as hero of his own myth by imagining this hero as the man "who by himself had slain the father" (here Friar/Medusa) who appears as "a totemic monster" (Ibid.).

Even though the poem concludes with an image of anticipated death-dealing violence, Merrill in many ways follows modern interpreters of the Medusa myth to suggest that monster and spectator are narcissistic mirrors of each other, both "still fixed as by a stone-eyed spell"; in this way the Medusa slays itself (Siebers 10–11). By imagining Friar gazing into the representation of his own self-image, it is Friar (and not Merrill) who is responsible for the fact that, from the very first lines of the poem, the "head, of course, had already fallen to disrepair / If not disrepute." Merrill's deployment of Yeatsian images in the poem is of a piece with this self-slaying in that Merrill thereby turns Friar's own gaze, his own characteristics and beliefs, against him.

But the imagined death of the father alone does not release the poet into his individuality. Freud explains it is "in the hero who aspires to the father's place [that] the poet now create[s] the first ego ideal" (18:136). Identity is constructed out of displaced representations of what one desires. Just as the hero sees himself taking the father/monster's place and power, so the poet sees himself as such a hero. But just as hero and monster are caught up in a self-mirroring economy in Merrill's "Medusa," so does Merrill imagine himself and Friar "turning each to the other," each turning into the other, in the poem. [This image is made even more pointed in revision: "Oblivion / Turns us to one another, as to stone." (In *From the First Nine*.)] Thus, in making Medusa's gaze also Narcissus's, Merrill not only figures Friar's narcissism, but his own—his own recognition of how much of what he desires in Friar's paternal autonomy is his own.

In summarizing Freud's models of narcissism and individualization, Tobin Siebers's study of ancient and modern magical thinking, *The Mirror of Medusa*, captures a great deal of the particular dynamic of Merrill's poem and its occasion. He writes that, for Freud, both narcissism and individualism "pivot on the desire to represent oneself as another" and continues:

> This is the double-bind of identity: superior [or desired] traits, whether imagined or real, must be imitated if the individual is to differentiate himself from another. He must become the other in order to win a victory for self. Just as Freud's first individual imitates the individuality of the primal father, the "narcissistic" individual imitates the one whom he believes is narcissistic, thereby attempting to recreate an imaginary form of omnipotence. His moments of megalomania occur when he has successfully rendered the superiority of the model [his image or representation of the desired other]. His self-reproach derives from his bitterness toward the model and, paradoxically, from the inner recognition that he has failed to achieve the model's false autonomy. (138)[32]

Surely Merrill's last line, "We raise our quivering swords and think to kill," approaches a vaunting (if not megalomaniac) elation at having "successfully rendered" the climax of Friar's personal myth. So too the entire poem is pervaded by bitter insight directed toward both Friar and himself.

Merrill's struggle to at once free himself from and define himself through (as well as against) the character, position, and beliefs of Kimon Friar continues well into the 1960s and may be seen most clearly when we consider passages from *The (Diblos) Notebook* as well as Merrill's later revisions to "Medusa."[33] Twenty years after writing "Medusa" for Friar, Merrill returns to the Medusa-image in *Diblos*, his "little fiction . . . perilously drenched with real life" ("Afterword" 149).[34] At first what we see is self-criticism following the suggestions of the earlier poem. The writer in *Diblos* representing the young Merrill declares that "the Gorgon's face was mine" (133) and thereby not only establishes his link to Medusa and Friar's symbology of "perfection in its absolute form," but also suggests two of Merrill's early dilemmas as a writer working under Friar's direction: first, his impatience with his own "unrelenting fluency" (S. 70), his fascination with and gift for a petrifying "glaze of perfection" ("Interview with Sheehan" 35) and second, the difficulty of seeking to see the Other through the mirror of his art and finding only himself staring back in a transfixing gaze.[35] This is the dilemma of aesthetic narcissism that Friar warns against ["he must drown, like Narcissus or Hart Crane, in the madness of introversion" ("Medusa-Mask" 5)] and that Merrill portrays in a number of early poems.[36] Even with the deployment of his fictive characters' mirroring personae, the young writer "never succeeded in getting a full view" of his own face (*Diblos* 133). All he sees is the stone mask of his artifice.

As we have seen, Merrill figures this moment of "self" recognition as a kind of blindness and tells us that the Medusa's gaze was always already "blind in its own right . . . / Brilliantly blind" ("Medusa").[37] Similarly in *Diblos*, an Oedipal, self-lacerating conjunction of blindness and insight links Merrill's unnamed writer with the Friar character, Orson/Orestes. "Blind I go," the young writer insists (34, 133) just as he tells us that O. impels his own punishment "out of his own blind hopeless allegiance to this country of his dreams" (143). In these images, Merrill shows us the effects and the nature of the Medusa-like, transfixing gaze his young writer first considers for a "more formal opening" for the novel (where Orestes is the Friar character and his brother represents Merrill):

> The snapshot seemed at first to show Orestes & his brother, in profile, face
> to face. But a closer look revealed that Orestes was there only in plaster effigy,
> as if transformed by something in the young, inexperienced
> the barely formed, mindless features of the other   (13)

Here the "mindless features" is a further trope for blindness and "the other" refers to the young Merrillian writer who is always also other to himself. In the mutuality of this petrifying narcissism, the younger poet is himself arrested in his power to transfix the older. The mirror gaze of artifice freezes both. Merrill in his "barely formed" poetic vocation realizes only the frightening Medusa-like facility of what Friar's gaze returns. The passage also suggests that Merrill is fully aware that he is presenting only a one-sided ("profile") version of Friar, a "plaster effigy" which is also "his lifemask . . . painted dull red" (37). But it is through these self-conscious distortions, this seeing by "halves of a clue" ("An Upward Look"), that Merrill makes his way forward against both Friar and Yeats.

We see this struggle and contentious progress perhaps most clearly when we consider the revised final stanza of "Medusa" along side the concluding pages of *Diblos*. In both, the avenging action is mental and given the pointedly ambivalent status of something imagined: "*In my head* he raised his beautiful clenched hand" (*Diblos* 144) and "Tonight may one of us / . . . raise his quivering sword, and *think to kill*" ("Medusa" emphasis added). In both, the avenging figure is allied with the writer: he is "one of us" and "*my* Byron" [Orestes' wife's son, but also, tellingly here, the poetic persona Merrill often adopts against Friar's, and his own, Yeatsian proclivities] (*Diblos* 137).[38] In both a thoroughly Yeatsian context saturates the imagined action. In the poem, an imagined Perseus arises, rebellious yet fated, and strides out into the Yeatsian perfection of "the coldest, roundest moon"; whereas, in the novel, "every action however brutal is nobly, inflexibly ordered" (145). Like Yeats enumerating his "old themes" in "The Circus Animals' Desertion," this figure puts aside the "noble mirror / Of lust and birdsong, waterplay and guile" and strips "his dreaming down," if not to "the foul rag and bone shop of the heart," then to "a cheap serpent horror" that animates his thought for the vengeful action, the same murderous action that Friar cast as the decisive gesture of poetry and that Merrill has consistently undertaken to turn against Friar (and himself) as a means of self-definition and poetic emancipation from his poetic fathers.[39]

"Medusa" was only one of the dozen poems Friar took with him to Greece in 1946 to publish there under the title *The Black Swan*.[40] It is a remarkable collection, not only for the poems that Merrill later published in *First Poems* ("The Black Swan," "The Broken Bowl," "The Green Eye," "Accumulations of the Sea," and "Medusa") but for those not subsequently collected until the posthumous *Collected Poems*: ("From Morning to Morning," "Perspectives of the Lonesome Eye," "Phenomenal Love Song," "The Formal Lovers," "Suspense of Love," and two of Merrill's "Embarkation Sonnets"). These previously uncollected poems suggest a good deal about the conflicted, largely closeted relations of Merrill and Friar's love affair. It is a relationship that depends upon, yet is also the victim of, the demands of artifice and secrecy ["Between, between our facing faces, not / Upon them, the secret of our loving lies" ("Suspense of Love"), "And the grand lonesome / Artifice is needed to mask the primitive // Sensation" ("Perspectives of the Lonesome Eye")]. It is a relationship that nonetheless tries to affirm that "form and fever / Have never once been separate" ("The Formal Lovers"), that "Bound by perspectives, we are loosed by love" ("Perspectives"). Theirs is a relationship that must imaginatively condense "Years of green loving" into what "these strict minutes have remembered" ("The Formal Lovers"). It is a relation that has no future, but is always already bound by retrospection, where "remembrance is a ritual" ("Suspense of Love"). It persists "fevered by / The creed of the impossible" ("The Formal Lovers") and requires daring, acrobatic feats of juggling to maintain ("Suspense of Love," "Embarkation Sonnets I"). In such a relationship, the lovers must be "chameleon-wise" and ever vigilant ("Phenomenal Love Song") to find their moments of unseeing Dark, which is "the perfect thing we have" ("The Formal Lovers"). Finally, it is a relation in which the lovers must find their consolations in art and in their separate feelings ["Pattern from passion, love from loss" ("The Formal Lovers")] since the season of these lovers is "fixed as by a stone-eyed spell" ("Medusa").

But in this context Medusa does not represent a petrifying formal perfection so much as the tyranny of social form and the "horrified opposition" of Merrill's mother to his relationship with Friar: "My mother flatly dismissed the life I dreamed of living. 'Society will not condone it,' she more than once told me . . . " (*Different* 19, 89).[41] It was at his mother's insistence that Merrill experienced his first "brush with

Prelude: Merrillian Influence, Kimon Friar, and Yeats

psychotherapy" soon after the enforced break-up with Friar—his mother, as was common then, thinking to have him "cured" of his homosexuality (Ibid. 89, see also 150–51).

One poem from this period preserves the remarkable distress Merrill felt at the loss of his lover and mentor and at his mother's role in what he saw as her killing crime. The opening section of "The Forms of Death" presents a scene Merrill would later develop in "The Drowning Poet."[42] A swimmer "lies unfurled" on the sand, a suicide who will never have the chance to fulfill his poetic promise: "His lips for learning syllables of the tide / Are locked." The first section ends leaving "him splayed in the noon / Like any dried medusa," merely "an agony / to smile upon,"[43] leaving us to wonder who would find such a sight a source of such seeming "tragic joy"? The implied answer and further Yeatsian echoes surface as the poem proceeds.

The second section reprises the Medusa-vision of the drowned swimmer's "marble eye [that] will never close" and asks the question the first section raises, "but who / Would mourn it more than yours?" The third section moves from "real death" to "the spoiled page" of the poet's notebook and concludes with a Yeatsian cry:

> Not blood, nor burning, not
> The bewilderment of dying,
> But the essential death from which is built
> The gaiety fastened to the poet's eye . . .

The fourth and fifth sections shift their focus from the dead (and then dying) poet to the woman ("you my mother") whose crime is to turn to tapestry, to art, the poet's agony and death. I give these sections in their entirety for the depth of animus they reveal and for the echoes of Yeats Merrill employs even here:

>   IV
> Only the satin lives, and you my mother
> Are featureless, your image overexposed:
> A photograph at the brilliant end of time.
> Shadows are feathered, but on your face my mother
> No gentle plumage is roused
> To do your meekness homage
> Or dim the white white countenance of your crime.
> Only the satin blazing where you sit
> Lives, being spiritless, knowing a death past damage,
> A death so exquisite
> That in your drawing-room
> Of gilt and feathery flowers there is no language
> To utter it before it fades, surpassed
> By the white epic of your face in the gloom
> Whose breakneck beauty finds its mark at last.

> V
> A woman while I slept stood by my bed
> And with a needle and gold thread began
> To stitch with gold each agony of my skin;
> Over my cheek, thin eyelid, willing thigh,
> Beneath her jabbing thread
> Gold like a jaundice spread
> Until I changed into a tapestry,
> Until as the last great cities that will come
> I shone in a gold nonchalance of doom
> Beyond those violences
> Of lust that spoils and lust
> That seems to spare. Nightlong I lay, all gold;
> And since that night, in moving through the world
> Within its poignant needlework, [44] my breath
> Halts like a gesture pedestaled in death.

Here and in "The Drowning Poet" Merrill responds with an outburst of self-elegy to what he clearly sees as not just a threat to the life he dreamed of living but to his viability as a poet.[45] His breath halts; his mother has transformed him into a gilded effigy that cannot sing. And perhaps most horribly, the speaker suggests his own sexualized complicity in her handiwork as she stitches over his "willing thigh." Merrill figures himself as the too-willing victim of his mother's fatal influence, so that the melodrama of his poem becomes his only vindication.

"The Forms of Death" represents the most extreme example of Merrill's self-elegizing, as well as what one reviewer of *First Poems* notes as "one of his most characteristic motifs . . . a watery death" (Harrigan 236). Yet as we have indicated, an elegiac, retrospective air clings to much of Merrill's love poetry from his *First Poems* as well—what Merrill calls "the obligatory note of sadness struck without exception by my early poems" (*Different* 70). Nowhere is this note more strikingly apparent than in the dedicatory poem Merrill writes for Friar as the frontispiece of *The Black Swan*:

> Keats on board ship for what we shall call Rome,
> In waterlight watching his shadow fall,
> Mingle with written water, observed that time
> Obliterates nothing but those public pulses
> Nibbling his wrist; so at the difficult prow,
>
> Feeling that all things fail but love that is
> Rainbowed by the last raveling of his hand,
> Illumined beyond hope, he and his world,
> As blood and seawater, meeting only in death,
> Retain like lovers their chemical sympathies.

Prelude: Merrillian Influence, Kimon Friar, and Yeats 31

Keats sailing to his death in Rome is Merrill's chilling trope for Friar's embarkation to Athens. Its echo of Yeats's imagined sailing to Byzantium and his alchemical sympathies is secured by the "blood and seawater" of the last two lines. A certain theatrical "Liebestod" floods the poem, an effort to assure the power and value of the love attested to by the ultimate index of death. But more than this, the poem serves as a proleptic elegy for his "departed" lover. In this "catastrophe" of their relationship, Merrill reaches for the strongest help he knows: the sacrificial economy of the elegy.[46] Merrill conjures with an imagined death in order to do more than forestall his own; he needs a death and the invocation of "an illustrious dead man" to launch him into his strength as a poet, so that imaginatively sending Friar to his death is what sponsors the poetry that is to follow (*Per Amica* 335).[47] The wish behind this poem's declaration of love and loss is that Friar's strength and all he stands for will descend to Merrill. The wish to be rid of a constraining, determining influence, and yet to have full benefit of its powers, always entails a certain psychic struggle, a willful blindness or violence directed either toward the self or toward the other (or both, as we see in "Forms of Death"). It is this wish for freedom *and* power and the concomitant internal struggle that characterizes Merrill's poetic relationship with Friar and, even more so, with Yeats, who has always stood behind Friar as an even more potent (and problematic) poetic "force" in Merrill's life (S. 492).

YEATS IN MERRILL'S EARLY POEMS: MOVING FROM FLOODEDNESS TO STRUGGLE

The previous discussion of Merrill's relationship with Kimon Friar and its significance for the poetic relationship between Merrill and Yeats has already taken us well into the realm of aesthetic "struggle." To see how Merrill moves from his early "flooded apprenticeship" to the self-quarreling "struggle" that marks his more mature work, it is important to go back to what Merrill terms the poems of his adolescence, *The Black Swan, First Poems,* and *The Country of a Thousand Years of Peace,* to poems written for the most part before Merrill's first experiences with the Ouija Board. In so doing, we not only observe how Merrill comes to identify Yeats's poetry as a voice that must be superseded—even as he recognizes in Yeats both appealing and troubling aspects of himself—we also gain a more comprehensive and dynamic appreciation for poems famously "finished" and gain clearer insight into the subject matter, structure, and motivation of poems typically accounted slight or obscure.

I

In the decade of Merrill's first published poems (approximately 1946–1956), Yeats's voice is just one of many influences that characterize his verse. This is the period of which Merrill remarks in his 1993 memoir, "Language at this stage uses him; years must pass before the tables turn, if they ever do" (*Different* 14).[48] Just whose language is at work in Merrill's early poems is readily apparent. In a 1987 interview, Merrill singles out certain writers whom he had read at college: Keats, Pope, Donne, Milton, Proust, and Dante, and notes that before he had graduated he'd read "all the modern poetry that, in those days, never appeared in the curriculum: Yeats, Stevens, Dylan Thomas, Pound, as well as lesser figures" ("James Merrill on Poetry" 5). As we have noted, Merrill points particularly to Proust and Dante as "emblematic, throughout my life, of what a writer can achieve" (Ibid. 5). And though Merrill's mature achievement calls for substantive comparisons with both Proust and Dante, Merrill's early verse owes a particular debt to the other figures in his college reading. We hear echoes of Keats and Dylan Thomas in Merrill's themes, imagery and the lushness of his diction, in his "joy in the cradle of calamity," and "love's warbler among leaves"; and echoes of Pope (and Byron) in Merrill's epigrammatic wit and the deftness of his versification.[49] Donne and Milton show their influence in Merrill's penchant for extended metaphor, vertiginous puns, and syntactic density. Stevens' luminous blend of abstraction with the concrete particular presides over whole poems, as does T. S. Eliot's doctrine of impersonality and themes of fragmentation and loss. And finally, Rilke's elusive plangency and keenness of vision hover over much of Merrill's earliest published verse.[50]

Yeats's voice, his diction, images, themes, and methods, is part of the "floodedness" with language that characterizes this early work. But Yeats's voice recurs with a special force. Merrill remarked in a letter to Ross Labrie that "Yeats must have meant a great deal to me. I tried to sound like him (in poems) around the time I graduated" (Labrie 6). Sometimes this "sounding like" Yeats consists of merely echoing characteristic elements of diction or emblematic phrases and does not entail any sustained engagement with the themes or arguments of Yeats's poems. Reading these early poems, it is often not so much Yeats one hears as certain Yeatsian notes struck in the midst of a host of other echoes. In a poem with "Transfigured" in the title, for example, and a section that ends (before revision) on the rhyme-word "gay," a poem with "wild wings," a little rooster that "flaps gold wings and crows" while "inside of it a thumbnail engine whirs," and a bird that sings "first of the past . . . then / Of fables, findings, . . . images in the minds of men; [then] Of love"—as if of "what is past, or passing, or to come"; a poem with phrases like "a panic in my blood," "the flood of time that flows," "Blow all away," and "let the fragments whirl," where a girl combing her hair gives the hair "lessons in simplicity / Till each long lock was docile and severe"—such a poem cannot help but evoke Yeats,[51]—just as "Her hair too much like the sun" says Shakespeare and a "bird, forever / Beyond, stops only if we stop, to trill / In the thicket yonder, loudest to a lover . . . while she dreamed and I was somewhat still" all but cries out Keats.[52] What is interesting about this element of pastiche in Merrill's "Transfigured Bird" is at once how lightly and how effectively it is worn. Here, in "sounding like" Yeats, or Keats, or Shakespeare, Merrill uses these echoes, as he uses the Dantean terza rima, to deepen the metaphysical luster of his linked meditations.[53]

At other times, Merrill's early poems address Yeatsian thematic concerns more closely and offer more than semantic echoes of the earlier poet. In such poems, "floodedness" includes taking on the thought and spirit of the earlier poet, as if to revisit favorite haunts, turn over again an old puzzle, or finger an old bruise. "The Parrot," for example, stands as Merrill's first and one of his closest acts of Yeatsian ventriloquism, sounding as if Merrill wrote "The Parrot" to address (if not "to parrot") Yeats's perennial themes in Yeats's own voice.[54] From the early poems to the late, Yeats told "much about old age / Beyond what is serene or quaint," and might have broached the topic in just this way. Merrill captures Yeatsian frustration and cadence with his opening: "I am impatient of the myth that numbs / A spinster as she hums / Sweet nothings to her parrot in its cage." (Compare: "I am worn out with dreams;" "I have heard that hysterical women say / They are sick of the palette and fiddle-bow . . . " "I sought a theme and sought for it in vain . . . ") Though Yeats surely would not have allowed himself "Our revels now are ended, pretty Poll," Merrill's poem continues to strike more and more Yeatsian notes. Merrill takes up Yeats's image of the mask and the necessary "as if" that governs human desire, especially desire for the promised depths of an "individual face behind the mask." Like Yeats, Merrill makes dance the ruling metaphor for the life lived and the life observed. Like Yeats in "The Circus Animals Desertion," he insists on both the "sad irrelevance" of the dream "Moment she had so long wanted" and the "enchantment" of that dream, the enchantment of art, of eye and syllable. In the manner of late Yeats, Merrill reflects bitterly on how a "bird of utterance" can dispel the personal,

"That frail and talkative ghost," as if he were remembering hopes placed on another bird, one that would preside on his translation out of nature and into "the artifice of eternity." Echoing the bird-like "comforters" in "Cuchulain Comforted," Merrill's parrot also "speaks with no human voice" and "destroys the personal," making "common," spectral and gray the human, which Merrill's disillusioned speaker tells us is but "pretense / Of gentleness and sense." Finally, like the late Yeats, Merrill concludes the poem with bitter, apocalyptic exhalation. Where Yeats variously lies down "In the foul rag and bone shop of the heart," is shaken from his dream by "A stricken rabbit . . . crying out," and sees "great sea-horses bare their teeth and laugh at the dawn" and "nymphs and satyrs / Copulate in the foam," the parrot's "ancient cry" wakes "jungles" within Merrill's spinster. The parrot's raucous music "inform[s] her dance," making music, dance and dancer one, "Until all music shook / To stillness in the bestial night." Thus, the primitive and fecund, the bestial and dark survive the personal and human, and music presides at its own undoing in a Yeatsian midnight of the soul.

Sometimes Merrill offers "corrections" to a particular Yeatsian argument or extensions of a particular theme, much as Yeats did in his own poems. Merrill's "The Broken Bowl," which, in its first version, seems motivated largely by the modernist reverence for "artifice / Informed in its flawlessness / With lucid unities," evokes the Yeatsian ideal of emotional and aesthetic coldness when it speaks "of colder flowerings where cold crystal broke."[55] There is something too of Crazy Jane's linkage of love with "the place of excrement" and lesson that "nothing can be sole or whole / That has not been rent" in Merrill's comparison of the play of light sprung from the shattered bowl to love—where, like love, the broken bowl "triumphs through inconsequence / And builds its harmony from dissonance / . . . And our last joy [is] knowing it shall not heal." In Merrill's poem, the "face / Of mathematic fixity" recalls Yeats's "plummet-measured face" not just as an image, but also thematically, since Merrill's face like Yeats's bespeaks the ideal, and idealized, space where "Love's projects green with leaves" signify the transforming quality of lovers' passion. Merrill's imagined constellation of "Cut structures in the air" establishes a "circumscription" within which "we may set / All solitudes of love"; just as in "The Statues," Yeats's boys and girls rise "pale from the imagined love of solitary beds" to bring "character enough" through their imaginative passion to the Pythagorean public image. Both poems also conclude by evoking the disparity between ideal Platonic forms "realizable" in glass or marble artifice and the press of time, death, and history that is also the freedom of love.

Yeats's last stanza is more positive in its denunciations and affirmations than Merrill's, but parallels persist. Yeats's speaker addresses the public and national realms where "We Irish," who are as haunted or inspired by Pearse as Pearse by Cuchulain, are beset by the "filthy modern tide" and "Climb to our proper dark, that we may trace / The lineaments of a plummet-measured face." As with the Greek boys and girls before us, Yeats suggests it is the horizons of our passion, "our proper dark" that will give character (though one may wonder whether it be "character enough") to the Irish national ideal. In contrast, Merrill emphasizes the ambiguity of "Love's monuments like tombstones on our lives," where the public (or private) monuments that celebrate also "mark off" or circumscribe our vision of love just as they come to mark the memorializing limits of our lives.

Revising this poem for inclusion in *From the First Nine* in 1981, Merrill "touches up" the poem, in this case "drastically" (*First Nine* 346), but in such a way as to extend and deepen its use of allusion. Yeatsisms do not vanish but grow more integral and make way for evocative echoes of Blake, Dante, Eliot, and Keats, so we see that, even as a mature poet, "doing voices" remains one of Merrill's choicest effects. Using one of Yeats's favorite devices, Merrill now opens the second stanza with a question, "Did also the heart shatter when it slipped?" recalling Yeats's question in "Leda and the Swan," "Did she put on his knowledge with his power /Before the indifferent beak could let her drop?" Most of the third stanza is likewise recast as a question, a question as syntactically rich and almost as portentous as the question Yeats uses to conclude "The Second Coming:"

>   What lets the bowl
> Nonetheless triumph by inconsequence
> And wrestle harmony from dissonance
> And with the fragments build another, whole,
>   Inside us, which we feel
> Can never break, or grow less bountiful?

If we lose the Yeatsian emphasis on coldness in the final couplet of the first stanza, we gain a more promising assertion. In the place of modernist "colder flowerings," Merrill now offers "A fledgling rainbow," the much more resonant figure of spiritual covenant and grace. In a couplet of almost Blakean simplicity and authority, Merrill still emphasizes the lesson of "Crazy Jane": "From piece to shattered piece / A fledgling rainbow struggles for release." But as Merrill has it, the promise *and* struggle implicit in these pieces, linked with the "fragments" of the third stanza and "ruin" of the fourth, also meld Merrill's revised poem to the comprehensive ambitions of Eliot's *The Waste Land*. Gone are the "splendid curvings of glass artifice," the "self-containing artifice" celebrated by middle-period Yeats and much high modernism. Merrill emphasizes now not "the simplicity of fire" but the contention of opposites, and of opposite visions of a present-day apocalypse: "fire, ice, / A world in jeopardy." The revelations of *Sandover* recently behind him, Merrill allows suggestions of nuclear fire and nuclear winter to deepen the implicit threat and urgency of the poem he revises.[56] With a world at stake, Merrill reaches for the most authoritative diction and stance. He answers his Yeatsian question, "What lets the bowl / Nonetheless triumph . . . " with the bald, stichomythic response, "Love does that."

The early poem cycle, "Theory of Vision," is not a particularly Yeatsian enterprise except as later revisions highlight Merrill's concern not just with the phenomenology of seeing but with the experience of poetic and spiritual vision.[57] But certain poems do reveal Merrill working with Yeatsian themes, again in ways that occasionally offer contrasts but may be said to work from within the spirit of the earlier poet. Set beside Yeats's "Lapis Lazuli," Merrill's "The Flint Eye," for example, reveals a host of significant parallels and contrasts. Both poems open with women openly disdainful of poets and end with images of a timeless, smiling beatitude. But whereas Yeats's women are "hysterical" and think poets superfluous, Merrill's tribal matriarch, "with eyes like arrowheads" and a witheringly bright, imperial gaze, personifies a more-than-human reason. She also dismisses poets as a frivolous epiphenomenon such as one might sift through for relics of the past. Although both poems emphasize the ephemerality of human life and achievement, with Merrill citing Isaiah that "all flesh is grass" and Yeats declaring that "All things fall," Yeats's "gaiety" celebrates both the relics and their makers; whereas, a tone of Cartesian bleakness pervades most of Merrill's poem. Under the timeless, flint eye of inhuman reason, what Yeats celebrates reduces to so much "skulls / And pottery" found "high in the shallowest stratum of the past."

Where Yeats delights to imagine his Chinamen climbing to their blossom-fragrant half-way house, listening to mournful melodies, and gazing out on the world, Merrill imagines his perduring matriarch deep within the darkness of some vast Platonic cave, in whose "vaults of perfect rock" her "eyes of artifact" had once cut "clean diagrams . . . / That no air dampens."[58] Yeats rises, Merrill descends. Yeats breathes blossom-scented air; Merrill suffers no air to dampen the design of reason, the "flint rituals" of inhuman language, of uninflected Platonic mind itself, pure and perfect as the rock darkness from which it is cut.

Although in this comparison I have emphasized differences between Yeats and Merrill, they are differences within the same Gnostic and neo-Platonic tradition. Yeats would, I think, quickly recognize Merrill's echoes and see the point of his interest in a metaphysical reality before "Language." In "The Gyres," which introduces "Lapis Lazuli" and its twin movements of disdain for present "coarseness" and "comfort" in a detached vision of recurrence, Yeats points to the realm of "old Rocky Face" out of whose "rich, dark nothing" the figures of the next era must be "disinter[ed]." Merrill's "The Flint Eye" in a sense allows Yeats to look behind his own Rocky Face and into that darkness out of which Yeats hears "that one word 'Rejoice.'" By the time Yeats writes "Man and the Echo," he has had occasion to delve into the stony dark "that broad noon has never lit" once again, this time haunted by his own mortality and less sure of what the rocky voice once seemed to promise: "Shall we in that great night rejoice?" Harrowed by the cry of animal mortality, he perhaps would be ready to recognize in the "long smiles" of Merrill's spectral "race of sober children" something like the mix of attraction and dread that he recognized in Pater's vampire Mona Lisa, "older than the rocks among which she sits."[59]

By the time Merrill writes "Parable," the third of "Four Little Poems" in his volume, *First Poems*, he seems to have become so comfortable with his Yeatsian mantle that he can, in turn, offer pointed advice to the earlier poet. Like Yeats's "A Coat," "Parable" tells a wry story of influence, and, like Yeats's poem, Merrill's draws on the Hans Christian Anderson story "The Emperor's New Clothes." By working with the same story, Merrill's "Parable" offers ironic commentary on the prior poem and on the effect of Yeats's shift from more elaborate to more "naked" diction. Yeats's speaker casts off his old style, his "coat / Covered with embroideries / Out of old mythologies" because other, lesser poets, the "fools," have taken it up "as if they'd wrought it." He is anxious that his song has been too influential. Its elaborate regalia no longer single him out or provide a clear distinction by which to "rule" or be effective. "For there's more enterprise," more to be gained, more advantage and power, the speaker famously reasons, "In walking naked." In contrast, Merrill's Emperor has not adopted nakedness as a conscious strategy to preempt imitation, or, like Yeats's or Anderson's emperor, to assert his full and unique authority. Once the deception and self-deception are revealed, Merrill's Emperor realizes his error: "yes, / He was indeed quite naked. What a mess." But the Emperor's example and the solemn music that attended his progress have had a larger effect than merely to evoke imperial "Embarrassment." Merrill tells us:

> The children, more impressionable for all
> Their accuracy, could not but recall
> The solemn music before the Embarrassment,
> And naked down the avenues they went.

In these lines, Merrill's tale presents the same situation that Yeats's speaker objects to in "A Coat": children, Yeats's fools or younger poets, have taken up the master's new style. Thus, Merrill tells us, nakedness suitably solemnized will be just as much a fashion as is any stylistic finery. Nakedness as a poetic stance offers no more authenticity, status or "enterprise" than any other style. Merrill's parable, aimed with the power of hindsight, seems designed to respond to Yeats's, or any other's, claims for the special virtues of poetic nakedness.[60]

Here Merrill, as a child of Yeats, seems to instruct his forebear not to worry about the indignities of influence: children will always follow what the master does—as long as the music, the power that the style conveys, is compelling. Perhaps, Merrill seems to suggest, we all do this as children ["ALL CHILDREN WANT . . . TO IMITATE THE FATHER" (S. 476)]. In this way Merrill at once makes clear his own dependent 'minority' and his adult authority in offering this parable to Yeats. By creating a parallel tale of poetic influence and linking Yeats's claim for the virtue of "walking naked" with Anderson's tale, Merrill's "Parable" also helps raise the question of how much self-deception is involved in Yeats's renunciation of his earlier style and in the apparent rationality of his facile concluding "For . . ." Thus, "Parable" shows Merrill again not just following but also instructing the master, recalling Yeats's poem while also "swerving" away to make its "correction," to use Harold Bloom's characteristic terms.[61]

II

The poems discussed thus far were in the publisher's hands before Merrill left for an extended stay in Europe in March of 1950. That winter, while in Mallorca, Merrill wrote several poems, then, for more than a year, wrote nothing.[62] "I was living alone and unhappy in Rome and going to a psychiatrist for writer's block," Merrill writes about this period (*Recitative* 6). In his first visit with his therapist, Merrill recalls explaining:

> I didn't know how to love, I didn't know how to live, but I did know how to write a poem. Did once and didn't now—hadn't since leaving Mallorca, months before. That was my reason for seeking help. I wrote, therefore I was; if I couldn't write, I was nobody. (*Different* 116–17)

Kimon Friar presided over Merrill's first transformation from "schoolboy imitator of Elinor Wylie . . . into this new person who read Hart Crane" and published in magazines (*Different* 19). But visiting Friar in Greece in April of 1950 had not proved similarly fruitful. Merrill began to feel particularly alone and at a loss as a writer, telling one interviewer:

> It had by then come to me that I had really nothing to do except to write, and a kind of stage fright took over. . . . So I wasted a great deal of time trying to make the transition from school discipline, where you were told what to write and when to hand it in, to the discipline which you imposed on your self" ("Exploring" 416).

After a year in therapy, Merrill, who "was not in the habit of doing things by myself" (*Different* 6), took several days by himself to visit Ravenna, in what was to be another transformative encounter. "Had Ravenna been a psychiatrist," Merrill declared, "today's hours alone would have cured me" (Ibid. 199).

Merrill says these were "hours alone," but it would be at least as accurate to say that it was Yeats who presided over Merrill's epiphantic experience before the mosaics of Ravenna—which Yeats had visited to similar stunning effect with Lady Gregory in 1907.[63] There, "*alive* and *alone*" and caught up in "the sheer hours on end of *seeing*" in the presence of the fabled mosaics, Merrill experiences his initiation, his calling, into the life and mind of the poet (200–01). Another Orpheus or Apollo, or better yet another Hyperion, he stands "as though in the mind of some young, wide-eyed god, extravagantly in love with detail, and grieved by nothing under the sun. . . ." He has given way to "a glow I try to resist." The dolphins he sees, "their heads thrown back, as on the last chord of some ecstatic universal tango," show Merrill confidently appropriating the vision of Yeats's Byzantium poems. He visits one church after another; "in Sant' Apollinare Nuovo, [he sees] the sages whom Yeats called 'the singing masters of my soul,'" attains "a sense of peace and plenty in the lee of history's howling gale," and walks "out into sunlight" and with the realization: "it is true—death doesn't matter." What is vouchsafed to him here is a spiritual and poetic rebirth, a new childhood, and the conviction that these "glistening states are still attainable" (*Different* 198–200).[64]

While earlier Friar mediated between Merrill and the "vast chamber full of voices" that were his poetic inheritance, here Merrill describes the experience of his poetic calling as mediated only by Yeats's prior words, Yeats's prior presence and "*seeing*." The Yeatsian spirit of Ravenna is still palpable in the new Merrill's first effort, a play titled *The Bait*:

> Tomorrow we shall stand in Ravenna, I suppose
> Quite as if standing in the mind of God.
> Much constellated gold, dolphin and seraphim
> Shall blind us with the blessing
> Of something fully expressed, the sense of having
> Ourselves somehow become expressive there. (122)[65]

Later in 1952, Merrill started a second play, *The Immortal Husband* as well as his first novel, *The Seraglio*, while also completing a number of poems—all before returning to New York in time for Christmas, when by one account he received his first Ouija board as a present.[66] As we shall see, Merrill's connection to Yeats is both reaffirmed and made more complex in this burst of productivity as he starts out on his new life as a poet.

Later, in the memoir, Yeats surfaces again, this time to suggest both the distance from the earlier scene of annunciation, of receiving his vocation as an artist, and the anxiety that attends both this distance and the realization of his vocation. Merrill and David Jackson are in Stonington:

> both writing novels [this is the summer of 1954] . . . I on a sideboard under the tin dome of the dining room we'd painted flame red, perhaps to placate the powers that one day, such was our delight in the old wooden building, might set it ablaze. (Sages standing in God's holy fire? Each time we left we shut our manuscripts in the refrigerator.) (202).

Merrill calls the "genetic angel" that strikes at this point to worry him with childlessness "a parody of the Annunciation," but soon notes, "the crisis passed. Another summer, and the house filled up . . . with Ephraim and Company, who were prepared, like children, to take up as much of our time as we cared to give, but whose conversation outsparkled Ravenna . . . " (Ibid.).

These rivalries—one that pits Merrill's accession into his own healthy, poetic "Childhood" in Ravenna against the "doom" of childlessness he only accepted a few years later, and the other that pits Ephraim's sparkling conversation against the Yeatsian call of Ravenna's mosaics—suggest that Merrill's anxiety or guilt does not concern his childlessness so much as his child substitutes—his poetry, "the little [metrical] feet that patter here" ("The Emerald"), and his nonchalant affiliation with

"Ephraim and Company . . . whose conversation *outsparkled* Ravenna" (203, emphasis added). In Ravenna, Yeats offers the young poet "the singing masters of [his] soul"; whereas, in this passage Yeats's sages stand in the "holy fire" of a jealous or offended God, whose ministers ["Powers . . . we've been avoiding"(S. 108)], might set his home ablaze, and will later rebuke JM ("UNHEEDFUL ONE") and call him to a daunting (and Yeats-haunted) task (S. 113).

III

The poems gathered in *The Country of a Thousand Years of Peace*, largely written after Merrill's visit to Ravenna, show him still working from within an imaginative identification with Yeats but beginning to struggle with that identification and with issues that are central to both poets. As Harold Bloom might suggest, in this collection we see Merrill advance "from the early phase where his precursor floods him, to a more Promethean phase where he quests for his own fire, which nevertheless must be stolen from his precursor" (*Figures* 9). Fittingly, in light of this remark, a number of poems collected in this volume (one or two for each section of the book) strongly operate as appropriative contestations of Yeats's "condition of fire" (*Per Amica* 356).

"Fire Poem" was originally published in *Poetry* in 1951.[67] "A View of the Burning" and "About the Phoenix" originally formed a kind of internal bracketing for Merrill's 1955 volume, *Short Stories*, "A View of the Burning" being the second poem in the collection and "About the Phoenix" the third to last. "The Dunes" and "The Charioteer of Delphi" do not address "the psychology of fire" as thoroughly as the other three poems. Instead, they build to culminating images that gain greater resonance in relation to the Yeatsian detail of the other poems.[68]

J. D. McClatchy points to two of these poems, "A View of the Burning" and "About the Phoenix," as examples of how "a poem's very elegance and equanimity serve to disguise the obscurity of its subject and treatment." He continues, "It is difficult to say how 'About the Phoenix' moves from one florid or puzzling point to another; it is difficult to say what 'A View of the Burning' is about at all" (McClatchy "Monsters" 129). Merrill himself has said, "A poem like 'About the Phoenix'—I don't know where any of it came from, but it kept drawing particles of phrases and images to itself" ("Interview with McClatchy" 76). I argue that reading these poems as responses to several specific Yeats' poems helps clarify subject matter, structure, and motivation for poems otherwise deemed particularly elusive.[69] These three poems, "Fire Poem," "A View of the Burning," and "About the Phoenix," also importantly set the terms and strategies for Merrill's revisionary struggles with Yeats in much of his subsequent poetry and well into his final decade.[70] More specifically, these poems demonstrate the intensity of Merrill's ambivalence, both his fear and fascination, before the initiatory fire of Yeats's elemental priority.

Merrill's "Fire Poem" draws on images from both of Yeats's Byzantium poems, but the poem as a whole shares even more with the third section of Yeats's "Anima

Mundi."[71] Just prior to this section, Yeats has been describing the sleeping and waking visions that seemed to give him access to "a Great Memory passing on from generation to generation"; these visions convince him of the persistence of minds who "still saw and thought and chose" (*Per Amica* 345–46). In section "III," he speaks of how difficult it is to confront the "minds behind the personifications," because the personifications, or visionary images, themselves are so "living and vivid" that the imagination clings to them and will not allow more than a passing "sense of contact" with the minds beyond (347). Yeats looks for an organizing form by which to understand both mind and image and seizes on the traditional (neo-Platonic) elements of earth, air, water, and fire, as if their symbolic authority could reveal or at least stand for the "certain aims and governing loves" behind the images, the mental fire "that makes all simple."

But Yeats cannot rest with this symbolic "understanding." The complexity and allure of the images reassert themselves. The images "themselves were fourfold," he insists. Yeats prevents himself from tumbling into the *mise en abîme* of an understanding founded on veils "hiding another four [elements]" only by resorting to and concluding with the image itself: "a bird born out of the fire." By allowing the image and its resonance to stand at the end for all he "longed to know," the passage replicates for the reader certain features of Yeats's own experience: a confidence in the presence of a mind behind certain images, mixed with longing for greater knowledge which only finds "fulfillment" in the lingering and finally specified image. The culminating image serves the reader as an instance of Yeats's original moment of vision, and thus seems to generate what leads up to it, phoenix-like, born and reborn out of a Gnostic desire for the mind behind the vision—the "fire that makes all simple."

Merrill's "Fire Poem" transforms this material into a haunting interior drama on Oedipal, as well as visionary themes. In dramatizing what in Yeats's prose is "merely" rhetorically dramatic, Merrill establishes one of his most constant means of responding to Yeats's writing. What Yeats presents as exposition or imagery, Merrill recasts as a vivid "scene of instruction," a flickering play of voices and personae. Where Yeats speaks of longing to know something, Merrill presents a scene of longing:

> How unforgettably the fire that night
> Danced in its place, on air and timber fed,
> Built brightness in the eye already bright.
> Upon our knees, held by a leash of light
> Each straining shadow quietly laid its head
> As if such giving and such taking might
> Make ripe its void for substance. . . .

Merrill's fire builds "brightness in the eye already bright," the eye already "flashing" in the visionary mode.[72] Looking at shadows, "held by a leash of light," the speaker sees the very emblem of longing in their quiet straining, "As if such giving and such taking might / Make ripe [their] void for substance." In this personifying formulation the shadows in part resemble passive captives in Plato's cave, and, by extension, suggest that we are also mere shadows who take empty shadows for substantial forms (in a sense, like Yeats, captive because captivated by the images we see). But this image does more than evoke an "unenlightened" condition; it offers a stronger sense of desire and annunciation. What's wanted is that out of the engendering give and take of light and shadow, that crucible Merrill's fire calls "the furnace of its form," something like Yeats's "living substance whose form is but change of form" will ripen into being.[73] Both Merrill and Yeats struggle with this paradoxical notion of form, finding it necessary to give substance to their vision. Like Yeats's images, which engender both desire for knowledge and the sense of a mind behind the image, Merrill's opening lines evoke a longing for the work of the demiurge.[74] Yeats's longing for knowledge of a mind behind the image leads back to the image of the "bird born out of the fire." Merrill's imagination goes further, offering the voice of such a mind as well as the image, dramatically answering the speaker's longing for "substance" with the speaking voice of flame.

> *If as I am you know me bright and warm,*
> *It is while matter bears, which I live by,*
> *For very heart the furnace of its form;*
> *By likeness and from likeness in my storm*
> *Sheltered, can all things change and changing be*
> *The rare bird bedded at the heart of harm.*
> We listened, now at odds, now reconciled.

The fire, in Merrill's poem, begins, as is very much also Yeats's practice, by an appeal to experience and to itself as a natural image that gradually reveals and then insists on its emblematic status.[75] The fire calls attention to its "natural" materiality, its contingency, and its status as an object of perception by first recalling its primary qualities of light and heat and then its dependence on "matter," not only for its "life" but for its "very heart." Even the darting, braiding syntax mimes the material flicker of flame. But "bright" and "warm" quickly announce a simplifying and beneficent cast to the image. The use of personification and the trope of direct address, as well as appeals to the auditor's experience, sympathy, and understanding, all gradually prepare a more emblematic stance first fully announced by the neo-Platonic "furnace of its form." From this point on we are already "out of nature" and into a Yeatsian vision of the consuming simplicity of flame, the purifying holy fire of Byzantium. In a sentence that recalls, in its repetitions, cadence, diction, and imagery, Yeats's voice in the Byzantium poems, the fire announces: "By likeness and from likeness in my storm / Sheltered, can all things change and changing be / The rare bird bedded at the heart of harm."[76]

Here is a storm-like image that also promises shelter from resemblances. Here universal transformation promises identity in unity; "all things" may become "*the* rare bird" (emphasis added). Merrill's bird offers something very like Yeats's transcendent "fifth element, "which is also "a bird born out of the fire" (*Per Amica* 347);

it too serves as an emblem as much (and as ambiguously) "out of nature" as Yeats's mystical bird of gold enameling. Though potentially all-consuming, Merrill's fire dances "in its place." Though it offers to take "all things" into "the heart of harm," its totalizing vision and pervasive music seem to offer "all music and all rest" (through "sheltered" and "bedded"), which Yeats says characterizes the Condition of Fire (*Per Amica* 357). Here at "the heart of harm" is the "agony of flame that [like the "straining" give and take of light and shadow of Merrill's first stanza] cannot singe a sleeve." It is a flame one could blithely ask to "consume my heart away."

But for all its Yeatsian moments, Merrill's poem ends with an ambivalent protest against the simplicities of Yeats's Condition of Fire.[77] The fire's voice that is so much Yeats's voice raises a number of questions. The fire contrives to rhyme "warm" and "harm," "form" and "storm"; yet how are these odd contraries to be reconciled? How does the emblematic fire relate to the fire "that night"? Which fire burns more brightly or gives a better light to live by? Merrill's speaker vacillates, "now at odds, now reconciled" with what the Yeatsian fire has said.[78] Like the later Yeats, Merrill's speaker proves unwilling to rest with either vacillation or a simple or tormented faith in images, and yet, like the Yeats of "The Circus Animal's Desertion" and the third section of "Anima Mundi," Merrill finds no other conclusion.[79] His poem also ends with the freighted image of bird and flame:

> I was impatient when the laughing child
> Reached for the fire and screamed. Pointless to blame
> That splendor for the poor pain of an hour.
> Yet fire thereafter was the burnt child's name
> For fear, and many ardent things became
> Such that their fire would have, could fire take fear,
> Forgot the blissful nester in its flame.

This third and final stanza domesticates the metaphysical drama ignited in the second stanza by the fire's words, thus reversing the usual trajectory of Yeats's poems, yet without any loss of power. Here the speaker's first person plural ("our knees," "We listened") divides into an "impatient" "I" and a "laughing child." In this way, an impassive voice of authority and judgment divides into Yeatsian "irritation" (*Per Amica* 365) and a Blakean child of nature.

In Merrill's poetry the "child" is almost always the autobiographical and Wordsworthian "father to the man."[80] This poem is no exception. Although a literal, dramatic reading insists on two separate persons in the third stanza, this separation dissolves as the voice of the narrating "I" takes on more and more the "interiority" of both man and child, so that the stanza leaves the strong impression of an adult voice commenting on his own childhood experience of being so attracted to the beauty of the fire that he burned his hand in trying to touch the flames. In a scene that Merrill will return to in "A View of the Burning," and with a similar instability and blurring of identity, the adult, Yeatsian voice first seeks to exonerate the beauty of fire of any blame for the child's injury. Yet if beauty is the "rare bird bedded at the heart of harm," pain and splendor are too closely linked to separate so easily.

In balancing splendor and harm, the adult voice seeks at first to minimize the child's "poor pain of an hour" but then acknowledges that the injury was traumatic enough that "fire thereafter was the burnt child's name / For fear," and, in the most difficult sentence of the poem, "many ardent things became / Such that their fire would have, could fire take fear, / Forgot the blissful nester in its flame." Here even syntax dramatizes the *complex*, rather than the simplifying, condition of fire. Weaving together both childhood experience and adult knowledge and longing, beautiful things have themselves become "ardent," invested with the longing they inspire. Their very attraction breeds fear and the desire not to be attracted, the desire to forget "the blissful nester in its flame." Although the sentence struggles to conclude with an image that "simplifies through intensity," its very difficulty keeps an agony in mind. Merrill's fire cannot deny its own beauty, cannot take away the fear that springs from its inevitable mix of splendor and pain. As much as the adult, Yeatsian voice struggles in this sentence to anesthetize the claims of pain and insist on the higher aesthetic and metaphysical claims of "the blissful nester in its flame," Merrill has contrived to frustrate just enough of the Yeatsian intensity of his final image that the precipitous fall from the "laughing child" to the "burnt child," from innocence to experience, shadows and chills the effect of this stanza, and of the poem as a whole.

We see that "bright and warm" is at once an innocent and a tempting, duplicitous, and indeed self-deceptive characterization of fire. The fire's Yeatsian voice proves finely Satanic in its vision of esoteric knowledge and immortality, that "rare bird" again. The adult voice cannot deny the fall into pain, but its whole effort thereafter is to reclaim the innocence of its childlike vision of the "blissful nester." This is the innocence-after-experience that Yeats recounts in "Vacillation IV" and in "Anima Mundi XXI," the innocence that Yeats identifies with the Condition of Fire and that underwrites his moments of vision and ecstasy. Merrill's poem longs to hold on to Yeatsian ardor, but in its effort "to hold in a single thought reality and justice," "Fire Poem" also resists Yeatsian simplification. Its unity is dramatic and refuses wholly to forget or metaphorize the experience of pain.[81]

"A View of the Burning" continues the meditation on Yeatsian themes begun in "Fire Poem." The sense of critique grows in this poem and carries over into "About the Phoenix." At first the poem promises simplicity: "A View." And yet, with the first phrase "Righteous or not," complexities, questions of perspective, identity, and motivation ramify throughout the text. Simplicities: the agent and the action—an angry man, dressed in crimson, face blackened "If only by the smoke of a self-purifying flame," thrusts his hand into the fire. Not quite so simple: his motive—he acts not so much out of a desire for self-punishment for "a moment's folly" as for self-mutilation: to "sear away" the useful part of his hand. Here fire seems to answer the need for cathartic pain and the "deliberate sacrifice" that Yeats associates not just with the "the Christian saint and hero" but with the poet as well (*Per Amica* 333). Yeats's poet is he "who has endured all imaginable pangs" to be rewarded with a view of "that dazzling, unforeseen, wing-footed wanderer" (Ibid. 332). The reference to Hermes, here in his phoenix-like association with alchemical fire ("I shall find the dark grow luminous, the void fruitful"), allows Yeats to confound the physical and metaphysical attributes of fire, even as he develops his case for the latter. It will be one of Merrill's tasks in this poem to keep in view what separates these two notions of fire, even as he sees how they also feed each other.[82]

According to Yeats, fire is the element "that makes all things simple;" in the Condition of Fire "is all music and all rest;" it is an innocence of hatred, anger, and fear that makes one love; it is Shelley's "fire for which all thirst" (*Per Amica* 346, 357, 364–65). It is the "holy fire" of Byzantium that will consume the heart "sick with desire." It is the flame "begotten of flame" where "all complexities of fury leave, / Dying into a dance, /An agony of trance, / An agony of flame that cannot singe a sleeve" ("Byzantium"). It is the condition of which Yeats wrote: "My body of a sudden blazed; / And twenty minutes more or less / It seemed, so great my happiness, / That I was blessèd and could bless" ("Vacillation"). In short, whether "righteous or not," it is just what an angry man might most desire, "a self-purifying flame." Taken to its height, Yeats tells us this condition grows so pure "and far extended and so luminous" it feels that all the world "would, like a country drunkard who has thrown a wisp into his own thatch, burn up time" (*Per Amica* 365); it is the moment "God shall burn up the world with a kiss."[83] What looks like madness is also divine. Here the "simplicity" in Yeats's formula for the Condition of Fire, "simplification through intensity," spins off toward both imbecility and the singularity of godhead.

In each instance in which Yeats evokes the Condition of Fire, although the overriding tone is one of beatitude verging on ecstasy, a masochistic dynamic of self- or cosmic immolation underwrites the passion of the scene. For example, in "In Memory of Eva Gore-Booth and Con Markiewicz," the speaker acknowledges the "folly of a fight / With a common wrong or right"—as if he is either beyond or trying to convince himself to surmount "the common condition of our life," which is hatred, "irritation with public or private events or persons"—knowing as he does that transcendence of terrestrial reality into the Condition of Fire happens "the moment I cease to hate" (*Per Amica* 365). "In Memory" seems most to capture the thirst for transcendence which is nonetheless still a straining and not "all music and rest" (Ibid. 357). Innocence and beauty can be saved from their enemy, time, only in the Condition of Fire, the conflagration. Thus the speaker calls on his "Dear Shadows" to "Arise and bid me strike a match / And strike another till time catch; / . . . Bid me strike a match and blow"—so that the fury of the last five lines belies with a breath all the seeming composure of the opening five. It is this frightening, holy *and* demonic masochism that Merrill treats most directly in "A View of the Burning":

> Righteous or not, here comes an angry man
> Done up in crimson, his face blackened
> If only by the smoke of a self-purifying flame.
> Now he is thrusting his hand into the flame
> To sear away not, as he said, a moment's folly
> So much as his hand, the useful part of it.
> I must confess this fails, after a bit,
> To produce the intended effect on us.
> We had loved each other freely, humanly
> With our own angers and our own forgiveness. . .

To start, the poem gives every indication that the "view" it will offer is a more or less objective one, that the speaker and the angry man he observes are quite separate and distinct. We are surprised to learn that the angry man's self-mutilating behavior is aimed not only at himself—that it is meant to produce an intended effect on the speaker and his partner ("us"), (although it fails to do so)—but this surprise does not detract from the security of a distinct observer/observed perspective. The reader almost certainly wonders about the identity of the speaker and his relationship to the angry man; and, as if to satisfy this kind of curiosity, we are told that the speaker and his partner "had loved each other freely, *humanly* / With our own angers and our own forgiveness"—as if such loving, reminiscent of the ambivalence and fervor of Auden's "Lay your sleeping head, my love, / *Human* on my faithless arm," were the cause or occasion for the other man's ire (emphasis added). The once seemingly distinct figures become more and more interrelated, however, as fire brings a unity to all it touches, whether it is the fire of anger ("Righteous or not") or the fire of love (faithful or not).

> We had loved each other freely, humanly
> With our own angers and our own forgiveness
> —Who now, made light of by his seriousnes,
> Gasses on which flame feeds, are wafted up
> With lyre and dart, public, hilarious,
>
> Two cupids cuddling in a cupola.

The couple are "made light of" by the seriousness of the angry man; and here Merrill's pun first openly ignites the possibility of the poem voicing an intra-subjective, masochistic identity. On the one hand, the phrase suggests a kind of condescending scorn in keeping with the angry man's hostility and pride; on the other, if taken literally, the phrase suddenly makes it possible that it is the couple themselves that the man has thrust into the flame. They are his other hand; they are what's burning:[84] "—Who now, made light of by his seriousness, / Gases on which flame feeds, are wafted up . . ." Although the appositive, "Gases on which flame feeds," having "his seriousness" as possible antecedent, still allows a shadow of the more objective reading—as one may still see the shadow of a burning log through flames—the rush of the succeeding lines more and more feeds the inflammatory, intra-subjective reading, and "Gases" more strongly harkens back to the "We" who are made light of. Self-immolation is suddenly rendered as baroque apotheosis: "With lyre and dart, public, hilarious, / Two cupids cuddling in a cupola." Merrill's "self-purifying flame" critiques Yeats's "holy fire." Both consume that "useful part," be it heart or hand, and both transport (gather or waft), or translate, the speaker into the realm of public artifice; but the resulting artifice for Merrill is not transcendent eternity. It is "hilarious," a laughing flame that makes light of ("lyre and dart") the pretensions of that liar—art.[85]

In the lines, "Two cupids cuddling in a cupola. / Useless to say he is acting for our sakes," the copulative "It is" which is elided beneath the "cupola" mimes a copulation elided in "cuddling." This absence also leads aptly to "Useless," which ("Righteous or not") so often marks or masks the anger (and self-anger) directed at masturbatory or homosexual practice. Thus, as if in reply to just this accusation, the missing copulative *is* thematically productive. "Useless" recalls the "useful" part of the hand being burned, for some unnamed offense, and suggests the desired result of the self-inflicted punishment, a hand that is "useless" to offend again.[86] But such recollection also reminds us that the punishment fails its intended effect on "us," the lovers or the hands. It is useless to say who "he" is by this point in the poem, whether some other angry man or an aspect of the speaker's self, just as useless as it is to say he is acting for the sake of the lovers—as if protecting them by rendering useless a possible instrument of his anger. It is useless to say he is acting for the sake of the hand he burns, keeping it from further usefulness, just as it is useless to say he acts for art's sake (so close in sound to "our sake" and so proximate to the cupola's baroque cupids), as if the artifice could justify the anger, or the desire. Merrill's lines insists on delivering all these "useless" possibilities, as if to underscore both the ramifying and refining effectiveness of such burning possibility.[87] Succeeding lines maintain this simultaneity of multiple valences and self-reflexivity:

> One does not care for those who care for one
> More than one cares for oneself. Divine or not,
> At the end he calls upon justice. But, my dear,
> Little shall startle from the embers, merely
> A grinning head incensed, a succulence
> On which to feast, grinning ourselves, I fear.

The first sentence gives a general rule meant to apply to this particular case. Sympathy, it is claimed, follows physical or economic rules of relative scarcity or abundance.[88] Since the angry man (or that aspect of the speaker) cares more for him than he does for himself, it is useless to ask the speaker to care for the angry man. Warmth does not flow from the cooler to the warmer object. We should not expect the poor to subsidize the rich (however much they notoriously do). Note too the play of dominance and appropriation in this situation: "those who care for one more than one cares for oneself" attain totalizing and objectifying prerogatives over those deficient in self-regard. A hand has been thrust into the flame. The one thus "cared for" may adopt something like the speaker's tone of defensive indifference, but this is the classic guise of resentment. It is after all the one who cares more, the one who acts, who is able to call on justice, whether "Divine or not," so that, in this almost Nietzschean dynamic, supervening "care" (or desire or need) both permits and justifies any act.

We recall how often Yeats declared himself "an angry man," how he called "hatred" his common condition and the common condition of people in general. We recall that he enters upon the Condition of Fire "the moment I cease to hate." Then, he is flooded with affection, looks "at the strangers near as if I had known them all my life," and, himself ablaze, feels "That I was blessèd and could bless" (*Per Amica* 365 and "Vacillation IV"). Thus, Yeats too moves through something like the stages of Merrill's poem, from anger, to the "self-purifying flame" of Merrill's "burning," and finally to the flood of "caring" that lets him thrust a hand into the flame, or throw "a wisp into his own thatch [and] burn up time" (*Per Amica* 365). In "Vacillation VII", he is at once "Struck dumb in the simplicity of fire," not effected, affecting indifference, *and* apt to call for "Isaiah's coal," (like Merrill's "Divine or not") and to say of fire that "salvation (like Merrill's "justice") walks within." Yeats's Vision system gives him the distance to look on "the burning town" of Troy, the conquests of Babylon or Nineveh, or "man's blood-sodden heart"—on all the tragic or merely indifferent scenes and declare with burning simplicity: "Let all things pass away" ("Double Vision," "Lapis Lazuli," "Vacillation"). In sharp contrast, what Merrill's "view" reveals is how fire provides no such distance, no such simplicity, and how both Merrill's arch tone and Yeats's ardent assurance may well be only masks for fear.

"But, my dear," Merrill's speaker begins his summation, "Little shall startle from the embers. . . . " Here it is the tone of social pleasantry (or is it real affection?) that strives to dampen or mask the horror to come. Who could the speaker be addressing now? The lover who shares his fate? The angry man who has reduced more than his hand to embers? Himself, as lover, hand, judge, and executioner? By this point in the poem, all questions of identity have become part of the flickering fascination of burning itself. With his pun on "incensed" and the final "I fear," rhyming so sociably with the sentence's opening "my dear," the speaker persists in the defensive badinage that has consistently marked the poem. These efforts continue the strain to see the burning as separate, manageable—the useful, friendly-frightening, domesticated flame. But they also remain so much bravery in Hell. The figure of Ugolino gnawing, bent over Ruggieri, shadows these lines: "A grinning head incensed, a succulence / On which to feast, grinning ourselves, I fear." Punning on "incensed" may seek to make light of the horror it also brings to light, but it is the persistence of overpowering anger somehow also sanctified ("Righteous or not," "Divine or not") that burns through the witticism. What remains in these lines is all the avidity of fire itself, "Gases on which flame feeds." The smoke of incense *is* "a succulence," and the rhyme reinforces the identity; it is the enflaming juiciness of desire feeding on desire. The speaker, too, now in all his aspects ("ourselves"), enters upon "the condition of fire," as a demonic, devouring flame.[89]

This "grinning head . . . / On which to feast, grinning ourselves" is Merrill's version of "flame begotten of flame." His tone and rhetorical effects mime the doubleness of Yeats's "agony of flame that cannot singe a sleeve." Like the later Yeats of "Byzantium," as opposed to the poet of "Sailing to Byzantium," Merrill does not belie the "agony" or the "furies of complexity" in his effort to attain the Condition of Fire ("holy" or not). And as in Yeats, at least one impulse in Merrill makes every effort to make sure that "his" burning is safe, even perhaps "useless" or mordantly "hilarious," that it "cannot singe a sleeve." But whereas Yeats consistently pulls a self-dramatizing grandeur out of the flames, what startles from the embers of Merrill's view of burning is the ambiguous, haunting play of the last words: "I fear." After this poem, Yeats's presentation of the Condition of Fire seems too simple. It presents a consumption too devoutly to be wished. Merrill's view of the burning is inside and outside at once, just as his view of identity flickers between self and other and multiple intra-subjectivities. Merrill highlights the sensationalism and masochism of his subject matter, this longing for a simple self-purification, a final totalizing justice. Yet Merrill's tone remains detached and unaffected, however archly critical and self-critical—and thus, in this sense, remains true to offering a "view."

Both "Fire Poem" and "A View of the Burning" present Merrill's ambivalent response to the primal scene of his Yeatsian instruction. Both show the allure of what Bloom identifies as a flame-like "love unconditioned in its giving, but wholly conditioned to passivity in its receiving," where the younger poet is "kindled" by the proffered flame of the precursor. Bloom continues, "at the start of every intertextual encounter, there is this unequal initial love, where necessarily the giving famishes the receiver. The receiver is set on fire, and yet the fire belongs to the giver" (*Map* 51). In both poems this unequal, consuming love, both fascinates and terrifies. The challenge comes in finding some form of accommodation with the "rare bird bedded in the heart of harm" that will nonetheless allow the poet his own "wavering center," his own sense of "justice," however embattled.[90] What is wanted is a vision of "loving kindness" that Bloom nominates "Covenant-love." But as Bloom explains, this "loving kindness" is subject to the irreducible ambivalence of "what Freud meant by 'antithetical primal words,'" so that the "root meaning" of such love "also embraces that kind of 'keenness' that moves from 'ardent zeal' to 'jealousy,' 'envy,' and 'ambition,' and so Covenant-love is uneasily allied to a competitive element" (Ibid. 53)—a progression that aptly characterizes the vacillating energy of these two poems and their "ardent" efforts both to acknowledge and correct the precursor poet. These poems, in contrast to the "merely" assimilative, oceanic poems of poetic incarnation (and sometimes dissolution) "Accumulations of the Sea," "Forms of Death," and "The Drowning Poet," powerfully show Merrill moving from his "flooded apprenticeship" into a strong period of revisionary, "loving strife" with Yeats, his most troubling precursor.

Chapter Two

PRELUDE: FIRST READINGS OF YEATS'S *A VISION*

IN THE INTRODUCTION, I INDICATED HOW, THROUGHOUT *SANDOVER*, MERRILL belittles Yeats. Judging from what is said about the older poet and from what is (finally) given Yeats to say at the end of the completed poem, a reader of Merrill's *chef d'oeuvre* would have little idea that Merrill took Yeats's spiritualism or his poetry with any seriousness at all. Yet the notes Merrill made while reading and rereading Yeats's *A Vision* and his *Essays and Introductions* show Merrill turning to the older poet with deliberation and studious interest, often in just those occult matters that most exposed both Yeats and Merrill to ridicule.

The earliest record we have of Merrill reading *A Vision* comes in 1955, just two weeks after the day he and David Jackson first sat down to the Ouija board.[1] September 7, 1955, is the date given in the marginal note in Merrill's second-hand copy of *A Vision* (page 25). Perhaps spurred by the revelations of the board and what he already knew about Yeats's spiritualist experiences, Merrill turned to the older poet for guidance. He read through the 1928 "Introduction," drew a line along the margin indicating almost all of section "XV," and, in the margin on this same page wrote, "Is this what I must learn?" With this question in mind we may still wonder what the particular lesson was that Merrill had discovered in Yeats's text. Is it merely the idea, directly opposite Merrill's note, that he has been "overwhelmed by miracle as all men must be when in the midst of it" and that he has taken this miraculous material quite literally, but that his reason must likewise soon recover? Or the lesson may be more comprehensive, extending to all the material Merrill indicates by his marginal line. In this famous passage, Yeats writes:

> Some will ask whether I believe in the actual existence of my circuits of sun and moon . . . . To such a question I can but answer that if sometimes, overwhelmed

> by miracle as all men must be when in the midst of it, I have taken such periods literally, my reason has soon recovered; and now that the system stands out clearly in my imagination I regard them as stylistic arrangements of experience comparable to the cubes in the drawing of Wyndham Lewis and to the ovoids in the sculpture of Brancusi. They have helped me to hold in a single thought reality and justice. (24–25)

By marking off this passage Merrill seems to indicate his hope that his encounters with the other world will lead him, as they did Yeats, to a "system [that] stands out clearly in my imagination," a system that will enable him to render "stylistic arrangements of experience" and which, ultimately, will help him "hold in a single thought reality and justice." These are large ambitions for a young poet.

Merrill certainly knew Yeats well enough that he would not mistake Yeats's "reality" for a narrow interest in empirical "facts" or his "justice" for concern primarily with the rigors of social equity. Indeed, the phrase can be taken as a touchstone for both Romantic and modernist aesthetic ideologies, both of which maintain the understanding that it is the power and vocation of art to reconcile divergent discourses and realms of experience in a "higher" discourse and discreet realm of experience. Merrill was particularly well schooled in this aesthetic at Lawrenceville, at Amherst, and through his own reading.[2] Indeed, Yeats's phrase fits well with the metaphysical and aesthetic ambitions of much of Merrill's early poetry and his reading at the time.[3] If for Yeats "reality" also includes the realm of spirits, and "justice" entails a pattern of fulfillment or completeness, Merrill has no quarrel with either term and has a poet's abiding interest in finding language that will enable him both to conceive and to convey his vision of "what is" with economy and a sense of wholeness (*Vision* 235–36; Bloom *Yeats* 276).

Merrill turned to this introductory passage in *A Vision* again and again over the years as interviewers asked whether he believed in the spirit voices his poems presented. The passage became a kind of touchstone on which he improvised, in no small part because the often-explicit allusions to Yeats it afforded provided Merrill with authoritative cover for his cagey "double mindedness" on the question of his belief. In a 1980 interview with Ross Labrie, Merrill makes this answer to the question, "How literally are you into spiritualism?" "As Yeats said, when you are caught up in it you believe it wholeheartedly; when you cool off you see it as a stylization of various things in your experience or in the world's experience" ("James Merrill at Home" 30). Here Merrill not only remembers the substance but the occasion of Yeats's remarks and, with his last phrase "a stylization of various things . . . in the world's experience," he suggests a way of circling back from pragmatic aesthetic skepticism to quasi-Jungian notions, which are in themselves a kind of belief.

In a 1982 interview with Jean Lunn, and in response to a similar question about belief, Merrill again offers a telling paraphrase of Yeats's sentences:

> *As for belief,* I've spent too much time trying to be of two minds—because that seemed to be the most fruitful way of writing the poem, and feeling about the

> material—I've spent too much time doing that to settle permanently for one or the other, for skepticism or credulity. I have been very skeptical, usually in the early stages; I've also been extremely credulous at high exciting moments, simply because there was not room left for doubt, there couldn't be—the excitement, the thrill of the patterns you saw consolidating was such that you did believe. But this is exactly what Yeats said: that in the heat of the dictation you shape things instinctively, your experience gets stylized in spite of yourself, kind of like the tulip that doesn't know it's growing. . . . I don't think that just because it turns out to be a system that there's anything against it; it seems to me that everybody's belief is a system of one sort or another. ("Conversation" 4–5).

In this passage the movement goes from initial skepticism to the enthusiasm of encounter to a rationalized understanding of the experience which is itself figured as a kind of possession: "in the heat of *dictation* . . . your experience gets stylized in spite of yourself" (emphasis added). Yeats makes no such claim, but Merrill uses this idea as a way of sidestepping apparent "responsibility" for belief. Merrill's final remarks about "system" point toward Yeats's holding "in a single thought reality and justice," and in a way that works to defend such systematic ambitions against seeming too grand or unlikely in a lyric poet.

Again, in a 1991 videotaped interview with Helen Vendler, Merrill returned to this passage as soon as the question of belief was raised:

> Well, as with Yeats, he said that there were times when it is extremely beautiful and there was no choice but to believe; but then as the experience cooled and as he distanced himself from it, he saw that, in a way, times, culture, and civilization—all these things that the voices are given to—were stylizations like the cubes and so on in a Wyndham Lewis drawing. In writing the poem I never wanted to be of less than two minds. It seemed to me that if I gave in and swallowed the doctrine, the system, hook, line and sinker, that there would be no, no way of saving myself or saving the poem as a piece of literature.[4]

It may be unfair to subject this spoken reply to the same kind of scrutiny as Merrill's written interview responses. But from this response we see that Merrill again follows the Yeatsian pattern of moving from overwhelmed belief to aesthetic distance. He even uses Yeats's references to "the cubes in the drawing of Wyndham Lewis" (*Vision* 25) to help bring his remark to a similar resolution. Yet the apparent thrust of his remarks, explaining the contingency of belief, again hides a notion more deeply subversive of empirical explanation: "times, culture, and civilization" are themselves "stylizations"; they are what Merrill's "voices are given to." If this last phrase means anything, it suggests a kind of Jungian account of how everything from a specific culture or civilization to Merrill's voices are alike "stylizations" of some shared unconscious ground—so that the question of believing in one more than the other simply drops away.

Merrill's concluding remarks are likewise revealing. The rhetorical stance of never being of less than two minds may be necessary to Merrill's ideas of what makes for successful literature (and mental balance), but what is interesting here is how closely his "public" language of skepticism, of not swallowing "the doctrine . . . hook, line and sinker," replicates the terms of his credulity. The climax of Merrill's play, *The Bait*, concerns the protagonist at once taking and literally being the bait, and at one famous point in *Mirabell*, Merrill characterizes himself and DJ as being "more the docile takers-in of seed" so that "No matter what tall tale our friends emit, / Lately—you've noticed?—we just swallow it" (S. 154).[5] In such passages, as we watch the movements of Merrill's doubt and belief, "whose elements [often] converge," variously "scissoring and mending," we glimpse another lesson learned perhaps from Yeats: "We must not make a false faith by hiding from our thoughts the causes of doubt."[6] Here faith, as "the highest achievement of the human intellect" (*Per Amica* 332) and "the only gift man can make to God" (S. 154), is a kind of keeping faith. It represents persistence in the work of attending to the world and endeavoring to "MAKE SENSE OF IT" (S. 337). In this way, Yeats's faith is the very like the gift the angels make to God B in *Sandover* and that Merrill's poetry consistently endeavors to make (S. 350–52).

As with any book Merrill was reading closely, his annotations to *A Vision* are sparse but show considerable engagement with both the rhetorical and thematic details of the text. Merrill underlines the imagistic "supersensual power intervenes, the steel-like plasticity of water where the last ripple has been smoothed away," but not the whole sentence which begins, "man is submissive and plastic: unless where supersensual power intervenes . . . " (*Vision* 82). On page 72, Merrill labels Yeats's interlocking triangles "subjective" and "objective" and adds arrows (—> <—) just as on the diagram of the gyre on page 71, to underscore the dynamic relationship between the double cones. Merrill also underlines Yeats's quotation from Blake: "Contraries are positive . . . a negation is not a contrary" (72), brackets the first mention of the "Four Faculties" (73), circles "Phase 15" in the diagram on page 79, and picks out this sentence: "Only by the pursuit or acceptance of its direct opposite, that object of desire or moral ideal which is of all possible things the most difficult, and by forcing that form upon the *Body of Fate*, can it attain self-knowledge and expression" (83).

Each of these markings point to material that is central to understanding Yeats's system, but Merrill's annotations also support his own account of only "half trying / To make sense of *A Vision*," since his notes do not extend beyond page 83 (S. 14).[7] This effort to study Yeats's *A Vision*, which was soon, and apparently easily, abandoned, fits Leslie Brisman and Henry Sloss's contentions that Merrill did not want to take his early encounters with the spirit world too seriously, even though these experiences seemed to offer a powerful link to the divine and the real. Such encounters with the occult were also threatening. As the speaker recounts in "Voices from the Other World":

> . . . once looked at lit
> By the cold reflection of the dead
> Risen extinct but irresistible,
> Our lives have never seemed more full, more real,
> Nor the full moon more quick to chill.

In a much later poem, Merrill makes explicit the connection between the full moon and the inhuman unity represented by Yeats's Phase Fifteen: "And Gravity's mask floats—at Phase XV / Oblivion-bright—above the stolen scene" ("A Room at the Heart of Things). What both attracts and frightens Merrill in these encounters is this chilling glare of oblivion. In these encounters, as with his relationship to Yeats, Merrill's art depends on manipulating forces both protective and conductive, forces that draw him to as they also insulate him from an unsustainable contact with the absolute (S. 424, 84). It was important for Merrill that he not become too enthralled and that he maintain as "brave" a front of nonchalance in the face of his encounters with Yeats and with the voices from the other world he was beginning to entertain.[8]

BRAVING THE FIRE:
POSTURES OF NONCHALANCE IN THE EARLY
OUIJA BOARD POEMS, 1957–1967

In Chapter One, I endeavored to trace the pattern of Merrill's relationship with Yeats in the poems before his encounter with the "voices" of the Ouija board. I argued that these poems revealed a pattern moving from a period of "floodedness" and fairly overt imitation and appropriation to more covert strategies of struggle and critique. Addressing Yeatsian themes was important for Merrill before he started working with the Ouija board, but his experiences with the board made Yeats's priority and influence even more of an issue. It is tempting to say that in subsequent work Merrill "braves" Yeats's influence, through strategies of nonchalance, trivialization, and silence, much as he does his early experiences with the board itself.[9] But this is only a partial truth, since Yeats's poetic voice and vision haunts the poems and prose leading up to "The Book of Ephraim" much more insistently than any of the more occult "voices" hailing from the "other world" of the Ouija Board. Nonetheless, the writing leading up to the highly Yeats-influenced 1969 collection, *The Fire Screen*, reveals how Merrill worked to keep Yeats's demanding example at a manageable distance, as well as his seemingly effortless work to "make light" of his ongoing, double-minded engagement with the older poet.

The following discussion focuses on two bodies of work: one, the early writings which more or less explicitly address Merrill's first experiences with the Ouija board and which also establish the theme and posture of "nonchalance" and, two, work written in the early to middle 1960s which show Merrill applying strategies of nonchalance to his continued relationship with Yeats.

I

In "Voices from the Other World," first published in 1957, which Leslie Brisman characterizes as pitting "Yeatsian urbanity against the desire for something as 'cold and passionate as the dawn'" (191), Merrill first establishes the theme of "nonchalance" in the face of the Ouija board's otherworldly "voices":

> Indeed, we have grown nonchalant
> Towards the other world. In the gloom here,
> Our elbows on the cleared
> Table, we talk and smoke, pleased to be stirred
>
> Rather by buzzings in the jasmine, by the drone
> Of our own voices and poor blind Rover's wheeze,
> Than by those clamoring overhead,
> Obsessed or piteous, for a commitment
> We still have wit to postpone . . .

Nonchalance staves off the threat of commitment to these "clamoring" voices—voices, as it were, of a "higher calling." Yet it is telling that the stance of nonchalance itself drops away in the poem and that Merrill chooses to evoke such a calling in particularly Yeatsian accents. His voices are the "cold reflections of the dead," and though "extinct," their influence proves all but "irresistible." Merrill announces his intention to postpone any commitment to this influence and tells us the strategy he will deploy again and again to hold it back—namely "wit." Yet the poem ends, not in a gesture of witty evasion, but with two lines which, in effect, allow Yeats to set the terms of Merrill's dilemma, "two lines," as Brisman says, "Yeats could have written" (Ibid.): "Our lives have never seemed more full, more real, / Nor the full moon more quick to chill." Thus, the poem also makes the first implicit connection between Yeatsian influence and Merrill's voices from the other world.

Merrill's loosely autobiographical novel, *The Seraglio* (1957), offers an account of Merrill's early experiences with the Ouija board that is consonant in many of its details with "Voices from the Other World" and the early sections of "The Book of Ephraim."[10] Yet in the novel, the Merrill character, Francis Tanning, is anything but nonchalant about his occult encounters. They transform him "in a new odd way that affected only half of his face" (237), an image for the self-divided, "torn" individual that Merrill will take up again in "The Thousand and Second Night."[11] In Francis, Merrill presents a cautionary portrait of false enthusiasm, figured very much in Yeats's terms of Dispersal. At first Francis represents himself has having achieved something like Yeats's "Unity of Being" following the revelations of the Ouija board:

> It left him free to snap his fingers blithely at history, at human reason. "Things that once upset me dreadfully," he was telling her, "simply don't concern me any more."
>
> . . .
>
> "I feel warmly towards people for the first time in my life. I need no defenses. I'm like a philosopher in his bath; all the hatred, all the fear has been let out of me, as by an opened vein, painlessly. Sometimes," Francis laughed, letting go her hand, "I don't even know what I'm saying, I who used to weigh every word! . . . I can't imagine fearing death. I can't imagine wanting anything—what I've been given's enough" (242–43)[12]

Yet we know that Francis is neglecting this world in his obsession with the "next" and has not learned to hold both worlds "in a single thought" (*Vision* 25). He neglects his friends and is no longer particularly kind toward his old friend, Jane, who could almost say with one of the "three good friends" in "The Thousand and Second Night," "You were nice, James, before your trip. Or so / I thought." In his obsession with Meno, his familiar spirit, he also neglects his new friend, Marcello—prophetically, as we shall see, in much the same way that Merrill will fear that his fascination with Ephraim's Ouija board revelations might undermine his relationship with

Strato several years hence.[13] Francis's elation is fragile, his security false. At a later session at the board, when he is unable to reach Meno, we see that far from being beyond want or fear Francis has grown dependent upon his contact with the "other world":

> "Meno, Meno," he was begging, "we are here, we are waiting, come to us! ... Can you see us? can you hear us? ... It is of the greatest importance that you give some sign. We may otherwise never again communicate! ... Meno, there's so much you haven't told me, so many ways you can help me...."
>
> ...
>
> "Is any body there?" asked Francis. "We want so much to make contact with somebody.... Please! ... Is anybody there?" (246)

Here is a character who is radically of two minds but, unlike Merrill, is unaware of the fact. Francis vacillates, but only we see it.

With this character, Merrill suggests that he knows that he will need more strength to begin to forge poems and a life that can productively accommodate his fears of death, his fears of "aging into" a character such as Francis, and his deep uneasiness as well as delight in the communications from the Ouija board. More than anything, Merrill wants to avoid aiming "so high" only to lapse "into such negligence" (236). Thus, Merrill self-consciously constructs Francis as his monitory False Mask, the persona that permits expression of what he dreads and must struggle against (*Per Amica* 335).[14] Francis is Merrill's pathetic caricature of a Tower poet, questing for sublime knowledge and the transcendent encounter, but undermined by his own desires and credulity. For this reason, it is particularly fitting that the chapter closes with Francis descending from the scene of his occult encounters "down the winding iron stair"—on his way to dinner and the opera (248).

Two years later, in 1959, Merrill returns to his explicitly occult theme in "Words for the Familiar Spirit." In this poem, Merrill evokes the Southwest landscape in terms Yeats would recognize from his experiences with mediums, ectoplasmic emanations, and the spiritualist rituals of The Golden Dawn:[15]

> i
> The tongues leap on the summit of your will.
> The dead shine back like planets. They don't know
> Whose livingness they shiver round, until
> A glancing shape leans up and out from it.
> This is yourself. Your body sits below,
> Clenched upon vertigo, mouth slack, brows knit.
>
> ii
> The speech condensing on your breath is mine,
> Is me. Thick, fast, gemmed round you, it exceeds

> Meaning. Tomorrow, blinking in sunshine,
> You won't recall it . . .

In the poem, Merrill makes his own use of Yeats's "rocky face" ("But down the sheer face / Behind your features it will have run in beads, / Seeking a level miles beyond this place") and the figure of Empedocles from "The Gyres" ("upon the gleaming lip / Of an immense and immanent cascade, / Sun, sky, volcano totter, shatter, slip") and evokes the gyres themselves as "more than eddies made / In blood by devils twirling on their toes." But his purpose in these images is not to convey the "inhuman remoteness from ordinary life" of either the natural or occult worlds, as Yeats does in "The Gyres" (Jeffares qtd. in Bloom *Yeats* 435). Instead, Merrill establishes an uncanny communication between the human, natural, and occult realms. Merrill thus employs Yeatsian images to revise Yeats's customary sense, which depends on more rigorous separation (indeed often antagonism) among these realms. Merrill also exploits the Yeatsian interplay of primary and antithetical, interior and exterior, up and down, dream and waking throughout the poem and, out of Empedocles' experience with the volcanic abyss, releases "the quetzal floating up and up" recalling Yeats's falcon in "The Second Coming"—but again reversing the meaning of this spiraling flight—from Yeats's image of anarchic loss of control to Merrill's sense of an apotheosis.[16] Here too Merrill writes lines that Yeats (had he ever visited New Mexico) could have written:

> iii
> Your body crouches on red earth beside
> The broad and inmost serpent of my drift
> Whose dream is only more and more to glide,
> As yours is to awaken from the dream
> Transfigured. Rippling, neither slow nor swift,
> The condor's shadow widens on the stream.

Stanza iv which begins "Poor savage, never once do you suppose / My river something more than eddies made / In blood by devils twirling on their toes" provides the basis for the later Balanchine tercets in Merrill's "Watching the Dance": "Poor savage, doubting that a river flows / But for the myriad eddies made / By unseen powers twirling on their toes." This later poem completes the Yeatsian vacillation between the expansive "god's own roar / . . . Then to endure, green fire in a soap / Bubble, the quetzal floating up and up" of the earlier poem and the inward, centering lesson of the dance presented in the later poem's second and concluding tercet: "Here in this darkness it would seem / You had already died, and were afraid. / Be still. Observe the powers. Infer the stream." By bringing the Balanchine section of Merrill's "Watching the Dance " back to its roots in the occult, Yeats-inflected landscape of the southwest, we also release the later poem from the nonchalant "mask" of its merely topical occasion—one in which Merrill contrasts the sublimity of Balanchine's New York City Ballet with the twitching "teenage plankton" of the poem's second section, "Discotheque." Allowed to stand next to the earlier poem, the Balanchine section of "Watching the Dance" slips beyond the glamour of a clever conceit and insists on the Yeatsian provenance of a spiritual theater (founded on the dance). This relation between the earlier and later poems also helps recover a deliberate theatricality implicit in "Words for the Familiar Spirit"'s second-person address. Finally, the dialectical relation between two poems several years and seemingly worlds apart (a Yeatsian relation in itself), is but one indication of how consistently Merrill employs Yeatsian idioms and themes when addressing his own early experiences at the Ouija board, even as he maintains a posture of his witty nonchalance regarding these same experiences.

II

Over the next several years (1962–1966) Merrill continues to make use of Yeats, all the while being careful not to engage either Yeats's poetry or his own occult experiences too directly. A brief survey gives an indication of the importance and range of Yeats's presence during these years. *Water Street* (1962) is bracketed by two poems, "An Urban Convalescence" and "A Tenancy," which announce, for Merrill, a renewed poetic vocation in terms Yeats would recognize as particularly telling. Yeatsian language and themes also figure prominently in "Childlessness," "Prism," and "For Proust"; and "After Greece" deftly evokes a Yeatsian alchemy of essential elements and a system that "[c]alls for spirits." Similarly, "The Thousand and Second Night" and "From the Cupola," [the second and second to last poems in Merrill's next volume, *Nights and Days* (1966)] lay claim to ambitious thematic territory largely identified with Yeats, while "Violent Pastoral" revisits Yeats's "Leda and the Swan." In this same volume, "Charles on Fire" and the first sonnet of "The Broken Home" lightly recall Yeats's "Condition of Fire." And in "Days of 1964," Merrill's "erotic mask" and assertion "A god breathed from my lips" echo Yeats's discussion of Mask and "sweetheart" and the lines "he knew another's breath came and went within his breath upon the carven lips" from *Per Amica Silentia Lunae* (336, 335).

As we have seen, Merrill also makes pointed but arch use of Yeats in his 1965 experimental novel, *The (Diblos) Notebook*. In each of these volumes, Merrill continues to mine his productive ambivalence toward the older poet, turning to Yeats for vital poetic resources, toying with Yeatsian rhetoric and imagery, recasting and extending Yeatsian argument, playing Yeats as a foil or mask, working to shake off Yeats's stony priority. Yet throughout these volumes, Merrill also works to keep Yeats at best a shadowy, background figure. Through the devices of glancing allusion, deliberate obscurity, irony, and a characteristic lightness of tone, Merrill maintains his posture of nonchalance toward the older poet—a nonchalance that also recalls Yeats's own commitment to the aristocratic value of *sprezzatura*.

Part of what haunts Merrill in the poems of *Water Street* is the question of how to make his way as an adult gay man and poet in a clamorous, conventional, calamity-ridden world. It is a question of whether the poems, the houses, made "Out of the life lived, out of the love spent" into which he would invite others to "be at home"—whether such a childless but poetically productive domesticity would suffice in the face of the world's claims. In "Childlessness" Nature, the speaker's "dream-wife" calls for the "gender of suns, large, hardy, / Enviable blooms" and threatens the apocalypse of the television war: "The erased metropolis reassembled / On sampans, freighted each / With toddlers, holy dolls, dead ancestors," "a world / Clad only in rags, threadbare, / Dabbling the highway's ice with blood." In the poem, it is as if because of Merrill's childlessness the world falls apart and the particular burden of this calamity, like a "cloak thrown down" for the world to wear, "Has fallen onto the shoulders of my parents / Whom it is eating to the bone." Yeats enters this poem as a goad to increase its self-inflicted bitterness. The "foul rag and bone shop" here indicts the heart that robs it of its "natural" issue. Nature's cloak "blown back / To show the lining's dull lead foil" engenders no "embroideries / Out of old mythologies." Instead, her "slow colors" burst along the speaker's limbs "Like bombs." Yeats threw down his coat at the end of *Responsibilities* because fools had taken it up. Nature, spurned by the speaker in Merrill's poem, wraps his parents in the corrosive cloak of generation as if to make them pay for his slight. Yeats, at the beginning of *Responsibilities*, begs pardon of the old fathers:

> Pardon that for a barren passion's sake,
> Although I have come close on forty-nine,
> I have no child, I have nothing but a book,
> Nothing but that to prove your blood and mine.

Merrill denies himself even that last claim: "But in my garden / Nothing's been seeded"—as if no book of his, no poem, could answer let alone "prove" the claims of blood the world, father and mother, requires. Yet this is exactly the challenge Merrill is determined to face.

Thus, if Merrill's project is to make art of sufficient "density" that it somehow answers the claims of life for more life, it can only do so by finessing the Yeatsian tension between art and life. The task is grandly compensatory, but it must also avoid grand aesthetic claims. Artifice, however golden, cannot eclipse the vital claims of time and nature. Perfection of the art must be seen to derive from efforts to make sense of life, to make a home for himself and others, to serve as host who can say:

> welcome, friend.
> Welcome to earth, time, others; to
> These cool darks, of sense, of language,
> Each at once thread and maze.   ("Little Fanfare for Felix Magowan")

If the child is to be Merrill's art ["The little feet that patter here are metrical" ("Up and Down")] that art must affirm (formally, since "Form's what affirms") all the promises and terrors of childhood and, within the medium of paper, ink, and metal, effect "the unstiflement of the entire story" ("The Broken Home"). In Yeats's alchemical terms, which Merrill takes up again and again, art's enchantments though "fiery" issue in the fixity of stone; though situated "in the midst of all," these stones nonetheless only "trouble the living stream" ("Easter, 1916"). The point, for Merrill, is to make the art serve as "stepping-stones" which take one again and again back into the living stream, there "Without clothes, without caution // Plunging past gravity" to reemerge, in one's own body and "In [one's] own mind," "astral with phosphor" ("Swimming by Night"). The transcendent moment happens bodily and mentally at once, within and for life. As Yeats has it:

> My body of a sudden blazed;
> And twenty minutes more or less
> It seemed, so great my happiness,
> That I was blessèd and could bless.   ("Vacillation" IV)

For Merrill, art "help[s] us brave the elements / . . . of terror, anger, love," and so always returns us to the "wear and tear [of] the lawless heart" and the question of "how we live" ("Dreams about Clothes"). Yeats too returns to a "lawless heart"; but for him this return to the "foul rag and bone shop" is always for the sake of the "ladders" of artifice and "masterful image" whereby he may climb once more into realms of "pure mind" ("The Circus Animals' Desertion"). For Yeats, entering into mastery entails the immolation of the heart, desire, and the dying animal self; it takes us out of nature, gathers us into artifice ("Sailing to Byzantium"). Merrill refuses the disjunction between nature and mastery, since the plunge into living waters may itself confer a kind of mastery. The swimmer emerges aware he has taken on the universe as a garment. Though this sublime raiment is only borrowed and far too grand, there is nothing of a sorcerer's apprentice ridiculousness here:

> You wear your master's robe
> One last time, the far break
> Of waves, their length and sparkle, the spinning globe
> You wear, and the star running down his cheek.   ("Swimming by Night")

Mastery happens, but only momentarily, in the midst of life, as an awareness (sensual and sensible) of the world at once vast and "wearable," fitting and infinite, an awareness too of being the object of a master's regard and care. This is the program of Merrill's art, and the bargain he strikes with nature and the "source of light"— again and again to make his art at once mirror and window, home and homecoming, child, mask, and means by which to give "in return" all he had.

Merrill first announces the terms of this "bargain with—say the source of light" in "A Tenancy," the final poem of *Water Street*:

> That given a few years more
> (Seven or ten or, what seemed vast, fifteen)
> To spend in love, in a country not at war,
> I would give in return
> All I had. All? A little sun
> Rose in my throat. The lease was drawn.

What is Faustian in this bargain (an extension of knowledge, life, power, and pleasure, gained at the cost of pledging his "all") is even more explicitly Keatsian: "Oh, for ten years, that I may overwhelm / Myself in poesy; so I may to the deed / That my own soul has to itself decreed" ("Sleep and Poetry"). Like Keats, Merrill pledges himself to what his own soul decrees—his vocation as a poet. As we will learn in *Mirabell*, Merrill's "source of light," his "S/O/L," is at once sun and soul and Dante's paradisal point of light; it is both "ROOTED IN THE LIVED LIFE and part of God B's "MAIN MAGIC [and chief gift to man]: IMAGINATIVE POWER" (S. 251).[17] Likewise, the lease drawn here on "some kind of house" ("An Urban Convalescence") bespeaks at once Merrill's Stonington home with David Jackson, his place within the "ROSE-BRICK MANOR" of the English language (S. 262), and the "little more than [his] own past" to which he bids friends and readers also "be at home" in "A Tenancy."[18]

Merrill's commerce with the "changing light" of this poem, like Yeats's depiction of glittering light in "Vacillation," does more than evoke passing time; the light itself is transformative and raises questions about the relationship of body and soul and how a soul is made:

> I let the light change also me.
> The body that lived through that day
> And the sufficient love and relative peace
> Of those short years, is now not mine.
> Would it be called a soul?[19]

Like Yeats, in his contemplation of changing lights and times "expired," Merrill moves into a meditation on death and life's transience. But unlike the Yeats of "Vacillation," Merrill does not linger over the contending impulses of Heart and Soul or the larger antithetical rhythms of history. Instead, Merrill follows body and soul into a regeneration beyond death. Here are "intimations of immortality," but in a richly Yeatsian mode:

> It knows, at any rate,
> That when the light dies and the bell rings
> Its leaner veteran will rise to face
> Partners not recognized
> Until drunk young again and gowned in changing
> Flushes . . .

This passage offers echoes of the Yeatsian marriage of body and soul that transpires between lives, as well as intimations of the Christian resurrection of the body. It is as if Merrill were himself ringing changes upon the thought that informs Yeats's lines: "I shall find the dark grow luminous, the void fruitful when I understand I have nothing, that the ringers in the tower have appointed for the hymen of the soul a passing bell" (*Per Amica* 332).[20]

Thus, "A Tenancy" offers more than a momentary flirtation with the Yeatsian occult. The poem at once announces and cloaks Merrill's "strong" poetic vocation. Domestic allusions and seemingly casual wit keep the poem's grander implications "under the surface" where Merrill wants them ("Interview with Bornhauser" 54). For example, the uncanny and potentially portentous evocation of "stereoscopic" writing "Through which to seize the Real" dissolves across the line break, even as it persists behind the "Real / Old-Fashioned Winter of my landlord's phrase."[21] By such means then, the poem establishes Merrill's characteristic tone of urbane self-depreciation, so that the poem's undercurrents of occult contact and metaphysical ambition pass, more felt than remarked upon.

"An Urban Convalescence" follows similar "deflective" strategies and also points to a turning point in Merrill's poetic career. Yet this poem speaks even more significantly to the continuing power of Yeats's influence in Merrill's major poetry. In "An Urban Convalescence" the poet confronts a moment of Yeatsian vision, in which he is able to stare "on all the tragic scene" of "what life does"—the depredations of collapse, of "wires and pipes, snapped off at the roots"—as on a series of emblems, or "Gospels" from the "massive volume of the world," a book not unlike Yeats's "Spiritus Mundi." The vision evokes a surprising promise from the poet, a promise that is telling for how poorly it describes Merrill's work (even in this poem), and for how much more closely it describes much of the later Yeats:

> Upon that book I swear
> To abide by what it teaches:
> Gospels of ugliness and waste,
> Of towering voids, of soiled gusts,
> Of a shrieking to be faced
> Full into, eyes astream with cold—
>
> With cold?
> All right then. With self knowledge.

In these lines Merrill evokes the "cold eye" of "Under Ben Bulben," the shrieking cry of mortality at the end of "Man and the Echo," and the scene of urban waste that opens "The Circus Animals' Desertion III."[22] Yeats too identified his moments of vision with "self knowledge," but whereas for Yeats this knowledge is ideally "cold and passionate as the dawn," Merrill abruptly refuses the Yeatsian identity of coldness and self-knowledge. At this crucial point in the poem ("With cold? / All right then. With self-knowledge."), the poet breaks off, and precisely on the submerged image of one who does in fact break up his lines to weep. It is here that Merrill tells an interviewer he stopped, "thinking [the poem] was going to be impossible to finish" ("Interview with Brown" 45).[23]

Merrill has acknowledged "Urban Convalescence" as a "turning point" both in terms of technique and in terms of how "very personal" the poem is ("Interview with Brown" 45–46). Part of how this poem marks its turn is this abrupt swerve away from taking on the (paradoxically austere *and* self-indulgent) mantle of Yeatsian pathos. The time is over (at least in this poem) for contending with Yeats as if Merrill were Yeats's better self, or Yeats Merrill's wayward other. Merrill turns away from the outer, other world overshadowed by a technological and mythic bird grown monstrous and devouring—his "huge crane" which, in its aspects both as machine and as icon of Gravesian myth, grotesquely parodies Yeats's miraculous bird. He turns away from systems of both progressive and cyclic time and toward the common interiority of *Time* (magazine) as an artifact of reported experience (countering Yeats's "artifice of eternity"): "Indoors at last, the pages of *Time* are apt / To open . . ." He turns to the interiority of quatrains which, as "housing," both reveal and withhold Merrill's public privacies (thus countering the extremities of Yeats's hermetic "death-in-life and life-in-death"), and he turns back to the interiority of his imagination, which is transcendent, but only in that it answers to a "dull need," the need "to make some kind of house / Out of the life lived, out of the love spent."

Yet the break from the "outwardness" of memory that leads to such Yeatsian posturing as "Upon that book I swear . . . " and the turn "Indoors at last" is never a turn toward solipsism. Merrill's indoors is also an eminently social realm, and the second half of the poem announces Merrill's entry into the accommodating "enclosures" of public literary traditions and communities of interest and tone that Yeats also shared. The poem repeats the conventional progression of many Romantic poems, moving from confrontation or identification with the external world (always Nature, although in this case particularly urban) through self-knowledge (usually figured as a crisis) and into the recuperative realm of the creative imagination (Hartman 307).

We note that Yeats took a similar interest in social- and self-criticism, in matters of the imagination, and in building "houses" both of stanzas and of stone, building both as products of and as vantages on his life lived and love spent. Thus although the poem announces a break away from one line of Yeats's influence, in its second half it may be said to turn toward another such line of influence or affinity. For some too, the second half of the poem might particularly suggest a "Yeatsian urbanity" or a "Yeatsian, aristocratic wit, coupled with a high seriousness and a graceful manner" (Brisman 190). These recognitions of how the poem's "inwardness" participates in more "general views" mark the particularly "urban" nature of its "convalescence," the ways it recuperates not just a personal need and knowledge, but a public poetic tradition in which Yeats's voice and model still cast their ambivalent charm.[24]

Besides these two major "turning point" poems, other poems of this period that reflect Merrill's ambivalence toward Yeats's voice and model include "Prism" ("Look, / You dreamed of this: / To fuse in borrowed fires, to drown / In depths that were not there.") "Table Talk" (Merrill's tongue-in-cheek "*Ars Poetica*" that hesitates before "swallowing" Charles's Yeatsian claims for poetry as *rara avis* "acrackle in its nest / Of spices") and, most significantly, "For Proust" where, as Stephen Yenser notes, "The phrase 'a thin gold mask' offsets 'The world' to the extent that it evokes some perdurable work of art, comparable to Yeats's bird of 'hammered gold and gold enameling,' that will have transfigured the world" (*Myth* 81). Even more, the poem describes the Nietzschean/Yeatsian need to return to the world "over and over" in the poet's mix of exasperation, disappointment, weariness, and desire (*Per Amica* 329, 337, 340). Thus, the poem presents what Yeats refers to as the "vigil of desire" out of which comes a transforming vision of the world, "the wheel where the world is butterfly" (Ibid. 338, 341)—where, in Merrill's words, "What happened is becoming literature." As in Yeats, the return to the world is always also a return to "defeat, disappointed love, and the sorrow of parting" (Ibid. 338):

> of that day she had sworn
> To come, and did not, was evasive later,
> Would she not speak the truth two decades later
> . . .
> And presently she rises. Thought in pain
> You let her leave—the loved one always leaves.

As Yeats would have it, the Daimon of the world is in "some secret communion" with the sweetheart (Ibid. 336).

But in the alchemy and martyrdom of composition ([you] "station yourself there, beyond the pale / Of cough or of gardenia, erect, pale") what transpires is a Yeatsian masking that fuses world and man. Through the mask, the poet/novelist stares out fixedly "upon a visionary world," as if a god breathed through his "carven lips" (Ibid. 335) and the world itself has "put on a thin gold mask." Thus, something miraculous is achieved, "past / All understanding," an image of Yeats's Unity of Being. Yenser continues: "Moreover, if the "thin gold mask" is a figure for dawn, it is simultaneously a tribute to the imagination's power to renew and a reminder of time's passage" (*Myth* 81). Here Yenser points to the two contending themes of Romantic vision, found as much in Yeats as in Proust or Merrill, that the mask, the image, seeks to hold "in a single thought."

There is one more poem from this period which shows significant engagement with Yeats but which Merrill chose not to include in *Water Street*. According to remarks made in a 1982 symposium on "Literary Tradition," Merrill wrote "Willowware Cup" in the early 1960s (*Recitative* 10), but only chose to publish it ten years later in *Braving the Elements*. "Willowware" would have made a fitting companion beside "Prism" or "Angel" or "Swimming by Night," but may have seemed to follow too closely on the teacups in the Ouija board scene in *The Seraglio* and "Voices from the Other World" from his previous volume of poems. The decided underpainting of "Lapis Lazuli" that helps structure the poem (the "Mass hysteria," plum tree and pagoda, wise old man who has "given up on earthly attachments, and all that") may also have seemed to raise the Yeatsian "temperature" of *Water Street* a bit too high.[25]

As in "For Proust" and many of the poems in *Water Street*, Merrill's approach to Yeatsian themes and images in *Nights and Days* is often masked—at once marking and disguising his engagement with Yeats's writing. Glancing allusions to Yeats's Condition of Fire make their way into both "Charles on Fire" and "The Broken Home." In "Charles on Fire" a threatened movement "out of nature" into a consuming "spiritual" fire that does not "singe a sleeve" nonetheless occasions a moment of panicked reflection:

> Steward of spirits, Charles's glistening hand
> All at once gloved itself in eeriness.
> The moment passed. He made two quick sweeps and
> Was flesh again. "It couldn't matter less,"
> He said, but with a shocked, unconscious glance
> Into the mirror. Finding nothing changed,
> He filled a fresh glass and sank down among us.

It is hard to imagine a more arch treatment of spiritualist and otherwise transcendent themes. Similarly, in "The Broken Home," the speaker conjures a moment of Yeatsian occult (albeit modulated by mocking self-regard):

> I have lit what is left of my life.
>
> I have thrown out yesterday's milk
> And opened a book of maxims.
> The flame quickens. The word stirs.
>
> Tell me, tongue of fire,
> That you and I are as real
> At least as the people upstairs.

Such are the most characteristic notes of Merrillian nonchalance. These lines in "The Broken Home" establish what will be Merrill's particularly light touch when approaching Yeatsian matters in the major poems that will follow.

Only twice does Merrill abandon this gallant, glancing approach in the works leading up to *The Fire Screen*: once in the 1965 poem "Violent Pastoral," which lifts the speaker into a Yeatsian apotheosis, and once again in Merrill's 1965 novel *The (Diblos) Notebook*. In Chapter One, I discussed how the novel helps us to understand the intense ambivalence Merrill felt toward his thoroughly Yeats-identified mentor and lover, Kimon Friar—a process figured as the disciplinary "punishment of the god" (*Diblos* 146). What I want to examine now is how much Merrill also uses Yeats to underscore his ambivalent relation with his own (earlier) writing self. But before considering *Diblos*'s project of self-criticism, we should see Merrill working in the contrary Yeatsian mode, that of exaltation.

"Violent Pastoral," the one poem in *Nights and Days* to take up Yeats's manner as well as his argument, presents a Yeatsian emblem of grappling contraries, echoing images from poems including at least "Leda and the Swan," "Byzantium," "and "The Second Coming," but without a hint of irony or pastiche. In this poem, Merrill presents a torment of identification, an image of struggle as consummation, in the agony of primary and antithetical beings locked "helplessly," in "one oriented creature": "the eagle / Mounts with the lamb in his clutch: /Two wings, four hooves, // One pulse pounding, pounding." If the question that climaxes Yeats's "Leda and the Swan" concerns a momentary union of divine and mortal knowledge and power, so too the unspoken question that animates Merrill's poem asks what kind of unity, what kind of understanding, is this that links predator, prey, and shepherd in one pact of identity? Merrill's image is "beyond Arcadia" indeed. We hear a note of release, of exaltation in the speaker's declaration: "Beyond Arcadia at last." By linking Yeatsian apocalyptic violence with no less Yeatsian distance and sense of cosmic assurance, it is as much the speaker as the lamb who is transported. If the poem presents an emblem of Merrill's own inner conflicts, it does so in a manner singularly striking in its dramatic intensity. The poem's "no longer" and "not yet" mark the timeless eternity of the violent moment, even as they plunge the reader back into the sweep of time and alteration. The knowledge of redemption—seen in the rainbow, the eagle and lamb as "wholly brothers" and, most triumphantly, in the shepherd's being able to look on and not be "turned to stone"—this knowledge only underscores the terrors of the poem, so that "Violent Pastoral" not only performs what its title announces, the difficult but not impossible conjunction of Yeatsian "terrible beauty," it also provides Merrill with a rare moment of seemingly direct access to a Yeatsian sublime.[26]

But just as "Violent Pastoral" ends by evoking the triumph of Yeatsian aesthetic vision in the figure of Kimon Friar's "Gorgon-proof" Perseus (who also found a way to look and not be "turned to stone"), so too does *The (Diblos) Notebook* culminate by evoking Perseus' imagined blows. Only now, instead of presiding over a moment of Yeatsian sublimity, this figure and the novel as a whole work to open questions about the aesthetic practice and moral standing of the young writer representing Merrill. In this way, questions of justice as well as questions of reality are never far from the surface of Merrill's novel.

As we have seen, *The (Diblos) Notebook* culminates in "a brutal, horrible action" (18) brooded on from the very start. This scene of "violence to which all the words had been leading" (129) proves to be that of the young writer's imagining and writing Orestes' punishment, which is also the sado-masochistic fulfillment of

Friar/Orestes' tragic view of life. As the narrator puts it: "his 'tragic' view, would never be wholly an illusion, once having interlocked so perfectly with his suffering" (143). It is a suffering, we are told, that brings the young writer nothing but "pure aesthetic pleasure" (Ibid.), although we are also soon given to wonder just how purely "aesthetic" such pleasure may be. Merrill's character achieves his writerly and emotional "satisfaction" in part by insisting on "how little any of it had been my doing" (142), thus showing voyeuristic passivity as but one mask of the writer's controlling intention. From the start, the writer's efforts at "mere" description self-consciously prefigure and license the "fated" action. Orestes, we hear, "had the self-conscious grace of a martyr by Botticelli:

~~masochistic grace, inviting harm~~" (58)

This overstruck line telegraphs the operation of the writer's barely repressed desire to be the instrument of such "grace," the vehicle of such fulfilling "harm." We watch both pleasure and guilt at work beneath the apparent transparency of the writer's self-censorship. Indeed, the crossed-through word, line, or paragraph is one of the principal stylistic devices Merrill employs in the novel for miming the contested interplay of the writer's conscious and unconscious subjectivities. The very first line of the novel gives the name "~~Orestes~~" crossed through, and this disfigured name evokes not only the haunted son of another infamously "broken home," but also, in its "cancellation," the writer's impossible desire not to face, not to mirror or fulfill such a heritage. As this figure is repeated through the novel (1, 3, 140), it becomes a proleptic emblem not only of the whipping the character receives at the end of the novel, and of the desires that propel that whipping; it also becomes an emblem of the violent and compulsive dynamic of objectification and identification that characterizes the writer's interior struggle with his mentor, nemesis, brother, lover, who is at once Merrill's mask for Kimon Friar and a portrait of his Yeatsian Daimon.[27]

Another, earlier, "sudden attack" of violence prepares for the later disciplinary scene and brackets Merrill's novel. The writer's seaside attack of diarrhea near the island's slaughterhouse reads like a violent parody of Yeats's "blood-dimmed tide," where "Like blood my own excrement ran glittering down the rocks into the sea which feinted & struck back, hissing" (17). The incident concludes with a vision of sharks' fins as if in answer to Yeats's dolphins (Ibid.). Where at the end of the novel the Friar figure, Orson/Orestes, suffers while attaining exactly the experience he needs to validate his "tragic" view, here, at the beginning, it is the Merrill figure who suffers, while also discovering a necessary insight: "I remain grateful for what I have seen. I have been shown something my story needs" (Ibid.) Merrill's pleasure in this scene may at first seem chiefly masochistic; but here too vivid strokes of description compel the reader to imagine both the writer's and his own pain. With a rhetorical question worthy of Yeats, Merrill ensures that Friar, and Yeats through him, likewise catches the edge of loathing that colors this scene:

> Years ago, in his lecture on Darwin & the Poetry of Science, Orestes made much of the chemical affinities of blood and seawater. If he, with his passion for dialectic, ever takes that walk, will he find in the slaughterhouse an antithesis to the serene harbor view, or a synthesis of that view & its beholder? (Ibid.)

Here, and with a vengeance, is the Yeatsian formula of joining violence and elegance. As the writer puts it, he has been shown "something" that his story needs—specifically, the multiple violences and play of pleasures that will later mark the scene of Orestes's whipping: "Something to be concealed *by* the story, by the writing—as in *Phèdre* where the overlay of prismatic verse deflects a brutal, horrible action" (18). Later, the young writer returns to this passage and pointedly contrasts the Yeatsian "master's lesson" with his own stylistic proclivities: "Haven't I only to remember the master's lesson, & dramatize the quarrel, the coldness? [Note Yeats's terms: "dramatize," "quarrel," "coldness."] Anything rather than let it be glimpsed cutting fishily through the shimmer of a phrase" (48–49). Here, with this "shimmer of a phrase," Merrill not only gives an apt characterization of his signature Piscean style, he also reveals the Yeats-inspired terms of his own critique of that style and its "relentless fluency" (S. 70).

As the novel moves to its insistently sadomasochistic climax, Merrill allows Yeats's language to take more and more explicit control. With a kind of hyperpoetic justice, Merrill insures that Friar/Orestes's punishment comes as much under the aegis of Friar's own beloved Yeats as by the hand of Byron (Orestes's wife's son, but again the poetic persona Merrill often adopts against Friar's, or his own, Yeatsian proclivities):

> In my head he raised his beautiful clenched hand. The riding-crop descended, once, twice, again, upon my
> once, twice, again, inscribed its madder penstroke upon my brother's face,
> at the tempo of a *slowly pounding tempo of a giant's drugged pulse*
> of the dolphin's progress through glittering foam
> at the tempo of those 3 blows whereupon the curtain of the Comédie rises to reveal, as foreseen, that universe of classical unity whose suns blaze & seas glitter & whose every action however brutal is nobly, inflexibly ordered & the best of each of us steps forth in his profound dark spotlight with poetry on his lips.   (144–45)

This scene, replete with its echoes of "Byzantium," "Lapis Lazuli," and the abstraction of Yeats's Noh-inspired drama [which was, in its own way, an answer to French classicism], is immediately preceded by the writer's meditation on the scene as an achieved emblem, an emblem which enables both Orestes and the writer to "hold in a single thought reality and justice" (*Vision* 25): "And he had carried it off, made it seem like justice. Even I, in the notebook's blackest depths, would never have dared to construct such a denouement—coincidence, melodrama, every earmark of life's (the rival's) style. Il miglior fabbro!" (143). The last exclamation, by appropriating Eliot's dedication of *The Waste Land* to Pound from Dante's *The Divine Comedy*, subtly turns attention away from life, the rival, and towards issues of poetic rivalry and indebtedness, the implicit motive for the scene of punishment that follows. The writer emphasizes this turn with his next crossed-out line: "How not to admit admire." Merrill employs these stresses in his "fabric of illusion" to draw "greater attention to what is being represented" (132), in this case the anxious complicity of the writer in his brother/lover/teacher's undeserved but self-fulfilling punishment.

The writer guiltily and ecstatically imagines not only the scene of punishment, but immediately follows by imagining himself caught in the act of this imaginative depiction. In one of Merrill's favorite tropes, the writer metaphorizes the fact of being read, not just to reinscribe the pleasures of his own guilt, but to place the reader in the writer's own guilty, voyeuristic position. We do as he has done; we watch him take his self-impelled stripes as he watched Orestes; guilt, pleasure and the semblance of knowledge leak over the page: "Had anyone discovered me up there, I would have been caught in flagrante with a myth-making apparatus every bit as vigorous as O's & probably a trifle more depraved" (145). The "myth-making apparatus" imparts its "telltale stains" in a veritable orgy of participation. Friar and his fictive representatives Orson (the brother) and Orestes (the character), Yeats (the indicated precursor), the unnamed writer of a novel which purports to have been abandoned, the anomalous reader, and Merrill himself, all join in the necessary and necessarily violence-tainted process of myth-making in the course of the novel.

Perhaps the chief myth self-consciously elaborated in the course of the novel is "the romance of accomplished individuality" (66), which, like Yeats's Unity of Being, is figured as a product of contraries. The goal is to reconcile "the two modes of being. The moon, the sun" (91), to accomplish "the sun and moon together in the sky" (92, 133)—without being seduced by the notion that such a unity exists in some transcendent state. Such unity, if it is achieved at all, is achieved "on a lower level," among the "living antagonists" of the personality (91). "The moon, the sun; the earth, the soul, the wife, the god," these are the contending emblems which taken together "quicken" and "cleanse" the heart (92).[28] Like Yeats in *A Vision*, the young writer in *Diblos* personifies and charts the attributes of these contending forces (90), lists legendary, fictive and historical characters to exemplify particular types (3, 62), and sees in art a path toward a Unity of Being, "The sun & moon together in the sky."

Where Merrill pulls up short in following Yeats in the elaboration of this myth is by swerving away from Yeats's ideal of "simplification through intensity." Rather than intensity, Merrill's young writer entertains the notion that "'the only solution is to be very, very intelligent.'" "Intelligence," the writer suggests, "will dissimulate itself, will *lose itself* in simplicity. By the same token, any extended show of Mind may be taken as the work of some final naïveté" (146–47). Too little intelligence, that is, and the Mind shows to the detriment of the unity or "simplicity" one would achieve. In such a formulation, Merrill may be offering a swipe at the "simple-mindedness" of Yeats's determination to use expository prose, charts, and figures to expound a metaphysical system in *A Vision*; but, even more, these remarks reveal some of the attitude behind Merrill's lifelong use of all the resources of his intelligence to keep his intellectual lights well hidden behind the elaborate pleasures of his poetry and fiction.

Those epiphantic moments in which self and world come together are part of the "romance of accomplished personality" that Merrill depicts in *Diblos*. Like Yeats, in "Vacillation IV," the young writer in *Diblos* is visited by a momentary but profound sense of "love and sweetness" (97). He savors the feeling of being blessed and the sense that he too could bless, wondering "how I might nurse it, keep it from draining out of my cupped hands into dust before it reached its proper objects," and echoes Yeats's diffidence—"I have something about me that, though it makes me love, is more like innocence" (*Per Amica* 365)—with his own: "It would seem that love, [agape], lives by its own laws, like a cat, & will not be commanded" (97). This surprising access to love is woken by a Daimonic visitation (from Chyryssoula's cat); but "this loving self of mine that had woken, that was digging its claws lightly, voluptuously into my flesh" is also the writer's own "self-loving" self (96) and, as such, is closely allied to the masturbatory, phosphorescent "ectoplasm" of the night-swimming "genie," which opens the book, "conjured up out of oneself, floating & sporting, performing all that's asked of it before it merges at last into the dark chilled bulk of its master's body stumbling over stones to sleep"(9). Something more-than-self precipitates and is awakened in these scenes, something strongly associated with writing [with "the poetry of the night" (9) or "its proper objects . . . the pages of my novel" (97)].[29]

What is striking is that another night encounter, which also speaks of love, this time more explicitly (hetero)sexual ["My heart went out to her. My flesh as well" (34)], is what evokes Merrill's critique of Friar, Yeats, and attributes he finds in his own writing self: "She was right. The soul's selfishness was worse [than the body's]. The thirst for pattern, whether of words on a page or stresses in the universe. The hubris that invents tragedy for the glory of undergoing it. As I saw O., Lucine saw me" (Ibid.). Merrill accosts his earlier writing-self here with Yeatsian self-dramatization—the very attitude he will later celebrate in "Matinees," asserting: "The point thereafter was to arrange for one's / Own chills and fever, passions and betrayals, / Chiefly in order to make song of them."

But in this heterosexual context, the charge is "selfishness," a selfishness that, remarkably, the solitary "loving self" avoids. The onanistic pleasures of writing and masturbation are figured as openings, as taking one out of one's self into vastness or mystery beyond what one could command; whereas, the "thirst for pattern" in phenomena outside of the self reifies both self and other. Ultimately, as Stephen Yenser notes, the young writer in *Diblos* realizes that he is "playing with [Orson and Dora] in effigy, loving the effigies alone" in much the same spirit as Yeats when he admits in "The Circus Animals' Desertion" that "Players and painted stage took all my love,

/ And not those things they were emblems of" (*Myth* 99). Ultimately, the Merrillian narrator realizes that Dora and Orson/Orestes, like Yeats's Oisin, Countess Cathleen, and Cuchulain, are "masks behind which lay all too frequently a mind foreign to them," a mind which is always only the writer's own (*Diblos* 133).

It is a slippery distinction Merrill is making here. Writing, when it operates as an "emanation," as Yeats might say, of the writer's inner quarrels with his Daimon, gives love, blesses and fills the writer with "love and sweetness" that he may in turn dispense. But writing that operates too simply as a theater of control diminishes the self and deadens its objects, yielding not so much a generative pleasure as a chilling, selfish pride. This charge of "coldness," of "selfishness," and of toying with "effigies" in his personal and artistic life is the self-accusation that Merrill brings against himself (and Yeats) a number of times in works leading up to *Sandover*.[30] It is one of the ways that Merrill identifies with the older poet and one of the reasons Yeats is continually evoked in scenes of Merrill's own self-quarreling.

In contrast to the quite explicit engagement with Yeats shown in "Violent Pastoral" and *The (Diblos) Notebook*, the most accomplished poems of *Nights and Days*, "The Thousand and Second Night" and "From the Cupola," approach their Yeatsian material much more circumspectly, marking a return to even more ambitious strategies of nonchalance. In these poems, the Yeatsian animus subsides, and what is figured as a both a reconciliation and an acceptance of the divisions inherent within and between the self and life and writing self-consciously forgoes any such single scene of "passionate intensity" as we have seen in *Diblos* or "Violent Pastoral." In these prismatic, multi-faceted poems, Merrill moves toward making sense "out of the life lived, out of the love spent," in such a way as to make complexity, rather than Yeatsian "simplification" his muse. Echoing the last line of "Sailing to Byzantium" ["I think," the speaker tells us in "The Thousand and Second Night," "Of what I have been, am, and care to be" (126)], Merrill appropriates from Yeats but always with a touch that opens questions, rather than making pronouncements. "These letters," the poet wonders in "From the Cupola," questioning the light of his own poetic vocation, "Show me, light, if they make sense" (163). In these poems, Merrill teaches Yeats the power of wondering as a means to wonder, the power of not writing as if one already knew. Yet in "The Thousand and Second Night," in particular, Merrill situates his poem on unmistakably Yeatsian ground, electing, as one critic puts it, "to risk a new Byzantine poem, using some of the same oppositions between East and West, life, death, and art that Yeats had made almost his own"; and yet so deft are his departures from Yeatsian precedent that he does this, "astonishingly, without inviting any damaging comparison," indeed without inviting any serious thought of Yeats at all (Hecht 331).

In "The Thousand and Second Night," Merrill returns to several of the sites of his first visit to Istanbul. There, on that visit in mid-August of 1952, "Byzantium glimmered a every turn," and, still under the spell of his Yeatsian annunciation in Ravenna, Merrill searched for "the mosaics promised by Yeats" and asks, 'Who could say but that the Bazaar might yield a bird "of hammered gold and gold enameling'?"(*Different* 234). Like Merrill's account of his visit to Ravenna, his reminiscences about his visits to Istanbul establish this city as another vital site linking him to Yeats. They also indicate, as does "The Thousand and Second Night," the ways in which Merrill wants to remake Yeats's city as his own.

In the memoir, Merrill's allusion to Yeats's golden bird eventually cascades into a particularly Yeatsian reverie on Istanbul's birds. For Merrill "Istanbul was a city of birds; a vortex of birds" (244). In his list of sightings ("sparrows and swifts, fishwife gulls, storks on chimneys") we are quickly "out of nature" and into the realm of artifice and language: "Storks, too, made of limber Arabic letters in the Calligraphy Museum—already migrating, in what I feared was a one-way passage, from Nature's realm to that of the Mind" (244–45). Here Merrill's "fear" is part of his ongoing quarrel with his own interior Yeats. One-way flights out of nature and into the mental world of artifice do not sit well with a poet who insists on seeing things both ways and also traveling back and forth. It is in light of this insistence on vacillation, on constantly moving between contending poetic registers and points of view—first given their fullest voice in "The Thousand and Second Night"—that we best understand Merrill's passion for the beaded-bird pendants he keeps returning to Istanbul to buy:

> ". . . it's the perfect souvenir: a translation into the demotic of Yeats's golden bird on its eternal bough. Swaying from the rear-view mirror of Claude's Volkswagen or basking in the glow of my mother's bridge lamp, the talisman (readily unstrung, but who isn't) keeps up appearances, reminding us how notions Joy or the Imagination—the Holy Ghost Itself, if it comes to that—out of some recurrent urge to be embodied, make for a Halloween trunk full of feathers and wings" (245.).

Every word counts in this paean to perspectival reversibility: Claude's "rear-view mirror," his mother's "bridge lamp," the puns on "unstrung" and "appearances," the notions of "reminding" and "recurrent," the double force of "make," the recuperative leap from "feathers" to "wings." Merrill affirms that "My beaded talisman could have come from no other place in the world"; but Merrill's Istanbul, for all its "monumental marble half submerged in dreamlike transparence" is pointedly not Yeats's Byzantium (Ibid.). Or rather, in the manner of the later poet, it both is and isn't: "No sooner does the real thing vanish than it returns," Merrill tells us; and, as in "The Thousand and Second Night," both "real" cities return "with a conniving wink, as folklore" and as "a translation into the demotic of Yeats's golden bird on its eternal bough" (Ibid.).

"The Thousand and Second Night" is a poem that in structure, manner, tone, narrative, and theme is built up of wholes divided, interrupted, and glimpsed as fragments. It argues a self divided against itself, mind, body, and soul, and asks what kind of cure or restoration of unity is possible. The first section, "Rigor Vitae" announces the poet's "absurd complaint"—his face is half paralyzed with Bell's Palsy and mind likewise "wrecked," bereft of its "precious sensibility." Images of paralysis, decrepitude, and near death pile up and force the question of how one keeps body and soul together.

Merrill first explicitly brings Yeats into the poem in this first section by quoting "The 'death-in-life and life-in-death' of Yeats' / Byzantium;" but this quotation does not celebrate Yeats's "superman" or such transcendent forms "as Grecian goldsmiths make." Rather, the image of the city Merrill evokes suggests that there is too much death-in-life, too much of a haunting life-in-death in this "entire city / Dissolved by rhetoric."[31] Yet even before this quotation, Yeats is certainly present in the conception of the poem, treating as it does so many of the thematic oppositions associated with Yeats.

For much of the poem, Merrill uses Yeatsian imagery and argument as a foil for his own meditations on the relations between body and soul, in this way "correcting" the older poet, but hardly in the spirit of modesty that his instructor persona suggests in section four (when told "the poet quotes too much"):

> Mightn't he have planned
>
> For his own modest effort to be seen
> Against the yardstick of the "truly great"
> (In Spender's phrase)? Fearing to overstate,
> He lets *them* do it—lets their words, I mean,
>
> Enhance his—

Merrill uses Yeats's words to enhance his, but not out of fear. Yeats (and Eliot, Valéry, Hofmannsthal) and the ventrioquized voices of friends and other personae provide the refractive elements that allow Merrill to generalize his personal dilemmas without the poem becoming "PERSONAL AS SHIT" (in WHA's phrase, S. 262) and without having to reach for the rhetoric of Yeatsian "intensity." Here, as in "From the Cupola," Merrill perfects his "anti-Yeatsian" strategy of making Dispersal a major source of his poetic power.[32]

Where Yeats calls for poems as "cold and passionate as the dawn" ("The Fisherman"), Merrill protests against the "cold" and notes how its chill has left him *dispassionate*. "Part of me has remained cold and withdrawn," the poet recounts. "The day I went up to the Parthenon / Its humane splendor made me think *So what?*" Thus, in this case, Art is not what "cures affliction" ("Farewell Performance"). Neither the Parthenon nor the "lineaments of a plummet-measured face" ("The Statues") excite a passion the poet does not already feel. Neither, for that matter, does a seemingly available Greek, "superb, male, raucous [albeit also] unclean, Orthodox // Ikon of appetite . . ." In this second section, the poet, shadowed by death, cannot bring himself even to act the part of his shared humanity. His physical affliction has "cracked / That so-called mirror of the soul," the body; and though the palsy is healed, his soul still feels broken. It may be, as Yeats's Crazy Jane affirms, that "nothing can be sole or whole / That has not been rent," but Merrill bids the reader focus on the difficulty and uncertainty of Crazy Jane's pronouncement ("It [body/soul] is not readily, if at all, made whole") and keeps alive the unspoken question of how such a "making whole" might happen. Against Jane's too facile call to "take the whole / Body and soul," fair with foul, Merrill offers the counter-voice of his depression.[33] And against Yeats's wish in "Sailing to Byzantium" to leave nature and the body and be instead pure artwork, singing of life and time while unaffected by either, Merrill answers that "what I have been, am, and care to be" seems like so many motes, "neon figments . . . / Of incommunicable energy," that appear and vanish behind blind eyes. No singing for lords or ladies is possible here, no answering back to the Bishop. With his rewriting of Yeats's concluding lines to "Sailing to Byzantium" and the single word "incommunicable," Merrill shuts his doors on any hope Yeats might offer his soul's despair.

The third section of the poem, "Carnivals," seems to continue Merrill's revisionary treatment of Yeatsian themes. David Kalstone remarks that "This sailing to Byzantium has led to an unexpected goal": not a singing master of the soul or incorporation into an artifice of eternity, but a dancer representing death, whose deathmask the poet begins to assume as the "mask begins to melt upon [his] face" ("Merrill" 147).[34] Stephen Yenser similarly suggests that Merrill's Rio de Janeiro offers further "counterpoise [to] Yeats's city of artifice and eternity" (*Myth* 134) and argues that "Unlike 'Sailing to Byzantium,' Merrill's voyage brings the speaker back 'home' to 'winter' and 'Real / Snow.' It is here, in the world, if anywhere he seems to insist to Yeats, that body and soul can combine" (135). But surely this is also what the Yeats of "A Dialogue of Self and Soul," "The Circus Animals Desertion," and at least one part of "Vacillation" seems to suggest. Here as elsewhere, to focus only on how Merrill writes against Yeats is to miss the ways in which Merrill's work also demonstrates his affinities with the older poet.

Toward the end of "Carnivals," the speaker seems to have found that restoration of body and soul he has longed for. His lines are celebratory and almost incantory in a Yeatsian mode:

> Love. Warmth. Fist of sunlight at last
> Pounding emphatic on the gulf. High wails
> From your white ship: The heart prevails!
> Affirm it! Simple decency rides the blast!—

This affirmation is darkened for a moment and cast into doubt by the sextain's concluding couplet: "Phrases that, quick to smell blood, lurk like sharks / Within a style's transparent lights and darks." But this characteristic moment of Merrillian self-conscious skepticism is swept away by the following stanza, which if anything heightens the Yeatsian tone:

> The lips part. The plume trembles. You're afloat
> Upon the breathing, all-reflecting deep.

> The past recedes and twinkles, falls asleep.
> Fear is unworthy, say the stars by rote;
> What destinations have been yours till now
> Unworthy, says the leaping prow.

What has restored the poet is, in Yeats's phrase, "the heart's purple" ("A Dialogue of Self and Soul"), compounded of the memory and experience of love—and war. "Voyages, I bless you," the poet is now able to affirm, "for sore / Limbs and mouth kissed, face bronzed and lined, / An earth held up, a text not wholly undermined / By fluent passages of metaphor."

In Yeats's "A Dialogue of Self and Soul" these are the terms, love and war, whose value the Soul questions: "Why should the imagination of a man / Long past his prime remember things that are / Emblematical of love and war?" The Self's reply, like each of his other speeches, emphasizes the values of history, family piety, social and material culture, and sensual experience. The second section of the poem, in which only the Self speaks, builds to a celebration of the embodied soul analogous to Merrill's lines quoted above:

> When such as I cast out remorse
> So great a sweetness flows into the breast
> We must laugh and we must sing
> We are blest by everything,
> Everything we look upon is blest.[35]

What leads to such a moment in Merrill's poem is first the "infantile /Memory" of falling asleep on his grandmother's lap that comes upon him unbidden on his way in "the modern town / Midway across the bridge," just as a similar moment came to Yeats inside "a crowded London shop" ("Vacillation IV"). The speaker is at once lulled and imaginatively stimulated by his grandmother's "beloved" presence—a memory, we later learn, emblematic of the infant state in which the soul "could not be told from the body." Memory of love also brings with it memories of war in Merrill's poem when the speaker recalls a starlit evening walk with a boy friend "in late fall 1943." [Merrill would have been almost 18, concerned about enlisting and the uncertain progress of the war.] His friend was such that "To die in [his] presence seemed the highest good"—a line that cements this particular tie of love and war. We learn that a war of sorts between the two young men followed, the friend turning out to be straight. And, of course, the poem itself centers on the poet's experience of being at war with himself, his face in rebellion, his spirit seemingly defeated—not unlike Yeats's "unfinished man and his pain / Brought face to face with his own clumsiness" ("A Dialogue of Self and Soul").

The lesson of war and memory is that wars end. "Our war was over," the poet declares. "We had made our peace / With—everything." Here Merrill's dash telegraphs the speaker's ambivalent surprise at his own affirmation. Ambivalent because, very much as in Yeats, sex and love are such troubling companion desires.

Where Yeats, looking forward, declares: "I am content to live it all again / And yet again . . . to pitch / . . . into that most fecund ditch of all" of a woman's sex, Merrill, looking back, exclaims: "A thousand and one nights! They were grotesque." What follows are scenes not from speaker's own sex-life, but from the obscene postcard collection of his libidinous "Great-Uncle Alastair," scenes which literalize the grotesque comedy of Yeats's "engender[ing] in the ditch": ". . . with muscle flexed // In resurrection from his underwear, / Gaining an underworld to harrow. / He steers her ankles like—like a wheelbarrow." The poet, far from being put off by such displays, is privately content to acknowledge his affiliation with his great-uncle's pleasures and, content to "live it all again," spends "the night rekindling with expert / Fingers—" precisely that manual "care of the soul" that "needn't be discussed."[36]

Body and soul are welded for a moment in those moments of "great happiness" which we grant ourselves and may later recall. Life then is a blessing, and our pleasure is to bless. Such might be the (eminently Romantic) moral of both Yeats's "Dialogue" and Merrill's "Nights," and part of Merrill's revisionary achievement in the poem is to include the experiences and memories of masturbation within the context of such an argument. But Merrill does not conclude with this ecstatic moment of the embodied soul. His final section takes up and continues Yeats's prior dialogue, but modulated away from the earlier triumphant tone both poets achieve. Instead a wistful, valedictory tone presides, fitting for a scene in which Sultan/body and Scheherazade/soul agree to separate.

In this Merrill is true to Yeatsian notions of cycles of conjunction and division. Our lives consist of a constant "scissoring and mending" between the real and reflection, objective and subjective, body and soul suggests Merrill in another poem with a Byzantine and "nautical" setting ("Yánnina"). What is remarkable at the end of "The Thousand and Second Night" is Merrill's use of Yeatsian diction to characterize his two characters. Scheherazade longs to "refresh / Her soul in that *cold* fountain which the *flesh / Knows not*," and the Sultan responds: "Free me, I pray, to go in search of joys / *Unembroidered* by your high, soft voice, / Along that *stony* path the senses pave" (emphasis added). Even Merrill's final lines catch the Yeatsian attributes: the soul is lunar, subjective, at one with her fictions; the body solar, objective, but blind and without understanding in the soul's absence.

> They wept, then tenderly embraced and went
> Their ways. She and her fictions soon were one.
> He slept through moonset, woke in blinding sun,
> Too late to question what the tale had meant.

Yet if Anthony Hecht is correct in his assessment of the poem as "a new Byzantine poem," very much concerned with images and issues "Yeats had made almost his own," how is it that Merrill manages this feat "astonishingly, without inviting any damaging comparison whatever" (331)? I think the answer lies in part in a shift in sensibility. Merrill revises Yeats in ways that respond to our times and experiences more directly than does Yeats and with such distinctive assurance in his own mastery of the many voices of the poem that there is little impulse to read for comparisons. What's more, through the "indispensable" commentary of his instructor persona, Merrill shapes how we read the poem's several direct and revised quotations.[37] We are told to think of these allusions as rhetorical devices deployed to "enhance" the poet's own intentions, so that even his best readers follow this cue and look no further. A 1967 interview with Donald Sheehan further suggests that these "little snippets from Eliot, Yeats, Hofmannsthal" operate "ornamentally" (32). Yet we should be alert enough by now to realize that one of Merrill's chief goals is precisely to write so that "ornament" or "artifice" also becomes inseparable from the "heart" and "matter" of a poem—once again a kind of unity of soul and body.

Then there is the matter of tone. Here Merrill turns to Byron, his surest antidote against Yeatsian "intensity." In the same interview with Donald Sheehan, Merrill comments:

> I *knew* that [Byron] had been an influence on "The Thousand and Second Night." When I checked, I found very much the tone I'd been trying for: that air of irrelevance, of running on at the risk of never becoming terribly significant. . . .You can't forego the whole level of entertainment in art. Think of Stevens' phrase: "The essential gaudiness of poetry." The inessential suddenly felt as essence. (35)

Many parts of the poem may sound "like badinage, casual, if not frivolous," but as Merrill suggests about talk in general, "something serious is usually going on under the surface" ("Interview with Bornhauser" 54). What Byron gives Merrill in this and other major poems is "that air of irrelevance" which keeps "the serious" lightly submerged.[38] It is this late-Byronic nonchalance then that allows Merrill to keep his Yeatsian material in such deft suspension so that his own voice dominates. Thus, on its "face," the poem offers little encouragement to anyone interested in making sustained comparisons with poems by Yeats; while, at the same time, it also amply rewards anyone who suspects that Yeats *is* nonetheless important to the poem, both as a positive and as a negative influence on much of the poem's argument and style.

Written a year after "The Thousand and Second Night," "From the Cupola" extends the both the prismatic strategies and the achievement of the earlier poem. The poem again addresses themes prominently associated with Yeats, the divided self and role of personae or masks in the work of self-knowledge and soul making, a necessary and yet thwarted love, the lover as Daimonic presence both within and beyond the self, the momentary possibility of unity, the confluence of history, fiction and myth, the truth of vacillating perspectives, of seeing truth by halves. What is largely absent is any allusion to Yeats's claims for the transcendent realities of art or soul or the coming apocalypse. It is as though Merrill has (for the moment) almost had enough of those particular arguments with the older poet, so that Merrill takes from Yeats only what he can fully appropriate as his own.[39] He need not avail himself of Yeats's or any other prior poet's words in order, coyly, to "enhance his" own. In this poem, it is enough to make the Yeatsian convention of externalizing an internal drama the basis for this Merrillian "Dialogue of Self and Soul."[40]

In the one passage which evokes Yeats most particularly, Psyche recalls a "world where nothing changed or died / unless to be reborn on the next tide," a "City half dream half desert where at dawn / the sprinkler dervish whirled and all was crystalline" and each house was "half brothel and half shrine." As Stephen Yenser notes:

> The description echoes in its rhapsodic repetition Yeats's vision in "Vacillation": "A tree there is that from its topmost bough / Is half all glittering flame and half all green / Abounding foliage moistened with the dew; / And half is half and yet is all the scene." Like Yeats's vision, Psyche's memory is of a world in which opposites such as the spiritual and the sensual unite. (*Myth* 145)

But importantly, what triggers this memory is Psyche's recollection of Eros's "letter from the South" in which he writes: "*A city named for palms half mummy and half myth / pools flashing talking birds the world of my / first vision of you Psyche.*" Eros's language neatly anticipates and parodies the unifying affirmations of Yeats's "Vacillation" that Psyche immediately takes up. It also casts a dubious eye upon the possible Yeatsian implications behind Eros's first "vision," his "talking birds," and pools "flashing." If Eros's first vision is Yeatsian in its transcendent pretensions, it is also flawed by the blindness of "first sight" and transcendent desire such as animates Yeats's Byzantium poems. Thus, Eros's (only) words in the poem qualify the Yeatsian unity of opposites Psyche's memory seems to achieve.

As in "The Thousand and Second Night," the memory of love does unite body and soul but only for that brief time in which one seems to "bloom // Where nothing died"—that ecstatic moment of "blossoming or dancing where / The body is not bruised to pleasure the soul" which Yeats also evokes in "Among School Children." Such memories gladden but also taste of literature for Merrill; they soon acquire the "dry gold [that] settles on my mouth" as Psyche says, about that remembered other world or city that we make real again out of illusion and want, "half desert and half myth." But as much as "From the Cupola" is about memory and the achieved, "thin gold mask" of literature, it is even more about the experience and work of coming to terms with the mysterious, soul-hurting and soul-healing gifts of love and language, and of making a self by trying to make sense of love-letters from an unknown source.

In his interview with Donald Sheehan, Merrill explains:

> In the poem there are, let's see, three stories going. There's the story of Eros and Psyche, which is, if not known, at least knowable to any reader. Then there is the contemporary situation of New England village Psyche and her two nasty sisters and of somebody writing love letters to her. And finally there is what I begin by describing as an unknowable situation, something I'm going to keep

quiet about. But, in a way, the New England village situation is transparent enough to let us see the story of Eros and Psyche on one side of the glass and, perhaps, triangulate the third story, the untold one. (30–31)

With this we can imagine the New England Psyche as a "transparent" medium through which Merrill offers a reflected view of his own Eros and Psyche, as one image, together "on one side of the glass." But Psyche and Eros [or "Maker and Muse"("The Thousand and Second Night")] also can't so easily be one. The letters must come from somewhere unknown, the unity must entail an all but impossible difficulty.

A year later, in another interview, Merrill strongly suggests that his own experience provided the occasion for the poem: "At first it was just a little poem in the first person. It was involved with a curious experience—receiving letters from somebody I never met, who seemed to know everything about me. I'm not paranoiac, but it was rather unsettling" ("Interview with Brown" 47). To readers of *Sandover*, the last section of "From the Cupola" evokes strong parallels with Merrill's experience at the Ouija board. The "shrunken amphitheater" of the typewriter that informs this section recalls Merrill's Ouija board: its "twenty-six / Footlights, arranged in semicircle" (S. 147), and when Merrill concludes "From the Cupola" with "I have received from whom I do not know / These letters. Show me, light, if they make sense," we hear, perhaps for the first time, the poet's plea and God B's directive to "MAKE SENSE OF IT" (S. 474). Merrill makes the connection even more clear at the end of "The Book of Ephraim" when we hear about "Letters scrawled by my own hand unable / To keep pace with the tempest in the cup— / These old love-letters from the other world" (S. 91).

We may speculate then that part of the reason for Merrill's decision to "keep quiet" about the "unknowable" and "untold" personal story "behind" the poem is his ambivalence about explicitly acknowledging or working from his Ouija board experiences. As he tells J. D. McClatchy:

. . . the spirit *we* contacted—Ephraim—was anything but simple. So much so that for a long time I felt that the material he dictated really couldn't be used—then or perhaps ever. I felt it would be like cheating, or plagiarizing from some unidentifiable source. Oh, I put a few snippets of it into *The Seraglio*, but that was just a novel, and didn't count. ("Interview with McClatchy" 66–67)[41]

When Merrill speaks of an "unidentifiable" source here, more is at stake than possible embarrassment at being identified with the "absurd, flimsy contraption" of the Ouija board ("Interview with McClatchy" 68). The source is unidentifiable because it is so strongly indeterminate. As Merrill explains, either Ephraim "was the revelation / (Or if we had created him, then we were)" (S. 32). In either case, divinity or mortal, we are in the realm of highest mystery. In the interview with J. D. McClatchy, Merrill explains further:

> Well, don't you think there comes a time when everyone, not just a poet, wants to get beyond the self? To reach, if you like, the "god" within you? The board, in however clumsy or absurd a way, allows for precisely that. Or if it's still *yourself* that you're drawing upon, then that self is much stranger and freer and more farseeing than the one you thought you knew. ("Interview" 66).

About Eros in "From the Cupola" Merrill also adds, "I think that a stranger who knows one very well is practically a metaphor for God" ("James Merrill at Home" 29–30). Thus, again, whether the source is God, "the 'god' within, or the self, it is irreducibly strange.

Both "The Thousand and Second Night" and "From the Cupola" are crisis poems in which what is at stake is the health of the self-divided soul and how that soul might be refreshed in love and self-fabling. Both draw on Yeatsian themes; but, even more, both show Merrill succeeding in clearing a space for his own words and silences out of the "glooms of meaning" planted by his poetic fathers.[42] Merrill succeeds in these poems largely by virtue of his anti-Yeatsian strategies of poetic dispersal, of refracting the "self" of the poem through various voices, personae, and rhetorical stances. More than any of Yeats's dialogue poems, "The Thousand and Second Night" and "From the Cupola" establish the self as a Bakhtinian play of voices, for whom self-quarreling is but one of the many available registers, and for whom questions of meaning, questions of sense, continue to be part of the ongoing quest of the poem. In moving from "The Thousand and Second Night" to "From the Cupola," we also watch Merrill move beyond reliance on postures of nonchalance to an increasingly various self-examination, based on the growing realization that "the self is extremely ambiguous. There are so many different selves" ("James Merrill at Home" 28).

INTERLUDE: RETURNING TO YEATS'S A VISION

In the period following Merrill's early encounters with the Ouija board (1955–61), we have evidence in the poetry and in Merrill's first novel, *The Seraglio*, of Merrill's experiences at the board and of his hoping to strike a "bargain" with the higher powers. (See *Seraglio* 243, "Voices from the other World," and "A Tenancy.") But particularly in the poems, Merrill is careful to present the material as manageable and under control. He and David Jackson had set up housekeeping in Stonington, Connecticut; they had traveled around the world, and, in 1959, began their custom of staying part of the year in Greece. These stays offered Merrill "a kind of anonymity" and escape from sounding "very leisured and privileged" ("James Merrill at Home" 20). In Athens, unlike Stonington, Merrill and Jackson began seeing people their own age, or younger, and made friends with people from different backgrounds, ("Interview with McClatchy" 62; "James Merrill at Home" op. cit.). Again unlike Stonington, or even New York, Athens during these years also offered both men a scene of heightened and yet domesticated sexual adventure. Early in 1961, Merrill began a friendship with a young Greek named Strato Mouflouzélis. This friendship would become an ongoing affair that gradually cooled over the next decade.

In February of 1962, while wintering in Athens, Merrill again picked up *A Vision*, noting the date beside Yeats's sentence: "And again and again they [Yeats's 'philosophic voices'] have insisted that the whole system is the creation of my wife's Daimon and of mine, and that it is as startling to them as to us" (22). A pencil check on page 54 marks the sentence (in a letter concocted by Yeats in the name of his rationalist persona, John Aherne) "I recall what Plato said of memory, and suggest that your automatic script, or whatever it was, may well have been but a process of remembering." The first passage suggests that Merrill is struck by the parallels between his spiritualist collaboration with David Jackson and Yeats's collaboration with his wife. It also recalls the number of times the spirit voices in *Sandover* express their startled delight or anxiety at the course of "events" and revelations of the board and their dependence on Merrill's efforts "TO MAKE SENSE OF IT" (S. 337).[43]

Both passages also suggest that Merrill is uneasy about the sources of his voices. Are they a "folie à deux" as his former "psychoanalyst" Dr. Thomas Detre, suggests (S. 30)? Are they Jungian tappings of a collective unconscious, and thus a kind of remembering? Are they "Reality [or] Projection" (S. 46)? Both passages suggest that it matters to Merrill at this moment early in 1962 more than before whether and how to believe the "revelations" coming to him via the Ouija Board. One reason may be that their friend, Maya Deren, had recently died, and Merrill reports that he and Jackson had received communication from her shortly afterward: "DAVID JIMMY I AM YOUNG AT LAST" (S. 64). How were the two to take this first spelled out "voice" of an old friend who has died? Was it "The gods own truth, or [a consoling] fiction"? Consolation, or bringing Maya back "in a whiff / Of blissful grief" is, after all, the explicit result of this "contact" (S. 63, 64). As we shall see,

Deren's death and subsequent communication also serve as occasion for Merrill's "contacting" Yeats in quite another sense in section "R" of "The Book of Ephraim."

Merrill's next annotation reveals much more directly how personally he takes aspects of Yeats's text. It also suggests a yet more complex nexus of credulity, doubt, and desire than do previous annotations. On the top of page 70, Yeats writes:

> Flaubert is the only writer known to me who has so used the double cone. He talked much of writing a story called "La Spirale". He died before he began it, but something of his talk about it has been collected and published. It would have described a man whose dreams during sleep grew in magnificence as his life grew more and more unlucky, the wreck of some love affair coinciding with his marriage to a dream princess.

In response to this story of a man who loses an earthly love in his enchantment with a "dream princess," Merrill writes in the margin of his copy: "Is failure to assert myself with S. leading to the revelations of E. [?]" It is difficult to determine when Merrill made this note. It may have been as early as 1962, when Merrill was in the early stages of an extended affair with his Greek friend Strato, the likely "S." in Merrill's note. But autobiographical evidence from the poems, and the understanding that Merrill and Jackson maintained fairly extensive contact with Ephraim only up until 1968 (S. 55), suggest that the date could be as late as 1968.[44]

With this note we see that Merrill finds in Yeats's summary an analogy and a cautionary tale for his own life. But, characteristically, it is an analogy with a difference. Merrill does not ask, "Is my enchantment with the revelations of E[phraim] leading to my failure to assert myself with S[trato]?" but instead asks the more psychologically attuned question of whether failure or frustration in an erotic relationship has not produced a compensatory response, namely the "revelations of E." (Here we recall that Ephraim's name in Merrill's lost novel preceding *Sandover* is "Eros," making the "revelations of E[ros]" another telling reading of Merrill's note.) The status of these revelations, however problematic they may appear in other lights, is not in question here. "E." is treated as concretely as "S." Here again, as with the note on page 25, "Is this what I must learn?" Merrill's questioning shows him turning to the older poet's most esoteric text for indications of lessons to be learned for his own life.

MERRILL'S DIALOGUES OF SELF AND SOUL, 1966–1976

If, as late as 1968, Merrill is returning to *A Vision* with questions about how his relations with the Ouija board are affecting his life and work, and if the board's revelations are particularly provocative at that time, this may help explain why Merrill's 1969 collection *The Fire Screen* bursts out with such so much explicit Yeatsian detail. As Stephen Yenser points out:

> ... Yeats figures especially often in *The Fire Screen*. In one way or another, he might be glimpsed in the background of "The Friend of the Fourth Decade," " More Enterprise," "Flying from Byzantium," "Last Words," and "Matinees." In this last poem Merrill alludes to "Sailing to Byzantium," "Byzantium," and "Dialogue of Self and Soul," as well as perhaps "Cuchulain Confronted," "The Circus Animals' Desertion" and "Meditations in Time of Civil War." Indeed, Yeats seems to be the "'father'" figure and dentist who has "'tampered with [Merrill's] mouth'" so that "'From now on, metal, music, myth / Will seem to taint its words.'" Since one form this figure takes is that of a Dr. Scherer, Yeats might be thought of as Merrill's secret Scherer in this sonnet sequence (though that title could also go to Wagner, whose own fire and gold recur throughout)." (*Myth* 348n. 6)

To this list we can also add the first and last poems of the volume: "Lorelei" for showing the poet well on his way to being another Yeatsian "Old Rocky Face," as "Love with his chisel / Deepens the lines begun upon [his] face," and even "The Summer People" wherein, as Yenser notes, "Jack dedicates his winters to a lonely creative activity that he carries on, like the poet in Yeats's 'The Phases of the Moon,' late at night in the tower of the former church" (*Myth* 173).

In this and subsequent volumes, Merrill moves beyond his earlier, largely appropriative and "nonchalant" responses to the resources and challenges of Yeats's example. Something seems to have happened late in 1967 or early in 1968 to galvanize Merrill once again into a more critical engagement with the older poet. Yet, after *The Fire Screen*, this direct engagement and commentary markedly subsides. Yeats's presence in *Braving the Elements* (1972), for example, is more covert than in *The Fire Screen*. Yeats's Condition of Fire informs Merrill's "Log" and "After the Fire," just as Yeatsian aesthetics inform "Dreams About Clothes" and "Syrinx"; but these poems, for the most part, avoid explicit allusion. "Willowware Cup" argues powerfully with "Lapis Lazuli"; but Merrill would rather we note the parallels with Keats's "Ode to a Grecian Urn."[45] Similarly, in the opening poems of *Divine Comedies* (1976) Merrill's use of Yeats seems markedly reduced, even with J. D. McClatchy's assurance that "Chimes for Yahya" is "an elaborate parody of Yeats's 'The Second Coming'" ("Lost Paradises" 317). Yeats seems to have become as transparent for Merrill as the air he breathes—no longer a figure to be parodied, wrestled with, or even pointedly avoided. Until Yeats's speech condenses once more in "Ephraim," we might think that Merrill has effectively "mastered" not only all the poetic resources but also the anxiety and ambivalence that Yeats's poetry and example has entailed.

But to conclude that Yeats gradually vanishes from Merrill's concerns in these later poems would be to dramatically "misread" them, especially given the "correction" that the subsequent volumes of *Sandover* afford.

Since no mere list of poems or passing allusions can indicate how or why Merrill was so variously engaged with Yeats during the first twenty-odd years in which he also ambivalently "entertained" the "voices" of the Ouija Board, we must turn back to the poems for insight into Merrill's ongoing dialogue with the "father" figure who seems to have "tampered with [his] mouth." What most stands out about the Yeats-inflected poems in *The Fire Screen* is the way Merrill uses Yeats as a vehicle for his own inner dialogue—much as he looks to Yeats for guidance in his reading of *A Vision*. The titles of two poems in *Fire Screen*, "More Enterprise" and "Flying from Byzantium," announce their role as commentaries on Yeats's "A Coat" and "Sailing to Byzantium." Yet only "More Enterprise" consistently uses its prior poem as a means of answering or "correcting" Yeats as a way of suggesting Merrill's own vacillating poetic "credo." "Flying from Byzantium" (and its envoi "Last Words"), "Matinees," and "The Friend of the Fourth Decade" all show Merrill to be much more engaged in his own "Dialogue of Self and Soul," rather than as direct confrontations with the earlier poet. In these poems, Yeats's "Dialogue" often hovers in the background and Yeats is often identified with a particular aspect of the Merrill's own poetic self, sometimes chastened and sometimes cherished, but in all events suddenly "present" in ways that distinctly color Merrill's characteristic self-scrutiny.

With the opening poem, "Lorelei," Merrill establishes the poet's relation to his precursor poets: they are "stones" which he follows: "Each strands you, then // Does not," and he is fast becoming one of them, another Yeats, another "Old Rocky Face," whose stone will some day guide those who follow after, helping them to "see that much further into the golden vagueness / Forever about to clear." Having made this sweeping, opening gesture, Merrill offers "The Friend of the Fourth Decade" as introduction the volume's Yeats-inflected project of masked self-interrogation. As Stephen Yenser has noted, a number of cues indicate that we are meant to see the "friend" in this poem as an alter ego of the poet (*Myth* 168). He may be a reflection of how others view the poet or an emblem of an aspect of his earlier self. He is the bored sophisticate ("'I'm tired of understanding / The light in people's eyes, the smells, the food. / . . . Tired of understanding what I hear, / the tones, the overtones'"). He longs for a "simplicity" of sorts (though quickly interjects, "I *despise* Thoreau") and desires the intensity of new, unmediated experience. It is not hard to identify the friend with certain aspects of Yeats-the-sensualist, who would drink his life entire, even though "the ditches are impure" ("Dialogue"). The friend's "rag and bone shop" which promises a phoenix-like renewal is "a dung-and-emerald oasis," where "'Individual and type are one. / Do as I please, I *am* the simpleton . . .'":

"I answer to whatever name they call,
Drink the sweet black condescending dregs,

Try on their hungers like a shirt of flame
(Well, a sports shirt of flame) whereby I've been

Picked clean, reborn each day increasingly
Conspicuous, increasingly unseen."

Here is flame that quite literally "cannot singe a sleeve" and though he knows himself to be something of a tourist ("Don't worry, I'll go back. Honeymoons end"), the friend's renewal seems genuine, marked as it is by the spiritualizing force of paradox ("increasingly / Conspicuous, increasingly unseen").

In contrast to the "friend," the speaker is much more "the poet as poet," the self who is not so easily rinsed clean of words, obligations of the heart, or memories (Yenser *Myth* 170). In the final section of the poem, the speaker's dream of the friend [which operates like Yeats's "dreaming back" (Ibid. 169)] links the two personae in one mirroring moment of self-recognition, which might also be a moment of rebirth (not unlike the friend's being "reborn each day") into the startling, liberating realization of the self as "the perfect stranger."[46] What Merrill initially divided with the trope of self-as-other into two Cartesian "knowables"—self and friend, earnest poet and bon vivant—comes together in a dream of release from identity, which is also a (dangerous) kind of joy. The release from identity the friend achieves, "gone where he was going . . . increasingly / Conspicuous, increasingly unseen," the poem also achieves as it ends on the open note of strangeness, of perfect possibility, which is the enabling dream of being a poet.[47] Thus, the poem ends as it began, as a fantasy of release from what Yeats would call one's Body of Fate, "the sum, not the unity, of fact, fact as it affects a particular man" (*Vision* 82). Yet by giving form and conscious expression to that desire, the poem also realizes Yeats's desire to "attain self-knowledge" for the poet (Ibid. 83).

Continuing the theme of self-definition (often with regard to Yeats) that is so much the project in *The Fire Screen*, "More Enterprise" reprises the dramatic situation of Yeats's "A Coat" only to draw attention to the many differences between Merrill's and Yeats's manner and judgments. In this way, the Yeatsian background to "More Enterprise" allows Merrill to bring his own poetic commitments into sharper focus.[48] In each poem the poet takes up a new, more "scant wardrobe" of poetic gesture after the "local heirs" have appropriated his former style. But whereas Yeats glorifies his past manner (it was "a coat / Covered with embroideries / From old mythologies / From heel to throat"), Merrill mocks "the old strait swank" of his earlier ways. "Strait," a delightful archaism, points directly to the constrictions, the exacting demands, and stylistic confines of Merrill's early stanzas and "decorative and glamour-clogged" manner—to use Richard Howard's phrase (407). The word points obliquely, too, through its play on "straight," to the distress and accumulating restriction Merrill felt at "having to" mask his homosexual love in the gender-neutral second person.

Whereas Yeats berates "the fools" who "caught" the manner of his old song and "wore it in the world's eyes," Merrill makes specific and indulgent mention of the locals who now wear what once was his. "Koula's nephew has the suit she shrank," "Andreas" gets the Roman shoes. Merrill's metaphor is clothes, just as Yeats's is; but Merrill's vehicle is freer. "Coat" does not reduce to "Song." Merrill's metaphor is more open to the literal occasion of a wealthy, American semi-expat who shares his castoffs. It is more free to take "style" as its tenor in a number of senses—habits of mind, manner of speaking and gesture—all more flexible than Yeats's tone of public rebuke and terse assertion that "there's more enterprise / In walking naked." The one link Merrill's clothes do not obviously make—to the manner of his earlier and present poetry—his title's clear allusion to Yeats's poem does for him. In this way, Merrill's allusion to Yeats's poem allows him to write about his own poetry and to protest against Yeats's manner and judgments without himself adopting the same manner.[49] Finally, whereas Yeats makes a brusque and perhaps bitter claim for the merit of the starker mode he has left him, Merrill "fills out" the pregnant ambiguity of the language he's been given: "that Yes of theirs." The Greek head shake that Americans may first take for "no" or as a sign of doubt and which instead means "confusingly, assent," may seem a scant poetic wardrobe; but it retains for Merrill an essential doubleness and thereby serves as emblem for the credulous skepticism (or skeptical credulity) that fuels his art. It is, for example, the enabling YES [& NO] of *Sandover* that he'll wear "into the grave."

At first Merrill's "Flying from Byzantium" promises an ironic "correction" of Yeats's "Sailing to Byzantium" in keeping with its title and the tone set by "More Enterprise." As the title promises, modern-day air travel updates Yeats's age-old voyage by sea and, what's more important, the announced goal, "The hour has come. I'm heading home" (the known place of daily living) in Merrill's poem challenges Yeats's announced arrival, "therefore I have sailed the seas and come / To the holy city of Byzantium" (the transcendent realm of artifice and eternity). We are thus prepared to expect simple inversions, with Merrill arguing for life, lived bodily experience, and the blessing of voyages (as we have seen most recently in "The Thousand and Second Night") and against Yeats's longing to be "out of nature," rid of his animal body, and transported into a realm of eternal song.

Certain contrasts are this direct. Merrill's speaker is torn by having to leave his lover; whereas, Yeats's speaker is only too happy to leave the "young / In one another's arms." Merrill's poem takes pains with the internal colloquy of separation: apostrophes to the lover, self-pity, self-exhortation, and rationalizing projections; whereas—once Yeats has summarily had done with "Whatever is begotten, born, and dies"—his poem focuses resolutely on the soul and "Monuments of its own magnificence."

But Merrill's poem is no simple exercise in pointed contrasts. We quickly learn that the Merrillian speaker is, like Yeats, devoted to images of "poignant recollection" ("An Image from a Past Life"): "I've kept my Kodak handy / To snap the last unfocused Kodachrome."[50] We learn that he is in part abstracted from the immediate emotional situation ("a near lightning," the speaker's migraine standing in here for Yeats's "holy fire," "sheets the brain. / I cannot take your hand for pain.") and wishes himself, if not wholly "out of nature," at least spared "from more living." Thus, "Flying from Byzantium" is not so much a critique spoken from outside of Yeats's concerns as from within them. To fly *from* Byzantium, the speaker must first have been there. Consequently, Merrill's speaker abounds with divergent Yeatsian postures. He vacillates:

> Now to say something I'll regret—
> It's not true, it's not true, and yet
> *God save me from more living.*
> I loved you, I am leaving.
> Another world awaits me? I forget.
>
> You, whose animal I am,
> My senses' mage and pentagram,
> Look, listen, miles above you
> I love you still, I love you . . .
> Then get in line to board the long slow tram.

He engages in self-serving, self-affirming internal dialogue:

> Up spoke the man in the moon:
> "What does that moan mean?
> The plane was part of the plan.
> Why gnaw the bone of a boon?"
>
> I said with spleen, "Explain
> These nights that tie me in knots,
> All drama and no dream,
> While you lampoon my pain."
>
> He then: "Lusters are least
> Dimmed among the damned.
> The point's to live, love,
> Not shake your fist at the feast [. . .]

And so on for three more stanzas, the "man in the moon" exhorting that he rise and shine ("So up from your vain divan / . . . I've shown you how to shine—") and be a man, and the more "soulful" voice of the speaker offers the rationalizing perspective of time. Looking forward he sees "no sign / That either heart had been hurt" [his or his lover's] and, as seeming master of "what is past, or passing, or to come," concludes: "The years shone back on yours [heart] / Free and immune from mine." This is as much actual Yeatsian parody as the poem allows itself. But we notice that Yeats is only secondarily its object. If anything, the poem uses Yeats's methods not so much to critique the older poet as to dramatize the limitations of the Merrill-identified speaker of the poem.

In the third section of the poem, Merrill makes a point of reminding his reader of miraculous golden bird of "Sailing to Byzantium." That "priceless metal bird," the airplane that transported him homeward and away from Byzantium, Merrill tells us, "came down at last," as if to emphasize the specific Yeatsian dichotomy his poem addresses—a dedication to life and love or to the work and art. But, again unlike Yeats's poem, this section focuses on the "He" that the speaker leaves behind; only in the last two lines do we see (rather than hear) what has become of the speaker, transformed into the enduring emblem of the artist caught at the first moment of beginning a work. In contrast, the "He" of the poem continues to be the speaking, fated child of earth who loves and suffers and who embodies "that sensual music" of Yeats's poem:

> Mountain lion, watersnake—
> As if the choice where his to make,   [choice of how to die, or be reborn]
> Kneeling there on the earth's crust.
>
> "Mother, I was vain, headstrong,
> Help me, I am coming back."
> He put his lips along a crack,
> Inhaled the vague, compliant song.

The poem's final quatrain abruptly divides between the voice of this Yeatsian self "content to live it all again" ("'That I may be born again / Lead the black fly to my flesh.'") and the equally Yeatsian image of the tower poet or soulful scribe ("Far off a young scribe turned a fresh / Page, hesitated, dipped his pen.")—who is presumably the speaker returned from his voyage now bent upon making "what happened" into literature. Here then is Merrill's figure for himself, or that writing part of himself most allied with "the artifice of eternity." We are struck by how small it is, as if seen at a distance or in miniature upon a page. This is clearly only one part of the poet's self necessary for life and poetry, a precious part but not the whole.[51]

"Last Words," which follows immediately, serves as the envoi for "Flying from Byzantium." It is addressed to the same lover and bespeaks the transforming, transporting power of love. Here the speaker is elevated into something like Yeats's "Thirteenth Cone" where time and knowledge and the refracted aspects of one's lives are all freely available, unconstrained, but focused on the unifying vision.[52] I give the whole poem:

> My life, your light green eyes
> Have lit on me with joy.
> There's nothing I don't know
> Or shall not know again,
> Over and over again.
> It's noon, it's dawn, it's night,
> I am the dog that dies
> In the deep street of Troy
> Tomorrow, long ago—
> Part of me dims with pain,
> Becomes the stinging flies,   [the "black flies" of sensual regeneration]
> The bent head of the boy   [head of the "young scribe" above his page]
> Part looks into your light
> And lives to tell you so.

In the exchange of loving glances that frame the poem, the speaker attains unity of knowledge and of being while being nonetheless a creature of "parts." He is both in and out of time, in and out of nature, animal and image, speaker and word, knower and known, glancer and the glance. The last two lines compress images of Dante the Pilgrim passing through the refining fire, drawn on by the grace of Beatrice's gaze, and Yeats's "holy fire" about which the Soul in "Vacillation" declares, "Look on that fire, salvation walks within." Thus, together "Flying from Byzantium" and "Last Words" operate as a dialogue, in which Yeatsian self-reflection and critique of the first poem is answered by equally Yeatsian affirmation in the second.

About "Matinees" Stephen Yenser has rightly said, "Yeats seems to be the 'father' figure and dentist who has 'tampered with [Merrill's] mouth' so that 'From now on, metal, music, myth / Will seem to taint its words'" (*Myth* 348 n. 6). The poem is quintessentially Merrillian in its unobtrusive, fluent sonnets, in its mix of tones and voices, in taking its occasion from the memory of his childhood introduction to grand opera, and in using this memory as a frame for varied reflections on the relation of art and living and the status of his current domestic relations. The poem is remarkably at ease with this material, material that in other poems has and will continue to evoke considerable ambivalence and anxiety. It is also remarkably at ease with its Yeatsian paternity. Merrill's own parents hardly figure in the poem (instead we have the family friend Mrs. Livingston and dentist Dr. Scherer), so that by their absence the poem seems to suggest that opera, that marriage of music, words, and spectacle, was the true parent to this child. And yet the poem also seems to unfold under the generous and watchful eye of parental guidance and concern. Perhaps this is part of its ease. [The presence of "my Mother" hovers just beyond concluding scene of the young poet writing his thank you note to Mrs. Livingston, "I will treasure the experience always— / [. . .] Ever gratefully, Your little friend. . . ."] Ultimately, the occult question of parenting, of how influence shapes us and what, in turn, to make of such influence, colors almost every section of the poem.

At first it is the experience of art that excites a child's clear-eyed openness ("No one believing, everybody thrilled") that allows its influence to operate:

> "The strains of Cimarosa and Mozart
> Flowed through his veins, and fed his solitary heart.
> Long beyond adolescence [. . .]
>   the aria's remote
> Control surviving his worst interval,
>
> Tissue of sound and tissue of the brain
> Would coalesce, and what the Masters wrote
> Itself compose his features sharp and small."[53]

This is Merrill's un-anxious account of what through *Sandover* he will learn to call "cloning." In an interview with C. A. Buckley, Merrill explained: "I've often felt something like that "cloning" in my own life. What if somebody had not told me to read Proust? The act of sitting there reading; I mean it was as if my mind was being permanently changed and tampered with" ("Exploring" 424). Or, as we hear about the Yeatsian Dr Scherer, "My father having tampered with your mouth, / From now on, metal, music, myth / Will seem to taint its words." "Tampering" and "taint" do suggest a certain amount of anxiety about such influence; but "its words" makes this process seem so matter-of-factly objective that there is little occasion for fuss. Influence is what happens. It operates on and through the body ("Tissue of sound and tissue of brain") and comes to "compose" us. Our words always come by "word of mouth."[54]

As if to demonstrate this process in operation, Merrill's next sonnet allows us to see the play of reading and experience. We see the Plato behind Yeats's "A Dialogue of Self and Soul" and then Yeats's "Dialogue" and "Sailing to Byzantium" behind Merrill's governing, operatic metaphor:

> We love the good, said Plato? He was wrong.
> We love as well the wicked and the weak.
> Flesh hugs its shaved plush. Twenty-four-hour-long
> Galas fill the hulk of the Comique.
>
> Flesh knows by now what dishes to avoid,
> Tries not to brood on bomb or heart attack.
> Anatomy is destiny, said Freud.
> Soul is the brilliant hypochondriac.
>
> Soul will cough blood and sing, and softer sing,
> Drink poison, breath her joyous last, a waltz
> Rubato from his arms who sobs and stays
>
> Behind, death after death, who fairly melts

> Watching her turn from him, restored, to fling
> Kisses into the furnace roaring praise.

By appropriating Yeats's "Soul clap its hands and sing, and louder sing," Merrill highlights how opera too is an "artifice of eternity." "Death after death," it sponsors the Nietzschean "eternal recurrence of all things."[55] It too culminates in that "holy fire" that gathers together audience and performer in one complementary, restorative act. Merrill's Yeatsian "Soul will cough blood and sing" also shows how influence cycles back on itself in the way it reflectively highlights the operatic in Yeats. [How easy after such a line to imagine Yeats's verses heroically staged and sung in some vast, resounding hall.]

But what the next sonnet demonstrates is that art need not operate only on what we think of as an "operatic scale." "One's household opera," Merrill tells us, also reveals its "magic fire, / Tongues flickering up from humdrum incident." In this light, however much one may think of the "domestic sublime" as a particular Merrillian specialty, one also remembers Yeats's "When You Are Old" or "Adam's Curse" or "A Prayer for my Daughter," or even "Meditations in Time of Civil War," to mention only a few poems in which Yeats works from a "household" or domestic setting, finding there, like Merrill, sufficient "passions and betrayals / . . . in order to make song of them."

A certain Yeatsian vacillation governs the last two sonnets of "Matinees." Before suggesting, in part by writing in his child's voice once more, that he would be "content to live it all again," the adult poet concedes that it would be "Kinder to remember than to play" or "Risk the real thing any more." Memory of "old beauties" seems enough. It is "Enough," the speaker suggests, "to know the score." These "records or transcription[s]" of past "passions and betrayals" will, in Yeats's phrase "Suffice the aging man" but not exactly as they did "the growing boy" ("Meditations in Time of Civil War"). The difference here is Blake's—between the voice of experience and the voice of innocence. What Merrill recovers in the poem, to place finally against the chastened, knowing, adult voice, is the child's joy in recurrence, the innocence of wishing "to live it all again":

> I play my record of the Overture
> Over and over. I pretend
> I am still in sitting in the theatre.

It is also ultimately the innocence that art is able to make of experience:

> I also wrote a poem which my Mother
> Says I should copy and send.
> Ever gratefully, Your little friend . . .

Such thanks seem to exemplify exactly that "ceremony" whereby the "soul recovers radical innocence" ("A Prayer for my Daughter") and provide Merrill's version of the high Romantic argument for innocence recovered through experience and art; or, as Yeats explains: "In the spiritual world . . . innocence . . . is now the highest achievement of the intellect" (qtd. in Vendler *Yeats's Vision* 185).

If Yeats is the "secret Scherer" in this poem (and, note, the poem asks us to speculate "as to what dentist and tooth 'stood for'"), he occasions remarkably little anxiety about the Conradian issues of competence, detection, or identity (*Myth* 348 n. 6). Whether as his soul's double or as a father-figure, in this poem, Yeats seems clearly to be part of what Merrill most wholeheartedly loves: the self-reflective, self-transformative passion of an art work that thrills one body and soul. Here Merrill also seems to understand the benefits of his relation with the older poet, since it is this father/dentist figure's "Plan [. . .] to fill my tooth with gold"—which is itself a benign trope for the shaping, reconstitutive forces of poetic influence and for the restoration of a kind of higher innocence through experience and art. The usual pain and anxiety attendant upon such operations is submerged in these verses beneath an idyllic childhood memory and the "ravishing din" of opera, whose "high airs," like a dentist's ether, are "light as lust." This operatic voice or "speech of birds" recalls the Byzantine enchantments of Yeats's golden bird, but also the bird voices of Cuchulain's "comforters" who counsel acceptance of a common fate.

It is as though Merrill recognized, that by putting defensiveness aside and taking up what "All must together do" in our collective *Gesamtkunstwerk* of making something "Out of the life lived, out of the love spent," he too would find his "mouth" or "tooth" remade "Of hammered gold and gold enameling." In this way, Yeats hovers over the poem, helping Merrill, "out of nature" so far as opera and memory and poetry can take him, to "sing, and *softer* sing" "Of what is past, or passing, or to come" (emphasis added). Here too, Merrill's "softer" singing not only reflects his self-conscious, belated diminishment in relation to Yeats's poetic "volume," it also makes a pointedly "naturalizing" correction to Yeatsian artifice, albeit from within the highly artificial conventions of grand opera! Such is the often dazzling music Merrill makes on the revisionary themes of Bloomian anxiety.

A more typical variation on Oedipal anxiety colors the poem from which *The Fire Screen* takes its title. "Mornings in a New House" concerns a "cold man" who "hardly cares" who lights his morning fire for him, a man ultimately warmed not so much by the fire in his room as by memories of his mother awakened by the "Crewel-work" fire screen she embroidered as a child. Her childhood needlework bids him imagine how she once must have cared for her doll (as if, even at eight years of age, "she had foreknown him"), how she had "nursed him . . . / Sewn his first dress, sung to him, let him fall, / Howled when his face chipped like a plate." Thus, the man stands bathed in the "holy fire" of his memories, "Infraradience, wave on wave," until caught up in a moment of transcendent, unknowable, "pleasure," a unity of being which shatters distinctions of time and identity:

>   . . . once more, deep indoors, blood's drawn,
>   The tiny needlewoman cries,
>   And to some faintest creaking shut of eyes
>   His pleasure and the doll's are one.

In these lines, Merrill weds the lessons of Proust and Yeats, the mother's fire screen being both a potent madeleine and a portal into sublimity, an operatic "screen *of* fire" (as Merrill insists in his note to the poem). The fire screen's "infraradience" marks the crossing over into that "great [bodily] happiness" of Yeats's "Vacillation IV" and the spiritual or "abstract joy" suggested by the trope of a doll's pleasure. As the "Valkyrie's baffle" of Merrill's note, the fire screen is "A STRONG FORCE BOTH / PROTECTIVE & CONDUCTIVE" (S. 424). Both barrier and beacon, it is "whatever draws us / To, and insulates us from, the absolute—" (S. 84). These seeming contradictions, between barrier and conduit, body and soul, child/man and doll, fire screen and screen of fire, should not distract from the unity, the "one," this poem moves toward. Indeed, they help constitute it. It is one of the lessons Merrill seems happy to rehearse in this poem, that unity only comes out of complexity, that "nothing can be sole or whole / That has not been rent," and that, here, warming the "cold man," mending his pain, comes at the imaginative cost of his mother's somehow compensatory, expiative, or fellow pain.[56]

The Yeatsian theme of expiation is broached in another poem of this period as well.[57] Written in 1968, in what seems to have been a particularly crucial year for Merrill, "Hourglass" (*The Yellow Pages*) revisits some of the imagery from Merrill's 1946 poem "Hourglass," written while Merrill was both Kimon Friar's lover and tutee. In the earlier poem the speaker watches the hour glass "that has been taught / Calm flowing such as you teach me" and concludes, "You / Are the kind gathering I most falter to. / Love only is replenishment of halves" [in a multiple pun that joins the Platonic myth of lovers reuniting separated halves, the "our glass" of Merrill's and Friar's relationship, which remaining always half full (or empty), and the notion that lovers give but what they already have]. In the later poem, the speaker has predeceased his lover, and reminds us that in Merrill's dedicatory poem to Friar in *The Black Swan* Friar is linked to Keats sailing to what would be his death in Rome ("Keats on board ship for what we shall call Rome, / In waterlight watching his shadow fall"). The figure of Keats dominates that early poem, just as he seems to introduce the later "Hourglass":

>   Dear at death's door when you stand
>   I will run to let you in.
>   You may know me by my grin
>   And the joints of this right hand.

If "this right hand" recalls Keats's "This living hand" in the same way that "the last raveling of his hand" does in Merrill's dedicatory poem, Keats again serves as a mask for Friar. Only now, Merrill imagines Friar not sailing to his death but speaking to (and for) Merrill from beyond the grave:

> I will say to Pluto's wife,
> "Please your Majesty, this shade
>
> Is my friend's who kept your Spring,
> Showed me how to wear your green.
> Twenty winters intervene
> Yet I glow, remembering."

Twenty winters before this poem was written Merrill had recently broken off his love affair with Friar. This second "Hourglass" seems to allow Merrill to revise the ambivalent pain of that parting, perhaps based on his experiences of renewed contact with Friar during his annual visits in Greece. In the poem, the speaker predicts that at the point of death the lover "will follow [him] unafraid / As one seldom does in life," quite possibly an allusion to Merrill refusing to follow Friar to Greece at the height of their earlier affair. To conclude the poem, Merrill fittingly (if the speaker stands for Friar) gives the speaker a fine enactment of Yeats's Dreaming Back:

> [Persephone] will then unlock a chest,
> Shake our senses out like robes
> Fine and warm to naked ribs,
> Make a sign when we are dressed
>
> For one hour in which we fill
> With ten thousand joys and pains.
> Then, reversed, the burning grains
> Back through her transparent will
>
> Drain, and the robes are blown apart,
> Two more bat shapes in the cave,
> Little dreaming now they have
> Blessed each other heart to heart.

Taken as a reconciling return to the Merrill/Friar relationship after the violent treatment in *The (Diblos) Notebook*, this "Hourglass" raises a number of biographical questions, especially in light of the host of other Yeats-inflected poems of this period. Again we want to know what happened in Greece in the winter of 1967–68 that may have led Merrill to return to reading *A Vision* and that helped inspire these poems. Why does he seem to imagine himself about to die in this poem? Why imply that he will never see his Greek lover again in "Flying from Byzantium" ("If only / I thought that I would look in them [his eyes] again!")?

The poems of Merrill's next volume, *Braving the Elements*, excite no such inquiries. In all but "Willowware Cup," the Yeatsian mode has been dampened down to a matter of glancing, self-referential allusion. But it would be a mistake to say that Yeats has suddenly ceased to engage the younger poet. Rather, the relative lack of interest in Yeats in these poems looks more like a pattern of avoidance, another kind of "bravery"—especially since Merrill will significantly renew his engagement with Yeats in his next collection, *Divine Comedies*, and since he seems to lose interest in Yeats during exactly the same time that he proclaims a "nonchalant" lack of interest in the Ouija board. *Braving the Elements* does open with two poems, which are meditations on experience in terms of the refining ambiguities of fire; but we will have to wait until "McKane's Falls," in *Divine Comedies*, before Merrill gives us his counterimage to Yeats's Condition of Fire.

"Log" opens *Braving the Elements* with division and diminishment: "Then when the flame forked like a sudden path / I gasped and stumbled, and was less." Here is choice, experience, and the depredations of time. Flames consume fuel, give off light and heat, and die, leaving ash. The poem ends: "Dear light along the way to nothingness, / What could be made of you but light, and this?"—a question that is its own answer. Here the speaker suggests that he takes the fire's light as fuel (or subject matter) for his imagination, whose fires in turn yield both the "light," the intelligible sense of the poem, and "this," its ash or physical remains on the printed page. But what distinguishes "light" from "this," poem-in-the-mind from poem-on-the-page? Everything and nothing. They are, in Yeats's terms, dance and dancer. Ending with a rhetorical question (like "Among School Children" or "Leda and the Swan") the poem also invites the reader into its own self-reflexive play. As reading moves like "intellectual fire" ("Blood and the Moon") over the printed text, we "see according to our lights" ("From the Cupola"), but what we see also remains "this." The forked play of reading and the read links the evanescent ("along the way to nothingness") and an inexhaustible, self-mirroring "artifice of eternity."

The next poem in the collection, "After the Fire" opens with a similarly flickering play of decisive undecidability: "Everything changes; nothing does." Fires of passion (lust, avarice, anger) die away and reignite leaving "embers that can't be handled yet." But ultimately all is caught up in a higher flame, that of loving recognition and transformation:

> The snuffed-out candle-ends grow tall and shine,
> Dead flames encircle us, which cannot harm,
> The table's spread, she croons, and I
> Am kneeling pressed to her old burning frame.

These flames are at once "dead" and "burning": a "holy fire" then "that cannot singe a sleeve" and yet gathers the speaker into an "agony" of devotion.

Merrill does not over-simplify or argue with Yeats in these two poems. Enough imaginative work has been done perhaps, enough understanding of how to use the precursor's fire as both conduit and insulation has been gained, that Yeats rarely rises to "trouble the stream" of the "unruly natural forces" Merrill so often takes as his text in this volume (Yenser *Myth* 160).[58] After the "tamed uprush" of Yeatsian moments in *The Fire Screen*, *Braving the Elements* provides only these introductory glimmers, the glancing variation on Yeats's "dying generations" in "Syrinx's" "fatal growths,"[59] and the vague echo of Yeats's "A Coat" and perhaps a flicker of Yeats himself as the "old-clothes man" in "Dreams about Clothes," Merrill's meditation on the vexed relation between art and life, which is given new urgency by his vision of the Angel of Death: "He passes me unseeing, yet how much / Of mine's already in his sack!"[60] The only poem to engage Yeats provocatively or deeply is "Willowware Cup," written a decade before the poems in this volume (*Recitative* 10).

Welcome anywhere, "Willowware Cup" nonetheless seems oddly placed here between the particularly middle-aged anxiety of "In Nine Sleep Valley" (where "Trying to read in Nature's book," one remembers "There was a day when beauty, death, and love / Were coiled together in one crowning glory," but now "Centimeters deep yawns the abyss") and the equally anxious feeling of inadequacy before lover and cosmos "celebrated" in "Banks of a Stream Where Creatures Bathe." The "version of heaven" the speaker finds, indeed holds, in "Willowware Cup" is predicated on loss ("You are far away.") and resignation ("The leaves tell what they tell."), but "something warm and clear" still flows; "the old odd designs / Crowd as before, and seem to concentrate on" the one he loves. This warmth and clarity must have seemed a welcome reminder in 1971, and the poem's pointed revision of Yeats's "Lapis Lazuli" a fitting continuation and correction of the numerous Yeats-involved poems of *The Fire Screen*.

In the period during which many of these poems were written (between the summers of 1968 and 1970) Merrill and Jackson had not been in keeping in touch with their familiar spirit Ephraim ["Why? No reason—we'd been busy living, / Had meant to call, but never quite got round . . . " (S. 55)]. We have earlier been told they did not feel themselves "equipped to face the Sphinx. // And slept again" (S. 52) in that postponing sleep of nonchalance that had so successfully kept "commitment" to his "Voices from the Other World" at bay. Yet after making contact with Ephraim again in the summer of 1970, Merrill begins to entertain notions of a "task / Deepen[ing]," "Craft narrowing to witchcraft," and "Obligations it is bliss to suffer" for the sake of "Stories whose glow we see our lives bathed in" (S. 53). Henry Sloss marks this as the point at which Merrill decided to begin the novel which was "to survey / The arteries of Ephraim's influence" (S. 66) and which signaled his "commitment" to the pressing powers and responsibilities Ephraim had just called him to acknowledge (Sloss 106):

> SOBER UP IT IS YR DRUNKENNESS
> SENDS THE CM [Cosmic Mind] LURCHING TO ITS FATE
> Wait—he couldn't be pretending YES

> That when the flood ebbed, or the fire burned low,
> Heaven, the world no longer at its feet,
> Itself would up and vanish? EVEN SO (S. 56)

It is one thing to acknowledge that the hands of "the doomsday clock" are "our own" when doom seems "merely" to betoken "megadeath" (as Merrill does just before this exchange, S. 55). It is quite another to take up responsibility for heaven and the Cosmic Mind. No wonder this is a task Merrill had shrunk from in the past and takes up only obliquely in the novel, where he is still too worried about matters of "artery" [forgive the pun] and "influence." [Ephraim will tell JM that the novel, whose purpose was "to survey / The arteries of Ephraim's influence" in his life, far from being a "step toward reality" was a step "AWAY" (S. 66).] "In the end," JM admits, "it's *Clio* I compose a face to kiss" (S. 53), but the (Yeatsian) task of once again marrying History and Reality to Metaphor and Myth will take him the considerable and unexpected length of *Sandover* to accomplish.[61]

Thus, if Merrill sees Yeats most closely associated with his own efforts to make sense of the revelations of the Ouija board, we might expect to see less of Yeats in the poetry not connected to occult matters or the ill-fated novel. In *Divine Comedies*, the waterfall in "McKane's Falls" introduces one element from the novel that seems to be both Merrill's (Piscean) version of and his answer to Yeats's "Condition of Fire."[62] The waterfall echoes the antitheses of movement and constancy, danger and attraction, the complex and the simple, the mundane and the transcendent that have always drawn Merrill to images of fire. It promises a perilous state of enlightenment grounded in, but incompatible with, usual existence (except for "moments only"). It is represents a nature beyond nature (Merrill's own "natural supernaturalism") and affords Merrill distinctive emphasis to contrast with Yeatsian fire.[63]

While the speaker in "Sailing to Byzantium" is the pilgrim-soul who would be purged of all that is mortal and natural, the speaker in the third section of "McKane's Falls" is the waterfall itself, the goal of a possible pilgrimage. It is as if Yeats had written from the point of view of the "sages standing in God's holy fire" or the golden bird upon its bough. Where in Yeats's poem it is the speaker who asks to be taken in, gathered into the "artifice of eternity," in Merrill's poem the waterfall calls on him (or us) to "Come live within me," evoking all the seduction poems which begin "Come live with me and be my love." Where Yeats's pilgrim turns his back on "that sensual music" and longs to be out of nature and out of time, Merrill's waterfall offers only the "lean illuminations" that can be had in time:

> Stay here a year or two, a year or ten,
> Until you've heard it all,
> The inside story deafening but true.
>
> Or false—I'm not a fool.

>   Moments of truth are moments only
>   . . .
>   All things in time grow musical.

Truths are provisional, not eternal: "the current changes course / . . . The golden voice [of Yeats's sages or golden bird] turns gravelly and hoarse." The waterfall calls for immersion in the full range of experience Yeats's speaker would leave behind: "Plunge through my bath of plus and minus both, / Acid and base." Merrill's waterfall includes in this "bath" of experience "The mind that mirrors and the hands that act." Thus, for Merrill, intellect and artifice dwell, not in some distant Byzantium, but as part of our living and dying "plunge."[64]

Nonetheless, as in Yeats's poem, a kind of higher knowledge is at stake in this encounter with the waterfall. Yeats's pilgrim longs to sing "Of what is past, or passing, or to come," to know time while being untouched by it; whereas, the waterfall counsels: "Get me by heart, my friend, // And then forget. Forgive . . ." Here highest knowledge is also a bodily state or act. Nor is it the ultimate, unless it can be let go and issue as forgiveness, a kind of blessing. Yeats tenders similar notions at times: in "Vacillation" the voices of history, civilization, and art all proclaim, "Let all things pass away"; in *A Vision* we learn that the soul between lives bathes itself in forgetting after revisiting particular experiences;[65] and in the concluding section of "A Dialogue of Self and Soul," the Self famously proclaims his willingness to "Measure the lot; forgive myself the lot!" to "cast out remorse" and find great "sweetness" and blessing. But Yeats's vision of the Condition of Fire (or Thirteenth Cone to which it is allied) implies a purely spiritual realm apart from incarnate reality, and this Merrill rejects.

As Yeats puts it, "There are two realities, the terrestrial and the condition of fire," where the terrestrial is the realm in which "all opposites meet" and "there only" does one find full freedom of choice, heterogeneity, and evil, which is "the strain one upon another of opposites" (*Per Amica* 356–57). "The ultimate reality," in contrast, "because neither one nor many, concord nor discord, is symbolized as a phaseless sphere, but as all things fall into a series of antimonies in human experience it becomes, the moment it is thought of, what I shall presently describe as the thirteenth cone" in which "all things are present as an eternal instant" (*Vision* 193). For Merrill, the divine is thoroughly implicated in the mundane, and there is but one reality. Mirabell, one of Merrill's spirit voices in *Sandover*, insists on this point: "LET ME PUT IT AS / FORCEFULLY AS I CAN: THE SOCALLED 'SUPERNATURAL' / DOES NOT EXIST" (S. 288). When asked about this statement in an interview with C. A. Buckley, Merrill elaborates:

> Perhaps the point is that the natural extends over a much vaster sphere than we would have thought. We made the distinction between natural and supernatural. If you agree that God is within us and that we are natural, think how vast nature is, both vertically and with circumferences everywhere. ("Exploring" 431)

In the cosmology of *Sandover* Nature is God's twin (S. 281) and "The heavens and all nature are [inter]dependent"(S. 132), "ALL CONNECTED / TO EACH OTHER DEAD OR ALIVE NOW DO U UNDERSTAND WHAT HEAVEN IS," Ephraim interjects, "IT IS THE SURROUND OF THE LIVING" (S. 59).

Like Yeats, Merrill opposes a reductive, thoroughly naturalizing vision of reality; the divine and the mundane are distinct, but not separate. It is the function of the daimonic to grant access to the divine, and through the daimonic that the divine acts in the world.[66] Merrill also allows that "we have instant access to it [divine sublimity]":

> As Michael says, all that protocol Mirabell wants before we meet the angels is perfect nonsense! I mean man has made the imaginative leap onto the palm of Michael for generations, for millennia. ("Exploring" 424)

For Merrill, it is under the categories of the imagination and the unconscious that we tend to think of the daimonic function at this time, and he points to Stevens and to Jung in establishing this connection between the imagination, the unconscious, and the divine (S. 66, 74).

We have come a long way from "McKane's Falls" and Merrill's watery rewriting of Yeats's Condition of Fire, but I think that giving full account of what is at stake in this revision helps us better appreciate what Merrill achieves by his shift in terms. Perhaps the best way to gauge this accomplishment is by bringing the relationship with Yeats's "Sailing to Byzantium" to bear on the second waterfall in *Divine Comedies*. This is a short passage from "Notes for the ill-starred novel" in "The Book of Ephraim" and concerns the relation between the familiar spirit, Eros, and the Merrill-character, Leo. [Note that Leo shares his name with Yeats's familiar Leo Africanus.]

> [Eros] Can feel his [Leo's] crippling debt to—to the world—
> Hearth where the nightlong village of desire
> Shrieks and drowns in automatic fire—
> Can feel this debt repaid in currency
> Plentiful and precious as the free
> Heart-high chamiso's windswept gold that frost
> Hurts into blossom at no further cost.
>
> To touch on these unspeakables you want
> The spry nuances of a Bach courante
> Or brook that running slips into a shawl
> Of crystal noise—at last, the waterfall.
> (It's deep in Indian land. Some earlier chapter
> Can have Sergei drawing a map for Leo.)
> Stepping through it drenched, he finds himself
> On the far side of reflection, a deep shelf
> Hidden from the nakedest of eyes.

> Asked where he is, Eros must improvise
> HE IS WITH ME   (S. 48–49)

In what I'll call the first stanza, the first three lines recapitulate Yeats's attitude toward "the world" in the first stanza of "Sailing to Byzantium." But Merrill replaces Yeats's watery depiction of "Those dying generations" with "automatic fire," a pointed and violent inversion, indeed, laced as it is with Leo's recollections of combat in Vietnam. Both poets first establish a lack, a "debt," in the common state of affairs. To redeem or redress this deficiency, Yeats's speaker evokes Byzantium and the consuming, refining, golden fire of artifice. In contrast Merrill takes us into nature, but in terms that chime with Yeats's "Byzantium"; as well as the echo of Yeatsian "gold," note the similarity between "gold that frost / Hurts into blossom at no further cost" and the "agony of flame that cannot singe a sleeve," as well as the antithetical relation between "frost" and "flame." In each case struggle, pain, or harm is transfigured into a beneficence. In each case, we have entered the realm of the "unspeakable" reality only metaphor can touch.

In the next stanza Merrill posits two paths to the waterfall or "these unspeakables" we want to touch upon. The first is art (or artifice), specifically music; but, unlike the eternalizing artifice and aristocratic social setting of Yeats's birdsong, Merrill's Bach seems almost thoroughly a part of nature—its "courante" is a "current," and "Bach" the ready German pun for "stream" or "brook." So it is no surprise that the other path is through nature (in turn domesticated, just as art has been naturalized), the "brook that running slips into a shawl / Of crystal noise—at last, the waterfall"; nor do we wonder that these two paths are so closely allied. What the waterfall reveals, like the walked-through flames of "Byzantium," is a renewed self or reality, deeper, hidden, beyond the touch of what reflects (just the other side of thought or language); it is whatever is original or true. This moment of spiritual homecoming is improvised under the sheltering aegis of Eros, at once personal daimon and personification of life and love.

Merrill's waterfall also serves at times in place of Yeats's gyres to offer the grand, universalizing perspective of history, physical processes, and the life of the soul. The end of "Lost in Translation," where "nothing's lost. Or else: all is translation / And every bit of us is lost in it / (Or found—," seems an expanded version of Mirabell's "NOTHING IS EVER LOST   THE WATERFALL WILL HOLD / YR 2 BRIGHT DROPS   & YOU WILL SPLASH INTO THE GREAT CLEAR POOL" (S. 117).[67] In such later passages, we see that in the waterfall Merrill has found an image to set beside Yeats's images of the Condition of Fire, the Thirteenth Cone, and the structured movement of the gyres.

There is one last waterfall to notice before leaving the poems that precede "Ephraim" in *Divine Comedies*, a waterfall that quietly announces what "Ephraim" and *Sandover* achieve in the ongoing dialogue between Merrill and his inner-Yeats. According to J. D. McClatchy, "Chimes for Yahya" is "an elaborate parody of Yeats's 'The Second Coming,' a mock nativity ode whose playful epiphany becomes an emblem of 'the pain so long forgiven / It might be the pleasure I rise in'" ("Lost

Paradises" 317). Aside from the plot, which climaxes on the revelation that the "rough beast" about to be "born" is, in this case, no more than a puppy, the poem strikes just enough mock-Yeatsian notes to support McClatchy's ascription of parodic intent.[68] But the object of parody here is never self-evident; the parody itself is not so much elaborate as esoteric. It enjoys the character of a glancing, private joke that runs through the more substantial pleasures of the poem. What is interesting is not so much the incidence and parodic placement of Yeatsian allusion as Merrill's desire to have Yeats serve in such a position in a poem which concludes in a rush of pain forgiven, pleasure risen to, and the self-conscious ringing of his own chimes. It is an apotheosis of Paterian aspiration ("Grazing music as I do") but told with a self-effacing wit Merrill characterizes as "children's doggerel." This voice and attitude is the actual revelation of the poem. Its juxtaposition with Yeats's "The Second Coming" announces a moment of particular assurance out of which the poem itself issues. It is as if to say: "Here is the counter-voice to Yeats's most famously portentous rhetoric. Falling or rising, it provides the diapason, the 'tingling spine of tone, or waterfall / Crashing pure and chill, bell within bell, / Upward to the ninth and mellowest.' It will serve." Thus "Chimes for Yahya," in making such subtle mock of Yeats, finds in the waterfall the voice that will characterize "The Book of Ephraim" and announces the strategies of parody and "counter-speech" elaborated in *Mirabell* and beyond.

Chapter Three

PRELUDE: READING YEATS'S *ESSAYS AND INTRODUCTIONS*

THE NEXT GLIMPSE WE GET OF MERRILL READING YEATS COMES IN 1971, IN the notes in one of Merrill's two copies of Yeats's *Essays and Introductions*.[1] Two essays receive Merrill's particular attention: "The Philosophy of Shelley's Poetry" and "A General Introduction for My Work." As with *A Vision*, Merrill's annotations tend to pick out a phrase or two that serve as the kernel of a thought or that could stand on their own as a compelling image. Longer passages marked out by underlining or lines in the margins are rare. In Yeats's "General Introduction," Merrill's underlining indicates a number of his perennial interests in matters of religion, prosody, and his own belatedness or displacement as a poet. He underlines, "Christ was still the half-brother of Dionysus" in a passage in which Yeats stresses the once common syncretism of pagan and Christian faiths (514). In Yeats's sentence, "Because I need a passionate syntax for passionate subject-matter I compel myself to accept those traditional metres that have developed with the language," Merrill underlines just two phrases: "passionate syntax" and "traditional metres," picking out what is central to his poetics, where "subject-matter" is as various as its tone and writing in traditional metres is more second nature than self-imposed (522).

Further down the page, Merrill draws a line beside "but all that is personal soon rots; it must be *packed in ice or salt*" (Merrill's emphasis).[2] There is more than modernist distrust of "the personal" here; Yeats offers Merrill a formula and metaphor for how formal discipline at once preserves and "cures" elements of personality in poems. This is a formula Merrill has long trusted, and though he has his quarrel with the fixity of Yeats's passion for ice ["but all must be cold; no actress has ever sobbed when she played Cleopatra" (523)] he does recognize and employ the icy qualities of emotional distance and intricate design. Even more, Merrill places his faith in poetic form as a kind of salt: the "food for thought" that sharpens taste and wit and which serves as both "fuel and stabilizer . . . raw *power* and its insulation" (S. 141). Like Yeats, Merrill trusts to the "salt" of formal verse to "lengthen out the smart / In the affections of our heart" ("In Memory of Major Robert Gregory" II).[3]

The one sustained passage Merrill indicates in this essay comes when Yeats discusses his reasons for using a variety of meters in the dance plays (524). It makes sense that Merrill, who found that his experience as playwright and novelist in the mid-fifties had encouraged more formal variety within subsequent poems, would be interested in such reasoning ("Interview with Bornhauser" 59). But there is something more personal at the heart of this underlined passage:

> When I speak blank verse and analyze my feelings, I stand at a moment of history when instinct, its traditional songs and dances, its general agreement, is of the past. I have been cast up out of the whale's belly though I still remember the sound and sway that came from beyond its ribs, and, like the Queen in Paul Fort's ballad, I smell of the fish of the sea. (524)

The first sentence points to Merrill's shared sense of a nostalgic connection to the past, to its traditional forms, and fictive "general agreement." But "when instinct . . . is of the past" more is at stake than temperamental conservatism. We hear a note of "belatedness" which the second sentence strongly reinforces with its image of being cast up Jonah-like onto the unregenerate land. For Merrill, this sentence would have even deeper familiarity. In his 1993 memoir *A Different Person*, Merrill recalls the dream he had in the summer of 1947 in which he had "become a fish, beslimed and barnacled" and unable to communicate his actual humanity to an onlooking man (117-18). Fish out of water, man in his wrong element, humans used as bait, ocean suicides, ocean swims, water as the ultimate and primal home are some of the recurrent themes of Merrill's Piscean writing.[4] Yeats's passage offers a Merrillian fusion of access to and insulation from the oceanic absolute, in its "sound and sway . . . from beyond the ribs," and salts this briny Platonism with the equally Merrillian deflation of the lingering fishy smell.

The most heavily annotated essay in the collection is "The Philosophy of Shelley's Poetry." I believe that part of the uncharacteristic density of notes is due to Merrill's having read the essay closely a number of times. For convenience, I have separated these notes into three kinds: those pointing to lines or phrases where the appeal of the image seems uppermost, those pointing to ideas bearing some thematic or other close relation to ideas or characters in *Sandover*, and those pointing to ideas of more general interest. I believe that at least some of the notes which point to material related to *Sandover* reflect a reading later than 1971, although except for one instance I have no way of offering a specific later date. What follows is a discussion of the passages showing possible relation to *Sandover*; the other annotations are left for a note.[5]

On page 72, Merrill's underlines an extensive passage having to do with the resurrected Adonais:

> When he is dead he will still influence the living, for though Adonais has fled 'to the burning fountain whence he came,' and 'is a portion of the Eternal which must glow through time and change, unquenchably the same,' and has 'awakened from the dream of life,' he has not gone from the 'young Dawn,' or the caverns and the forests, or the 'faint flowers and fountains.' He has been 'made one with Nature' . . .

Elements of the passage recall the prospective fates of Auden and Maria Mitsotáki, "reborn" respectively to mineral and plant worlds (S. 303). Yeats's précis of stanzas 41-43 of Shelley's poem (which includes material Merrill did not underline) gives Merrill all he needs for his own "translation" of Shelley's lines in *Sandover*:

> THEY WILL BE OF THE RULING ORDERS
>   But with no way for us to get in touch.
>   THEY WILL MAKE THEMSELVES
> KNOWN TO U BOTH THEY WILL CHARGE U WITH ENERGY & WAIT
> TO LEAD YOU TO THEIR MASTERS
>   Localized—here Daphne in young leaf?
>   There the chalk face of an old limestone cliff?
>   AH THEY WILL RIPPLE THEY WILL
> JOLT THRU THE WAVES OF TREES & WARPS OF THE EARTH THEY WILL CARRY
> MESSAGES IN THE GRAIN OF ROCK & FLOW IN THE GREEN VEINS
> OF LEAVES, FOR THOSE 2 GODS' VAST NETWORK KEEPS THE GLOBE INTACT
>
>   Like "Adonais"—all of life imbued
>   With the dead's refining consciousness. (S. 310)

At the very least, it seems significant that the passage Merrill underlined and this passage from *Scripts for the Pageant* point to the same sections of "Adonais." My reasons for thinking that Yeats's essay provides a likely source for the passage in *Scripts* will be apparent after considering Merrill's next annotations.[6]

A newspaper clipping from the Associated Press, headlined "Famed Poet Robert Lowell Dies at 60," acts as a bookmark interleaved between pages 74 and 75. This clipping and its placement strongly suggest that Merrill was reading and annotating Yeats's essay in the fall of 1977—the year that the events and lessons of *Scripts* take place, concluding on David Jackson's fifty-fifth birthday on October 16. On page 74, Merrill indicates the first lines of the second paragraph: "Intellectual Beauty has not only the happy dead to do her will, but ministering spirits who correspond to the Devas of the East, and the Elemental Spirits of mediaeval Europe." Since Yeats immediately conflates Shelley's "Intellectual Beauty" with "that Memory of Nature the visionaries claim for the foundation of their knowledge" (74), this note shows Merrill's interest in determining the relationship of Nature to the idea of "Elemental

Spirits." Merrill's angels clearly represent such spirits [Michael, the Angel of Light; Emmanuel, the Angel of Water; Raphael, the Angel of Earth; and Gabriel, the Angel of Fire and Death (S. 281)] and the relationship Yeats points to between Nature and her angels is as crucial for Merrill as is the pronoun "she," since Merrill sees the sensual world informed by the spiritual and personifies Nature in all her traditionally ambivalent femininity.[7]

On the next page in Yeats's essay, Merrill puts a line beside "'the guardians' who move in 'the atmosphere of human thought,' as 'the birds within the wind.'" Again, Merrill's angels in *Sandover* are just such "guardians," but guardians who, especially through their connection with Psyche/Nature/Chaos, the female twin of God Biology, also wake moments of dread—and none more so than "the shy brother," Gabriel.[8] Thus, it is with a particular shock that we come upon Merrill's next annotation. Where Yeats writes: "It is these powers which lead Asia and Panthea, as they would lead all the affections of humanity . . . beyond the gates of birth and death to awake Demogorgon, eternity, that 'the painted veil called life' may be 'torn aside,'" Merrill underlines "Demogorgon" and pencils beside that spirit's name the question "Gabriel?"

In placing the question mark after Gabriel's name, Merrill is clearly considering more than the question of identity between his most formidable angel and Shelley's "Spirit of Necessity." If Merrill penciled this question around the time of Lowell's death in mid-September 1977, he is returning to Yeats just as he and Jackson are receiving Gabriel's last lessons at the board. Again Merrill seems to be looking to Yeats for guidance at a crucial moment. Will Gabriel, in his potential for apocalyptic violence, tear aside "the painted veil" of life and reveal something of eternity in his last lessons? Merrill himself may not know as he reads these lines and writes the angel's name. What we know is that, in the nineteen pages of *Scripts*'s last lessons, Yeats is mentioned far more often than in any other section of *Sandover* and that, in these pages, Merrill finally allows "WBY" to speak his lines of self-abnegation and praise for the younger poet, JM (S. 473-92).

With this note, we lose sight of Merrill reading Yeats's prose.[9] In examining these annotations, we have followed Merrill almost all the way through his experiences at the Ouija board and the long project of *Sandover* as he repeatedly turns to Yeats for guidance, affirmation, and a rich store of "metaphors for poetry" (*Vision* 8). Yet Merrill's spare annotations in *A Vision* and *Essays and Introductions* indicate more than a tutelary relation in which Merrill acts as the attentive, inquiring, and independent-minded student. They also suggest ways in which Merrill constitutes Yeats as a vital collaborative presence. As collaborators do, Merrill's Yeats both helps and hinders his work. In this, Yeats is like his own spirit voices, which were both "communicators" and "Frustrators" in transmitting his vision system (*Vision* 13). For his part, Merrill both freely appropriates from and learns to resist Yeats's influence through the course of his career. The annotations in Merrill's volumes give us a glimpse of the private Merrill; but he is always the poet who, while reading strictly for himself, is nonetheless never alone—a poet for whom reading is a ghostly dialogue between distinct yet "co-operating" lives.[10]

What Merrill's annotations help us see is how much his poetry takes full advantage of the trope of writing as intertextuality, and how much these intertextual relations are similar to and carry the force of relations between people. In reading, one commonly argues and assents almost as if listening to another person; but Merrill's poems and annotations help us see more than this. Reading conjures the felt presence of "a different person" in Merrill's sense, "different" in being both distinctly other and, as a mental voice, an aspect of the self. Such vital reading reveals how permeable and multiple any "given" self may be. In Yeats's terms, such reading is palpably daimonic in the way it challenges the reader and permits the expression of what, in the self, the reader lacks or desires or dreads (*Per Amica* 335). Merrill's annotations and poems help us see that there is something irreducibly occult in reading *per se* (and perhaps in a poet's reading in particular).

Even without the aid of Ouija board or otherworldly voices, new meanings and new subjectivities arise as we read. They rise out of the unlit ground between assumed and conjured meanings, assumed and conjured subjectivities. This is not to diminish the impact or authenticity of Yeats's or Merrill's occult experiences, but only to suggest how their experiences help "explain / The miracle [of reading] as if it were mundane" (S. 286). (One wonders how much poetic mysticism is founded on the intense otherness and interiority of the reading experience and how much our everyday myths of self-identity and self-presence operate as defenses against the force of such experience.) Merrill's annotations in Yeats's critical and metaphysical prose ask us to give particular attention to the internalized intersubjectivity of reading. They ask us to consider how and why reading gives rise to texts that include otherworldly readers and staged scenes of reading and instruction, and how such texts both reflect and shape what Tilottama Rajan calls "the life of signs in literary communities and in psychic life"(11).[11]

Returning to the evidence of the poetry, we continue to encounter poems in which Yeats is explicitly evoked, as well as passages in which something like Yeats's voice, his images and concerns arise to "trouble the stream" of Merrill's poetry. Particularly in the volumes that make up *The Changing Light at Sandover*, we also encounter an increasingly complex and ambiguous relationship, one predicated on the difficulties of negotiating a productive relation between Merrill and his most demanding precursor.

OBSERVING YEATS THROUGH MERRILL'S CHANGING LIGHTS

Merrill's version of Yeats in *Sandover* is a motivated misreading, a reduction of Yeats to something like the monitory figure who also haunted W. H. Auden: "my own devil of unauthenticity, of everything which I must try to eliminate from my own poetry."[12] But where Auden speaks of trying to remove all traces of Yeats's influence, Merrill brings this devil into his poetry in order to wrestle with him there. Poems as early as "Fire Poem," show Merrill achieving, through this contest, a compelling complexity *and* intensity of vision, as if in answer to Yeats's "simplification through intensity." Merrill's Yeats represents aspects in his own ethos that he can neither fully accept nor easily disregard: his pride, elitism, simplifying mystical aestheticism (and his aesthetic mysticism). His Yeats represents the "errors" of ambitions that Merrill finds troubling yet in some ways also shares: the public and political ambitions of Yeats's art and the desire for knowledge and systems of knowledge beyond the limits of the unimaginative fact.

Thus, Merrill uses the figure and language of Yeats to sustain a quarrel with himself. As Yeats puts it, "We make out of the quarrel with others, rhetoric, but of the quarrel with ourselves, poetry. Unlike the rhetoricians, who get a confident voice from remembering the crowd they have won or may win, we sing amid our uncertainty" (*Per Amica* 331). In *Sandover*, Merrill brings this internal quarrel, elaborated through Yeats and his many other voices, to its most sustained and elaborate height. Through this dialogic interplay, Merrill attains at once the "confident voice" of a master rhetor and the generative uncertainty that issues in song. Yet for all the strategies of denial and depreciation, parody and "correction," covert linkage and appropriation that Merrill employs in *Sandover* to create and to best his phantom-Yeats and haunting mirror-self, Merrill succeeds in achieving a most Yeatsian kind of complementary. Both poets are chastened and elevated as *Sandover* turns back towards its beginning, and Merrill's quarrel stays uncannily alive as much by the authority of Yeats's example as by the power of Merrill's poetry.[13]

Merrill's reasons for wanting to establish his distance from Yeats so pointedly, and from the very outset of "The Book of Ephraim," hold for his campaign of diminishment throughout *Sandover*. By dissociating himself from Yeats, Merrill works to prevent the kind of narrowly reductive reading of influence and comparison that would lead readers to focus more on parallels and contrasts and less on his own achievements. He is also careful to distance himself from exactly what, to many, seems most naive, scandalous or silly in Yeats's spiritualism, so that by stage-managing our dismissive attitude toward Yeats and by anticipating our reactions to his own moments of enthusiasm, he positions himself to control our nervousness about how to take his Ouija board revelations.[14] Finally, I would argue that Merrill's ambivalent opening gesture toward Yeats in "The Book of Ephraim" and the pattern of slights and ironies, veiled citations and anxious plotting elaborated subsequently throughout the poem reflect Merrill's ongoing ambivalence about Yeats's priority both as poet and as prophet "of a new divinity" (*Vision* 27).

As we shall see, "The Book of Ephraim" establishes the ghostly importance of Yeats in the midst of an explicit campaign of diminishment. It establishes the manner of Yeats's "materialization" within JM's language and the dramatic possibility of his eventual "presence" as one of the otherworldly participants in the Ouija board sessions. *Mirabell's Books of Number* then builds on each of these elements, heightening the campaign of slights, strengthening the pattern Yeatsian language, and cultivating the drama of Yeats's absence, while at the same time offering a parodic account of elements of Yeats's *A Vision* as it also draws covert lines of affinity between JM and the older poet. In *Scripts for the Pageant*, Merrill moves away from parody. Parallels (and contrasts) between Yeats's and the angel's doctrines surface without the earlier rhetorical edge. Anxious ties of affinity and identity likewise give way in a gathering elevation of JM's own poetic authority, so that the Yeatsian voice and vision finally become little more than just one particularly valuable "merel," or counter, in the poem's ongoing game of language and meaning. With Merrill's coda, "The Higher Keys," Yeats finally vanishes into the fabric of what *Sandover* as a whole has largely become: the narrative of the maturation of a "strong poet," in Harold Bloom's sense of the phrase.

I. Yeats in "Ephraim": The Master's Ghostly Presence

In the five years during which Merrill composed the four sections of *Sandover* (1974–78) his explicit attitude toward Yeats remains remarkably consistent, although each book handles that relationship differently. "The Book of Ephraim" commences the campaign of diminishment against Yeats with the "bombshell" announcement from Ephraim: "POOR OLD YEATS / STILL SIMPLIFYING" (S. 14).[15] But Merrill's more subtle tactic is to "concede" Yeats's pertinence and then provide only Yeats's absence. Yeats is the only character listed in "Ephraim's" "Dramatis Personae" who does not have a speaking role or the minimal dignity of reported speech or action. Even the one acknowledged fictional character, "Smith, Rosamund," has more to do and say in "Ephraim" than Yeats. So why is Yeats listed among the "cast," and in what sense is "Yeats, W(illiam) B(utler)" "dramatis" if he is listed only to be discounted and put aside?

Firstly, this listing enables Merrill both to establish an affinity between the present book and Yeats's *A Vision* and to deny that Merrill's work might in any way resemble or derive from Yeats's.[16] Yeats is "the celebrated / Poet," and Merrill subtly trades on this prestige; but describing Yeats's mythagogic work as a "maze of inner logic, dogma, dates—" sets a tone meant to shield Merrill's work from similar characterization and to divert the suspicion that Yeats's work might prefigure or influence Merrill's.

Secondly, Yeats's felt absence becomes vaguely dramatic in "Ephraim" as Yeats's language and thematic concerns are heard to support some of Merrill's most effective poetry. Nonetheless, in terms of overt drama, this first mention of Yeats only raises expectations that must wait for subsequent books to fulfill. If after "Ephraim," Merrill indeed had no idea of continuing to write based on his experiences at the board,[17] the listing of Yeats in section "D" and the one acknowledged quotation in section "R"(S. 65) make for a very ghostly and unfinished kind of textual drama. But, as we shall see, even in "Ephraim" there are more than just these "bracketing appearances."

JM's early "Hymn to Nonchalance" (S. 31-2) points back to "Voices from the Other World" ("Indeed, we have grown nonchalant / Towards the other world.") and forward to the urgency of "YR NONCHALANCE / IS THE SLEEP OF A VAST TRAVAIL & TIME RUNS OUT" in *Mirabell* (S. 124). This passage not only develops what Leslie Brisman calls the stance of "Yeatsian urbanity" (191) from the earlier poem, it also raises the Yeatsian issues of vision as projection or dream, particularity giving onto universality, and the interpenetration of system and image. But these echoes are understandably faint; it would not do to have strong recollections of Yeats's remarks on similar themes if Yeats's absence and irrelevance are what Merrill wants first to establish. Nonetheless it is telling that this first shadow of Yeats's presence in the language of Merrill's text comes in section "I"—thus offering not just the faintest ghost of an appearance but the first wisp of his Yeatsian self-identification.

Only with section "R" does the incidence of Yeats's language slowly increases until, in the last sonnet of the sequence, Yeats in effect "materializes" in the body of Merrill's direct quotation from "A Dialogue of Self and Soul." To see the ghost appear, it may be best to observe him fully manifest and then recall how his presence is evoked.[18] (But before turning to this the last sonnet, note how the phrase "dimmed by time," which immediately precedes it operates like a muted echo, as from a horn in the wings, preparing the ear and mind for Yeats's "entrance." Yeats's "blood-dimmed tide" haunts Merrill's "dimmed by time," not just through "dimmed, " but also through the mediating association of tides with time and the shared rhyme and metric.)

> Leave to the sonneteer eternal youth.
> His views revised, an older man would say
> He was "content to live it all again."
> Let this year's girl meanwhile resume her pose,
>
> The failing sun its hellbent azimuth.
> Let stolen thunder dwindle out to sea,
> Dusk eat into the marble-pleated gown.
> Such be the test of time that all things pass.
>
> Swelling, sharpening upwind now—blade
> On grindstone—a deep shriek? The Sunday stadium.
> Twenty thousand throats one single throat
>
> Hoarse with instinct, blood calling to blood
> —Calling as well to mind the good gray medium
> Blankly uttering someone else's threat. (S. 65)

The opening line gives us JM, not only because he is the sonneteer of this section, but because the "eternal youth" is one of Merrill's most cherished roles: forever the child of a broken home and the witty young man. These are roles that *Sandover* both sustains and challenges. As in the earlier fire poems, Merrill at first identifies with the younger man, while the older recalls Yeats. Here this identification could not be more explicit since the older man speaks Yeats's words. But also as in the earlier poems, the division between younger and older, Merrill and Yeats, collapses as the poem develops. Here it may be the sonneteer grown older who revises his earlier views, no longer interested in the artifice of a youthful eternity, he would be "content to live it all again," to climb back on the wheel of generation and not just to relive, in Yeats's phrase, "the ignominy of boyhood." Again as in earlier poems, the opening quatrain plays on themes of youth and age in a way that both recalls and inverts Yeats's "Sailing to Byzantium." It is the old man here who assents again to "Whatever is begotten, born, and dies," while "this year's girl" resumes the eternal artifice or pose of youth—whichever girl she may happen to be—perhaps even JM, seen and seeing through the mask of Maya.[19]

In the next quatrain, the "failing sun" resuming its "hellbent azimuth" recalls Yeats's "gaze blank and pitiless as the sun," especially given Merrill's earlier "blind, sunset-invaded / Eyeball," while "azimuth" recalls the soul's "star that marks the hidden pole" ("A Dialogue of Self and Soul"). (But even here echoes of Yeats also shelter Merrillian self-references: what is the "Book of Ephraim" if not an A-Z Myth?[20]) "Stolen thunder" is exactly what fuels this passage and robes the apparition of the older poet. It is not so much that Merrill, in appropriating Yeats's language, is stealing his thunder, as that Yeats's previous poems at once allow and qualify the pitch of thunder Merrill would achieve in this concluding sonnet. Even if Merrill is figured as stealing from Yeats, he steals only thunder, only "someone else's threat," not the Promethean fire of original creativity.[21] Given these intimations of Merrill's anxious belatedness, his "stolen thunder" can only "dwindle out to sea," even as the mere mention of "sea" in this context increases its contrast with Yeats's "mackerel-crowded" and "gong-tormented" seas. Merrill's "marble-pleated gown" further recalls the works of Yeats's Callimachus in "Lapis Lazuli," which poem, with "Vacillation VI" and perhaps "Sailing to Byzantium," also governs the last line of the octave (although through the an unmistakably Merrillian pun on "test" and "pass"): "Such be the test of time that all things pass."

In the sestet image mounts on image, assembling a frightening evocation of mass enthusiasm that links an Athenian soccer match with fascism and then surprisingly draws the parallel to how mind and language, in Whitmanesque guise as "the good gray medium," possess the speaker, and draw him as well into "Blankly uttering someone else's threat." At the same time, the cascading density of Yeatsian reference continues to call forth both the older poet's power and the anxiety of the younger before his daemonic possession. Merrill's "blade / On grindstone" gives at once Time's or Death's scythe and Sato's blade unsheathed. Merrill's "deep shriek" unsettles with the mortal "shriek [and] struggle to escape" of "Among School

Children." It is also the sudden rabbit's cry in "Man and the Echo" and Yeats's cry when confronted with the mass beast, "That thing all blood and mire . . . drunken with singing as with wine" ("Her Vision in the Wood" 25-32).[22] Merrill's "Twenty thousand throats one single throat // Hoarse with instinct, blood calling to blood" melds the "comforters" of Cuchulain with the tumult of "mire and blood" in "Byzantium" and the "passionate intensity" of the "worst" in "The Second Coming." The phrase, "good gray medium" does introduce a note of spiritualist banality, but one that underscores rather than relieves the tercet's building sense of menace. If the octave materializes Yeats's ghost, the whole weight of the sestet is to establish an ensuing scene of possession. Here is JM, now thoroughly caught up in the Yeatsian prophetic mode, speaking in tongues, and "blankly uttering" the stolen thunder of Yeats's "threat"—the threat, perhaps, of having the poem not really be his own. ["maddening—it's all by someone else! . . . / I want it mine," Merrill will later say (S. 261).][23]

The sonnet travels a remarkable distance, from the blithe sonneteer to the medium possessed. Section "R" itself is remarkable for its diversity. The heart of the section confronts Maya Deren's stroke, death, and first communications from the other side. But the opening points back to the apocalyptic threats of section "P" and threats of another sort of dissolution.[24] The section, like its would-be "original," is death haunted and resisting. Maya is explicitly "brought back" at the center, but Yeats gathers allusively at the margins. Having seen the compelling presence Yeats achieves in the final sonnet, it is now easy to see the earlier elements before they assemble. "[B]lind and old" put us in the realm of "A Dialogue of Self and Soul." "Remake it all into slant, weightless gold" gives, via Dickinson, hints of "Lapis Lazuli" and the "miracle . . . golden handiwork" of the Byzantium poems. "That whatever had been, had been right," although in the idiom of Pope, recalls the last line in "A Dialogue": "Everything we look upon is blest" and a similar moment in "Vacillation IV." Images from "Vacillation" accumulate in the second sonnet, especially in the first quatrain and first tercet.

> "Here I'm divided.
> Wrong things in the right light are fair, assuming
> We seize them in some holy flash past words,
> Beyond their consequences and their causes.

Although, like Yeats, JM opens with the theme of self-division (JM too is divided, Self and Soul), the impulse is toward a transcendent vision achieved in the "holy fire" of "A brand, or flaming breath" that takes us out of time ("beyond their consequences and their causes") and the mundane "antinomies" of right and wrong. In characterizing this "holy flash" as "past words," Merrill illuminates why for Yeats it is his wordless "body" that "of a sudden blazed." The light that follows in this sonnet is as equivocal as Yeats's insistent "half and half." Maya's eyeball is "sunset-invaded." What is lucent here is mere "spittle" (recalling, especially given its proximity to "blind," the "frog-spawn of a blind man's ditch" in "A Dialogue"). "Gloom" is matched with "gleam," "What light there was" with "a mind / Half dark." Thus, though the impulse is toward transcendence, here and through the first four sonnets, Merrill too insists on a vacillation between "joy" and "grief," between "god's own truth, or fiction," that yields two ambiguous apparitions: Maya "RESTORED" to JM's "blissful grief" and Yeats, at once "content" and threatening.

The final sonnet of "R" marks at once Yeats's most focused and most troubling presence in "Ephraim." Merrill's subsequent "quarrel" with the older poet in this book proceeds through a double mediation. In section "V," Venice takes the place of Yeats's Byzantium and a pseudo-Proust stands in for Merrill's Yeats. The subject of this internal quarrel is the dying "heavenly city" of art. A great part of Merrill is haunted by nostalgia for the timeless, time-defying powers of the caught image, "To be forever smiling, holding still," and the artifice of transcendent transformation, the way "anybody's monster breathing flames" may be "Vitrified in metamorphosis / To monstrance" (S. 75, 77). But another part insists on the petrifying limitations of this vision and its inability to adequately serve the artist "justly" in our day.

The first lines of section "V" set the terms for this internal quarrel. On examination, both "Proust" and his "Venise" soon dissolve into masks for Merrill as aesthete and son of Pater, Yeats, and Proust. The opening words JM says Proust wrote, "Justly in his day," are not Proust's at all; they are Merrill's staged ventriloquism (Polito *Guide* 106). "Venise, pavane, nirvana, vice" represents what the Proust-like part of Merrill would have had Proust write,[25] while the city itself is represented by and represents the "monumental / 'I' of stone," a "titanic ego mussel-blue / Abulge in gleaming nets of nerve" (S. 75).[26] Thus, both writer and city serve as speaking emblems of a vision that JM feels compelled to renounce.

Proust may be the explicit representative and "GREAT PROPHET" of the aesthetic vision in this section, but Yeatsian images also echo repeatedly through the fretwork of Merrill's neo-Proustianisms. Most constant is his repetition of the word "images" itself. Merrill's repeated "There. Come." and "Some have come form admiring . . . " (S. 75-76) recall the music of Yeats's "therefore I have sailed the seas and come," his repetition of "come" and its rhyme with "Byzantium." Merrill's "dull red mazes caked with slime" (S. 75) may be a nod to Yeatsian "mire or blood." Merrill's passage also concerns the relation of "undying" monuments and "dying generations," but it offers a parodic inversion of the "plot" of "Sailing to Byzantium" and thus enacts his criticism of the transcendent, aestheticizing vision Merrill associates most strongly with Yeats.

In Merrill's Venice the monuments are sinking and the "once fabled" few who commissioned and sustained them, the "lords and ladies" Santofior and Guggenheim, are dying. Like Yeats's "young / In one-another's arms," Merrill's tourist couples are ablur with "generation": the products and agents of population explosion, many "by now, have reproduced." And "caught" with dying, they enter "the dark / Ark of the moment . . . / Hurriedly, as by hazard paired . . . for a last picture" (Ibid.) But, unlike the youth in Yeats's poem, they do not "neglect /

Monuments of unageing intellect." They swarm them. Instead of "salmon-falls," Merrill sees the tourist-crowded city. It is the young, not the old, who anxiously have themselves made into images in Merrill's version, snapshots "(gloom coupleted with artifice)" (S. 76), which are emblems plucked from time that, like Yeats's golden bird, all the more insistently tell of time. When Merrill allows that the monuments all these people gather in or stand beside, like the *Tempesta*, are "timeless," but "timeless in [their own] fashion" (Ibid.), he makes sure that the idea of there being *fashions* of timelessness strips much of the redemptive aura from Yeats's "artifice of eternity."

Although Yeats's images are themselves "dolphin-torn," and "gong-tormented," they are also miraculously beyond perturbation: "all complexities of fury leave" and no storm can disturb them. But Merrill insists that such transcendence is emphatically not the case, even for the greatest images. His passage is animated by storm; its images are beset with ruin, anxiety, loss, the blur of mass regard, and the contingencies of fashion, history, and natural event. He works to counter Yeats's Byzantine tales of annunciation and arrival ("And therefore have I sailed the seas and come") with antithetical gestures of renunciation and departure. Prospero-like, Merrill abjures his former magic, associated through Yeats, Eliot, and Proust with the timeless-time-recalling stasis of the image ("Never again / To overlook a subject for its image, / To labor images till they yield a subject") and delivers his measured judgment of the eternalizing emblem: a mere "Dram of essence from the flowering field" (S. 76).

At this point, what is wanted seems to be access to the "lightning strike," the "naked current" [27]: the living field of experience more than its meager distillate, movement more than the momentary illusion or the disciplined constraints of holding, or being held still: "No further need henceforth of this / Receipt (gloom coupleted with artifice) / For holding still, for being held still. No—" (Ibid.). To pursue the artifice of the Yeatsian or modernist image, Merrill seems to say, is masochistic and diminishing ("Pictures in little pieces / Torn from me"). Therefore, Merrill writes from a Venice/Byzantium he is preparing to leave ("I fly tomorrow to New York"), in contrast to Yeats who has already journeyed and writes now from within the "walked-through frame" of his holy city.

Yet what follows the opening passage of blank verse is no easy departure. It is instead a carefully crafted quarrel of competing impulses and competing loyalties. The "semi-detached" quatrains that follow (S. 76-77) offer a vivid example of a "field" of energetic experience, alive with the allure and peril of nakedness ("needle-keen transparency"), yet highly mediated by the insulation of conspicuous literary devices. The breathless cascade of noun phrases in the first quatrains presents a sensual, yet myth-conscious, immediacy: gust, pungency, bellying shirt, air and water—a wrestling with Protean elements, "who, clung to now, must truthfully reply." Yet for all its glancing impressionism, formally this passage also signals its allegiance to the intricate weave and considered constraints of craft.[28] What is at stake here is truthful telling, a counter-speech or answering account, of "lightning" that will be commensurate with Merrill's struggle to both sustain and contain it.

Among the contending elements in the second quatrain are those of tone. Merrill at once evokes and deflates the rhetoric of Romantic struggle to attain transparency of self-consciousness before the elements of nature. On the one hand, the contest is reduced to a game of blind man's bluff between the storm and Merrill's "unsurrendering gooseflesh," while at the same time—and authorized by this shift in tone from what verges on the bluff of "sheer windbag" set-painting—the blind speaker (Oedipus, Tiresius, as well as the rain-blinded JM) *is* "buff," both naked and strong, and, even in the vulnerability of his "gooseflesh," unsurrendering. Merrill's insistent paranomasia pushes toward a simultaneity of multiple sense impressions. It offers a kind of immediacy that "releases" the present tense "streamlined" within a contraction ("blind / Man[i]s buff"). But "gooseflesh / Streamlined from conception" mingles so many registers of lofty and low, mind and flesh, born and made, that the mind reels.

As if in response, whether as sympathy or rebuke or comic-book aporia, or all at once, the thunder speaks ("crack! boom! flash!"). The thunder's voice more than interrupts; it appears to redirect the speaker's gaze—"soaking inward" now—and initiates a shift in the poem's mode: from agitated fragments of present action to a self-assembling, self-regarding fragment of recollected reverie. That is, from "anybody's monster breathing flames" to a "monstrance clouded then like a blown fuse / If not a reliquary for St James' / Vision of life" (S. 77). It is thus that Merrill's verse, turning inwardly reflective and retrospective, nonetheless maintains a performative presence. Here the conceit (monster → metamorphosis → monstrance) points backward both toward experience and its aftermath and toward their con-current representation, while also tracing the paradigmatic Romantic progress from Nature to the division of Self-Consciousness to the elevation of Imagination.

Merrill's "monstrance . . . like a blown fuse" stands, like the poem itself, as evidence of both a system challenged by an excess of "naked current" and a successful strategy of insulation. (Thus, it is, in its own way, also evidence of "An agony of flame that cannot singe a sleeve.") The miracle that the sudden rush of religious diction announces is always the body on view: the body of the poem, of word made flesh (even "gooseflesh"), and the body as reliquary for a "Vision of life." This latter is the beatifying moment for Merrill (for that moment, "St James"). It is also what has become of Venice, now both material scene (seen) and sign of transforming vision:

>   her least stone
> Pure menace at the start, at length became
>
> A window fiery-mild, whose walked-through frame
> Everything else, at sunset, hinged upon— (S. 77)

Far from ending in renunciation and departure, a turn away from artifice, devotion to the image, or the moment of transcendent vision, as the section earlier intimated it might, the passage ultimately concludes with a triumph of high-modernist annunciation. After (Yeats's stolen?) thunder, "anybody's monster breathing flames" becomes a window onto a Yeatsian scene of being "gathered," or having walked through, into the "holy fire," that everything depends upon. The "breathing flames" achieve Yeats's spiritualized suspension of contending elements, at once fire and "framed" as a window might be or a mosaic wall. It is a Yeatsian suspension made even more compactly in the phrase: "fiery mild."

But as always with Merrill, this is Yeats with telling differences. Merrill's refining fire is explicitly "mild"; his agon, or inner quarrel, so apparent in the body of the verse, need not be worn upon its sleeve in postures of Yeatsian "agony." "St James" is vouchsafed a "Vision of life"; whereas, Yeats's *A Vision* focuses more on a system of lives and the mechanics of existence between lives. Yeats's ambition is to "proclaim a new deity" (*Vision* 27) and hail the superman called "death-in-life and life-in-death" ("Byzantium"). And Merrill's "reliquary" does suggest a spiritual interpenetration of life and death; but the metamorphic content of his vision emphasizes a successive narrative of visionary experience rather than a "timeless" and transcendent image. As in "About the Phoenix," Merrill's echoing "came" and "became" sets this moment of vision in the past tense. He leaves us with a past event, as opposed to Yeats's eternalizing present. It is a crucial, or hinging, event, but one that finally returns us to, rather than lifts us above, the processes of time, so that movements and departures are still possible. Merrill concludes this passage in "a minor scale," in contrast to the major chords of Yeats's Byzantine endings. Imagery and sound (and modulation through Williams' "So much depends upon . . .") give Merrill's final lines their "dying fall." Yet in these last four lines Merrill progressively slows the momentum of his verse so that a kind of stillness is at last achieved—in order "to let the silence after each note sing" (S. 85): "A window fiery-mild, whose walked-through frame / Everything else, at sunset, hinged upon—" (S. 77). Thus, the quarrel with Yeats continues even into this last gesture. Merrill's Mallarmesque performance of a singing silence counters Yeats's description of his singing bird, and yet it is uncanny how much performance and description, silence and bird, have the same reverberant effect.

II. Yeats in *Mirabell*: Parody and Affiliation

If Yeats's "role" in "The Book of Ephraim" is largely a felt absence bracketed by the dismissive evocation of "D" and the ghostlier returns of his repressed authority in "R," "V," and perhaps in "Y,"[29] Yeats is much more present in *Mirabell's Books of Number* because the book operates in large part as a parody of Yeatsian spiritualism and system building.[30] The element of parody in the book is elaborate and deliberate. Just as Yeats's "The Second Coming" is the parodic source for Merrill's "Chimes for Yahya," much of the elaborate machinery of *Mirabell* springs from a few passages of Yeats's "The Phases of the Moon," the verse prologue to *A Vision*.

Merrill marks two passages from this poem in his copy of *A Vision*. One is a check mark pointing to Aherne's brief lines, "Before the full / It sought itself and afterwards the world" (*Vision* 62). For Yeats's system of personality incarnations based on the phases of the moon, these lines provide an overview of the soul's movement toward greatest subjectivity before the full moon and toward greatest objectivity after. For Merrill, the lines suggests the movement from the focus on self in "Ephraim" and the poems before "Ephraim," before the fullness of "the Powers [he's] been avoiding / Take possession," and toward the "POEMS OF SCIENCE" demanded of him after "Ephraim's" "PROLOGUE" (S. 108, 109, 113).

Merrill's other annotation is a line bracketing the last italicized quatrain of the poem:

> *And then he laughed to think that what seemed hard*
> *Should be so simple—a bat rose from the hazels*
> *And circled round him with its squeaky cry,*
> *The light in the tower window was put out.* (64)

This passage allows Aherne (Yeats's rationalist, conventional man, and here the credulous prompter of the true adept, Robartes) the last laugh at the expense of the tower poet, who is also Yeats before *A Vision*.[31] The complex interplay of voices in "The Phases of the Moon," where the authoring poet presents a previous self and divergent aspects of his present self, including the visionary and the mundane, has long informed Merrill's poetry. In *Mirabell* and then again in *Scripts*, Merrill develops this interplay to its fullest complexity. Specifically, Aherne's laughter at Yeats authorizes both Merrill's parodic use of Yeatsian material and all the knowing lightness of his manner. It is laughter against the other who is also the self, and thus laughter that has a way of turning back on the "speaker"—here for presuming to think so simple what was indeed so hard.

Yeats knows this, and Merrill develops the lesson. It is, after all, not the laughing ease of superior knowing that ends Yeats's poem, but the mystery of circled flight, a bat's cry, and light put out in the tower. In his parodic appropriations from Yeats, Merrill repeatedly reverses this movement from laughter to mystery, but to a strikingly consonant effect. In incident after incident in the completed epic, Merrill allows no mystery, no dread or elevation that does not dissolve in sociable laughter. Yet, ultimately, it is the moments of mystery that linger, like Yeats's squeaky bat's cry, seemingly launched by Aherne's laugh.

A third passage from "The Phases of the Moon" provides Merrill with *Mirabell*'s central miracle as well as numerous suggestions for plot and character:

> Because all dark, like those that are all light,
> They are cast beyond the verge, and in a cloud,
> Crying to one another like the bats;
> But having no desire they cannot tell
> What's good or bad, or what it is to triumph

> At the perfection of one's own obedience;
> And yet they speak what's blown into the mind;
> Deformed beyond deformity, unformed,
> Insipid as the dough before it is baked,
> They change their bodies at a word.   (*Vision* 63)

It is part of the parodic thrust of *Mirabell* that, whereas Yeats places supreme value on the unity of Phase 15,[32] Merrill makes the productive chaos of Phase 1 into one of the leading sources of his images for this volume. Yeats's spirits of the "Dark of the Moon" are creatures of darkness, like Merrill's bat-angels who loom out of a "DARK CLOUD" (S. 114). They lead an "automatic" existence, like numbers or formulae. They too are "BOUND TO THE IMPLACABLE UNIVERSALL WHEEL" (S. 113). Merrill's bat-angels, like Yeats's "unformed" disincarnate spirits are allied to chaos (S. 113, 173) and involved, through their R/Lab, in a kind of bakery for souls (S. 116, 140, 145-46). They too have been "cast beyond the verge," God B after their fall having told them: "OUT OF MY SIGHT" (S. 121). They are "MESSENGERS" (S. 130, 167, 186, 246), "BLACK SQUEAKERS" (S. 114), who "HAVE NEVER EXPRESSD A THING" (S. 172) on their own, who only "speak what's blown into the mind"; "WE ARE ORDERD, THEN WE SLEEP" (S. 130). They exist without desire or feeling (except for what Yeats would call the "joy of complete plasticity"), without knowledge of good or bad (or of manners): "TO OUR EYES THESE ETHICAL / RIGHTS & WRONGS ARE SO MANY BLANKS IN YR CANVAS" (S. 173). They are ugly, "QUIET REPULSIVE ENTRE NOUS" (S. 114), and unformed, "WE HAVE ONLY A DARK SHAPE" (S. 116) and yet, capable of form and change, they "change their bodies at a word." Bat-angel 741 famously becomes a peacock (S. 157) and, Tinker Bell-like, transforms again at the concerted thinking of the word, "Please" (S. 234).

More generally, just as Yeats's *A Vision* purports to give systematic understanding of human history and psychology, and our links to the spirit world both in life and between lives, so too do *Mirabell*'s bat-angels. Yeats's "Twenty-eight Incarnations" presents a clock-face anatomy of human character types.[33] As the polarized "hands" labeled "Will-Mask" and "Creative Mind-Body of Fate" turn in opposite directions around the "face" of Yeats's twenty-eight phases, they pick out distinctive personalities and suggest individual destinies depending on the present time in the cosmic Great Year. It is a system of willful complexity that nonetheless promises the apparent simplicity of a dial. Merrill's bat-angels give him digital readouts to much the same effect. Yeats (along with Dante, Shelley, and Landor) is at 17/3/13/27 (for phases of Will, Mask, Creative Mind, and Body of Fate respectively) (*Vision* 140-41). 741 dictates DJ's and JM's "Vastly simplified *Basic Formulas*" thus:

    JM: 268/ 1: 1,000,000/ 5.5/ 741
    DJ: 289/ 1: 650,000/ 5.9/ 741.1
      —Number of previous lives; then ratio

Of animal to human densities . . .
Then what might be called our talent rating:
U ARE BOTH PARTIAL 5S ADJACENT TO OUR IMMORTALS (S. 143)

741 also elucidates the "IDENTITY NUMBERS" of their guides, which encode information about the "STAGES" their living "representatives" will attain and at which stage they were first contacted (S. 144). Just as Yeats is interested in "placing" historical and literary figures in his system, locating everyone from Walt Whitman through Dostoevski's Idiot, Shakespeare, and Napoleon to Queen Victoria and Socrates, so Merrill's bat angels reveal a bit of the code for the likes of Artur Rubinstein, Eleanor Roosevelt, Lindbergh and "PEOPLE OF PHYSICAL PROWESS / & LEGENDARY HEROES" (S. 143).[34]

In *Mirabell's Books of Number*, what JM objects to in Yeats's *A Vision*, "the maze of inner logic, dogma, dates" (S. 14) always threatens to overwhelm Merrill's poetry, so that the struggle between "Merrillian" lowercase and often parodically "Yeatsian" uppercase elements heightens our sense of aesthetic peril as a form of dramatic tension throughout the volume. One form this aesthetic peril takes is thematic, as time and again Merrill's uppercase spirit voices ring unnerving changes on Yeatsian dogma. Themes of hierarchical elitism dominate Mirabell in ways that serve as a parodic reminder of Yeats's own elitist and quasi-fascist tendencies.[35] Not only are souls ranked numerically according to their "density," their purity is assessed and manipulated in the R/Lab in starkly racial and nationalistic terms. "JEW" becomes the term for what's most essentially human, "man par excellence" (S. 138), while "THE TEUTON & ARAB NURTURE BRUTES" (S. 123). This partial inversion of Nazi values is an emblem of the uncanny effect of Merrill's parody.

Where simple parody exaggerates or diminishes, fragments or inverts so that the reader achieves a distance from the object of parody, Mirabell's parodic doctrines insinuate themselves even as they seem to repel. JM warns us not to take these terms in "any easy ethnic sense" (S. 138), since the bat-angels "USE WORDS: SOUL, JEW, MIND ETC" (S. 144) metaphorically, in place of the chemical formulas that would be meaningless to JM and DJ. But the "easy ethnic sense" is never distant. Having "GREEKS / [stand] NEXT IN LINE OF DENSITY TO THE JEW" (S. 141) unsettles with its "easy" reassertion of the traditional terms of western cultural hegemony. The plea that such language operates merely as "metaphors for poetry" also sits uneasily within the over determining project of the R/Lab, with its program of eugenic engineering, its totalizing ideology of service ("ALL WILL BE USED"), and sponsorship of plague, war, and suicide to create the next god-like race and an "EARTHLY ETERNITY WHEN IT COMES"—notions troublingly reminiscent of other twentieth-century enthusiasms for the end of history (S. 145, 116-17).[36]

In certain realms Merrill's stance of ambivalent parody seems to modulate toward outright affiliation.[37] The emphasis on manners and of a constructed "WORLD OF COURTESY" (S. 155) in *Mirabell* recalls Yeats's regard for a privileged aristocracy "much compounded of high courtesy" ("Adam's Curse"). Yeats's regard for the mix of "courtesy and passion," of vibrant talk with "courtly images," is like Merrill's, for the most part, nostalgic and paternalistic—although, like Merrill, Yeats was aware that the freedom "to choose his company and choose what scenery pleased him best" set him uneasily apart from "the people" ("The People"). Setting attendant issues of elitism aside for now, we notice that Merrill's commitment to the ceremonial grows progressively more pronounced in each subsequent volume of *The Changing Light at Sandover* and that Merrill's dictum that "Manners are for me the touch of nature, an artifice in the very bloodstream" ("Interview with Sheehan" 33) catches much the same paradox as Yeats's famous "ceremony of innocence" ("The Second Coming"; see also "A Prayer for my Daughter").

Another Yeatsian theme to which Merrill is allied is the wisdom of vacillation, of insisting on being "of at least two minds" on vital questions, able "to hold in a single thought" both Yes *and* No (see S. 119, 137, 162, 232). This theme becomes the very shape of *Scripts*, as WHA puts it "2 GOLDEN TRAYS OF 'YES' AND 'NO' WITH '&' / AS BRIDGE OR BALANCE" (S. 328), but instances in *Mirabell* serve primarily to embrace and dramatize what Ellmann calls "Yeats's old trick of evasion" in questions of belief in his theories and supernatural visitations (199). Merrill is intent on showing the dynamic tension of balancing between credulity and skepticism throughout *Sandover*, as he puts it:

> No opposition graver than between
> Credulity and doubt, or thumb and forefinger
> Of a same hand, that, as we watch, commence
> Twirling the hypnotic bead of sense.   (S. 125)

But, again like Yeats, Merrill also highlights moments of poise in which this tension gives way to a blessed plenitude.

These are the "Arcadian" moments such as Yeats describes in "Vacillation IV," moments of rare happiness and vision coming out of a world of "half and half" antinomies, where even a tree appears "half all glittering flame and half all green" ("Vacillation II"). Merrill first hints at this relation in typically allusive fashion: "And Marvell was half tree? / Sidney's *Arcadia* is really yours?" (S. 152). "ARCADIA SURROUNDS US UNREALIZED / FILLING EACH OF US FOR THE LENGTH OF A LOVE OR A THOUGHT" is how Mirabell puts it; we have only to realize that we already inhabit the Arcadian surround. WHA prompts JM's understanding with his own version of "Upon Appleton House":

> IS NOT ARCADIA TO DWELL AMONG
> GREENWOOD PERSPECTIVES OF THE MOTHER TONGUE
> ROOTSYTEMS UNDERFOOT WHILE OVERHEAD
> THE SUN GOD SANG & SHADES OF MEANING SPREAD
> & FAR SNOWCAPPED ABSTRACTIONS GLITTERED NEAR
> OR FAIRLY MELTED INTO THE ATMOSPHERE? (S. 262)

Moments of Arcadian vision and innocence (as Yeats describes them in "Anima Mundi") are largely denied to JM, except as witness, but given to those surrounding him: DJ (mainly in *Scripts*), Mirabell, and WHA.[38] Here is such a moment for Mirabell as he tells about the lessons to come:

> WE SHALL BATHE THEM IN LIGHT WE SHALL HOLD THEM TO THE WINDOW
> TO SEE DENSITY BECOME THE HARMONIC STRUCTURE &
> CHEMISTRY THE ORCHESTRATION & AH SOULD THE HEARING
>   Peacock, peacock—
> MAY I ASK A ? DO TEARS PAIN ONE?
>   Yes. No. Pain and bless.
>   MY EYES BURN RED
>   (S. 157)

Finally and perhaps most pervasively, Merrill works to "correct," and to some extent fulfill, Yeatsian notions of drama and patterns of self-dramatization. When Yeats interrogates himself about the conditions that shape his voices: "Was he constrained by a drama which was part of conditions that made communication possible, was that drama part of the communication . . . was communication itself such a conflict [wherein one sees that 'all gains of man come from conflict with the opposite of his true being']?" (*Vision* 13), he presents the dynamics Merrill will literalize throughout *Sandover* but particularly in the lessons of *Mirabell* and *Scripts*. One of Yeats's communicators tells him "Remember we will deceive you if we can," and Yeats's comment, "as though it rested with me to decide what part I should play in their dream," again anticipates what will be much of the drama of JM's relation to his spirit voices (*Vision* 13). How will he respond to their revelations, as well as their occasional deceptions, their "PEARLGREY LIES" (S. 145)? Will he be able to "make sense of it"? Is he a real "catch," or will he be, like Yeats, "THE ONE THAT GOT AWAY" (S. 478)? Will he hear, as Yeats did, confirmation from on high: "you have said what we wanted to have said" (*Vision* 17; see S. 332, 478, 481, 555)?

In *Mirabell*, we are promised that "CURTAINS WILL RISE ON A VISION" but in the very next breath that "WE MEAN TO KEEP U ENTERTAIND" (S. 198). In keeping with this prospect of an entertaining revelation, Merrill opposes an arch and flexible comedic sense to Yeats's "rage" for tragedy and hierophantic prose. Where Yeats declares:

> As life goes on we discover that certain thoughts sustain us in defeat, or give us victory, whether over ourselves or others. . . . Among subjective men (in all those, that is, who must spin a web out of their own bowels) the victory is an intellectual daily re-creation of all that exterior fate snatches away, and so that fate's antithesis . . . We begin to live when we have conceived life as tragedy.
> (*Autobiography* 128)

Merrill persists in setting his "chronicles of love and loss" in the comedic mode, where "nothing either lasts or ends" and ultimately "loss turns to profit."[39] Thus, Merrill's poetic relies on serendipity, on a receptivity to what fate gives, the readiness to "make room" in the design for unforeseen event, ever intent to "make sense of it" (S. 376, 427).[40] Both poets make themselves the chief players in their own mental theaters (see S. 147-48 and Yeats's "The Circus Animals' Desertion"), and both see themselves humbled and lifted to considerable heights. Nonetheless, Yeats is "disciplined" in Merrill's poem partly by being made a figure in the comedy and then made to serve the "hide and seek" textual drama of Yeatsian "presence" in the poem.

We see this structural role best by tracing the pattern of Yeatsian influence as it weaves in and out of explicit references to the older poet as the volume unfolds. The first faint echoes are heard at the end of "Book 0." The conclusion of Merrill's reverie on a "biophysichemical textbook" nods to Yeats's understanding of the New Moon and builds to a Yeatsian pitch in part by adopting the concluding cadence of "The Second Coming." Where Yeats asks "And what rough beast, its hour come round at last, / Slouches toward Bethlehem to be born?" Merrill gives, "And on the dimmest shore of consciousness / Polypeptides—in primeval thrall / To what new moon I wonder—rise and fall" (S. 110). The next subsection, "0.9," includes Yeatsian gyres, both as "a spiral forever / widening" (S. 111) and, at Avebury, as a system of lenses "whose once outrippling arcs / Draw things back into focus" (S. 112). A parenthesis on Avebury as "both a holy and a homely site" also plays on some of the terms and sweep of time in Yeats's "Lapis Lazuli": "(Whenever the stones blink a century / Blacks out)" (S. 112).

Book 1 introduces us to the bat-angels and "THE IMPLACABLE UNIVERSALL WHEEL" of Yeatsian determinism already discussed in relation to Yeats's "Phases of the Moon" and echoes Yeats's discussion of "concurrent dreams" in the bat-angel's formulation: "WE ARE U   YOU ARE WE   EACH OTHERS DREAM" (S. 117; *Per Amica* 358).[41] The book commences with the demanding voice, "UNHEEDFULL ONE   3 OF YR YEARS MORE WE WANT   WE MUST HAVE / POEMS OF SCIENCE" (S. 113), which echoes the hectoring tone of the intrusive voice in section "U" of "Ephraim: MYND YOUR WEORK   SIX MOONES REMAIN." Both passages recall something of the exacting tone of Yeats's communicators, in their penchant for setting deadlines and their chiding the seemingly unprepared poet. As Yeats recalls: "though I had mastered nothing but the twenty-eight Phases and the historical scheme, I was told I must write, that I must seize the moment between ripe and rotten" (*Vision* 18). JM, driven by his own frustration at the obscurity of such occult intelligences, calls out, "Stop shifting ground!" (S. 122), just as Yeats, in describing his Frustrators, explains: "They shifted ground whenever my interest was at its height" (*Vision* 11). We also hear the bat-angels take credit for Merrill's *Divine Comedies* in terms that disclose a whole system of poetic influence and which also covertly point to Merrill's anxious drama concerning Yeatsian influence.[42]

Book 2 provides further insight into the workings of the "Research Lab," Merrill's parodic echo of the "soulwork" accomplished at Yeats's Phase One. Besides the passage from "Phases of the Moon" already quoted, Yeats gives these descriptions of Phase One, including that "not being human," this phase admits of "No description except complete plasticity"(*Vision* 183). Merrill responds both to this indescribability and to the governing spatial metaphor with the Miltonic variation, "AN EMPTINESS PACKED FULL" (S. 140). Yeats continues:

> ". . . there is complete passivity, complete plasticity. Mind has become indifferent to good and evil, to truth and falsehood; [Here we are reminded of the bat-angels "reluctant" traffic in "PEARLGREY LIES" (S. 145)] . . . and mind and body take whatever shape, accept whatever image is imprinted upon them, transact whatever purpose imposed upon them, are indeed the instruments of supernatural manifestation, the final link between the living and more powerful beings. . . . All plasticities do not obey all masters, and when we have considered cycle and horoscope it will be seen how those that are the instruments of subtle supernatural will differ from the instruments of cruder energy; but all, highest and lowest, are alike in being automatic" (*Vision* 183-84).

Merrill takes over the factory imagery of "imprinting," "imposing" shape and function in his discussions of the "masterful" R/Lab, including the concern for the variable quality of the "raw material": "souls ranging in quality / From the immortal Five to those of lowest / Human density. . . . Even animals / . . . May serve as spare parts" (S. 140).

Continuing in Book 2, Merrill's paean to salt on page 141 may have been suggested, in part by the passage on ice and salt and the nearby passage evoking "the fish of the sea" that he marked in Yeats's "General Introduction for My Work" (522, 524).[43] Pages 143 and 145 present the Merrillian analogs to Yeats's personality "readouts" from the "Twenty-eight Incarnations," as well as the notion of a nearing historical crisis or time of cultural transformation. Yeats famously hailed the transition to "the coming *antithetical* influx" (*Vision* 262) as a time when "Things fall apart." Merrill's bat-angels seem to feel much the same way, explaining, "QUALITY FAILS" (S. 145). In a passage that makes us wonder "what rough beasts" are slouching forth to be born, 741 informs us that the R/Lab is having to resort to "SOULS OF DOMESTIC ANIMALS MOST RECENTLY THE RAT" and that by 2050 (a near millennial date consistent with Yeats's charting of the coming antithetical "turn") when "THESE TWO WILL BE EXHAUSTED" the Lab will have to turn to "WILDER STRAINS MOUNTAIN CATS & FOREST MONKEYS" (S. 145-46).

Yeats is first mentioned in *Mirabell* in the dismissive context of his "intellectual's machismo," bent on erecting theories, disseminating thought, and doctoring what his voices told him (S. 154). And though JM and DJ ("docile takers-in of seed") affect an almost "complete passivity" in sexual terms that shed light back on the sexual content of Yeats's Phase One, Merrill as poet situates himself more complexly. He too "erects theories and disseminates thought"; and the objection that the theory and thought are not his but dictations and that these theories prove unreliable and "self-revising" in the course of *Sandover* cannot wholly mask the fact that the resulting questioning of originality and the stability of truth are Merrill's thought and theory too.[44] Merrill's "doctoring" hand is most obviously apparent in the clearly "shaped" syllabics of the bat-angel's voices and iambic pentameter of his human speakers, metrical conventions evident enough even without attention being drawn by JM's discussion of such matters with WHA (S. 240).[45] Manuscript evidence also reveals a number of instances of more "substantive" authorial intervention, so that the apparent distinctions JM draws between himself and Yeats in this passage should not be taken at face value.[46] The impulse to repress any "affiliation" with Yeats while parodic and more straightforward similarities abound seems to govern this and similar dismissive mentions of the older poet.

Book 3 includes 741's induction into "THIS WORLD OF COURTESY" (S. 155) and metamorphosis into a peacock, in seemingly naive fulfillment of Robartes' description of such beings in "Phases of the Moon" (S. 156-57). When Maria takes her leave from this session with the playful "UNTIL TOMORROW AT THE PEACOCK'S CRY!" (S. 159), we hear a typical Merrillian modulation on the moment in "Meditations in Time of Civil War III, My Table" when "it seemed / Juno's peacock screamed." As in Yeats's poem, the talk has been of getting into Heaven, here of Maria and WHA preparing to "MEET OUR MAKER." JM is uncannily like Yeats's "most rich inheritor," who "Knowing that none could pass Heaven's door / That loved inferior art, / Had such an aching heart / That he . . . / Had waking wits." And in both poems, the peacock's cry is prelude to revelation.[47]

With Mirabell's announcement that he represents fire, Merrill launches into an extended alchemical interlude, set in his signature "Black Swan stanza." This passage (S. 159-161) is replete with Yeatsian echoes in part because of Merrill and Yeats's shared interest in alchemical lore and imagery.[48] Yeatsian images of music and dance as part of "a universal transmutation of all things into some divine and imperishable substance . . . the transmutation of life into art" ("Rosa Alchemica" 267) inform JM's first and fifth stanzas, as well as the first stanza spoken by the elements themselves at section 3.7. JM's stanzas build to a moment of ecstatic vision (stanza three), governed by the fiery "tongues at matter's core" where JM "can no more / Speak than unlearn" as if "Struck dumb in the simplicity of fire" ("Vacillation VII"). His Yeatsian "pride and purpose" are consumed, and he is gathered into an "Embrace of cherubim" that recalls Yeats's imagery in the third stanza of "Sailing to Byzantium." JM's stanzas back away from this apotheosis (in part via more echoes from "Vacillation"), but even this "descent" from the "holy fire" of Yeats's Phase 15 to intimations of the "BLACK / HANDS" of chaos is mediated by WHA's prayer and the elements' admonition to maintain something like the "Unity of Being" the participants' "FIVEFOLD UNION" represents.

This is one of the major set pieces of the poem, and Merrill does not simply drop its Yeatsian reverberations. Mirabell, "Our incandescent bird" (S. 161), is more than ever a representative of "the fifth element, a veil hiding another four, a bird born out of the fire" ("Anima Mundi" 347). In this mirror world behind the mirror, he responds to JM and DJ with fascination and fear, as if they were the fire ("I FELT

/ YR CHARM I HAD FEARD U"), even though he locates himself "HERE IN YR VERY HEARTH OF HEARTS TO BURN" (S. 162). From the emotional intensity of such echoes of Yeats's Condition of Fire, Merrill again moves to more varied notes of "Vacillation." Mirabell queried about these "diametrics of the mirror" responds, "YES NO PERHAPS I STILL VIBRATE TO OUR DIAPENTE," WHA tells JM and DJ, "WE HAD A TASTE OF PARADISE TODAY" (Ibid.), and the book ends with Mirabell's reminder that those Arcadian moments which fill "EACH OF US FOR THE LENGTH OF A LOVE OR A THOUGHT" are not ends in themselves, but intimations of "P A R A D I S E" (S. 165).

Book 4 recalls the images of lenses first mentioned in the context of Avebury in Book 1. As before, Merrill's lenses are related to Yeats's gyres. The lens focusing light makes a cone. A pair of such lenses in array form an interpenetrating field through which the play of objective and subjective meaning "Discourses just beneath the skin / No less than from the farthest reaches / of Time and Space" may be observed in all their "crystalline / Reversibility" (S. 174). As Helen Vendler reminds us, Yeats's gyres "are always double . . . there is no separating subjective and objective, aesthetic and moral, emotional and rational. As one diminishes, the other increases . . . " (*Yeats's Vision* 7). Just as Yeats's system of "double cones" is central to *A Vision*, so Merrill's lenses are explicitly declared "Central to this bOOk," meaning the whole of *Mirabell*, and then, by extension, *Sandover*. What principally distinguishes the two emblems is a difference in stance or perspective hinted at in Merrill's typographic pun ("BOOK"). Both symbols are presented as means for "looking through" to achieve coherent vision. But Merrill makes his lenses synonymous with "THE IMAGINATION," the mode of vision; whereas, Yeats's image emphasizes what the mode of vision reveals. Where Yeats's diagrams, although of dynamic interactions, insist on the stability of design, Merrill's "toy spyglass" points out both the contingency of looking and its embeddedness within the conventions of literary language (the B and K of 'book').

Book 4 also contains Merrill's second explicit, albeit glancing, reference to Yeats: "Yeats' wife, between snores, / Gave utterance to an immense conceit" (S. 178). As usual, the allusion, although it allows a somewhat respectful reading, is dismissive. George's snores and Merrill's pun on "conceit" see to that.[49] But again Merrill's dismissive rhetoric does not wholly supplant an undercurrent of authority. Yeats keeps company here not just with Hugo, but also with Milton and Blake, whose visionary experiences are given more weight,[50] and the passage as a whole shows that JM's dismissive attitude is part of his problematic "nonchalance" in regard to otherworldly matters. He has been told "YR NONCHALANCE / IS THE SLEEP OF A VAST TRAVAIL & TIME RUNS OUT" (S. 124) and, here, learns that "The innate / Role of the Scribe must now be to supplant / Religion" (S. 178) a role Yeats recognized, as have all the sons of Pater.

All of *Sandover*'s elaborate and continuously revised explanations of reincarnation and historic and personal determinism also parody Yeats's elaborate and revised explanations in *A Vision*; and Mirabell's "NOW LET US FURTHER / DESIMPLIFY" (S. 189), as he begins one such explanation reads like a direct, if passing, jibe at Yeats's would-be "simplifications." The "NO ACCIDENT" clause in particular, which after Book 5 dominates *Mirabell,* echoes as it parodies the rapt determinism of Yeats's Vision system.[51] But it is not until the middle of Book 6 that Yeats begins, in effect, to assert himself more fully again, first in echoes of doctrine and imagery, then as positive revelation. WHA's experience literalizes Eliot's doctrine of impersonality but in the distinctly Yeatsian context of dissolution as apotheosis, the dancer made one with the dance: "THE WIND LET / OUT OF HIS BEING   HIS (M) PERSONALITY GONE   ITS / LOSS A COMPLETENESS IN THAT DANCE UNDER THE POWERFUL / LIGHT FLOODING THE LENS" (S. 211) As in Yeats's "Soul in Judgment," JM sees that this "STRIPPING PROCESS" is "*lived through*" (his emphasis).[52] Then, just as Mirabell is presenting his ghostly account of poetic influence (with Rimbaud at Eliot's elbow "WHEN TSE WROTE HIS V WORK"), we learn that "YEATS MOVES DJ'S HAND" (S. 217). With this first suggestion that Yeats has an active and substantive role guiding the Ouija's willowware planchett, an early typescript proceeds, "2 (M) SLIDES / ALIGND ON GOD B'S MICROSCOPE." But before publication Merrill adds these intervening lines for JM:

> What? The energy that activates
> These very messages, you mean, is Yeats?
> (Still, after the first stupefaction, why
> Not? Who but Yeats could have pulled, from the same high
> Hat as *his* talking bird of Grecian gold,
> Our friend here?)[53] (S. 217)

The effect of this seeming swift and breezy response is at once to highlight and to dismiss the aptness of Yeats's intimate involvement in the poem as a whole. Thereafter not much more is made of Yeats's strong connection to the workings of the board.

The two questions that might seem to interrogate this connection operate more powerfully to diminish any lingering sense of its significance: "If David's guide is 741.1 / Where does that leave Yeats" 'Still simplifying'?" (S. 218) and "DJ: Here on my palm / A lump's been forming—painlessly, but still . . . / What is it? Is Yeats raising a molehill?" (S. 220). The sweep of the poem impels the reader on to new "thrills and chills"; but if we pause to notice the attention that has already been paid to DJ's hand, and thereby, in retrospect, to Yeats, this is what we see: "CAN U NOT FEEL YRSELF SHAPING EVEN / NOW THIS PHRASE? WE CD READ IN THE DARK BY YR HAND'S WATTAGE" (S. 142), "DJ YR HAND IS A MAGIC WAND" (S. 211), "& LAST THE SHAPING HAND OF NATURE (DJ)" (S. 159).

This last phrase deserves some comment. Here is Merrill's gloss: "According to Mirabell, David is the subconscious shaper of the message itself, the 'Hand,' as they call him. Of the two of us, he's the spokesman for human nature, while I'm the 'Scribe,' the one in whose words and images the message gets expressed" ("Interview with McClatchy" 68). Merrill calls this "a fairly rough distinction," and we must agree. Its roughness does considerable violence to Merrill's usual insistence on the identity of message and manner (Lehman 25). A great deal having to do with authorship is being repressed here, and not only in matters concerning David Jackson's role and whether "the trilogy shouldn't have been signed with both our names—or simply 'by DJ, as told to JM'" ("Interview with McClatchy" 68).

In this section (6.8), JM also raises the related issue of Pound's role in the composition of Eliot's *The Waste Land*, eliciting Mirabell's witty retort: "AS IN SHAKESPEARE WE LET THE CASE REST ON A POUND OF FLESH" (S. 219). It was all just a matter of judicious cutting, as it were. Thus, Merrill's "ghostly" presentation of the drama of poetic influence diminishes the "shaping" role of "Uncle Ezra," as if Merrill felt compelled to covertly raise, while also brushing aside, the question of who might be "il miglior fabbro," the better maker, for his poem. "Shaping" is an etymon of *poesis*, and any "shaping hand" evokes God's hand and the story of creation. In this light, it is DJ/Yeats who becomes the Maker and Merrill the Scribe who follows after.

Anxiety about such issues is reflected in the record of additions and deletions that Merrill's manuscript provides. Where by implication the published poem leaves Yeats "Still simplifying" (S. 218), the typescript shows Merrill not quite so ready to dismiss: "David's guide, you've said, is 741 / .1—are you divisible like amoebas? / And Yeats, [is he] 'still simplifying'? *Clearly not*" (emphasis added). Why this "Clearly not" which is not published? By the logic of the poem, Yeats cannot be "still simplifying" if he is "the energy that activates / These very messages"—unless *Sandover* is itself a kind of Yeatsian simplification.[54] In manuscript there were no lines from Mirabell interposed between his punning reference to Ezra Pound's role in reshaping *The Waste Land* and JM's petulant, "Still, Eliot thought he thought his poem up" (S. 219). The lines Merrill adds for Mirabell to speak show the poet again trying to come to terms with the necessity of poetic influence. Mirabell responds to JM's dismissive "Thank you, that will do" by saying, "NO JM   FOR THE (M) OUNCE OF FLESH U CAN CLAIM AS YRS / LIVES BY THESE FREQUENT CONTACTS WITH YR OWN & OTHERS' WORK" (S. 219). This is what might be called the "daimonic theory of reading" and points toward the necessary and vivifying power of literary influence. The tutelary voice of Merrill's daimon has already instructed him in the mixed ingredients of souls (S. 189) and will later insist on JM's own status as a "composite voice" (S. 266). Mirabell comes close to adopting Harold Bloom's argument in this remark, urging JM to understand that what is original in his work and life as a poet depends on what he makes of poems already "given."[55] This remark also anticipates WHA's further prodding of JM to "SEE PAST LONE / AUTONOMY" to "THINK WHAT A MINOR / PART THE SELF PLAYS IN A WORK OF ART" (S. 262).

We gain some insight into how difficult this lesson proves for Merrill, especially in regard to Yeats, by seeing how, even in revision, the lump developing on DJ's palm is pressed into service as a means of keeping the notion of Yeatsian influence at bay. Where the published version aligns the laughable prospect of "Yeats raising a molehill" with "A BENIGN MUSCULAR CYST," the manuscript version reads: "DJ: I've been developing this bump / Here on my right palm. It seems to come / From how

I touch the cup. It doesn't hurt. . . . ." There is no mention of Yeats, only the lingering reminder of some significance in Mirabell's reply: "NOTHING O HAND IS EASILY ABSORBED," as if any touch or taint of Yeatsian influence were necessarily problematic. [Indeed, we learn in *Scripts* that this disturbance in DJ's hand will last only as long as the dictation; when it ends Yeats will "LEAVE YR HAND / MY DEAR MUCH AS HE FOUND IT" (S. 424).]

As further testimony that these issues are not lightly resolved we have the compulsive disciplinary history of DJ's hand being pressed and hurt (S.73, 108, 213), as well as Merrill's ongoing, yet subtly ambivalent, campaign of diminishment directed against the older poet. On the surface, references to Yeats in Mirabell 6.8 continue this campaign. As we have seen, JM's question, "If David's guide is 741.1 / Where does that leave Yeats? 'Still simplifying'?," recalls Ephraim's dismissive formula from the earlier book. But the analogy of Rimbaud "ghostwriting" Eliot's *The Waste Land*, if not glossed over, suggests a very different relation. Eliot and Rimbaud share the same guide number, with Rimbaud having "THAT SAME NUMBER / POINT ONE"(S. 219). This correspondence of guides acts as a conduit, a "feed": "WE HAD TO APPOINT RIMBAUD   HE WROTE / THE WASTE LAND   WE FED IT INTO THE LIKE-CLONED ELIOT" (Ibid.). But Mirabell also tells us that Yeats and DJ stand in the same relation as do Eliot and Rimbaud (a reversal of the expected order). DJ's guide is 741.1, as Rimbaud's guide differed from Eliot's by .1. By analogy, we may infer that Yeats's guide is 741, and thus that Merrill and Yeats both share his daimonic services. Thus, while the alphabetic language Merrill most depends on (and the "stupefying" news that Rimbaud wrote *The Waste Land*) diverts attention from the Merrill/Yeats relation, "reading" Merrill's numbers establishes once again an uneasy line of influence between Yeats and Merrill.

After this passage, explicit reference to Yeats disappears from *Mirabell*. His "presence" is felt only as a shaping element in JM's language. One of the best examples of such "presence" and of how Yeatsian imagery and thematics help underwrite Merrill's most impressive poetry comes in section "7.6," JM's "starstruck hymn to Mother N[ature]" (S. 235). Stephen Yenser characterizes this passage as "a highly wrought, wildly associative lyric in double quatrain stanzas, riddled with Yeatsian vacillations, that ultimately posits the union of mind and nature" (*Myth* 276).[56] "Mind" is "that [Yeatsian] battiness" Merrill explicitly connects with an "artifice" opposed to "random time and gale;" it is an "artifice of eternity," a shining, silvery, moon-like fire that consumes without singeing, but cast here in the most pejorative terms: an "argent grub" that leaves only "The crust, the mirror-meal."

Like pure mind, pure nature, with "her clinging vine / And the forgiving smother of her humus," poses its threats. What's needed is a way to marry both. And what Merrill finds is a way at once Yeatsian and "eminently me."[57] The trick is that "once [via the alchemy of poetic imagination] out of nature, a mercurial / Inch," one must remember to "look back!" Nature "so distanced," could then "be the way / Of [making] our own world"—a poesis that is also consonant with "the way of the world" (S. 232). Thus, like Yeats, Merrill sees the making of an alternate world of his own as a dynamic, dialogical relationship between mind and nature (objective and subjective gyres) alternating "by 'turns' as in a music hall."

As the Hymn continues, the second quatrain of the fourth stanza offers a particularly Merrillian spin on Yeats's system of gyres and moods:

> Not that the faint alarm pre-set
> In "Strato's fear of mind" goes off upon
> Impulses pure as those of the snowflake pun
> She [Nature] utters when *her* mood is zero . . .   (Ibid.)

The "faint alarm pre-set" domesticates the apocalyptic role of the peacock's cry that announces the moment the gyre of mind attains its pure fullness and nature, in a mood of "zero," reasserts her cascading multiplicity through the body of a "snowflake pun." Like Yeats, in more objective moods, Merrill sees this conception as a myth, a "stylistic arrangement of experience" (*Vision* 25), best served by the "two-minded" wisdom of "Vacillation." Merrill's sixth and seventh stanzas further allude to the "widening gyres" of bird flight and ringing song, the "lashing hail and rapturous farewell" of cycling incarnations, and the disincarnate "humming black . . . stardust in negative," like Yeats's "Dreaming Back," "between the rings" of incarnation. The poem concludes with Merrillian "bemusement," that glad communing between Mind and Nature that approaches, but is not yet Yeats's "Unity of Being."

If, as Yenser has it, this poem is an epithalamium of Mind and Nature (*Myth* 277), it is important to note how early the Mind (like Merrill's father, and again associated most pejoratively with aspects of Yeats) drops aside, leaving only the speaker's voice to carry on an imaginative, displaced and Oedipal exchange with both mother and Nature which, although it fails as "communication," does "sweep [him] away." Merrill's calling home to "maternal Nature" cannot come easily, compacted as it is with "terror" and deferral and the knowledge of having made, to some extent, "our own world"—a phrase telling for its hermetic gestures of both inclusion and separateness. Some kind of at least "passing" union is figured here, but one that will barely pass as "straight." The Hymn seems more to celebrate the uneasy marriage of aspects of Yeats and Merrill; it enacts a kind of "communing" that gets the speaker as pregnant as he is going to be—that is, "two-minded" and "bemused."

In the ten "RECUPERATIVE," countdown lessons, starting at the end of Book 7 and running through the end of Book 9, the Yeatsian elements become largely thematic. In keeping with the focus of the second half of *Mirabell* on the "stripping process," which is at once a purgation and a convalescence, these lessons echo themes from Yeats's "The Soul in Judgment." Mirabell, in these last lessons, becomes ever more clearly an instance of that Yeatsian miraculous bird ["Mercy! what a speech—from what a bird!"] "singing of what is past [his account of the rise of culture, story, and religion from the earliest "APECHILDREN" to the Koran (S. 241-43)], and passing [the workings and rules of the Greenhouse, also the weather (S. 244-47)] and to come [the days of "MAN IN PARADISE" (S. 247-48) and the voice of angels]. In one of his last "appearances" in the volume, Mirabell is suddenly made a "key-stopped" toy emblem of Yeats's "immortal song"—a song whose autonomy still clearly troubles the younger poet. Thus from Mirabell, "our dear bird // Outpouring numbers—music to his ears— / Fill the page, cage of our lifelong / Intolerance of such immortal song" (S. 267).

With his paean to Mercury, Merrill has JM confront his alchemical alter ego and ponder the cycle of reincarnation. As in Yeats's system, the whole is seen as a Great Wheel and "Life after life leaves uncompleted the full reversal" (S. 249). With the word "reversal," instead of "cycle" or "revolution," Merrill shows another affinity for Yeats's system of apocalyptic reversals when, for example, antithetical progress shifts into primary retrograde. JM ends with images of the soul between death and birth having cast off the old self "like raiment / Worn only once, on such-and-such a day" and envisions a "secret backward flow," this last image suggested perhaps by the names of two of Yeats's purgatorial stages, the "Return" and "Dreaming Back" (*Vision* 226-29). Finally, with an angel's insistence on "A CEREMONY OF MANNERS" (S. 249) Book 9 suggests ways in which all of *Sandover* takes an important theme from Yeats's "A Prayer for my Daughter." Through storms that echo apocalyptic anxiety about living in and through an atomic age to images of births and rebirths and of education presided over by ceremony and custom (manners), humans alive and dead are being prepared for how "the soul recovers radical innocence." In *Mirabell*, such preparation allows JM and DJ to "LOOK! LOOK INTO THE RED EYE OF YOUR GOD!" (S. 276) and, at the epic's close, it will enable JM to stand "self-delighting, / Self-appeasing, self-affrighting" and read "Admittedly, I err . . . " assured that his "own sweet will is Heaven's will."

III. YEATS IN *SCRIPTS*: ABJECTION AND APOTHEOSIS

In contrast to the sometimes "rough justice" of *Mirabell*'s parodic use of Yeats's *A Vision*, and the more covert patterns of affinity between the two poets established in that volume, *Scripts for the Pageant* draws away from overt parody and seems to offer Yeats considerable respect when he finally speaks from the board.[58] Yeatsian language continues to "materialize" at appropriate moments, but rarely with the threatening force or vivid taste of argument found in earlier apparitions. Yet *Scripts* does continue Merrill's epic campaign of diminishment against Yeats, even as it builds upon the long dramatic delay that finally issues in Yeats's only speaking "appearance" at the board. Merrill highlights the "quarrel" between Auden and Yeats as a means of externalizing and gaining more distance on his own ambivalent relations with the older poet. He also continues to "correct" Yeats throughout the volume, gradually inflecting Yeatsian Tragedy more and more through his own bittersweet Commedia, until Yeats has been charmed into an unspoken, but presiding presence at its ceremonious Finale—a presence that above all underscores Merrill's own poetic authority.

Yeats has very little place in the opening, affirmative section of *Scripts*. We may see something of the final stanza of "Byzantium" in the typographic representation of an image astride an idea in Merrill's opening lines:

> Nothing eludes the angel. And since light's
> Comings and goings in black space remain
> Unobserved   (storm-spattered midnight pane
> Until resisted,   a strange car ignites)
> Why think to change our natures?   (S. 285)

But this is perhaps as attenuated as an allusion may become. Some pages later, the scientist, George Cotzias, broaches the Yeatsian themes of vision and justice in his discussion of scientific inspiration (S. 298-99), but here too the published echoes are few and far between.[59]

Leslie Brisman has pointed to WHA's description of the angel Raphael, also known as the "Earth Brother" Elijah (S. 306-07), as a representation of "the old granite face and rocky voice of Yeats" and explains:

> With "wicked, merry eyes" [Merrill's Elijah] represents gaiety in the old sense, the hardened sensibility of one who learned to cast a cold eye on life, on death. It is against this wisdom of old age that Merrill's "younger" sense of gaiety restores the pathos and the importance of the life of the affections. (197)

Although there is a good deal in Elijah's brief remarks (as well as WHA's description) that indicates Yeats [particularly Elijah's "death-in life and life-in-death" confession that "I HAVE IN ME THE IRRADIATED METALS, I WHO MOST / DREAD THEM" (S. 307) and his description of the cosmos as a reciprocating, gyring dance with his watery twin: "MY TWIN DRAWS BACK & I ADVANCE, AND NOW OUR DANCE / REVERSES" (Ibid.)] and, although Brisman is certainly correct in his general characterization of the quarrel between Merrill and the cold, ascetic aspect of Yeats; nonetheless, what is remarkable in this passage is how warm and generative of the affections Elijah's speech is. Elijah concludes his comments in a tone of self-deprecating affection and fellowship: "BUT NOW MY SMALL BROTHERS, FOR ARE WE NOT ALL OF THE COMMON CLAY, / (Here at the close, a strong, dancing motion) / FAREWELL! I WILL ANOTHER TIME BE WITTY" (Ibid.). It is true that Elijah withdraws seemingly at "THE SIGHT OF [DJ'S] TEARS," but DJ's emotion, his "Reaction to the thrill" of Elijah's words and being able to "talk back and forth . . . with angels," is occasioned by the angel's words. There is no critique of emotion in the angel's departure. Rather we observe the courtly, even witty, enactment of Earth making way for the "watery" advance of DJ's tears and Wystan's mildly anti-Yeatsian lesson:

> FOR IS IT NOT OUR LESSON THAT WE COME
> EACH TO HIS NATURE? NOT TO ANY VAST
> UNIVERSAL ELEVATION, JUST
> EACH TO HIS NATURE PRECIOUS IF BANAL (S. 308)

In keeping with the affirmative nature of this section of *Scripts*, Merrill evokes Yeats as if to show how correction of the older poet is possible within his own terms. The reciprocating dance of opposites need not be an agony or battle of enemies, but may instead entail the interplay of mutual regard. When WHA comments after Elijah's words "I DO BELIEVE OUR SPRINGTIME WILL BE GAY / IN THE OLD SENSE" (S. 307), he evokes, but does not directly engage, the "hardened sensibility" of Yeats's gaiety. Instead we see how gaiety in the "OLD SENSE" of a sociable delight may be taken back into Yeats' rocky voice to transfigure in turn the "Gaiety transfiguring all that dread."[60]

Lesson 3 of "YES" opens with "Thunderclaps" (S. 328) that recall Merrill's anxiety about Yeatsian "stolen thunder" (S. 65, see also 77 and Yeatsian thunderheads in "Violent Pastoral" and "Willowware Cup"). The section builds to Gabriel's survey of "all the tragic scene": man's "PRIDE, AMBITION, [and] SENSE OF SENSE IN ALL HIS SENSELESSNESS" (S. 330). It offers a countervailing moment of light operatic "gaiety" (Offenbach, "La Périchole") and Merrill's version of "mournful melodies": "limpid bel / Canto phrases—raptures of distress" (S. 331). With this last phrase, Merrill indirectly evokes the power of Yeats's verse (and potent masochism of Yeats's vision) by borrowing "raptures of distress" from Auden's "In Memory of W. B. Yeats." But WHA is quick to turn this incipient evocation of Yeats against Merrill's Yeatsian quietism. "WHERE," he asks, "IN ALL THIS IS THE AFFIRMATION?" JM's reply, "In the surrender, in the forward motion—"is sharply countered by WHA's parody of a famous line from "Lapis Lazuli" so that WHA's rhetorical question satirizing JM's posture of surrender, "POWER BLAZING ON SHUT LIDS?" also reaches back to challenge Yeats's visionary "Black out; Heaven blazing into the head" as well as the posture of detached aesthetic "gaiety" that marks Yeats's poem. WHA underscores another critical departure from "Lapis Lazuli" at the end of Lesson 3. In characterizing Gabriel on his knees and weeping at the end of his speech as "THE UNIVERSE'S GREATEST ACTOR" (S. 332), Wystan reminds us that actors do indeed "break up their lines to weep" and that, as Leslie Brisman puts it, "it is as much the function of poetry to move us to tears as to regain a final composure over womb-felt agony" (193).

By bringing Auden's quarrel with Yeats into his poem, Merrill not only finds another way of "personifying" or externalizing elements of an ongoing internal quarrel, he also gains a certain mastery over (and through) his own carefully cultivated ambivalence. It is ironic, but, as we shall see in further instances of this instrumental relation between the poets, what once occasioned "raptures of distress" in Merrill's relation with Yeats will increasingly constitute simply another contending element in a scene Merrill's "accomplished fingers" orchestrate and which he has come to view through eyes glitteringly gay, at once Yeatsian, sociable, and queer.[61]

It is not until "Samos," the masterful canzone which opens the bridging section "&" in *Scripts*, that Yeats again figures strongly in Merrill's language—particularly the following passages with their echoes of Yeats's Byzantium poems, where "Soul clap its hands and sing and louder sing" and the speaker longs to be gathered into and consumed by "Gods' holy fire":

> ... We who water
> The local wine, which "drinks itself" like water,
> Clap for more, cry out to *be* this island
> Licked all over by a white, salt fire,
> *Be* noon's pulsing ember raked by fire,
>
> Know nothing, now, but Earth, Air, Water, Fire!
> For once out of the frying pan to land
> Within their timeless, everlasting fire!
> Blood's least red monocle, O magnifier
> Of the great Eye that sees by its own light
> More pictures in "the world's enchanted fire"
> Than come and go in any shrewd crossfire
> Upon the page, of syllable and sense,
> We want unwilled excursions and ascents,
> Crave the upward-rippling rungs of fire,
> The outward-rippling rings (enough!) of water ... (S. 369-70)

Both poets evoke "excursions and ascents," both the elevating movement of fire and the "outward-rippling" movement and plenitude of water—Yeats's "mackerel-crowded" and "gong-tormented" seas. But, as in "Swimming by Night" and "McKane's Falls," Merrill's echoes of Yeats once again also revise. Where Yeats contrasts fire and water, Merrill links them together. Where Yeats unequivocally imagines that, "once out of nature," an "artifice of eternity" awaits the speaker, Merrill finds his "timeless, everlasting fire" *within* rather than outside of Nature's elements. Where Yeats's "blood" is often blind, inchoate Nature, Merrill's is allied, not to mire, but to the seeing light of the sun, and it is Nature's art and intelligence more than any "shrewd crossfire" of poetic artifice that offers him something he dearly values: "More pictures."

Part of Yeats longs to "Break [the] bitter furies of complexity, Those images that yet / Fresh images beget" in order to attain "the simplicity of fire"; yet "Byzantium" famously concludes with just such a proliferation of images. Part of Merrill too cries "enough!" but this is only because mere proliferation of images is linguistically too simple. Here Merrill finds his faith, not in transcendence or a "simplification through intensity," but in "some details" of dailiness. They may be "Trifles"; yet this is where his God resides—not only in the "timeless, everlasting fire" but also in the quotidian light of memory, where "things that fade" may also "especially make sense" (S. 370).

In his interview with Fred Bornhauser, Merrill remarks:

> And isn't 'God lurks in the details' the motto of the Warburg Institute? The best
> I could hope for from a reader is that he keep one eye on the ever-emerging (and

self-revising) whole, and another on the details. A lot of the talk sounds like badinage, causal if not frivolous, but something serious is usually going on under the surface. (54).

Merrill's ideal reader is an esoteric reader. He comments in another interview, "I'm afraid I don't see how you can separate art from a degree of elitism" ("Interview" *Lawrentian* 9). Readers discover Merrill's "something serious" not so much through a hermeneutic of suspicion as through an attentive double-mindedness—which is also Merrill's constant manner and message.

In a manuscript note opposite these lines about trifles and memory, Merrill writes, "not the things themselves but what happens to things give them value / interest." A reader attends to what happens to things, here very basic things: "Earth, Air, Water, Fire!" And part of the "plot" of what happens to these elements is precisely the glitter of Merrill's formal play. In discussing "Samos" and the canzone form, Merrill acknowledges that he "copied Auden in this tiny, streamlining impulse" of reducing Dante's six-line envoi to five (the numbers twelve and five being "crucial to the doctrines behind the long poem"). He continues:

> I picked the most constricting form imaginable, yet the poem, which got written in only a day or two, came flowing forth, as if from a part of my mind I'm all too seldom in touch with. Rilke used to believe in keeping his 'instrument' in good working order. This meant writing all kinds of short, not-too-demanding poems in a variety of forms, always humbly waiting for the day when a completely different muse would sit down at the keyboard. When I'd finished "Samos" I understood as never before what Rilke meant. ("James Merrill on Poetry" 4-5).

It is wonderful to hear about this "flowing forth," but that is exactly the dazzling effect of the poem—whatever pains it might have cost in composing. Yeatsian sprezzatura, where lines must "seem a moment's thought" ("Adam's Curse"), and Yeatsian "Double Vision" are the hallmarks, not just of lyric set pieces such as "Samos," but of *Sandover* entire, as well as the rest of Merrill's oeuvre.

Though Blake is the poet most often explicitly alluded to, section "&" also begins to develop *Scripts*'s overarching theme of "Resistance" in terms that often recall Yeats's interest in the "Contraries," as a dynamic play of "Primary" and "Antithetical" forces.[62] Once again George Cotzias speaks in images Yeats would authorize. He pictures that "HEARTBEAT OF ATTRACTION AND REPULSION" that drives all universal processes in terms of Yeats's gyres:

> NOW IN THAT WHIRL IS A REVERSE WHIRL
> MAKING, AS IN THE BEATEN WHITE OF EGG,
> FOR THICKENING, FOR DENSITY, FOR MATTER.
> YES, FROM THIS OPPOSITION, WHICH HOLDS SWAY
> NO LESS WITHIN MAN'S SOUL, LORDS, CAME THE FIRST
> MINUTE PASTE THAT WAS GOD'S MATERIAL. (S. 396)

With this passage in mind, we recall Merrill underlining in his copy of *A Vision* Blake's assertion, "Contraries are positive" (*Vision* 72). When Psyche takes "BLAKE'S FAITH" as her text "AND PHYSICS LAW AS MY LESSON," she recounts God B's decision to give man a divided nature, "FOR IN DUALITY IS DIMENSION, TENSION, ALL THE TRUE GRANDEUR WANTING IN A PERFECT THING" (S. 408). Merrill's dualistic monism shares strong affinities not just with Blake's "Contraries" and Yeats's interplay of "Primary" and "Antithetical" forces, but also with Kimon Friar's "aesthetic theory of tension" and with Gnostic doctrine of a fallen and divided creation.[63] For Yeats, it is man's uncertainty, his "PUZZLEMENT," that make him a poet (*Per Amica* 331); for Merrill these same qualities are required to make him "COMPANY" fit for the divine (S. 408).

In this section, there are also intimations in Psyche's lesson that human beings are constituted according to predetermined "TYPES" that operate according to a "COMPLETE DESIGN," and thus it seems all together fitting that Psyche takes the Yeatsian full moon as her sign (S. 410). Merrill's Psyche, like the disincarnate beings of Yeats's "Full of the Moon" or "Phase Fifteen," "inhabit[s] a world where every beloved image has bodily form, and every bodily form is loved" (*Vision* 136). Like Christ at this stage, Psyche is also seen as an intercessor for humanity, and WHA prayerfully bids her "TIP THE SCALE" on behalf of threatened humanity (S. 410); and though she is "complete beauty" (*Vision* 135)—"the chatelaine of *Sandover*— / . . . A face so witty, loving, and serene / . . . [the] fairest face of Nature" (S. 407)—Psyche is also aligned with her opposite, the Chaos of Yeats's "Phase One" (S. 409).

Yeats is destined to make his long awaited "appearance" in the next section of *Scripts*. But before he does, Merrill lays important groundwork. It is not enough that the section "&" is saturated with the Yeatsian thematics of "RESISTANCE" or that Yeatsian language also surfaces briefly, as in MM's phrase, the "IMAGE-THWARTED PATHS BY WHICH WE THINK" (S. 414).[64] We are also reminded to associate Yeats with David Jackson (rather than Merrill), reminded too that Yeats's *Vision* is limited and being superseded. We learn that Yeats suffers—and wonder, does he suffer because of his errors, from being suppressed or under-acknowledged, or from being surpassed?—and are quietly supplied with a rationale for the relative enfeeblement of the most illustrious human figures encountered via the board, including Yeats.

When WHA reports that "AMONG THE GERMANS . . . GOETHE TURNS OUT QUITE MY DEAR / AS DULL AS RILKE," DJ fittingly supplies the reason (since his figure shares much the same fate): "*They're* mined out, / Densities fueling readers here below" (S. 292).[65] Plato, in his "tattletale gray nightgown off one shoulder" (S. 158), may be the most prominent casualty of this process. As Mirabell explains: "INDEED HE IS NEARLY A SHELL / BUT OUR HAUTE CUISINE IS STOCKD WITH HIS LIVE SOUL" (S. 189). Thus, it is no accident that of the "GREAT SCRIBES" encountered on the "other side," those who seem most hollowed-out, dull or diminished, are also the souls most fully put to use, particularly in the world of the poem. Wallace Stevens, for example, has become "THIS DRY SCRIBE" who is nonetheless "A PERMANENCE / TAPPABLE BY LESSER TALENT" (S. 429).

DJ has supplied the inverted index of Merrillian influence (and, of course, such a rationale also provides Merrill with considerable rhetorical cover against charges that he slights the very figures to whom he is most indebted.) *Sandover* is clearly informed by a reading of Rilke[66] and Goethe (*Faust* II), and Merrill has also acknowledged the Platonism of his trilogy ("James Merrill at Home" 35), so that it is no wonder that these "scribes" always appear more or less effaced in his poem. We realize that, of Merrill's chiefest lights, Proust and Dante can only be evoked in the poem, asked after, never described, and only once (at the very end) located, because they are so much in use. If Wallace Stevens, or even Auden, appear less than their proper selves, DJ gives us the reason; they too are being mined (Being/Mind) by the poem their voices contribute to. Yet none of these significant precursor souls suffer quite as extensive or consistent campaign of belittlement as Yeats does throughout the length of *Sandover*. By the wily logic of the poem, this too is "NO ACCIDENT" and only underscores the importance of Yeats's influence.

Since *Mirabell* we have known to associate DJ's hand with Yeats, as well as with his role as partner to Merrill's "Scribe"(S. 217-19). The instances in "Ephraim" and Mirabell in which DJ's hand is hurt are dramatic enough that when Maria concludes her lecture on the plant world "LORD MICHAEL, / LORDS, POETS, DOCTEUR, AND DEAR SORE HAND" (S. 389), we are accustomed to DJ's lowly and long-suffering status in the poem's hierarchy, even though there has been no recent occasion to draw attention to his pain. The epithet simply resonates, and prepares for the explicit connection between DJ's and Yeats's suffering made three lessons later when WHA announces:

> THE MOMENT IS LONG PAST WHEN YOU LM
> MIGHT HAVE BEEN DEVOURED BY THE CHIMERA   [of system]
> LLIKE POOR LONGSUFFERING YEATS. MUCH THAT U KNOW
> WAS DICTATED TO HIM BY THE OO (S. 424)

"But does Yeats suffer *now*?" JM asks. The passage continues:

> ANSWER DJ
> YOU ARE THE HAND
>   DJ, uneasily:
> Well, there's this bump on my palm. It doesn't hurt . . .
> What else? Often before I know the message
> I feel its beauty, its importance. Tears
> Come to my eyes. Is that Yeats being moved?
> Often it's tiring or obscure. I fumble
> Along, JM finds answers, I feel dumb.
> Is that Yeats too, still making the wrong sense?
> Why can't *he* ever speak? WHEN THE DICTATION

ENDS I THINK HE MAY & LEAVE YR HAND
MY DEAR MUCH AS HE FOUND IT   Good enough.
Meanwhile, he's visible? FAINTLY IN THE DARK
A WORDLESS PRESENCE

Merrill's manuscript is even more explicit in its faultfinding and in linking Yeats's suffering to the sessions at the board. It reads after "MUCH THAT U KNOW / WAS DICTATED TO HIM BY THE OO":

ALAS IN FORMULAIC LANGUAGE: HE
SUCCUMBED TO CHARTS INSTEAD OF POETRY
But does Yeats suffer *in these sessions?* (emphasis added)

Merrill's indictment (echoing Kimon Friar and voiced by WHA) is this: Yeats's *A Vision* was devoured by the chimera of number and succumbed to the rhetoric of charts, a kind of seeming certainty, where it should have been governed by the uncertainty, the inner quarrel that in Yeats's own account yields true poetry (*Per Amica* 331). Thus Merrill has Yeats given over to the parodic number-crunching realm of 741 in *Mirabell* and condemned to a kind of Dantean justice throughout the length of *Sandover*. Yeats is made to suffer the parody of his errors and, what may be more, the knowledge of the younger poet's accomplishment, "its beauty, its importance" and his inadequacy, "still making the wrong sense." He is reduced to a pathetic shadow by these later lights, "A WORDLESS PRESENCE" (S. 424).

Of course little of this is stated out-right, and most is couched in the form of very Yeatsian questions. To this indictment can also be opposed a quiet tribute, so that although Merrill's deliberate double-mindedness is weighted heavily against Yeats, it also retains its sometimes precarious poise. DJ's stigmata (to press my point) and Yeats's suffering also reveal a redemptive underpainting. Yeats gives access to beauty and importance even before the message is spelled out; he is wordless precisely because so fully used. Intimations persist that Dante, Yeats, and JM have all shared the same intelligence [linked both by the OO and 741—who is, like Ephraim (here given the number "279"), "A STRONG FORCE BOTH / PROTECTIVE & CONDUCTIVE" of the "naked current" of sublime revelation]. MM tells us:

AND 741 [the "guide" Yeats and JM share]
HAS PLAYED A PART N'EST CE PAS? HERE IN VOL III
Who else spread wings above you when God B
Sang in Space? OUR ST BERNARD   JM: Who—
Isn't it St Bernard—helps Dante see
Our Lady? AH   THE PATTERN BLEEDING THROUGH (S. 424-25)

But as always, when the mood lifts to such a "hush of wonder," an answering impulse prompts its deflation. Here the shift is effected sharply with a last jab at Yeats, aimed seemingly out of the blue by Robert Morse: "PSST CUT YR QUILL, MR

YEATS!"—as though this whole passage were meant to reveal nothing so much as Yeats's outmoded obtuseness (S. 425).

Merrill's typescript provides some insight on the motivation of Morse's remark. Where the published version of this passage ends with the couplet, "A hush of wonder Robert punctuates: / AU RESERVOIR PSST CUT YR QUILL, MR YEATS!" the earlier version has a quatrain that pointedly praises JM for his success in Dante's mode:

> They go. BOB HERE: CHARMED BY YR TERZA RIMA
> (I've been at work on *Mirabell,* 8.8) [Merrill's elegy to Robert Morse]
> SEE ME, DO U, AS A CUNNING SCHEMA?
> AU RESERVOIR A NEW QUILL, MR YEATS!

It is as if Merrill and Yeats are in competition, in Morse's view, and Yeats will have to get a new and better instrument if he wants to challenge Merrill after such a performance by JM. Tact, and an eye to weak verse, would be enough to dictate Merrill's revision. But what is most important to see is that, above all, Merrill chooses to retain the slap at Yeats and allows it to seem even more gratuitous and abrupt in the published version than in the typescript. When Merrill gave readings from *Scripts*, he indicated the end of a passages marked in the text by a star with a brisk snap of his fingers. On the tape he made of *Sandover* for Eleanor Perenyi's blind mother, the snap that follows Morse's words at this point comes with a particular dismissive sharpness.

This brief section also presents the first explicit appeal that Yeats finally be heard from, and thus helps build anticipation and lay the groundwork for Yeats's long-delayed "appearance" in the last major division of *Scripts*. Since Yeats's role will be to praise JM and offer him heaven's blessing, part of preparing for these scenes is the elevation of JM (through association with the thieving Prometheus), as well as the continued abasement of Yeats, so that blessing and praise seem appropriate. The Prometheus motif is first sounded very early when Ephraim tells JM and DJ "U & I WITH OUR / QUICK FIRELIT MESSAGES STEALING THE GAME ARE SMUGGLERS & / SO IN A SENSE UNLAWFUL" (S. 59). This early note of an elevating, dangerous conspiracy is retrieved and heightened in *Scripts*, first in relation to God B ["GOD AS PROMETHEUS?" (S. 453)], and then as Gabriel ascribes the Promethean sin to all mankind ["MAN'S THEFT OF GOD'S MATERIALS"—the divine fires of Time and Feeling (S. 455)]. In response, MM argues that since "MANKIND [or at least those such as Cotzias "OUR FAITFUL / FAULTLES GREEK"] MUST DO / IMMORTAL WORK" this theft is not only justified but sanctioned by heaven (S. 455-56). MM's emphasis on "IMMORTAL WORK," the "V work" most prominently given in the poem to humanity's "great Scribes," its scientists, musicians, and poets, tilts the argument toward "THE GODLINESS OF CREATION" (S. 458) so that ultimately JM will realize "The rock I'm chained to is a cloud. I'm free" (S. 462).

This progression from God's "fall" as Prometheus to JM's elevation to almost vatic heights via Shelley's *Prometheus Unbound* ["joyous, beautiful and free" (IV 577)] is shadowed by reminders of the fate Merrill has given Yeats in *Mirabell*, and begs the question of whose fire Merrill may be said in these contexts to have stolen. When JM wonders (following Yeats's ambitions for the tables and symbolic charts of *A Vision*) "mustn't we at last wipe clean / The blackboard of these creatures and their talk, To render in a hieroglyph of chalk / The formulas they stood for?" these are the terms by which WHA reminds JM of his proper freedom:

> U MY BOY
> ARE THE SCRIBE   YET WHY? WHY MAKE A JOYLESS THING
> OF IT THROUGH SUCH REDUCTIVE REASONING?
> ONCE HAVING TURNED A FLITTING SHAPE OF BLACK
> TO MIRABELL, WD YOU MAKE TIME FLOW BACK?
> SUBTRACT FROMHIS OBSESSION WITH 14
> THE SHINING/DIMMING PHASES OF OUR QUEEN? (S. 461-62)

WHA reminds us as well as JM that Yeats's passion for simplicity yielded the joyless, reductive reasoning that Merrill parodied in the doctrine and flitting black shapes of the OO and the unregenerate 741. Even the bat-angel's obsession with 14 serves to parody (by trimming neatly in half) Yeats's reduction of the "SHINING/DIMMING PHASES OF OUR QUEEN" to his codified "Twenty-eight Incarnations" or "Phases of the Moon." Thus the freedom JM celebrates at the end of this speech is particularly the freedom not to follow Yeats.[67] And yet, as we shall see, JM nowhere achieves the freedom of outright divorce; theirs is a life-long, lovers' quarrel.

When Yeats finally does make his speaking appearance in the poem it is within a prolonged drama of ambivalence. He emerges from "OUR ESTEEMD (& HIDDEN) HAND" as one who has also been "MOST PUT UPON" (S. 486) and is clearly aggrieved. First, he takes up the matter of his maligned obsession for "CHARTS AND FORMULAS." Defensively, he, who has always been mocked for making the wrong sense, asks the higher powers, "WAS I THEN WRONG, WITH DNA UNKNOWN, / TO BUILD MY WINDING STAIR OF MOONSTRUCK STONE?" (S. 474). What follows is in part grudging vindication of Yeats's "rage" for charts. As Gabriel dictates the emerging symbol of man, JM archly allows: "In a work this long, / Madness to imagine one could do / Without the apt ideogram or two" (Ibid.).[68] The reference is to Pound, but the focus remains on Yeats. As the first figure appears, JM remarks in terms that still mock, though they also appeal to the force of Yeats's diagrams: "a touch simplistic, but complete. / Plus a surprise resemblance—though in Yeats / The double cone, if I recall, gyrates" (S. 475). While JM smirks, Gabriel patiently takes his cue from this mention of the animating motion of Yeats's double gyres to reveal a similar dynamic at play in his graphic construction: "RUNNING UP" and "RUNNING OUT," "THE TWO MINDS OF MATTER"(Ibid.).

Discussion of this "ENIGMA, OUR 'IT'" (S. 474) soon evokes the long-standing quarrel concerning Yeats's "Condition of Fire." Gabriel himself, whose element is fire, is drawn into the anxiety: "'IT': CHILD'S PLAY? or a deadly game / *Fire fighting itself—fire its own screen— / Fades on a yearning whisper to our Queen:* / 'LEAVE THE DOOR OPEN, MOTHER WE CANNOT SLEEP IN SUCH DARK'" (S. 475). Gabriel's frightened appeal to Nature (Queen Mum) for some light, some way out of this enigma receives no readable response (S. 476) and bespeaks the conflicted inadequacy of Yeatsian fire to serve as its own self-transcending screen. And yet, Merrill also suggests that beneath the undecidable fascination of viewing art and the human condition as child's play or deadly game is a deeper, more compelling response to the Enigma, that of Yeats's prophetic dread. In an interview with C. A. Buckley, Merrill acknowledges that Michael's speech immediately following Gabriel's graphic dictation, with its dread pronouncement "ACCIDENTS HAVE BEGUN," its "FIRST FAINT TWIRLS OF SMOKE," "MONITOR'S BREATH," and its animus against "THE DULLWITTED, THE MOB, THE IDIOT IN POWER, THE PURELY BLANK OF MIND" (S. 476), "seems to be their version" of Yeats's "The Second Coming" ("Exploring" 427-28).

Almost grudgingly, Yeats comes to seem more and more central to aspects of the very process and achievement of Merrill's poem. Michael explains that the higher powers had tried to reach JM through dreams and inspiration but to no avail, and thus turned to "S A N D O V E R" and "2 OLD ZEN MONKS [in a scene revising the last of "Lapis Lazuli" and "Willowware Cup"] (DJ & WBY)":

> RAKING DESIGN AFTER DESIGN, STRUGGLING FOR THE SENSE OF IT
> WHILE THE ABBOT-SCRIBE SQUINTING MADE OUT WAVES, PEAKS,
> DRAGONS, RAINCLOUDS, [and this American mirror-epic] EAVES OF GLASS.
> (S. 478)

It is for his Yeatsian understanding (of a "Grand / Design outspiraling past all detail . . . that history's great worm / Turns and turns as it does because of twin / Forces balanced and alert within / Any least atom") and in direct comparison with Yeats that JM receives Gabriel's praise: "O FATHER, TWIN STAR, BROTHERS, SISTER, HEAR THEM: THEY HAVE MADE SENSE OF IT. / DID NOT OUR DEAR ONE REPORT 'AND WHAT A FISH!' (YOU, GOOD YEATS,. WERE THE ONE THAT GOT AWAY)" (Ibid.). But we notice that each nod to Yeats's importance also carries the sense of an ever-anxious comparison: Yeats and DJ the monks / JM the abbot; JM the landed Piscean prize / Yeats the one that got away.

Yeats's next "appearance," full of uneasy interplay, is prompted by a question ["And Yeats—will he emerge at last?" (S. 480)] that makes it seem as though Yeats has not already spoken—as if JM wanted both to evoke and to repress his presence and the recent unanswered question of whether Yeats was right or wrong. Yeats's exchange with JM is reluctant and self-deprecating: "WELL / IF THERE'S TIME I MIGHT COME OUT WITH A STANZA / Ah, we'd be thrilled. YOU WOULD? I OFTEN FEAR / I LEFT IT ALL BACK IN BYZANTIUM" (S. 481), and JM's manner is unusually formal and stiff.

But Yeats pointedly ignores next JM's question: "From your present viewpoint, Mr Yeats, / Was our instruction of a piece with yours?"—a question asking, much as Yeats did, "were we right?"[69] Instead of answering, Yeats turns much more familiarly to DJ: "DO ME A FAVOR? DJ, LET ME SHAKE / THE OTHER HAND. YOU WERE NEARLY AS GOOD AS A WIFE" (Ibid.)—a remark that immediately opens not only all the questions about how the relationship between JM and DJ compares to that between Yeats and his wife George, but also about the relationship between Merrill and Yeats.

If the gist of Yeats's remark is to say that DJ has served JM "nearly as" well as George served him (perhaps an allusion to the later couple's childlessness or need for other liaisons), one cannot escape the backhanded slight given DJ, but aimed it seems at Merrill. A covert, reluctant impulse toward some kind of self-administered "expiation" or "justice" (both Yeats's terms)[70] rules these lines as Merrill takes Yeats's wife as mirror to his own relationship with David Jackson. Yeats certainly compelled his wife to endure prolonged periods of discomfort and boredom in the service of his communications with the other world. He mined her reams of automatic writing for his own purposes and took the lion's share of credit for what he found there. But so has Merrill. DJ chafes under the Ouija regimen;[71] he is the one who is shown to suffer. Although Merrill wonders "if the trilogy shouldn't have been signed with both our names—or simply "by DJ, as told to JM" ("Interview with McClatchy" 68) [note the priority given to DJ's "experience" here] and although he acknowledges *Sandover* as "*Our* poem, now" ("Clearing the Title"), his is clearly the glory.[72] More remains to be said about this persistent triangulation among Merrill, DJ, and Yeats (where George now disappears behind DJ), but for now it is enough to say that Yeats and DJ both take their place beside JM, but tellingly not quite on his same "plane." We see this most graphically by comparing Yeats's first "appearance" in the poem "FAINTLY IN THE DARK / A *WORDLESS PRESENCE*" to how DJ "Takes his place, *beyond words*, at [JM's] side" just as *Scripts* draws to its ceremonious close (S. 424, 515, emphasis added).

As always, the notable silence that characterizes the presence of DJ and Yeats can be read in at least two ways. The first we notice is that, at key moments which affirm JM's accomplishment, Merrill imposes a wordless supplementarity upon both of the "partners" on whom he most relies: DJ for his necessary "hand" in the workings of the Ouija board and his long domestic relationship with Merrill, and Yeats too for his necessary "hand," that is his writing and its shaping influence.[73] We have seen this pattern before in *The (Diblos) Notebook,* when Orestes (Friar) is both appalled and fascinated "beyond speech" by Arthur Orson's superior sociability and Merrillian "cleverness" (101-02).[74] This enforced speechlessness, together with the Yeatsian color given the Orestes/Friar whipping make the later disparagement and disciplinary suffering of DJ and Yeats in *Sandover* seem significantly part of the same pattern. As Orestes/Orson/Friar blends "brother" and "lover," so in many ways does DJ—albeit in very different terms and admitting very different resentments. The connection between these figures suggests that much of the violence and enforced wordlessness in *Sandover* is part of Merrill's continuing resentment of lover and precursor, and their too-telling influence on his life and writing.

But as much as resentment seems to taint these relations, so too does a sense of an almost reverential regard. To be "beyond words" or a "WORDLESS PRESENCE" is to touch on the "unspeakable," that which surpasses even the fullest range of poetry to express. Andrea Mariani concludes his account of Merrill's use of Dante's language by asserting, "both in Dante and in Merrill, then, the highest achievement of poetry is limited by the inexpressible" (Polylinguism 209). But it is exactly with this limit that both poets conjure with divinity. In these particular instances, it is not that DJ's silent presence or Yeats's much-mined wordlessness is itself an indication of the Absolute; rather, each points to a profound feeling words cannot reach and, in marking this limit, suggests a reality beyond language. In both readings, then, Merrill attains a heightened power: in one because his is the more accomplished and determining voice, and in the other because, by finding ways to "let the silence after each note sing" (S. 84), he succeeds in gathering into his poem intimations of sublime presence.

Yeats's part in "Gabriel's Masque" serves as the culmination of many themes we have been observing: how in his identification with DJ's hand, he too suffers; how he is mocked and belittled; how his language and images are both parodied and appropriated to lend particular notes of grandeur; and how he stands in close association with, although always on the margins of, DJ and JM's "marriage." [As we come to Yeats's stanza, we must imagine that we hear Schwarzkopf singing Anne Truelove's aria, Act I scene iii, from *The Rake's Progress* (S. 484): "Has Love no voice?"] I give the passage in full with only limited underlining as commentary:

> Plato: MOTHER, WHAT USE FOR THAT ONE OF OUR BAND
> MOST PUT UPON, OUR HAND?
> DJ. (Hand poised but trembling from the strain) Who? Me?
> Nature: HA, FROM WITHIN IT DO NOT I
> A CROUCHING ELDER SPY ESPY?
>
> As in *Capriccio* when poor *Monsieur Taupe*
> Emerges from the prompter's box (of course
> In this case DJ's hand) there scrambles up
> Stiffly at first a figure on all fours.
> He straightens as one wild cadenza pours
> Through the rapt house; whips out pince-nez and page.
> A deep, sure lilt so scores and underscores
> The words he proffers, you would think a <u>sage</u>
> <u>Stood among golden tongues, unharmed,</u> at center stage.
>
> WBY. O SHINING AUDIENCE, IF AN OLD MAN'S SPEECH
> STIFF FROM LONG SILENCE CAN NO LONGER STRETCH

>   TO THAT TOP SHELF OF RIGHTFUL BARD'S APPAREL
>   FOR WYSTAN AUDEN & JAMES MEREL
>   WHO HAVE REFASHIONED US BY FASHIONING THIS,
>   MAY THE YOUNG SINGER HEARD ABOVE
>   THE SPINNING GYRES OF HER TRUE LOVE
>   CLOAK THEM IN HEAVEN'S AIRLOOM HARMONIES.
>
> Nat.   NOT RUSTY AFTER ALL, GOOD YEATS.
>   (The record ends.) NOW BACK INSIDE THE GATES
>   OF HAND. BUT FIRST MARK WHAT I SAY:
>   YOU ARE TO TAKE THAT HAND ON 'JUDGMENT DAY'
>   AND PLEAD ITS CASE
>   WITH YOUR OWN ELOQUENCE IN A HIGH PLACE,
>   THAT IT NOT BE DIVIDED FROM
>   OUR SCRIBE IN ANY FUTURE SECULUM.
>   Bowing, Yeats crawls back under DJ's palm.   (S. 486-87)

Perhaps the first thing to notice about Yeats's stanza, later called one of "THOSE TRUE MIRACLES" of the previous day's proceedings (S. 491), is the role Yeats seems to cast for himself. Yeats's speech "stiff from long silence" echoes not only his own "Speech after long silence"("After Long Silence") but also Dante's first description of Virgil "chi per lungo silenzio parea fioco" ("one whose voice seemed weak from long silence" *Inferno*, I. 63)[75]—as if Yeats were casting himself in the role of Virgil to Merrill's Dante—which is exactly the kind of claim Merrill has been at pains throughout the poem to avoid. For all its attitude of praise and blessing, Yeats's stanza is subtly permeated with typically Merrillian ambivalence—an ambivalence that heightens and undermines the authority of both poets (although, as usual, Yeats "suffers" disproportionately). Not only does Yeats's allusion to Virgil seem to finally proclaim Yeats's role as Merrill's principle poetic guide, but Yeats, with his characteristic nonchalance about spelling, makes a "Merel," a mere counter-piece for a board game, out of the younger poet—raising the question of influence again: who toys with whom in this passage? Certainly one suggestion that Yeats's speech allows is that perhaps Merrill too moves by another's hand.

Yet by far the strongest impulse of the passage is one of praise for the younger poet. It is Yeats's praise that noticeably accelerates the approach of Merrill's poetic apotheosis; and whatever heights Yeats's figure achieves in this passage, little survives the comic spectacle of him first "crouching," then "scrambling," and finally "craw[ing] back under DJ's hand." We subsequently learn that, for all its obvious richness in "authentic" Yeatsian imagery and form, Yeats's stanza is not so entirely Yeats's (or perhaps so much a miracle) after all. Once again, after the moment of miracle and revelation comes the requisite deflation. What is new in the following passage is the disconcerting whiff of JM arranging not only his "Own chills and fever, passions and betrayals" ("Matinees"), but his own self-polished praise and blessing, since JM admits "To having been up tinkering since dawn / With Yeats's stanza" (S. 492).

In form, the stanza is a Merrillian adaptation of what Helen Vendler terms "the Yeatsian *ottava rima*," since it inverts the traditional form and concludes with Merrill's signature abba quatrain ("Ottava Rima" 43). Merrill also takes on Yeats's authorial role and identity when he "remakes" Yeats's stanza [as Yeats puts it in an untitled poem: "When ever I remake a song, /. . . It is myself that I remake"][76] and signals this appropriation in the line referring to Auden and "Merel" as those "WHO HAVE REFASHIONED US BY FASHIONING THIS"—the "us" here growing to include not only Yeats, but Auden and Merrill as well. The stanza is further marked as importantly Merrill's by the deft allusion to Anne Truelove's aria ("THE YOUNG SINGER HEARD ABOVE / THE SPINNING GYRES OF HER TRUE LOVE") and the Merrillian pun on "heirloom." "AIRLOOM HARMONIES" points to Merrill's element "air" and finesses the problematic connotations of influence operating as a kind of hereditary property. By such light means, Merrill suggests that instead of entailing the Yeatsian privileges and obligations of a designated heir, heaven's harmonies are as free and accessible (and as difficult to hold) as air or love itself.[77]

Finally, in confessing to his "tinkering," JM allows himself a touch of elliptical innuendo at the expense of the older poet. Yeats's stanza it seems "came through a bit . . . " (S. 492). The ellipsis here covers tactfully for any possible criticism of medium or message Merrill might mean to suggest. Rendered all but completely abject by this gesture, Yeats breaks in: "MR M, I MADE A HASH. YOU'VE MADE IT CLEAR. / THANK YOU" (S. 492). It is not clear how much polite irony, or actual sincerity, governs JM's reply to this remark, but the cloying duplicity of WHA's response taints the whole exchange. Here is JM followed by an unbelievable Yeats: "Oh please, Mr Yeats, you who have always / Been such a force in my life! WYSTAN, U HEAR?" WHA responds:

> MAITRE, I HAVE EVER HEARD
> THE GOLDEN METER IN YOUR WORD
> AND KISS YR HAND (This with the straightest of faces
> As Yeats withdraws into the palm's oasis.) (S. 492)

Amazing animus rules the surface of Merrill's text at this point, so that it is a wonder that Merrill merely has Yeats "withdraw" where in every other way the "CROUCHING ELDER SCRIBE" is made once more to crawl.[78]

Yeats does not speak again in the poem. But neither does he disappear. As a character, he persists as the object of occasional mention. At the level of language, Yeatsian idiom, image, and cadence continue to inform and, now in a very resonant sense, to "authorize" many of Merrill's most powerful effects. Merrill's "double-minded" strategy of disparaging what he also cannot do without governs the last pages of *Scripts* as much as it has the rest of his poem. Notes on Merrill's typescript also show that he was aware of at least part of this process, the part of his continued indebtedness. Just a page before the last brutal encounter with Yeats, Merrill writes the names "Yeats / Pater // Arnold" and the phrase "& passionate as the dawn" in the margin beside this quatrain [with "Mild and gray" as a gentle dampening of Yeats's "cold / And passionate"]:

> —Till silenced, and ourselves brought halfway down
> To Earth, by a couplet mild and gray as dawn:
> ENOUGH UNI. YOU & I
> HERE ALONE IN EMPTY SKY.[79]   (S. 490)

As Robert Polito notes, "Merrill later renders his parody of Yeats's ringing resolutions still more particular and barbed" (*Guide* 260). Polito offers Merrill's Venice as "*Sandover*'s mocking equivalent of Byzantium" (259), citing these lines from *Scripts*'s "Venetian Jottings" as evidence of Merrill's critical, parodic intent: ". . . this drowning, dummy paradise / Whose nude, gnawed Adam and eroded Eve // Cling to their cornice, and September flies, Revolve above the melting tutti-frutti" (S. 502). What Polito's example and discussion fail to show, however, is just how "particular and barbed" Merrill's "burrowing into Yeats's lexicon" has become. Polito argues that Merrill employs his Yeatsianisms "not to launch the performing self but to enact his own vanishing" (259). What he does not see is how much such a passage is part of a larger struggle to effect Yeats's "vanishing," an erasure whose traces always work to reinscribe the troubling priority of the older poet. Polito's commentary also neglects the extent to which Merrill's successes at "vanishing," at self-transcendence (that high Romantic mode) or becoming "sufficiently imbued with otherness" (S. 89), are the necessary preliminaries to moments of staged self-apotheosis throughout the poem, but especially at the end of *Sandover*.[80]

In these "Venetian Jottings" (S. 502-06), Merrill attempts to see human existence as "Maya dancing," and strives to imagine a future out of which he has vanished—all as part of making "one last shot" at authentic prophesy: "dawn, the bare beach. 'Happy Ending?'" (S.506). But beneath this deliberately ambiguous view of humanity's future (do we take hope at the dawn or despair at the bareness?) remains the dogging question of the soul's immortality: what "if a trace remains"? It is the poem's central question, but still too burning to take up directly: "Let that be" the poet cautions himself. Yet for all the evasions and demurrals and however masked in the modesty of parenthesis, what remains in Merrill's "Venetian Jottings" is the confusing, contested, hoped for linkage of "Dance, Gods, Time, Stars" and Merrill's own "(ah, me)" (S. 506).[81]

Maya Deren and Yeats (linked again as in "Ephraim's" section "R") form the positive and negative terms out of which Merrill builds this terza rima interlude. Whereas the deceased Maya Deren both "is here and isn't"—in that her work and her memory are lovingly invoked, Yeats both isn't here and is—in that he is never mentioned yet his poetry and enduring concerns continue to haunt Merrill's text.

Like Maya Deren's, Yeats's "dyings live" in this passage; but they live particularly in the violent transformations Merrill's use of Yeats enacts. Merrill's "Venetian Jottings" takes us behind the scenes of Yeats's "golden smithies," behind the wall of holy fire, into the "glory hole" of artifice. Whereas in the disciplinary vision of Yeats's Byzantine "singing school," souls are gathered and consumed to be transformed "out of nature," Merrill wickedly literalizes this scene of instruction in terms of a fiery, "unnatural" sodomy:

> a blast of heat
> So powerful we've paused: it's the glass-blowing!
> A glory hole roars, pulses. Color of peat
>
> Artisans dip the long rod into glowing
> Pots, fire within fire, grasping conflate
> Ember with embryo   (S. 504)

Parodic "inversions" accumulate, some gentle, others again similarly violent. Thus, where Yeats celebrates the finished "artifice of eternity," Merrill watches "the rose-hot blob translate // Itself to souvenir," and in so doing modulates both artifice and time into more modest keys. Where Yeats propounds a transcendent vision, Merrill portrays a "vision [that] ducks too late and winces, scarred" (S. 505). Where Yeats has his "Marbles of the dancing floor," Merrill focuses on the "Dirt of the ceremonial dance floor." Where Yeats evokes the glory of his golden bird, Merrill uses the apocalyptic threat of Yeats's own "blood-dimmed tide" to ring the pretty singer's neck and offer in its place the sacrificial "headless, blood-slimed bird."

Yet Merrill's parody (if that is the word) is not all inversion. His affinity for elements of Yeats's thought is too strong for total dismissal. Just as Yeats, writing about Byzantium in *A Vision*, imagines that "the painter, the mosaic worker, the worker in gold and silver, the illuminator of sacred book, were almost impersonal, almost perhaps without the consciousness of individual design . . . " (279-80), so Merrill's peat-colored artisans work "by rote foreknowing," a formulation which evokes a similarly idealized kind of impersonality. Although Yeats imagines a process of imaginative transformation cut off from the world of nature (no storm disturbs it, nothing material feeds its fires, nor do its fires "singe a sleeve") and his "golden smithies" may strive to "break the flood" of nature's images, nonetheless the end of "Byzantium" opens itself to just such a flood of "images that yet / Fresh images beget." This is the self-quarreling Yeats that Merrill draws closest to, even as he continues to resist what Polito aptly calls Yeats's "ringing resolutions"—and even as he builds to similarly grand effects. Yeats's ringing concluding lines—

> Marbles of the dancing floor
> Break bitter furies of complexity,
> Those images that yet
> Fresh images beget,
> That dolphin-torn, that gong-tormented sea.

—echo through the middle of Merrill's "Jottings" describing Maya Deren's Haitian film Divine *Horsemen*:

> Action slowed by the soundtrack's
>
> Treacherous crosscurrent, if not swept clean
> Away by particles that so bombard,
> So flay an image to the bone-white screen
>
> That vision ducks too late and winces, scarred.
> It is the flak fired outward from time's core. (S. 504-05)

As we have seen before, what Merrill aims for in many of his encounters with Yeats is a recomplicated, "corrected," view of Yeats's "Condition of Fire." That such "correction" occasionally requires a measure of pain and suffering for Yeats is something Merrill's voices have long sanctioned. What is remarkable throughout this section is the mix of violent parody, milder "correction," and a kind of chiming affinity. If Merrill uses "The Second Coming" to throttle the aestheticism of Yeats's Byzantium, he also turns to "Among School Children" and "Vacillation" IV to affirm the vision of Maya dancing. This vision is partial, Merrill admits: "The frown, the flood of tears, and all the rest / Will have been cut, or never filmed" (S. 505), insisting too on our awareness of the consuming, stripping process of artifice. What remains is nonetheless a Yeatsian miracle of self-transcendence, here rendered for once as more than a passing moment: "Delight / Alone informs her dance, *unself-possessed*" (emphasis added). Maya, translated into film, achieves what Yeats's speaker prays for in "Sailing to Byzantium." She is "received one summer night / . . . Into the troupe, glowworm and lunar crescent, / That whole supreme commedia dell' arte // Which takes a twinkling skull for reminiscent / Theatre, and soul for master negative" (S. 505-06). Merrill's redaction catches so many Yeatsian elements (the being taken up, the glowing company, the lunar and metamorphic images, the governing metaphors of artifice and theater, the force of time past, passing, and to come, the determining notion of a "master narrative" for souls) that it is a further miracle that these "Jottings" avoid pastiche. It is as though quarreling with Yeats, opposing his "Tragedy wrought to its uttermost" with "commedia dell' arte," tempering his effusions with deflations and interruptions, appropriating Yeats's images and concerns and transforming them are exactly Merrill's surest means of achieving his own modest and yet resounding "(ah, me)."

Thus, continuing their productive quarrel, Yeats accompanies Merrill to the very "Finale" of *Scripts*. In a passage added to an earlier manuscript (from "6:00. Stone and words . . . " to DJ "at my side"; S. 514-15), Merrill allows his quarrel with Yeats to slip into a scene introduced by the sustaining, opposing, support of WHA. JM presses down upon the balustrade of Auden's "STONE & WORDS." The vertigo of a simplifying vision possesses him, tempting him ("How simply, too") toward whizzing traffic with the dead and his own "three-story drop." But, dream-like, the scene shifts to "here inside my head," JM (perhaps) behind the wheel of his own poetry, seemingly in control: "But here inside my head / No question of total blackout" (S. 514).

No question that is of "total," Yeatsian "blackout," of "Heaven blazing into the head" ("Lapis Lazuli") or even of the self-consuming conflagration the life's work being done: the self's "bare chimney . . . gone blackout / Because the work had finished in that flare" ("1919" XI). JM's anxious transposition from would-be Empedocles, observing and drawn to the whizzing vortex, to one who would drive homeward and away is precariously, blindingly, yet sustainingly illuminated, by Merrill's precursor poets: "Lights all along / Following closely, filling the rear-view mirror / Forcing upon whichever of us drove / Illumination's blindfold" (S.5-14-15). This drive, like taking dictation from the other world is a shared task, so that now, at the end of this book, when JM feels these following lights (and lights he has followed) "gather[ing] / Speed to pass," he and his partner have to make their way home guided only by "Our own weak dashboard aura, / Our own poor beams." Yet it is not to his partner in the car that JM turns when he says about this "homeward ride," "Still not alone." Rather, it is "that disappearing car"—one of Merrill's precursor poets speeding past—that will "make things round the bend / Shine eerily"— a poet in whose light he has driven and whose after-glow gives back "a tree, an underpass of bone," or "miles from now" will set "a dip between hills" "glow[ing] in recollection" (S. 515). It is not odd to identify the poet "Passing on the road that night" ("Crazy Jane and Jack the Journeyman") with Yeats, whose poetry is filled with such passings, as well as such haunting illuminations of tree, bone, and hill. What is odd is that, for JM, the "recollection" comes just "As DJ / Takes his place," like Yeats "A WORDLESS PRESENCE," "beyond words, at my side" (S. 424, 515). Yeats "is here and isn't." He has gone on ahead and, in his linkage with DJ, stays behind at Merrill's side.

The ritual breaking of the mirror that concludes *Scripts* (S. 516-17) suggests a renunciation, the giving up of a "whole / Lifetime of images," but it also announces a marriage, the "*indestructible union*" alluded to in *Scripts*'s epigraph from *Jean Santeuil*. Maria and WHA are released into their next incarnations, but JM, DJ, and Yeats remain, the latter partially in the characteristic rhymes on "flood" and "blood," "bird-beak shape" and "undestroyed heartscape" that pattern these last verses and partially in the atmosphere of ceremony itself, an atmosphere whose "gaiety" encompasses the bubble-flight of poetry and the stark signals of God B. It is not a customary marriage, this "'wedding trio'" (presumably from *Les Noces*) scored by the composite art of Pergolesi and Stravinsky (S. 516), but it attains to both the beauty and knowing innocence even Yeats could recognize.

IV. Yeats in "The Higher Keys": Fading into Mastery

On the face of things, Merrill's coda, "The Higher Keys," continues Merrill's epic campaign of diminishment against Yeats until the figure of the older poet fades away into a footnote, a mention on a guest list, and brief fits of gossip. In the first ceremony, Merrill dramatically clears his scene: the schoolroom, its little desks and chairs are gone, "gone too, the blackboards with Dantesque / Or Yeatsian systems" that served so prominently at the end of *Scripts* (S. 532).[82] Merrill's gesture, which for the first time almost unequivocally acknowledges Yeats's importance to the ideograms of *Scripts* only allows this acknowledgment in its act of erasure. Yeatsian and Dantesque systems do of course continue to inform the matters of RM's and MM's rebirth and JM's ceremonious colloquy with the divine. [Indeed, JM rises further in his state of grace when he puts in his own words the divine gospel of Dante's Point of Light (S. 555), and although Proust exchanges seats with Dante before JM's reading of the poem, it is so that the novelist, not the poet, can literally take a back seat (S. 557).] No by-play greets Yeats's name on the Guest List (as it does Dante, Pope, and Proust) (S. 546-47). But we do hear now-familiar, Merrillian variations on the themes of Ice and Salt (S. 535), suggested by Merrill's reading of Yeats's "General Introduction for my Work" (*Essays* 522), and (in parenthesis) the old news that JM and Yeats share the distinction of having had their revelatory texts suggested by divine dictation (S. 555).

The Auden-Yeats "exchanges" early in the "Coda" are what best shows Merrill's Yeats anxiety still very much at play. "The Higher Keys" opens on a moving apostrophe to Auden ("O Ariel"), suggested in part by Nature having given WHA that name on the final page of *Scripts* (S. 517). The poem, which uses Auden's trademark apocopaic rhymes, presents Auden as the agent of DJ's and JM's connection with the divine; his (or as the poem archly puts it "hers") is the "golden / Lidded compact" that "beamed DJ's / And JM's profiles into heaven" (S. 523). But this connection, via a kind of reflective signaling, is established through a mirror sense of Yeats's phrase "Heaven blazing" ("Lapis Lazuli").[83] In Yeats's poem heaven blazes "into the head" of the poet. Inspiration is figured downward in an archetypal moment of the "egotistical sublime." Merrill uses Auden/Ariel's compact to invert this movement, it being the reflective object and agency of Auden's language that "beams" the coded information (DJ's and JM's "profiles") upward into heaven. Merrill's image is of a baroque apotheosis seen through a Star Trek lens, intelligence gathered upward, a linguistic "Ascension" leaving the material (and mediumistic) appurtenances of table and cup behind. This Merrillian reversal of direction is no less "elevating" than Yeats's image. Indeed, it is a particularly dramatic case of the workings of Blakean contraries, where the opposite of a truth is also true.[84]

As in the passage that this lyric "answers" in *Scripts* (S. 514-15), what is at stake here is the anxiety of continuing to write in a world illuminated most strongly by the (reflecting) lights of other poets. Where the *Scripts* passage wondered about JM's power to see his way "homeward" by his own "poor" lights, here too, in the opening lyric of "The Higher Keys," the question is one of destinations and of how to achieve them: "Now to what destination does one write?" (S. 523). Where the *Scripts* passage offered the eerie light that lingered with Yeats's passing as a segue to JM's "down to earth" relationship with DJ, expressed as being "beyond words," this opening lyric offers a Dickinsonian "slant" on "birdsong" which owes only slightly more to Yeats than to Keats.[85] "Down to Earth" now, we nonetheless follow the speaker's view upwards "through boughs in sparkling bloom too high to pluck" (Ibid.). This upward seeking gaze remarking at the beauty of flowers beyond its powers to appropriate restates the anxious position of the poet "following closely" in the path of his precursors.[86]

Merrill's concluding couplet gives in miniature what he has learned about writing in this belated, blossom-tented state: "This onionskin in the shower puckered / Will soon be dry enough for words." Tears prompted by the pungent, empty page as well as the page itself "Will soon be dry enough for words." Words follow feeling, but only after a certain dryness has been attained. This is Merrill in his quintessentially lyric mode. The process is Wordsworthian and Richard Sáez provides the defining account of this "personal genre":

> Each poem begins after a physical or emotional crisis has enervated the poet, effecting something like Proust's intensified sensibility after an asthmatic attack. . . . When the focus has narrowed sufficiently to burn through the poet's self-absorption, remaining under the thin gauze of ashes is the poem: a cooling artifice that coalesces and refigures the past. (45)

But the process also recalls Yeats's insistence on not writing "of personal lover or sorrow in free verse, or in any rhythm that left it unchanged" (*Essays* 522). Like Yeats, Merrill finds his dryness, his cooling distance, and transforming salt in the chosen discipline of traditional forms. Like Yeats, and Auden after, Merrill could affirm: "even what I alter must seem traditional" (Ibid.).[87]

The next mention of Yeats also involves an uneasy interplay between Auden and Yeats as well as a displacement of JM's own "footnote anxiety" with regard to Yeats's *A Vision*. Robert Morse explains the "OVEREXPOSURE" of WHA's mocking subservience to Yeats—"MAITRE, I HAVE EVER HEARD / THE GOLDEN METER IN YR WORD, / AND KISS YR HAND"(S. 492)—as "THAT 'BOYISHNESS' / VIS A VIS YEATS THE SOUPCON OF A GLOAT / AT BEING TEXT TO WBY'S FOOTNOTE" (S. 527). WHA's pride this late in the long poem does seem a 'happy' answer to JM's initial fear that he'd be stuck editing and supplying footnotes to "The New Enlarged Edition" of Yeats's *A Vision* (S. 14), and RM's description does indeed give the relative status of WHA's and Yeats's explicit contributions to *Sandover*—WHA's "input" seemingly far and away the more central, with Yeats's meager and belated contributions appearing as mere asides.[88] But, as we have seen, WHA's texts often turn out to gloss more fundamental encounters with Yeats's prior word, and Yeats's presence in the *Sandover*'s text is hardly limited to his explicit "speaking" role.[89] The footnote, as Merrill shows in *The (Diblos) Notebook*—and as we have seen in JM's ongoing "quarrel" with Yeats—often reveals where the "living antagonists" actually contend for the "THINKING MIND" of the poet (*Diblos* 91; S. 527).[90] Besides, as Alice Tolkas reports Gertrude Stein saying (and as DJ remembers), a person is "damn lucky to be a footnote in letters" (Jackson "Conversation" 41). Even the fine speech Merrill gives WHA in *Mirabell* 9 makes an analogous point: "IT WAS THE GREATEST PRIVILEGE TO HAVE HAD / A BARE LOWCEILINGED MAID'S ROOM" in the "ROSEBRICK MANOR" of the mother tongue (S. 262). Given the "crystalline / Reversibility" of *Sandover*'s "toy spyglass" which shows us "Now vastness and impersonality / Brought near, now our own selves reduced to specks" (S. 174), we should not be surprised about this anxious-making *and* productive instability between footnote and text, commentary and original. Throughout *Sandover*, Merrill dramatizes both the anxiety and the exhilaration of poetic production and takes "YEAT'S WEARY PROUD FORBEARING SMILE / AS OF AN UNREAD VISION ON THE SHELF" as both goad and blessing to his project (S. 527).[91]

Yet this image of Yeats as a kind of neglected Buddha, perhaps smiling like one of the Chinamen of "Lapis Lazuli," is not the last glimpse of the older poet Merrill allows himself in *Sandover*. It is perhaps still too demanding, too haunting, bearing as it does the weight of both his knowing smile and the unread evidence of Yeats's proud priority. Commanded by Nature: "NOW POET, READ!" and accompanied by intimations of Wordsworth's "Ode" ("A splendor / Across lawns meets . . . its own eye"), JM prepares to ready his completed poem to the assembled friends and powers.[92] Anticipating some of the responses, he wryly notes: "Should rhyme / Calling to rhyme awaken the odd snore, / No harm done" (S. 559). This is more than a gesture of self-deprecation, since at this point beside "the odd snore" in his typescript Merrill writes, "WBY."

Thus, Merrill's last image of Yeats, as he both finishes the poem and begins to read, is of his old daimon Yeats, finally put to sleep.[93] Does this private, marginal note signify the last hollowing out of Yeats's authority in the poem, or is it a sign that Merrill recognizes how much *Sandover* owes to the older poet—since the poem has so thoroughly "mined" Yeatsian energies that perforce the older poet nods? *Sandover* is, after all, that "long poem based on Yeats's system: spiritualism, the phases of the moon, the gyres of history" that had been "Kimon [Friar's] dream, only [now Merrill] was realizing it in his stead" (*Different* 27). The answer is of course, "both at once." This private moment, which so diminishes Yeats's authority in the poem, simultaneously releases JM into his greatest poetic achievement and a performance that also operates as an apotheosis.

The reading of *Sandover* is a command performance ["SOME / FANS OF YOURS IN HEAVEN, A SMALL CROWD, / HAD HOPED TO HEAR THE POEM READ ALOUD" (S. 540)] before the audience, fit though few, that Merrill cares for most: beloved friends, living and dead, a personal alphabet of influential writers, Austen to Yeats, and two divinities, Nature and Michael/Ephraim, or more simply the self-regarding "M/E" (S. 546-47, 551). As Willard Spiegelman notes: "the last lines of the coda . . . remind us that in Merrill's work the ascent to spiritual revelation is rooted in personal affection, Yeats's foul rag-and-bone-shop, and returns to it at the end" (199). If Merrill returns to personal affection as the source, culmination, and continuing motive of his poetry, this final, private gesture, aimed seemingly so dismissively at

Yeats, also prepares for the material shadow of Merrill's self-elevation, that is the mere self-echoing of JM's voice: "Admittedly . . . I err" (S. 560, 3). Merrill's recycling conclusion, which refuses to conclude, both releases Yeats into his prior stature as precursor poet outside of the poem and entraps him within the poem's own determining gyres. Even with the return to the beginning of *Sandover* and JM's return to his own diminishment and error, Yeats is not freed from Merrill's influence. Merrill has succeeded in uniting the fates of both poets. We must now always read them in their "crystalline reversibility," the one living the death of the other and dying into his daimon's life.

Chapter Four

A HAUNTED MASTERY: YEATS AFTER *SANDOVER*

YEATS DOES NOT FIGURE IN ANY OF THE POEMS FOLLOWING *SANDOVER* THAT draw on dictations from the Ouija board: not "From the Cutting Room Floor," "The Plato Club," or "Nine Lives." Nor is he mentioned or directly quoted in any of the later poems. Nonetheless, evidence of Merrill's continued engagement with Yeats persists. Occasionally Yeatsian echoes surface as little more than rhetorical tags, pieces of wit, or tokens of affinity. Yet at other times (and sometimes within the same poem), we see continuations of Merrill's "inner-quarrel" with Yeats, or with those aspects of himself represented by Yeats that he can neither wholly accept nor reject. The work following *Sandover* further refines Merrill's confident mastery of the Yeatsian idiom even as he more and more subsumes it into his own. What once haunted him has become a cherished inner voice and a resource with which to look back on a life lived and forward, "colder and wiser," into "the grave dissolving into dawn" ("An Upward Look").

In *Late Settings* (1985), "Clearing the Title," strongly continues the double movement of *Sandover* towards Merrill's self-apotheosis within a more "selfless," cosmic perspective. The clown, whom Merrill first presents toward the end of the poem, seems a clear emblem for himself as the author of *Sandover*:

> Cat-limber, white-lipped with a bright cerulean tear
> On each rouged cheek, rides unicycle, hands
> *Nonchalantly juggling firebrands.*   (emphasis added)

This same clown returns in the last lines of the poem transformed into a majestically juggling sky-god and angel of light: "Sky puts on the face of the young clown / As the balloons . . . float higher yet, / Juggled slowly by the changing light." Yeats is here only in Merrill's sense of his own accomplishment and in the "changing light" of his most ambitious poem. As must be clear by now, these are Yeatsian firebrands the clown/poet juggles; and the balloons, reduced or refined to an elemental simplicity ("Mere hueless dots now, stars / Or periods") are the units of substance, light, and language that the poet/sky-god keeps aloft and spinning—so that cosmic juggling hands become Merrill's apt "personification" of Yeats's opposed, yet ontologically constitutive, gyres.

"Bronze" offers hints of Yeats's "Vacillation," "The People," and "A Coat." The ancient statues speak from a vantage "well out of [nature]" ("Nature / Is dead, or soon will be. And we / Are well out of it"), in a rocky voice nonetheless well schooled in the attitudes of Marianne Moore and Rilke. Merrill's childhood bust, like Dorian Gray's portrait, suffers for him: its patina coarsens; it offers no perch for either wisdom or song ("owl or nightingale"). Its eyes "deeply-bored" are also deeply bored in the world-weary sense of the glance Yeats identified with Romans ("the first to drill a round hole to represent the pupil") and "characteristic of a civilization in its final phase" (*Vision* 276). But Yeats is little more than an occasional resource in this poem. Not until "Santorini: Stopping the Leak," the penultimate poem of the collection, does Merrill explicitly gesture toward Yeats's relevance to the entire poem.

In its first stanza's concluding couplet ("—Whereupon, sporting a survivor's grin, / I've come by baby jet to Santorin") Merrill's "Santorini: Stopping the Leak" announces that an awareness of Yeatsian precedent will at least be part of the wit of the poem. As the poem progresses, subtle allusions to Yeats accumulate, and the poem's ottava rima form, which at first shares more affinities with Byron, gathers Yeatsian depths of tone and subject matter.[1] Indeed, as Stephen Yenser has noted: "Though [the poem] weaves in as well the various lights of Marvell and Blake, it takes its fire from Yeats" (*Myth* 326). But unlike earlier poems that evoke a Yeatsian "presence," "Santorini" betrays little anxiety in its echoes or departures. The Yeatsian notes struck here and there have become one more voice in the polyphony of Merrillian meditation.

"Santorini" follows its own gyring "Golden Climb" to austerities of vision balanced by interludes of wry interiority and social grace. Here, elegance attends on violence with Yeatsian aplomb; momentary vision strikes like sudden and terrible lightning—at a table over drinks: "Out of the blue the loss, / Young, of her twin brother flickers, searing / Us both for an instant; . . . Dear soul." —and we are reminded of the lightenings of *Per Amica Silentia Lunae* (340) that Merrill transports into sections R and V in the "Book of Ephraim." Merrill grouses, like Yeats, at the depredations of modernity ("Taverns torn down for banks, the personnel / Grown fat and mulish"); and, as Yeats's poems depend on his returning to the "rag and bone shop of the heart," Merrill's poems too grow out of the body—in this case Merrill's wart-afflicted foot, as well as the body of Gaia, the earth's "sun-thrilled body," sent spinning by the fictions of Apollo's "great Lyre." "Santorini" weaves its dialogues of self and "sole" (Merrill's pun) on the Yeatsian question of how the powers of art, language, and the senses may suffice in the face of the "grave dance" of history and indi-

A Haunted Mastery: Yeats after Sandover

vidual mortality: "as if catastrophe / Could long be lulled by slim waists and shy faces."

Yet even within Merrill's considerable ease with his Yeatsian "fire," we still sense moments of contention. Where Yeats's speaker in "Sailing to Byzantium" abandons a country of "sensual music" in order to attain "Monuments of unageing intellect," the speaker in "Santorini" champions the sufficiency of the *artifice* of the senses to "hold steady" against the "nothingness / Threatening forever to unmake / The living form it sees through." Here Merrill makes the "anti-Yeatsian" point that the senses are the basis of all artifice and that there is no clear or easy separation between the sensual and the artificial as Yeats sometimes implies. Merrill prepares his palette with the colors of experience: "White, silver, black, night purple, dab of lake." His "brushes" are his senses, "[t]hese five of mine," "these suffice" to stave off (for a time) the constant threat of uncreation. Merrill also insists on exposing the anxiety covered over by Yeats's trope of the climactic question. Instead of "Did she put on his knowledge . . . ?" or "How can we know the dancer from the dance?" Merrill gives us: "No lasting cure? No foothold on the void?"

> [Are] Our lives unreal
> Except as jeweled self-windings, a deathwatch
> Of heartless rhetoric I punctuate,
> Spitting the damson pit onto the plate?

In that "deathwatch" of "jeweled self-windings" Merrill's questioning probes the sinister mechanism of Yeats's miraculous, clockworks bird (what could such a device sing but "heartless rhetoric"?) and underscores the solipsism behind Yeats's notion of the soul's "radical innocence," which is famously "self-delighting, / Self-appeasing, self-affrighting" ("A Prayer for my Daughter").

In two stanzas of enormous power, Merrill once again interrogates the terms of "Sailing to Byzantium" and the powers of language, art, and flesh to withstand the volcanic force of "long-pent-up emotions" and cataclysmic event:

> Innermost chaos understood at first
> As Gaia's long pent-up emotions crippling
> Her sun-thrilled body, spun to the great Lyre;
> Pent up, but all too soon unleashed—outburst
> Savage enough to bury in its fire
> The pendant charms she wore, palace and stripling,
> A molten afterbirth transmuting these
> Till Oedipus became Empedocles—
>
> Leaper headlong into that primal scene
> And deafening tirade. The mother tongue
> At which his blood boiled, his brain kindled. Ash
> Of afterthought where once the sage had been,
> Louse in a log . . . Or else, supposing flesh

> Withstood temptation, could a soul that clung
> To its own fusing senses crawl as last
> Away unshriveled by the holocaust?

In this depiction of Santorini's fabled volcano, Merrill at once literalizes and extends the metaphor of Yeats's "holy fire." The "great Lyre" [liar] art is powerless to preserve either monument or man. The promise of Yeatsian transfiguration, based on traditions of male, Zeus-like, intellectual birth, pales before the image of Gaia's "molten afterbirth." The Yeatsian grandeur of Empedocles' legendary plunge, his questing after knowledge and transcendence, takes on Oedipal coloring so that any claims of esoteric sublimity must first and last face the universal inane of this "primal scene" and tirade of earth's "mother tongue." The pretensions of Yeats's sage could not be dispensed with more dismissively than in "Ash / Of afterthought where once the sage had been, / Louse in a log"), but Merrill also attempts to make sense, in his terms, of Yeats's image: how can a living soul outlast the furnace, the "holocaust," of its sensual living? What temptations must be withstood for the "agony of flame" not to "singe a sleeve"? The next stanza offers no direct answer, fleeing from the question of a soul's annihilation, but instead offers the comfort of a possible physical analogy: millennia later, after the curtain of volcanic destruction has rained down "on a universal hiss," life returns, "Vineyards wax," and a "plume of smoke with airier emphasis" (looking for all the world like a quill pen in its ink stand) "Slant[s] from the inky crater." The emblem of writing no sooner arises but "Paperbacks / About Atlantis map the looking glass / Rim of that old disaster." The physical analogy affirms restoration, but through transformation and loss. In Merrill's view, it is not, simply, that "all things fall and are built again." Literate culture (the soul) may return, but who can measure the amount of transformation and loss between Atlantis and our paperback treatments of legend and archeology? (And who can say whether an embodied soul returns "unshriveled" by its holocaust?)

We also note that whether in parody or in earnest, Merrill's speaker in this poem strives to adopt something of the attitude of Yeats's ancient Chinamen. Looking out over scenes of legendary, historic, and personal devastation and kinds of renewal that nonetheless betoken loss—"on all the tragic scene" that is—the speaker practices the "gaiety" of nonattachment.[2] "We must be light, light-footed, light of soul, / Quick to let go," we are told, "The good word's goodbye" and "leave the bulk behind," sounding not unlike Yeats's "great lord of Chou," who cried: "Let all things pass away" ("Vacillation"). Yet Merrill's speaker is not "out of nature," not a carven image or voice from legendary history. His is a gaiety no sooner found (or at least enunciated) than lost.

In one remarkable passage, Merrill also seems to complete a missing component within the poetry of Yeats's vision system. Where in "Vacillation IV" and the final stanzas of "Byzantium," Yeats celebrates a visionary moment of transcendence and exaltation, here Merrill uses much the same language as Yeats's two poems to recount a visionary confrontation with his daimonic Opposite:

A Haunted Mastery: Yeats after Sandover

> Aching for sleep. There comes to me instead
> —Brilliantly awake but cased in lead—
>
> A cinéma-mensonge. Long, flowing fits
> Of seeing—whose? Utterly not my own:
> Bayonet fixed, on olive-skinned Iraqi
> . . .
> In depth a double, phantom yet complete
> With skills and jokes, cradle to winding-sheet;
>
> His moonbaked slum, muezzin cry and tank
> Rumble, the day Grandfather plucked the goose,
> The sore in bloom on a pistachio-eyed
> Tea-shop girl above the riverbank
> —Vignettes as through a jeweler's loupe descried,
> Swifter now, churning down the optic sluice,
> Faces young, old, to rend the maître d's
> Red cord, all random, ravenous images
>
> Avid for inwardness, and none but driven
> To gain, like the triumphant sperm, a table
> Set for one—wineglass, napkin, and rosebud?
> Or failing that, surrender to blue heaven
> Its droplet of pure ego, salt as blood?
> The warm spate bears me on, helpless, unable
> Either to sink or swim . . .

Here indeed is Merrill's opposing double: "Avid for inwardness," where Merrill has portrayed himself as wanting nothing more than to be "sufficiently / Imbued with otherness" (S. 89). But the passage offers something more. It brings the incarnate, historically embedded double into the churning phantasmagoria of this life, rather than the after-life. Merrill's "avid" Iraqi is not just his opposite; he is also the gyring complement to Yeats's dead friend, whose journey into the after-life is depicted in "Byzantium."[3] If Yeats had written a portrait of his relation to his nemesis, Major John McBride, in the manner of "Byzantium," this passage would be its echo.

Instead, the passage fills a gap in Yeats's visionary poetry and, as such, represents a particularly heightened form of Bloom's Tessera, the microcosm of this unbidden vision representing the macrocosm of all that the subject is not, the vision of the other enforcing a masochistic passivity against the subject's own self (*Map* 98). Merrill's "ravenous images" provides the Yeatsian counterpart to the proliferating images at the end of "Byzantium" ("images that yet / Fresh images beget"). Merrill's blood and semen, "pure ego" and "table / Set for one," answer Yeats's "mire and blood," his plurality of spirits and ceremonial of the "dancing floor." What Merrill shows us, in a visionary moment of "Psychic incontinence," is that this life is as much an overpowering suspension between triumph and surrender, sinking and swimming, as any Yeatsian journey into and through the purgation of the after-life, carried "Astraddle on the dolphin's mire and blood." But further, this "completing" vision enables Merrill to locate "whence / My trouble springs": it is "a ghost-leak in the footsole." Here, the mock grandeur Merrill employs in naming his plantar's wart also points to the power of his ghostly father to infuse the soul of each poetic foot. What is at stake is the contest between two "drained" selves (one "ghostly," one "Behind a twitching human curtain"). If Yeats figures here behind this "ghost-leak," his diminishment is only in proportion to Merrill's own. This Bloomian Kenosis ("humbling or emptying-out") prepares the answering "Symbiosis with the molten genie" and the ascent to "once more attain the double // Site of our last excursion"— figures that charge the poem with abrupt shifts of perspective: up and down, single and double, early and late.

Throughout the poem, "Santorini" operates as a vacillation between extremes of perspective: touristic and social, introspective, geological and historical, visionary, and associative, occasionally bringing this vacillating movement to the level of the line: "*My* drained self doesn't yet . . . yet does! / From some remotest galaxy in the veins / . . . Alive and ticking, that I'd thought destroyed." In its final movements, the poem depicts the hollowing out of prophetic and spiritual tradition in a manner that neatly parodies Yeats's high regard for the spiritual achievements of Byzantium:

> . . . this nocturnal
> Limbo of straw children, scarecrow sleeves
> Lifting their Book of Life mute with neglect,
> While overhead a flickering in fetters
> Descended on the office of the dead letters.

Once this moment of undermining Yeats's metaphors (in Bloom's terms, once this Substitution operating between the ratios of Askesis and Apophrades)[4] is put behind, the poem concludes with a final swing between (and within) the constitutive antimonies of sun and shade. The Sun is Merrill's paramount symbol for the absolute or "naked current" that sustains and attracts both life and intelligence, while also requiring insulation (S. 84). Here "Our Friend" both gives and receives "the bare, thyme-tousled world we'd stumbled on" and startles with the devastating power conveyed by a mere "split-second glance." Shade, in turn, becomes cognate for the shadow-self, "Our 'worst' in part lived through, part imminent."[5] And since "shade" evokes both ghost or spirit and relative dark, it allows Merrill to play interior against exterior, spiritual against physical, and emphasize by the force of a pun the travails of soul-making in his last three lines:

> Our "worst" in part lived through, part imminent,
> We made on sore feet, and by then *were* made,
> For a black beach, a tavern in the shade.

Like "Santorini: Stopping the Leak," the Yeats-inflected work in Merrill's subsequent volumes shows him now fully in command of his Yeatsian patrimony. In *The Inner Room*'s "Monday Morning," Merrill lightly rings his changes on the ground of Yeats's "Byzantium" ("I see, by all that's holy . . . / Less bird, after all, than mensch / 'Free as a bird'—its ghost // Face cocked."). The poem nonetheless concludes on a grander Yeatsian note (though its grandeur is kept well in check) announcing the risks and object of his poetic vocation: "I keep risking collision / . . . To fix that unseraphic / Duo within my vision," where the "duo" here refers not to Yeats's "reality and justice," but the more Merrillian "all that's holy" and "one instant hedonist." More substantially, "A Room at the Heart of Things" draws on Yeats in both its details and theatrical context. A series of seven "sonnets" each comprised of seven rhymed couplets, the poem addresses Merrill's actor-friend and lover, Peter Hooten, at one point declaring, "'Light of my life, I've made a play for you!'"[6]

The second and third sonnets allude to Yeats's theory of the Mask, that role which "calls upon self and the eclipse thereof // By second nature," and the saving "weakness" of a life lived theatrically. "Active virtue," Yeats affirms, "is therefore theatrical, consciously dramatic, the wearing of a mask" (*Per Amica* 334). Similarly (though also with characteristic irony) the speaker here asserts:

> Life gave the palm—much the way God once did—
> For "living biographically" amid
>
> Famines, uprisings, blood baths, hand to heart,
> Saved by a weakness for performance art.

The fourth sonnet amplifies the poem's fond satire on things theatrical even as it builds to concluding lines that make no sense without knowledge of Yeats's "Phase Fifteen": "And Gravity's mask floats—at Phase XV / Oblivion-bright—above the stolen scene." Phase Fifteen, represented by the "oblivion-bright" full of the moon, is the inhuman apogee of Yeats's symbology; here "contemplation and desire, united into one, inhabit a world where every beloved image has bodily form, and every bodily form is loved. . . . Chance and Choice have become interchangeable without losing their identity" (*Vision* 136). Gravity and tragedy, the lots of human kind, are suspended. This may be the highest promise of art. It is an "artifice of eternity," a transfiguring gaiety. But, here in this world, Merrill insists, it is also always a momentary and ramshackle affair, its "ivory towers" improvised from wooden steps and "one slapdash coat of white," this "whitewash keep[ing] faith with tenements of dew."

Yeats also highlights the impermanence of human artifacts, but he celebrates the enduring vision that builds them again ("All things fall and are built again / And those that build them again are gay."). Merrill, more darkly, acknowledges such rebuilding as theft. The best scenes are always "stolen." But stolen in at least two senses: one, in that the artist is always indebted to others for his material (as Merrill signals here his debt to Yeats) and, two, in that, to succeed thoroughly, an artist must so command or so transform what is given (or taken) that the scene becomes unmistakably his (as has been Merrill's quest throughout the mature poetry). Merrill's art is always in both these senses Promethean as well as Mercurial (since Mercury is god of thieves); his originality always springs from a willingness to "risk collisions" while "nonchalantly juggling [others'] firebrands."

The fifth sonnet of "A Room" risks just such a considerable collision. Here Yeatsian "gaiety" all but touches the simultaneously sacred and profane arcanum of gay sex. With a "touch that wrestles tact," Merrill appropriates the risks of "Crazy Jane Talks with the Bishop," mixing "bodily lowliness" with "heart's pride," moral instruction with a leering and self-serving glance. Here "the celebrant attains // A chamber where arcane translucences / Of god-as-mortal bring him to his knees"— these are all but hackneyed, stolen words, risking the cliché of sexual religiosity, which the speaker marks by commenting, "Words, words." Yet, having nothing but words, the poet presses on, juggling the same vacillating registers of high and low. In "Vacillation," the speaker's body famously "blazed"; here we are offered "'set alight,'" but in a context that silently shouts the etymology of "faggot" ("to be 'tarred' and 'set alight' crosswise by 'Nero's guard'"). This in-rush of history gives sudden weight to what had threatened to be mere "words." All these words now, "and others," preside in the crossing from a "complex / Clairvoyance" (the most it would seem that we could ask of poetry or any human speech) to "some ultimate blind x" (which is at once the speechless site of "raw luster" and the site of visionary blindness beyond speech)—in both senses then the poem transports us beyond our customary, "human guise." Having led in a sense beyond words (toward both anima and animal), the sonnet concludes, like "Lapis Lazuli," by focusing on the characters' eyes. Taken by sex and the god-as-mortal, enacting a scene as momentary and enduring as any in art, one gaze gyres inward and down, the other outward and up: "The lover shuts, the actor lifts his eyes."[7]

The sixth and seventh sonnets round out Merrill's appropriative transformation of Yeatsian imagery. Merrill takes up the "twenty-six / Millennia" of Yeats's Great Year from *A Vision*,[8] comments, as does Yeats, on the "Earth-shaking figures, Christ or Emperor" [see especially "The Great Year of the Ancients" and "Dove or Swan," e.g. "Caesar and Christ always stand face to face in our imagination" (*Vision* 244)], and builds to intimations of Yeats's gyres, especially within the apocalyptic context of "The Second Coming": "Stylite and columnist / Foretell the early kindling of that nest // —Whence this rustle, this expectant stir?" [Merrill's "rough beast" being the self-immolating, self-resurrecting Phoenix]. For a moment Merrill "domesticates" the Yeatsian image, making a "theater-in-the-round's / Revolving choirs and footlit stamping grounds" out of Yeats's gyres. But then we are more fully released into the anarchic, "widening gyre" of Yeats's poem ("Only far out, where the circumference / Grazed the void, does act approach nonsense // And sense itself . . . / Matter not a speck."). In the last lines, Merrill seems to bring us back from this dizzying edge to a more properly domestic scene, the "You" and "I" "made room for." But before

A Haunted Mastery: Yeats after Sandover

we can settle into this chamber-theater with its "swordplay or soliloquy or kiss," the poem transforms both its characters into the simplest of constellations and places them "in the bright way of stars."

Although similarly rapid movements from the domestic to the sidereal famously shape the conclusions of "When You are Old" and "Adam's Curse," Merrill's final line owes more to his reading of Dante's *Paradiso* (modulated through "stars of stage and screen") than to Yeats. In a poem so dense with Yeatsian allusion, to end with Dante suggests what Harold Bloom might call a "daemonizing" turn, one in which Merrill concludes his poem by calling forth the power of a precursor prior to Yeats. By coming to Dante through Yeats, Merrill places the Yeatsian sublime within the context of a larger tradition, thus not only "generaliz[ing] away the uniqueness of [Yeats's] work," but affirming his connection to the sublime vision of the earlier poet (Bloom *Anxiety* 15). That the whole poem handles its many allusions to Yeats and finally to Dante in a lightly ironic manner, playing with the presence of and distance from the precursors alluded to, marks it as a characteristically blended form. Merrill delights in pulling an answering or counter-sublime out of a pervading irony. This movement and tone is his signature "YES & NO" and, as such, a hypertrophied descendent of Yeats's own evasions.[9]

"Losing the Marbles," which opens with the ironies of "A Room at the Heart of Things," leads to a dramatic Yeatsian influx at its very center. The poem addresses the depredations of time and chance, failures of body and mind, "decrepitude / in any form." But it also mimes acts of restoration, recovery, and imaginative renewal—the "long work of knowing and hard play of wit." It is a poem that contemplates art as that which might in some sense endure when everything passes; a poem that links serendipities of weather and friendship, particulars of personal and historical event, flashes of political critique with flights of wit and reverie; a poem that moves from the mundane "Morning spent looking for my calendar" to achieve in the "Here and now . . . a kind of heaven," beneath "cloudy brilliances above." In each of these qualities and in the poem's masterful structural diversity, "Losing the Marbles" is extravagantly Yeatsian, but with a lightness of manner particular to Merrill. Unlike other poems that show Yeats's imprint in details of diction, cadence, and theme, which stand out as rhetorical touchstones or objects of contention, "Losing the Marbles" shows Merrill's Yeatsian debts and arguments more fully mastered, the Yeatsian voice more fully integrated into Merrill's own most characteristic polyphony.

In Harold Bloom's terms, the poem opens with a Clinamen by playing ironically upon Yeatsian themes of "rage," "heaven blazing" (rendered here as "These dreamy blinkings-out"), and the justice of purgation between lives, or "*Out* of time." But only at the very middle of the poem (section 4) does a Yeatsian voice come into notable prominence. Where the structure of the poem as a whole may recall "Meditations in Time of Civil War," "Nineteen Hundred and Nineteen," or "Vacillation," this passage from section "4" wakens associations with "Lapis Lazuli," "The Statues," and "Byzantium":

>   Does the will-
> To-structural-elaboration still
> Flute up, from shifting dregs of would-be rock,
> Glints of a future colonnade and frieze?
> Do higher brows unknit within the block,
> And eyes whose Phidias and Pericles
> Are eons hence make out through crystal skeins
> Wind-loosened tresses and the twitch of reins?
> Ah, not for long will marble school the blood
> Against the warbling sirens of the flood.
> All stone once dressed asks to be worn. The foam-
> Pale seaside temple, like a palindrome,
> Had quietly laid its plans for stealing back.
> What are the Seven Wonders now? A pile
> Of wave-washed pebbles. Topless women smile,
> Picking the smoothest, rose-flawed white or black,
> Which taste of sunlight on moon-rusted swords,
> To use as men upon their checkerboards.

This is not bald ventriloquism. Merrill, fully as much as Yeats, is brilliantly apparent throughout (although one may particularly delight in the "counter-spin" Merrill gives to Yeats's guileless, idealized women at the end, and to Sato's "changeless" blade). The passage operates largely in the way Merrill describes seeing the features of his father looking back at him in the mirror: "a face not longer / sought in dreams but worn as my own . . . the rival two beam / forth in one likeness" ("Arabian Night")—a stunning image for what Harold Bloom would term Apophrades, or the Return of the Dead. It is in this section more than any other that we hear the "return of lost voices and almost abandoned meanings" (*Map* 97). [10]

The poem concludes in what Bloom would term a Daemonization, appealing beyond Yeats to a Buddhist counter-sublime, the sea of jewels that is Buddha Mind, "a kind of heaven / To sit in."[11] Thus, although Yeats takes his place at the center of the poem, he is not allowed to dominate. Merrill's urbane persona persists throughout. The interrogating cadences of Job's voice from the whirl-wind intervene in section "6" ("Who gazed into the wrack . . . ?" "Who was the friend, the steward / Who bent his head . . . ?"), as well as the voices of gossip and fable, so that, at the end of the poem, Yeats has become one of the many "risen, cloudy brilliances above" which the poem suggests we may remain "largely mindless of" given their "Here and now" reflections in the present poem.

As we have seen, Yeats also figures in many of these same ways in *A Different Person*, Merrill's 1993 memoir. As well as recalling how Yeats served as an important model for his early verse (15) and how his Sandover project represents the fulfillment of Kimon Friar's Yeats-inspired plans (27), Merrill uses Yeats and Yeatsian references as convenient figures for the transcendent claims of his art. The authority of

Yeats's Byzantium poems is sometimes accepted as sovereign and sometimes gently mocked, and sometimes, arguably, both at once, as befits Merrill's determination to remain of two minds on this matter.[12] By the time Merrill writes this memoir, Yeats has come to serve as a largely domesticated yet still mysteriously sovereign, household god, not unlike those figures that the Santero fashions and refurbishes in "The Image Maker."[13] Like the *santos* in that play, Yeats has become one of those potent effigies that the poet must periodically "Repair, freshen, efface / So that unswerving grace" may continue to flow through him and bless Merrill's always more than Yeatsian enterprises.[14]

"Repair, freshen, efface," these three words might well serve as Merrill's motto for how to deal with the older poet. "Repair" points to all the ways Merrill has striven to "correct" Yeats, to complicate Yeatsian "simplicity," to modulate Yeatsian "intensity," and to extend the range of voices heard so that the Yeatsian injunction to dramatize the play of ideas and "moods" might be better served. "Freshen" recalls Heinrich Zimmer's injunction that "The powers have to be consulted again directly—again, and again. Our primary task is to learn, not so much what they are said to have said, as how to approach them, evoke fresh speech from them, and understand that speech" (Qtd. in S. 62). Yeats has been such a power for Merrill, someone he has consulted again and again, and, through the force of Merrill's "repairs," Yeats continues, brought to fresh speech "again and again," in the younger poet's work. Finally, "Efface" bravely acknowledges the strategies of parody, distortion, erasure, trivialization, and masking that Merrill has employed as a sometimes gentle, sometimes violent form of discipline against the influence of the older poet. It seems certain that, for Merrill, without such "effacement" of what amounts to another self, no "fresh speech" would be possible—just as it has always been Merrill's privilege and practice to buy his freedom as a writer through self-disciplines displaced onto others or other selves. Yeats "effaced" is part of what allows Merrill his formal fluency. Yeats "effaced" is part of what impels his Santero's prayer, "Lord, make us unlearn / The skills that wound us, blind and burn" ("The Image Maker").

Again and again Merrill protests against the wounding, blinding, burning demands of art and life—even as he employs the same skills, even as he suffers and evades and sees and gives others to suffer and evade these same injuries. Yeats is Merrill's internal "voice of the father." He calls to the painful necessity of "love and loss." He is also something of the child's voice of protest and denial, of wish fulfillment, magic, and wonder. Neither voice is ever long silent or ever quite holds the upper hand. A mediating, adolescent skepticism and impatience, the need for distance and for the clear artifice of a stance of one's own, weighs in as well in Merrill's work, a voice that finds little use for either of the Yeats-inflected voices, child or man, except in the overt pleasure in being able to "wear" either style (as style) and a covert longing to inhabit both at once without either the pain of Yes or the pain of No. The drama and the wit of Merrill's achievement is not merely that all these voices are "his," or that he finds so many ways to let them sound coherently and almost at once, but that he gives these contraries such scope and *thus* retains his own most characteristic voice and manner.

In *A Scattering of Salts*, Merrill's 1995 posthumous collection, the Yeatsian voice is largely subsumed into the urbane polyphony of Merrill's disease-haunted, valedictory poetry. Yet something of Yeats's ambivalence toward stone marks the self-critical meditations on his life that Merrill presents through the rocky conceits of "Alabaster," "The Pyroxenes," and the conclusion of "Rescue" in which

> childlike I called for help. Was heard—
> only then turning to instinctive stone.
> Shame upon me: I had shut myself to
> life even as it uplifted
> and heaved me into a green haven.

"Home Fires" continues Merrill's project of self-appraisal by reprising each prior, Yeats-inflected meditation on Merrill's own Condition of Fire. We hear the vacillating "give-and-take" of Merrill's "Fire Poem," see the sage in his "roaring garret," the cold heaven and "shy" destructiveness of flame. "Life's brave disguise— / Rages and fevers, worn to tantalize—, " shows the self-conscious theatricality of the heart (which is not quite Yeats's "rag and bone shop" and more the coat of Merrill's previous poetry). In the confluence of civil unrest and mediumistic intelligence ("The riot had been 'foretold' . . . by glass ruby at / The medium's throat."), in the choice of the Yeatsian speaker, Empedocles—Yeats is everywhere and nowhere in the poem. The Yeatsian presence flickers largely through the medium of Merrill's previous poems, having been so thoroughly introjected that it is now Yeats who stands in Merrill's holy, home[ly] fire, needing the "mortal stuff" of Merrill's verse for warmth and embodiment.

Taken together with "Home Fires," "Self Portrait in Tyvek (TM) Windbreaker" gives us Merrill's valedictory "The Circus Animals' Desertion." Together the poems reflect on his career, reveal a speaker meditating on his own failings and those of his times, and recall powers left behind. In "Self-Portrait" these powers are sometimes implicitly Yeatsian ["I should confess before the last coat dries— / The wry recall of thunder does for rage"], sometimes more clearly Merrill's own ["From love to grief to gaiety his art / Modulates effortlessly, like a young man's heart"], sometimes both mixed:

> Styles betray
> Some guilty knowledge. What to dress ours in—
> A seer's blind gaze, an infant's tender skin?
> All that's been seen through.

Like Yeats, Merrill dreams of returning to where "all the ladders start"; he continues to seek out "the eloquence to come," hoping to "restage" "childhood's inexhaustible . . . jewel-bright lives . . . under our new skies' / Irradiated lucite." But the times are

A Haunted Mastery: Yeats after Sandover   167

unpropitious, time is running out, and "~~more than time was needed~~" to recreate the "breathing spaces" of Merrill's art and life.

The last stanza in "Self-Portrait" shows the poem (and the poet) in Yeats's "rag and bone shop," the workshop of the heart and poetic composition. [Again, Merrill dramatizes in his text what Yeats merely declares.] Its gaps speak eloquently of a mind and body riven by collapsing stars, black holes that yield no light, black stars [or viruses] that must continuously be struggled with in order to achieve the chastened, "brilliantly recurring" hope: "To keep the blue wave [of life and artifice] dancing in its prison" [whether it be body or stanza]:

> Love, grief etc. **** for good reason.
> Now only ******* STOP signs.
> Meanwhile***** if you or I've ex-
> ceeded our [?] ***~~more than time~~ was needed
> To fix a text airless and ** as Tyvek
> With breathing spaces and between the lines
> Days brilliantly recurring, as once *we* did,
> To keep the blue wave dancing in its prison.

Thus, Merrill concludes the poem by marshaling rage, resignation, and a witty bravery ["AH MY DEARS / I AM NOT LAUGHING I WILL SIMPLY NOT SHED TEARS" (S. 17)] and, in so doing, demonstrates a poetic heroism Yeats would recognize, compounded as it is of his loss of a "debonair" world to both disappointment and defeat.[15]

In "Vol. XLIV, No. 3," we hear again a barely contained bitterness, to which Yeats's "The Second Coming" contributes a decidedly apocalyptic stance:[16]

> Room set at infrared,
> Mind at ultraviolet,
> Organisms every stranger,
> Hallucinated on the slide, fluoresce:
>
> Chains of gold tinsel, baubles of green fire
> For the arterial branches—
> Here at Microcomiscs Illustrated, why,
> Christmas goes on all year!
>   . . .
> Dread? It crows for joy in the manger.
> Joy? The tree sparkles on which it will die.

Both poems rely on ironic allusion to the Christmas story for their sardonic force. But where Yeats's poem looks forward with expectant dread to the beast whose birth announces a new antithetical age, Merrill's poem sees "Invasion by barbaric viruses" as the death of joy. Where Yeats's "rough beast" is another sphinx, a figure of pitiless wisdom, with which Yeats identifies, Merrill's "beast" points to HIV infection, an unequivocal enemy within.[17] If a Nietzschean Schadenfreude animates Yeats's pronouncement that "the best lack all conviction and the worst are full of passionate intensity," Merrill shudders in stark contrast as he recounts how "Defenseless, the patrician cells await / Invasion by barbaric viruses, / Another sack of Rome. / A new age. Everything we dread."

The blithe assumptions behind Merrill's "patrician cells" may remind one of Yeats's similarly problematic regard for aristocracy and cries against the infection of mass, urban culture; but between these two poems, Merrill's clearly reveals the more immediately embattled speaker. As always, Yeats's grandly prophetic poem commands the rhetorical high ground of authoritative public pronouncement; whereas, Merrill's poem at once enlists and deflects this authoritative tone in order to better represent the ambivalent complexity of giving public voice to "the life lived . . . the love spent" ("An Urban Convalescence"). "Vol. XLIV, No. 3" concludes by mocking the blindness of those who, like Yeats, would celebrate the second coming of barbarism as "a new age." While the impending barbaric dispensation "crows for joy in the manger"—more sex, more indiscriminate rolls in the hay—Merrill warns that the "tree sparkles on which [such joy] will die." What looks like Christmas ("Here at *Microcosmics Illustrated*, why, / Christmas goes on all year!") is more like Calvary, where the branching tree-image announces the virus's traces and effects, seen in the fluoroscope as "chains of gold tinsel, baubles of green fire / For the arterial branches."[18]

In this poem, Merrill powerfully rewrites the apocalyptic terms of Yeats's "The Second Coming," not so much in an effort to "correct" or argue with Yeats (that need is long past), but rather, in a sense, to allow Yeats to respond in his own terms to the new dispensation of HIV infection and AIDS. In Bloomian terms, Merrill, in this final phase, "holds his poem open" to the influence of the precursor so that, particularly in the last six lines ("Defenseless, the patrician cells await . . . "), we have the uncanny effect not merely of Yeats in a sense "underwriting" Merrill's poem but of "Vol. XLIV" reaching back to make us read Yeats's poem with AIDS in mind.[19]

By the time we reach "An Upward Look," the final poem in this, Merrill's final volume, Yeats's words, as Auden says, "are modified in the guts of the living," but they nonetheless persist—in Merrill's alchemical "salt," in the "bright alternation" and "halves of a clue," each a counterpart of Yeats's "vacillation," and the grave "dawn," as well as "gallant," "blind," and "lover." What is more importantly reminiscent is the bitterness, almost the rage, that suffuses the defeated lover returning one last time to the world and finding "the world turning // toys triumphs toxins into / this vast facility the living come / dearest to die in." In such lines Merrill matches Yeats's own dying bitterness, a bitterness, as Bloom remarks of Yeats "that possesses aesthetic dignity" (Yeats 457). What is also Yeats's in this poem is the otherworldly, inhuman, yet coldly reassuring distance from which he surveys the ultimate, "recrystalizing" fate of "each and every // mortal creature."[20]

A Haunted Mastery: Yeats after Sandover

> In bright alternation minutely mirrored
> within the thinking of each and every
>
> mortal creature halves of a clue
> approach the earthlights Morning star
>
> evening star salt of the sky
> First the grave dissolving into dawn
>
> then the crucial recrystallizing
> from inmost depths of clear dark blue

The poem's concluding "clear dark blue" is Mallarmé's austere suggestion of possible intelligibility. But it is also Merrill's own (Emersonian) gaze, "the light in his blue eye"; it is that "Cosmological Eye" that sees only what it has already made, being at once original ocean and ultimate sky, which are always figures for both reality and the answering and positing, sufficient imagination.[21] Thus, Merrill's last book concludes with a final paean to the "crucial recrystalizing" powers of the imagination against death. Behind these lines is an assurance that Yeats did not so fully share, that "the ultimate eye," the imagination of which we are a part, does not die.

CODA: YEATS'S MERRILL, MERRILL'S BLOOM

I. Yeats's Merrill

We have seen how, through Friar, Yeats becomes established in Merrill's mind as the voice of the Gorgon-monster, the unliving-stone, the fireplace of his father's house, which is pointedly not the more inviting "Rosebrick Manor" of the Mother Tongue (S. 262). We have also seen the ways in which Yeats represents those paternal values Merrill both struggles with and to some extent shares: qualities of detachment mixed with family piety, regard mixed with carelessness for history and other people's lives, a willingness to "Let all things pass away" and a keen appreciation for material culture and sensual pleasure, as well as a conservative elitism and fondness for tradition. It should be clear by now that Friar introduced Merrill not so much to the "father who read Yeats" as to the poetic father who was Yeats: "the voice of the other, of the *daimon*, ... [of] a dead man (the precursor) outrageously more alive than himself" (Bloom *Map* 19).[22]

Unlike many of the other precursor-poets Merrill has chosen to acknowledge (Wylie, Rilke, Stevens, Pope, Byron, and Auden) Yeats represents more than a set of forms and freedoms, attitudes and manners upon which to draw.[23] Yeats also offers Merrill a significant voice to write *against*—not only thematically but in the sense of one poem "written against a poem of a different kind, one that reflect[s] a different tradition. Wordsworth against Pope, Byron against Wordsworth" (*Recitative* 22). One way that Merrill writes against Yeats, and has made himself a master of writing poems "of a different kind" than Yeats's, is by extending several of Yeats's chief "devices." Yeats's vacillations (his generative self-quarrelings) operate largely from period to period and poem to poem and, at times, from section to section within a poem, so that, for the most part, each poem or section appears rhetorically conclusive. By contrast, Merrill brings vacillation, self-questioning, interruption, and indeterminacy into the fabric of individual poems and even individual lines. Similarly, although Yeats argues that the "active virtue" of even a poem resides in its being "theatrical, consciously dramatic, the wearing of a mask" [and takes Wordsworth to task for the lack of "theatrical element" in his poems] (*Per Amica* 334), it is Merrill who more consistently fulfills this injunction, by distinguishing qualities of voice not only among characters and personae but also by capturing the dramatic play of voices within a particular consciousness or speaker.[24]

But Merrill writes most strongly against Yeats because Yeats represents a particularly compelling voice of power. Harold Bloom has said that power was "once the only true subject of poetry" (*Map* 66), and Merrill turns to and against Yeats as a personification of a particular kind of poetic power. Yeats deploys "the Promethean fire of consciousness" (*Map* 10) in order to forge a simplifying yet grand intensity that Merrill often finds dangerous, foolish, or blind to nuance and multiple possibility. Yet Merrill remains drawn to such power, even as he works to diffuse or insulate its effects. As a Promethean (that is daemonic) figure, Yeats commands Merrill's respect. Yet in Merrill's view, Yeats is clearly a thief who has not made the best use of his stolen fire; and it is perhaps as a better thief among a "race of thieves" that Merrill hopes to surmount the burden of his own belatedness.[25] As Maria puts it, "WILL NOT OUR RACE OF THIEVES /HAVE EMERGED AS THE ELDERS IN A RACE OF GODS?" (S. 456). In an earlier scene of similar effect, Mirabell speaks of JM and DJ as if they were already "powers," already manifestations of Yeats's "holy fire" and he "AT LAST" able "HERE IN YR VERY HEARTH OF HEARTS TO BURN" (S. 162). After Merrill's treatment of Yeats in "Fire Poem" and "A View of the Burning," it is hard not to hear Merrill's Yeats behind Mirabell's confession, as if the older poet were coming to warm himself by the fire of the younger:

>   ALL POWER ATTRACTS
> & MUST BE DENIED US   FROM MY 1ST STEPPING FORTH I FELT
> YR CHARM   I HAD FEARD U   I HAD HITHERTO RESPONDED
> ONLY TO FORMULAS (S. 162)

Here Merrill not only suggests a number of lessons that he might wish Yeats to speak—that Yeats had been mistaken, "DEVOURED BY THE CHIMERA" of number (S. 424), to have previously responded only to formulas, that Merrill's "charms" are also fearful, potent in their own right, and off-limits to any latter-day poaching by Yeats, and that, in this sense, the earlier poet is now constrained by the later; these lines also suggest lessons about Yeats's influence that, at a deeper level, Merrill might also need to acknowledge himself. The doctrine that power attracts but must be denied is another version of Merrill's fascination with "whatever draws us / To, and insulates us from, the absolute" (S. 84), as well as a restatement of the Bloomian doctrine of the productive ambivalence a later poet feels towards his precursor. When Mirabell says, "I HAD HITHERTO RESPONDED / ONLY TO FORMULAS," we may be hearing an echo of the older Merrill reflecting on his earliest poetry, as when he says about Elinor Wylie's poems: "There's a glaze of perfection to contend with, but I ate it up; it never put me off—not at least until I went on to Yeats" ("Interview with Sheehan" 35). In both passages, by this light, Yeats seems to be the pivotal figure in Merrill's "stepping forth" as a poet, a figure whose power both charms and frightens.

As much as Yeats is Merrill's antithetical figure of poetic power, out of and against which he writes, Merrill's stance is never one of simply "speaking truth to power." From his earliest poems, Merrill has known Foucault's lesson that truth is an effect of language, and that powerful truth-effects (like beauty and moral, emotional, and even intellectual knowledge) are the products of powerful language. Merrill's argument with Yeats's poetic power is often an argument with the tone or stance of Yeats's truths. In any given utterance, Yeats is a master of authoritative pronouncement [which is also the ninth heaven and all-but-ultimate sense of God B (S. 351)]. The statement may be vatic or limpid, freestanding or immediately challenged by the antitheses of vacillation or dialogue, but it attains a fixed intensity, which Merrill often seeks to qualify. The Yeats Merrill quarrels with is precisely the one who strives for "simplification through intensity," the Yeats who, at the level of the sentence at least, affects to stand "out of nature" and speak *about* life, *about* "what is past, or passing, or to come." Though this voice is also song, it is a song that starts and ends as if constructed of time-defying stone or precious metal. This authoritative tone and objective (or objectifying) stance is a traditional voice of power, as well as the archetypal "voice of the father." Merrill does not abandon or simply deny such power, but repeatedly undermines, interrupts, questions or supplements it, while also appropriating its chief effects. Harold Bloom nominates Yeats "the last of the High Romantics, the last of those poets who asserted imaginative values without the armor of continuous irony" (*Yeats* 471). But Merrill's ironizing itself serves the imaginative values of renewal and transformation in the face of time's depredations that are themselves fundamental to the Romantic tradition. Merrill's poetic truths (or truth-effects) are provisional and self-revising, yet they too contrive their (momentary) holds on time.

In writing "out of the life lived, out of the love spent," Merrill writes "out of" time in two antagonistic senses: there are moments of Yeatsian pronouncement as if from a timeless aesthetic vantage ["THE GREAT SCRIBES EXIST OUT OF TIME IN RADIANCE" (S. 217)]; but in the mature poetry these moments are powerfully qualified by the ongoing operations of subjectivity, imagination, and natural event, which also constitute the capricious or pressing forces of time itself. In this sense of "out of time," Merrill brings time into the fabric of his poetry. "Time! The forbidden, the forgotten theme" (S. 438). If, as Bloom suggests, all strong poetry attempts to vouchsafe the poet a victory over time and his own mortality, Merrill's strength is often in precisely avoiding the simplifying intensity of a victory.[26] If time is the great devourer and Merrill would be an "eater of time" ("Interview with Sheehan" 26), his poetry attains its mastery by strategies of emptying out of the self, identification with and incorporation of the other, openness to sensation, event, impulse, and the vagaries and strictures of language—precisely strategies of Dispersal and Receptivity which do not so much oppose as make use of both time and Yeatsian intensity.

For all Merrill's willingness to incorporate "otherness," interruption, and divergent modes in his writing, his receptivity nonetheless falls under the Yeatsian heading of Interest. He is not the Receptive Man of Yeats's Phase 23, although he often seems to see "all things from the point of view of his own technique" (*Vision* 164) [Maria reports (as much about Merrill's poetry as about the other world) that "ALL THINGS ARE DONE HERE IF U HAVE TECHNIQUE" (S. 104) and Michael, who is "THE LIGHT IN EVERY EYE" and Merrill's most sympathetic angel, "IS TECHNIQUE ITSELF (S. 548).] Like Yeats's Receptive Man, Merrill also "touches and tastes and investigates technically" and finds, in the generative work of composition, "perpetual surprise [as] an unforeseen reward of skill" (*Vision* Ibid.).[27]

But Merrill has little interest in "general humanity experienced as a form of involuntary emotion and involuntary delight in the 'minute particulars of life'" (*Vision* 165). Merrill's interest in the "particulars of life" is precisely a reflection of his interest in himself and his own imagination. Merrill is not a man who "must free the intellect from all motives founded upon personal desire, by the help of the external world, now for the first time studied and mastered for its own sake" (*Vision* 164). Rather, as he explains to Ross Labrie:

> What I mean by the outside world are the things we see, our experiences, those around us, our friends, strangers. You can render yourself, see yourself reflected by these people and things so that you wouldn't know you had a self except through these surroundings. ("James Merrill at Home" 28)

Merrill's definition of "the outside world" in this passage echoes Yeats's explanation of the Body of Fate: "the physical and mental environment, the changing human body, the stream of Phenomena as this affects a particular individual" (*Vision*, 1925, qtd. in Croft). Like Yeats, Merrill is chiefly interested in this "series of events forced upon him from without" as a ground upon which to "attain self-knowledge and expression" (*Vision* 83). Not such a man as "wipes his breath from the window-pane, and laughs in delight at all the varied scene" (*Vision* 165), Merrill sees the world primarily through the idealized features he has first projected upon the scene; his pleasure, unlike the Receptive Man's delight, always entails a loss of vision and a compensating vision of loss which informs his own self understanding:

> One winter morning as a child
> Upon the windowpane's thin frost I drew
> Forehead and eyes and mouth the clear and mild
> Features of nobody I knew
>
> And then abstracted looking through
> This or that wet transparent line
> Beyond beheld a winter garden so
> Heavy with snow its hedge of pine
>
> And sun so brilliant on the snow
> I breathed my pleasure out onto the chill pane
> Only to see its angel fade in mist.
> I was a child, I did not know . . .
>
> (from "A Vision of the Garden")

"I breathed my pleasure out onto the chill pane [we hear, of course, the pun on "pain"] / Only to see its angel fade in mist" could be the emblematic scene of Merrill's fruitful deployment of Yeats's Dispersal.

Yeats has little to say about Dispersal (his False Mask from Phase 3), but like all false masks, we may infer, it represents the particular form of the Ought ("or that which should be") most apt to lure one away from the most difficult desires which also promise completeness or justice (*Vision* 73, 83; Bloom *Yeats* 276-77). Yeats tells us that Dispersal is what "weakens men of Phase 17 when they try to live in the *primary tincture*" [the "tincture" of service, rather than that of their native antithetical creativity (*Vision* 85)] and tells us that Dispersal derives from Interest (from Phase 13), which offers "delight in all that passes," provided "[the person's] senses and subconscious dominate his intellect" (*Vision* 90, 108).[28] To the man of Phase 17, Yeats explains, Dispersal offers the images of innocence, of shepherds, lovers, and sages, that so attracts lyrical poets, as well as considerable sensual allurements ("he who kisses the joy as it flies / Lives in eternity's sunrise"); but these come at the price of not being able (or desiring) to make much sense of the world (*Vision* 108-09).

Here, under the aegis of Dispersal, Yeats almost seems to point to Merrill's characteristic concerns, his "CHRONICLES OF LOVE & LOSS" (S. 176), as well as to the antithetical concern of his angelic voices that the poet join them in sensing and "MAKING SENSE" of what he can (S. 370). Yeats's discussion of Dispersal also echoes the archangel Michael's "FIRST, AFFIRMATIVE TEXT: / THE MOST INNOCENT OF IDEAS IS THE IDEA THAT INNOCENCE IS / DESTROYED BY IDEAS" (S. 321), a notion that soon leads to the conclusion that IDEA or thought is inherently destructive, a Yeatsian conclusion that *Sandover* largely rejects (S. 321-23).

What seems clear from Yeats's fragmentary discussion is that Dispersal, as a vision of the Ought, has considerable authority of its own and that, as a means of directing one's gaze toward what "delights" as well as what "passes," it offers at least as much grasp of the ambiguities of reality and justice as Yeats's true Mask of "simplification through intensity." Characteristically, Merrill's poetry works to recuperate Dispersal, making it his "True Mask," while not totally denying the power of Yeats's "simplification."[29] For Merrill, "anything worth having's had both ways" (S. 174) and, while willing to shift the balance away from Yeatsian intensity toward Dispersal, Merrill sees little sense in accepting the exclusionary economy that governs Yeats's distinctions between False and True, when both so richly serve.

Many examples could be cited of such Merrillian insistence on the principles of Dispersal and "double mindedness." But the concluding stanzas of section "X" in "The Book of Ephraim" offer what may be the best instance, and one that is also particularly apt in terms of its themes:

> What I think I feel now, by its own nature
> Remains beyond my power to say outright,
> Short of grasping the naked current where it
> Flows through field and book, dog howling, the firelit
> Glances, the caresses, whatever draws us
> To, and insulates us from, the absolute—
> The absolute which wonderfully, this slow
> December noon of clear blue time zones flown through
> Toward relatives and friends, more and more sounds like
> The kind of pear-bellied early instrument
> Skills all but lost are wanted, or the phoenix
> Quill of passion, to pluck a minor scale from
> And to let the silence after each note sing.
> So Time has—but who needs that nom de plume? I've— [30]

Coda: Yeats's Merrill, Merrill's Bloom

> We've modulated. Keys ever remoter
> Lock our friend among the golden things that go
> Without saying, the loves no longer called up
> Or named. We've grown autumnal, mild. We've reached a
> Stage through him that he will never himself reach.
> Back underground he sinks, a stream, the latest
> Recurrent figure out of mythology
> To lend his young beauty to a living grave
> In order that Earth bloom another season.
>
> Shall I come lighter-hearted to that Spring-tide
> Knowing it must be fathomed without a guide?
> With no one, nothing along those lines—or these
> Whose writing, if not justifies, so mirrors,
> So embodies up to now some guiding force,
> It can't simply be written off. In neither
> The world's poem nor the poem's world have I
> Learned to think for myself, much. The twinklings of
> Insight hurt or elude the naked eye, no
> Metrical lens to focus them, no kismet
> Veiled as a stern rhyme sound, to obey whose wink
> Floods with rapture its galaxy of sisters.
> Muse and maker, each at a loss without the
>
> —Oh but my foot has gone to sleep! Gingerly
> I prod it: painful, slow, hilarious twinges
> Of reawakening, recirculation;
> Pulsars intuiting the universe once
> More, this net of loose talk tightening to verse,
>
> And verse once more revolving between poles—
> Gassy expansion and succinct collapse—
> Till Heaven is all peppered with black holes,
> Vanishing points for the superfluous
> Matter elided (just in time perhaps)
> By the conclusion of a passage thus . . . (S. 85-86)

In these lines Merrill again and again approaches the high Romantic moment of encounter with the sublime: the absolute, time, the mysteries of the self, world and language, heaven and the universe. With each approach the object of encounter seems to shift, but remains always the unsayable that only "goes," only operates, Merrill insists, "without saying." What may seem like evasion, a lack of power or an unwillingness to persist in the high mode of Yeatsian intensity is for Merrill more a form of tact—and a tactic by which to avoid the fixity of only one mode or direction of approach. Merrill disperses his terms, shifts ground, draws near enough to the "naked current" to let what is suggested about such energy, about the identity of self and time, language and world, have their singing, silent moments before falling back into lived experience, memory, or reverie once more.

Power in Merrill's verse is a force of recurrence, reawakening, recirculation, a breathing pulsation between expansion and, if not "collapse," then "modulation" into other keys. It is not just that "the powers have to be consulted again directly—again, again, and again" and that we must "evoke fresh speech from them" (Zimmer, qtd. in S. 62), but that by constantly refreshing his speech ("—Oh but my foot has gone to sleep!") Merrill tactfully draws renewed power into his poetry ("Pulsars intuiting the universe once / more"). Heinrich Zimmer counsels Merrill in the way of the dilettante, who is "always ready to begin anew" and for whom no vision is final: "It can only be a preliminary glimpse . . . an inspiration and a stimulation [inviting] further insights and differing approaches" (Zimmer 6). But this is also the way of Dispersal, Yeats's false mask. Rather than find his power against time by seeking "simplification through intensity," Merrill makes Dispersal his true mask and seeks delight, the power of pleasure in what complicates, multiplies, diverges, interrupts, and resists and yet also includes moments of resolution among the profligacy, mending as well as scissoring, and ways of beginning anew out of what is surrendered to time and "the problematics of loss" (Bloom *Map* 18).

II. MERRILL'S BLOOM

Harold Bloom has haunted this study since its inception. I have found it productive to evade and quarrel with his work as a "strong" critic quite as much as to employ his insights in the service of reading Merrill's relationship with Yeats, his most problematic precursor. It is time now to attend more directly to Bloom's roles in understanding the relationship between Merrill and Yeats.

Quite simply, Harold Bloom's theory of poetic influence is relevant to Merrill's engagement with Yeats's poetry in two ways: the first concerns how Bloom's theory applies to this relation, and the second concerns how Merrill himself applies Bloom's theory to his most ambitious work. Regarding the first, it is not hard to see how Merrill moves from early Yeatsian "floodedness" ("The Broken Bowl," "Medusa," "Transfigured Bird") quite quickly into a posture of swerving away to counter or correct Yeats with an influx of Stevens, Mallarmé, Auden, or Rilke ("Cloud Country," "The Grape Cure," "Marsyas," "The Charioteer of Delphi"). This "Clinamen," or swerve away from Yeats, never lasts long. Soon Merrill takes up the more contentious task of answering or "completing" Yeats's poems by reversing the meaning of Yeats's key terms—Bloom's ratio "Tessera" seen, for example, in "Fire Poem," "About the Phoenix," "Urban Convalescence," "Willowware Cup," and "The Thousand and Second Night." These poems interrogate, ironize, and parody Yeats's prior language sometimes brashly, more often covertly. Merrill's poems of "Kenosis," or self-emptying, often perform a characteristic spin on the Bloomian model. In these poems, Merrill's tone of a chastened and chastening modesty calls into question Yeatsian intensity in ways that ultimately elevate the younger at the expense of the older poet ("A Tenancy," "Childlessness," "The Thousand and

Second Night" "More Enterprise," "Flying from Byzantium," "Log"). Then there are the poems in which Merrill, in effect, appeals over the head of Yeats to a prior, and higher daimonic authority, sometimes Nature, sometimes Proust or Dante, sometimes the uncanny voices of the other world (be these the voices of the angels, god, the unconscious or the unbound imagination). Thus, in response to the Yeatsian sublime, Merrill evokes a counter-or-prior-sublime, in the revisionary ratio Bloom nominates "Daemonization." We see this ratio in effect in such poems as "For Proust," "Violent Pastoral," "From the Cupola" and "McKane's Falls" and a good deal of *Sandover*. Merrill's most striking example of Bloomian "Askesis," the curtailing of the poet's imaginative endowment in such a way as also to truncate or diminish the imaginative authority of the older poet (*Anxiety* 15), surely takes place in the book of *Mirabell*, with its remarkable displacement of Merrill's characteristic voice by the bat-voices of 741 and his cohorts. Similarly, the last lessons of *Scripts* make "holding open" the poem to Yeats one of that volume's most telling effects. This climactic instance of Bloom's "Apophrades" is even staged so that Merrill does in fact write or rewrite Yeats's "example" of "the precursor's characteristic work" (*Anxiety* 16).

In the poems written after *Sandover*, Yeats continues to play a number of roles; but, increasingly, Merrill allows his accommodation with Yeats to sponsor a swerving away that also holds open, or an ironizing allusion that also sponsors the Daemonic influx of a prior or counter-sublime. We have seen these and similar "blended" patterns of influence in our discussion of such poems as "Santorini: Stopping the Leak," "A Room at the Heart of Things," and "Losing the Marbles." Merrill's masterful ease with a figure who is still demanding enough to require mastery also characterizes Merrill's use of Yeats in *A Different Person*. It is not until what one might call the "death poems" of *A Scattering of Salts* that Bloom's Apophrades, or Return of the Dead, seems to preside, whether bitterly or bravely, almost unalloyed.

Certainly a good deal more could be said of the ways in which Bloom's theory of influence applies to Merrill's poetry. But what I more particularly want to argue is that shortly after completing "The Book of Ephraim" Merrill realized he could use Bloom's theory of poetic influence as a dramatic device to help structure the burgeoning transcripts of what would become *Mirabell* and *Scripts*. Bloom's *The Anxiety of Influence* (1973) and the subsequent volumes expounding the theory, *Map of Misreading* (1975) and *Figures of Capable Imagination* (1976), were much discussed as Merrill was finishing "Ephraim" and starting *Mirabell*. There is no doubt that the general outline of Bloom's ideas was available to him.[31] The problem Merrill faced particularly in 1976 and into 1977 was how shape the "enormous" transcript that was accumulating. He tells J. D. McClatchy that "what you see in [*Mirabell*] might be half, or two-fifths, of the original" ("Interview with McClatchy" 64).

Shortly after Bloom began teaching *Divine Comedies* late in 1976, he and Merrill began to speak and correspond with some frequency. Their conversations extended through the period during which Merrill composed *Mirabell* and *Scripts*, and Merrill sent Bloom "chunks" of *Scripts* as he went along. They discussed Yeats and Bloom's theories of influence, and Bloom recalls that Merrill read parts of his study of Yeats on his recommendation.[32] Given these exchanges, it is surely "NO ACCIDENT" that lines such as these find their way into Merrill's poem: "YR DC [*Divine Comedies*] CAME IN THIS WAY THRU OUR INFLUENCE" (S. 121); "WE COME MUCH AS FLOWERS CUT FROM THE STEM BELIEVE / IN THE BLOOM TO FOLLOW . . . WE MAKE ROOM" (S. 329); "& RAISE IN MM'S DREAMBEDS / HIDEOUS BLOOMS TO STIR UP RIVALRY AT HIGH LEVELS" (S. 193); "A FINAL / BLOOM OF CHALK AS WE DISSCUSS THE UNWRITTEN SIN: / MAN'S THEFT OF GOD'S MATERIALS" (S. 455) or the previously cited, "Down to Earth a ray slants true as birdsong / Through boughs in sparkling bloom too high to pluck" (S. 523). In each case the otherworldly or poet's voice echoes the anxious thematics of Harold Bloom's account of poetic influence. [We also have the manuscript evidence of Merrill explicitly addressing Bloom in the lines that once read, "And Harold Bloom / Pleads for no more big speeches in small caps" (see S. 499).][33] Yet, significantly, none of these possible references to Bloom and his theories of influence occur in "Ephraim."

My sense is that Merrill, ever resourceful, ever the "magpie" ("Interview with McClatchy" 66), decided that he could trump the "strong" critic (who was already setting the "apocalyptic" tone for "Ephraim's" reception) by putting Bloom's ideas on influence to work as he was composing the ongoing poem.[34] Bloom argues that poets are critics [since "the meaning of a poem can only be another poem" (*Anxiety* 94)] and critics are, or ought to be, poets.[35] Out of such a collapse of distinctions, in which poets' and critics' misinterpretations differ only "in degree and not at all in kind" (Ibid. 94-5), Bloom's unspoken ambition seems to situate him, as one critic has noted, as "our most sublime poet" (Molesworth 157), for whom all other forms of criticism "reduce to rival conceptualizations"; whereas, "we reduce—if at all—to another poem" (*Anxiety* 94).

Although Merrill most likely welcomed Bloom's anti-reductionism, he probably chafed against the totalizing claims of Bloom's theory of poetic influence. How satisfying then, in effect, to make a meal of Bloom's revisionary ratios by incorporating them into the structure of his most ambitious poem. Bloom may argue that introjection offers only a fantasy defense against an outside threat (*Map* 103), but *Sandover* itself testifies to the "GENERATIVE USES" of such defenses (S. 121). In the creative contest for priority and power between poet and critic, it is Bloom who must ultimately make due with the relatively meager resources of argumentative prose; whereas, *Sandover* releases Merrill into the full range of his poetic powers, including as we have seen the pleasures of appropriation, ironic allusion, indirection, and erasure—all aimed at the "HIDEOUS BLOOMS" of critical rivalry (S. 193).

Once aware of Bloom's theory, Merrill would have seen that the disparaging way Yeats is announced in the early sections of "Ephraim" but then seemingly dropped from the poem already serves as an opening Clinamen or ironic swerve away from the troubling precursor. Similarly, the final sonnet in section "R," which allows Merrill to "body forth" his own anxiety regarding threat of "stolen thunder" in a quotation from Yeats's "A Dialogue for Self and Soul," and the Yeatsian thematics of the Venice section, in which Merrill offers an antithetical reading of Yeats's own terms, also already serve as Tesserae.[36] With Yeats thus already installed in "Ephraim" as the rival precursor, Bloom's progressive theory of "some half-dozen steps" by which the "strong poet . . . attempts to convert his inheritance into what will aid him" (*Figures* 10) then provides Merrill the basic structuring principles for *Mirabell* and *Scripts*.

In accord with the "limiting" ratios of Kenosis and Askesis, JM must be emptied out, must undergo a "stripping process" and his characteristic voice suffer radical curtailment for substantial stretches of the next parts of the poem. (This "emptying" and "curtailing" of Merrill's characteristic voice is especially prominent in *Mirabell*.) But Yeats must suffer more; in both Kenosis and Askesis, Bloom tells us "the precursor is emptied out also, . . . the precursor's endowment is also truncated" (*Anxiety* 15). By having Yeats suffer taunts, theft of his language, and parodic appropriation of his vision system, by having him linked to DJ, especially in moments of disciplinary pain, Merrill extends Bloom's ideas by dramatizing the sado/masochistic dynamic inherent in Bloom's ratios of "limitation."[37]

Indeed, although Bloom's theory of influence offers a richly nuanced account of how "poets have suffered other poets" [specifically their processors] (*Anxiety* 94), Bloom says little about the ways a younger poet may make his precursor suffer. Merrill performs something of a Tessera on Bloom in this regard, offering what amounts to an antithetical (and perhaps parodic) completion of Bloom's "agonistic" model of influence. Certainly Yeats is made into a pawn, a "merel," and subject to considerable metaphoric humiliation and violence in Merrill's poem. Perhaps part of the animus of this campaign also derives from uses and abuses Merrill makes of Bloom's theory. "We get happiness," Yeats's instructors told him, "from those we have served, ecstasy from those we have wronged" (*Vision* 239).[38]

Bloom's ratio of Daemonization suggests that, to offer an effective "countersublime" to Yeats's, Merrill will want to move beyond Yeats to the very elemental powers that the earlier poet attended to—in this case, to the bat-angel voices of the "OO" who, we learn, once dictated to Yeats (S. 429), and beyond these voices to the solar vision concluding *Mirabell* and the revelations of the archangels, triune Nature, and God B in *Scripts*.[39] Lastly, in the ratio of Apophrades, Bloom's theory would suggest the poem should ultimately be "held open" to Yeats himself, not only so that the precursor seems to speak or write again, but so that Merrill would seem to have "written the precursor's characteristic work" (*Anxiety* 16). Merrill makes almost programmatic use of this description. Not only does Yeats emerge from DJ's hand to deliver his long-awaited stanza, but we also later discover that Merrill has had a hand in rewriting this piece of "characteristic" work (S. 492).

It is in this mode of Apophrades that Merrill again revises Bloom. The concluding passage of *Scripts*, in which we again hear God B's plangent song, and, even more strongly, the recycling conclusion of "The Higher Keys" and *Sandover* proper, in which JM commences his reading of the poem we have just finished, both seem to make of their "belatedness an earliness" (*Map* 100): the one by moving from the renunciation of a "whole / Lifetime of images" to the aboriginal image of inspiration, the "whirling point of Light" (S. 517) and the other by contriving in its concluding line a revisionary reading of how the poem begins, who it is written for, and how it asks to be read. In each case what Merrill actually achieves is a belatedness transformed into an earliness, which nonetheless insists on its own belatedness. In this, Merrill is closer to Bloom's insistence on the necessary belatedness of poetry than Bloom is himself.[40]

God B's song is a projection of the belatedness of the poet. He signals out of his solitude, back toward the "Pantheon" to which he is no longer joined (S. 330, 362); he sings of survival and resistance, of "self-preservation" as the principle quest of an embattled being thrown into creation by the presence of a rival, "MONITOR GOD" (S. 476).[41] Similarly, in ending, *Sandover* recommences, but now specifically "for *their* ears," for the great company of precursors who have always already gone before. In "The Higher Keys," Merrill stages a wholly celebratory Apophrades, or Return of the Dead, presenting a "powerful instance of a poet subsuming all his precursors and making the subsuming process much of the program and meaning of his work" (*Map* 103) as we prepare to start the work again. But this subsuming process [now proleptically or "preposterously" prepared, as Bloom would say "in the root sense of making the later into the earlier" (Ibid.)] always takes place for a reading that is only just beginning, and what's more, a reading that is intended for someone else's ears (an "over-reading," if you will, that displays all the difficulties of an overhearing). Here Merrill reveals another side of Bloomian anxiety: not only is the poet always too late to be self-begotten (the violence of origins), he is also too late to control how he will be read (the violence of endings and of mortality).

The dynamic of Apophrades also suggests that the poem should spiral into an apotheosis of self-begetting authorized by the power of the later poet who has now indelibly placed his mark on his precursors. But here too Merrill revises Bloom. Just as the violence Yeats suffers in *Sandover* seems to mirror more fully part of the Oedipal dynamic Bloom's theory requires, so the accession of the younger poet into his full power and into his mistaken, but full appropriation of the role of the older poet leads not only to a sense of completion and fullness but also to a hollowing out, a dispersal of power and identity. Bloom speaks of the "triumph" of the strongest poets in being able almost to overturn "the tyranny of time" (*Anxiety* 141); in this, they are like gods. What Merrill reveals most clearly in the un-concluding pages of *Sandover* is that the fullest poetic incarnation of a god is always also a withdrawal.

"Reject your parents vehemently enough," Bloom tells us, "and you will become a belated version of them." As we have seen, this is the formula for part of Merrill's method in *Mirabell* and *Scripts*, particularly the parodic Yeatsianisms of *Mirabell.* "But compound with their reality, and you may partly free yourself" (*Map* 38). In this next sentence, Bloom suggests the formula for the other part of Merrill's method in *Sandover*. By taking Yeats *in* as well as taking him *on*, by enlarging the scope and depth of his poetry Merrill has made room for Yeats in ways he earlier could not allow.

But questions remain for both Merrill and for Bloom. Bloom's criticism would have us ask whether Merrill is seduced by his own "sunnier" account of influence? (Under Bloom's spell too, we note the buried and anxious pun on "son" in this formulation.) Do Merrill's poems lose power by subscribing to too "affable" a relation with other poets? Does Merrill finally refuse to forge his fullest strength in anxious contest with his strongest precursors, being too much enamored of the wishful fancies and defenses of a child? And is such a refusal (if it is such) always a diminishment? To put these last questions this way is already to ask whether Bloomian "agon" provides a complete or the only significant account of poetic influence. (We have already seen how Merrill is able to supplement Bloomian theory, very much in its own psychodynamic terms.) Might there not be significant imaginative values in poetry that refuses to see poetic influence primarily in terms of single combat with a poetic father or fathers? [42]

To the first questions about a weakening of Merrill's poetic power out of a refusal to fully engage with his poetic inheritance, I think the answer is clear. Merrill continued to deepen and extend the range and power of his work throughout his life. Reviewing *Divine Comedies,* Bloom called it "an American book that dares everything in order to achieve what Emerson called the essential American trope of power: *surprise*" ("On Poetry" 1976, 20). Merrill continues to dare and to surprise throughout the reaches of *Sandover*. For sublimity few could ask more than the finale of *Mirabell,* God B's song and Wystan's commentary, or the breaking of the mirror at the end of *Scripts*. "Samos" astonishes with it range of vision and tone, its technical facility, and the unblinking humanity of souls who have "taken fire." The elegies, appreciations, and testimonies in many voices that occur throughout *Sandover* show Merrill to be one of our premier poets of friendship and personal reflection. [I think particularly of section "L" ("Life") in "Ephraim" and "About Maria" in "The Higher Keys."] Long esteemed (and discounted) for his wit, with *Sandover,* Merrill demonstrates how wit itself opens onto philosophy and wisdom.[43] All of which is not to imply that *Sandover* represents the culmination of Merrill's achievement. We see all these strengths further extended in poems such as "Bronze," "Santorini: Stopping the Leak," "Morning Glory," "Losing the Marbles," "Farewell Performance," "Nine Lives," "Home Fires," "Press Release," "Family Week at Oracle Ranch," "Overdue Pilgrimage to Nova Scotia," "Self Portrait in Tyvek (TM) Windbreaker," and "An Upward Look."

To the later questions about the adequacy of Bloom's theory, especially as it applies to Merrill, the answers are multiple. With regard to Merrill's relationship with Yeats, Bloom's account of the young poet's ongoing struggle to master the disturbing priority of an imposing poetic father is both helpful and illuminating. It alerts the reader to often covert signs of anxious affiliation and, with Bloom's six revisionary ratios in mind, draws the reader into a closer understanding of how a particular Merrill poem may be responding to a poem of Yeats's. The triadic relationship between Merrill's father, Yeats, and Kimon Friar also suggests that a strongly psychodynamic approach to the Merrill/Yeats relation should prove fruitful.

But whether Bloom's agonistic approach will prove equally fruitful in parsing the influence of Proust or Dante, Valéry or Rilke, Ponge or Cavafy, Auden or Bishop is far less certain. With these figures, a relationship much more like Merrill's amenable "good student" may pertain. Bloom is puzzled when faced with such "genial" forms of influence ("On Poetry" 1977, 24). But he needn't be. His own strong humanism, which bids him value in Yeats "a growing natural joy" and the "joy of natural knowledge" over Yeats's claims to an antithetical "tragic joy," should also suggest to him the value of more "primary," rather than "antithetical," forms of influence (*Yeats* 455). Bloom writes movingly about the mystery of Yeats's "Cuchulain Comforted" and explains that this mystery centers on the "unique knowledge of the shrouds," a knowledge which bids the hero exchange his "individual meditation on wounds and blood" [an apt image for Bloom's typical account of genesis of the "strong" poem] for "a sharing in a communal activity of stitching, and of singing a communal song" (Ibid. 463). In this last phrase, Bloom provides himself with an alternate approach to the "mystery" of poetic influence. Yet he remains convinced that such communal stitching and song is no longer effectively available to modern poets, as it once was to Dante and to Shakespeare, regardless of the testimony of poets to the contrary.

Poets may often lie about such matters, as Bloom says (*Map* 10); but it seems that their poems shouldn't. Wystan's great speech about "THE ROSEBRICK MANOR [and] . . . GREENWOOD PERSPECTIVES OF THE MOTHER TONGUE" (S. 262), with which he answers an eruption of JM's anxiety of influence ["it's all by someone else!" (S. 261)], may be a wishful, Arcadian fantasy, a kind of manifest dream that screens latent Oedipal anxieties from conscious view. But so much in Merrill's poetic practice, as well as the work of other poets, argues otherwise, or at least argues for the productive and singularly humane agency of this particular fantasy: that language is the communal house of man, our "LIFE RAFT" (S. 119) and that we can approach those who have built it and lived in it—the "SWEET WILLIAMS & FATE-FLAVORED EMILIES / . . . THE DULL THE PRODIGAL THE MEAN THE MAD / IN BED AT PRAYERS AT MUSIC FLUSHED WITH PORT"—and know it "THE GREATEST PRIVILEGE" to both find and make a place therein. That the dead are alive in the living—and indeed in some senses, "outrageously more alive" in their work than the poet feels himself to be—fails in this light to outrage. As Merrill puts it: "If I am host at last / It is of little more than my own past. / May others be at home in it" ("A Tenancy").[44]

Eve Sedgwick voices this hospitable or compassionate view of influence in her most Merrill-inflected book, *A Dialogue on Love*. Out of her haibun, a mixture of prose and haiku that Merrill transported into English in "Prose of Departure," a voice in small caps more and more frequently arises, culminating in this:

Coda: Yeats's Merrill, Merrill's Bloom

> THE MODEL OF A TRUE AND REVELATORY RELATIONSHIP IS THE GRATITUDE AND TENDERNESS BETWEEN MOTHER AND CHILD/TEACHER AND STUDENT—THE UNIQUE IDEA THAT YOU CAN TELL IF IT'S TRUE BY THE FEELINGS OF TENDERNESS AND GRATITUDE (NOT OEDIPAL-STYLE ENVY, LACK, VIOLENCE)—THAT THIS IS ALSO THE RELATIONSHIP BETWEEN YOU AND THE UNIVERSAL LUMINOSITY WHICH IS (ALSO) YOU. (215)

This voice is perhaps too serene to be typically Merrillian, but it is one that Merrill would recognize from his encounters at the board.[45] "THANK YOU" is, after all, one of the board's most common expressions, and mutual tenderness and affection one of the emotional hallmarks of the relations among JM, DJ, and their voices from the other world. Critics wear blinders when they slight the productive force of such emotions. Especially with a poet such as Merrill, delight and affection matter as much as anxiety and pride, and we need to hear all these registers too if we are to attempt to "hold in a single thought [the] reality and justice" of JM's declaration: "Oh please, Mr Yeats, you who have always / Been such a force in my life!" (S. 492). As Merrill's writing shows again and again, Yeats was indeed a generative, guiding force in his life—a force born always out of both resistance and devotion.

Appendix A
Merrill's Antithetical Use of "Sailing to Byzantium" in "About the Phoenix"

IN "ABOUT THE PHOENIX," MERRILL CONTINUES HIS INSISTENT WRESTLING WITH the lofty rhetoric and masochistic longing for simplicity that accompanies Yeats's Condition of Fire. In Bloom's terms, "About the Phoenix" represents Merrill's fullest early revisionary effort, moving from the swerving away of Clinamen to Tessera with its patterns of completion via antithesis and inversion of terms and structures (*Anxiety* 14, *Map* 98). With this poem, Merrill contrives almost the converse of Yeats's "Sailing to Byzantium." Merrill's opening deflates Yeats's conclusion. His ending revises Yeats's opening; and, throughout, Merrill's poem elaborates a pattern of inversions, transvaluations, and contrasting parallels. Both poems open with "complaints." Yeats avows, "That is no country for old men," and Merrill, "But in the end one tires of the high-flown." Merrill's "in the end" marks a recurrent concern of his speaker, and the phrase thus chimes with the concerns of Yeats's old man, since both poems explore scenarios of dying into a new life. But "in the end one tires of the high-flown" also works as pointed commentary on the rhetorical flights of Merrill's early poetry, as well as Yeats's poem, particularly, its golden bird "set upon a golden bough to sing / . . . Of what is past, or passing, or to come."[1] Where Yeats's opening signals the dissatisfaction that motivates a journey, Merrill's signals the desire for rest. Where Yeats's first stanza figures life as a cyclical tumult of "dying generations," pointedly plural and "mackerel-crowded," "About the Phoenix" presents a "rosy," and perhaps Rosicrucian, fantasy of one body's easeful transit, its wondering walk "into that other world":

> But in the end one tires of the high-flown.
> If it were simply a matter of life or death
> We should by now welcome the darkening room,
> Wrinkling of linen, window at last violet,
> The rosy body in its chair, relaxed,

>And then the appearance of unsuspected lights.
>We should walk wonderingly into that other world
>With its red signs pulsing and long lit lanes.

Where Yeats presents a sensuous cycle that his old man wishes to flee, Merrill presents an ethereal linear progression that anyone "should by now welcome," out of the body and into lights, conceived reassuringly as "signs" and "long lit lanes"—but only "*If* it were simply a matter of life or death," of Yeats's "whatever is begotten, born, and dies" (emphasis added). Merrill's conditional holds everything unobtrusively up for question.

Yeats makes his speaker's disaffection with living and dying the occasion for his (imaginary) journey to Byzantium to study "Monuments of unageing intellect." Merrill, in contrast, makes his speaker's dissatisfaction with an imagined, or intellectual, journey beyond life and death the occasion for his turning to a scene of annunciation and desire. Merrill's phoenix, though clearly a "bird born out of the fire" (*Per Amica* 347), has nothing of Yeats's avowed "simplicity" about it. It is "ambiguous / As the city itself," perhaps as ambiguous as Byzantium, and certainly as ambiguous as Manhattan (or even Phoenix) at night. The presence of the real city pours ambiguity back into the immediately preceding lines. Once read easily as a crossing over into "that other world" after death, they now also evoke the "violet hour," the haven of a city apartment, "And then" the attraction of a walk into "that other world" of evening streets, now pulsing with stop lights and streaming head lights—which, like the scenario of dying into light, might offer welcome relief, *if* "it"—everyday life, perhaps—were so simply serious as "a matter of life or death." But it is not so simple a matter, Merrill implies. And no journeying elsewhere is needed, since Merrill's bird, unlike Yeats's, itself comes to call (or "caw"):

>But often at nightfall, ambiguous
>As the city itself, a giant jeweled bird
>Comes cawing to the sill, dispersing thought
>Like a bird-bath, and with such final barbarity
>As to wear thin at once terror and novelty.
>So that a sumptuous monotony
>Sets in, a pendulum of amethysts
>In the shape of a bird, keyed up for ever fiercer
>Flights between ardor and ashes, back and forth;

Merrill's phoenix is no singing master of the soul, intellectual monument, object of desire, or transcendent self. Rather it seems an emblem of the mechanism of desire. Merrill's "giant jeweled bird" is like the pulsating night city itself, ambiguous and alluring. Although Merrill's phoenix is as much a work of art as Yeats's singing cloisonné bird (it too is a clockworks, "a pendulum of amethysts / In the shape of a bird keyed up for ever fiercer / Flights . . .") what is Art's song for Yeats is, for Merrill, Desire's cawing, animal and disturbing. Where one sees an enduring, courtly diversion, the other sees a wearing barbarism. Where one imagines a timeless and disengaged perspective on the human stuff of time, the other evokes the felt monotony and entrapment of compulsive repetition in time. Merrill's bird "comes cawing to the sill, dispersing [that is, ambiguously, both dispensing and dispelling] thought / Like a bird bath, and with such final barbarity / As to wear thin at once terror and novelty." Thus, all Merrill's emblem seems to offer the speaker is the "sumptuous monotony" of "ever fiercer / Flights between ardor and ashes."

When Merrill continues, "Caught in whose talons any proof of grace / . . . Fades," we are in much the same predicament as the numbing "back and forth" of birth and death, ardor and ashes, that Yeats evokes when he characterizes his "dying generations" as "Caught in that sensual music." But whereas Yeats's bird of fire is meant to embody a way "out of nature" and off the wheel of generation, the compulsive mania of Merrill's phoenix points to the limits even of art to stave off the depredations of time. What Yeats's holy fire burns away is human particularity and desire; what it yields is the enduring purity of gold and art. For Merrill, too, fire, whether of ardor or of art, destroys particularity. At the height of passion, the lover is "featureless"; and, in the recollections of a "cooling love," his face becomes "a fading / Tintype." Neither the generalizing power of passion nor of art provides what Yeats aspires to: the timeless, golden innocence of flame or song. Both fade according to the vagaries of desire, "the creature's whim."

> Caught in whose talons any proof of grace,
> Even your face, particularly your face
> Fades, featureless in flame, or wan, a fading
> Tintype of some cooling love, according
> To the creature's whim. And in the end, despite
> Its pyrotechnic curiosity, the process
> Palls. . . .

By this point midway in his poem, Merrill appears to be finished contending with many of the issues raised in Yeats's "Sailing to Byzantium." But he is not through interrogating the terms of his own argument. If Merrill is tired of "high-flown" rhetoric, such as Yeats's, that strives to woo or overwhelm the listener, he also rejects simple prescriptive prose, which seeks to tell us what to do, as if simple imperatives such as "live" or "die" were equally simple to fulfill. If Merrill takes issue with the simplifying urgency and the sense of choice that characterizes "matter[s] of life or death" (such as is felt in the ease of Yeats's formulation, "once out of nature. . . "), he also objects to the trivializing that corrodes matters deemed "less than a matter of life or death" and that turn us away from questions of *how* to live or die. Thus, if Merrill finds the first "rosy" scene of moving into "that other world" suspect, it becomes even more so when he presents its initially more realistic counterpart:

> One night
> Your body winces grayly from its chair,
> Embarks, a tearful child, to rest
> On the dark breast of the fulfilled past.
> The first sleep here is the sleep fraught
> As never before with densities, plume, oak,
> Black water, a blind flapping. And you wake
> Unburdened, look about for friends—but O
> Could not even the underworld forego
> The publishing of omens, naively?
> Nothing requires you to make sense of them
> And yet you shiver from the dim clay shore,
>   Gazing . . .

The first scene of movement into an afterlife is presented under the timeless aegis of the subjunctive, of wish fulfillment and dream. In contrast, the second such scene insists on the order and ravages of time. It happens "One night" that "Your body winces grayly from its chair." What was once an impersonal, generalized "rosy body" now confronts the lover, and the reader, personally with its pain.[2] The wondering walk of the first scene, which affirms the subject's continued agency in the other world, becomes a woeful embarkation in the second scene, evoking a passive ferry ride over the "Black water" of Lethe. In this scene, gray answers rosy, dark answers light, time answers timelessness, and pain and tears answer wonder, just as a sense of being borne away rebukes the earlier image of autonomy. But Merrill is not offering a cold-eyed realism to counter the first scene's fantasy. What he presents instead is another myth, or rather myths, since his account of the classical "underworld" slides so effortlessly into a critique of museum culture and the tales of History:

> There in the lake, four rows of stilts
> Rise, a first trace of culture, shy at dawn
> Though blackened as if forces long confined
> Had smoldered and blazed forth. In the museum
> You draw back lest the relics of those days
> —A battered egg cup and a boat with feet—
> Have lost their glamour. They have not. The guide
> Fairly exudes his tale of godless hordes
> Sweeping like clockwork over Switzerland,
> Till what had been your very blood ticks out
> Voluptuous homilies. Ah, how well one might,
> If it were less a matter of life or death,
> Traffic in strong prescriptions, "live" and "die"![3]

I have divided this middle section of the poem into two sections: a journey to the underworld beginning "One night . . ." and the museum scene given above. But this division is forced. The first section blends into the second with the sentence, "There in the lake . . . ," which reads as both a continuation of the scene in Hades and as a description of a museum diorama. The second section similarly blends into the last passage of the poem with the sentence, "Ah, how well one might . . . ," which expands on "Voluptuous homilies" and prepares for the counter argument beginning, "But couldn't the point. . . ." Merrill depicts the underworld in classical if also characteristically Merrillian terms. The soul is a child again. Hades is social but shadowy and "dim." Departed souls rest unburdened after their "fulfilled past." Sleep is fraught with "densities," a word Merrill will use especially in *Mirabell* to categorize qualities of soul, but which here points more to the opacities, the impenetrabilities, of death's kingdom. "Plume" suggests the floating quality of both feather and smoke and elusively prepares for both the bat-like "blind flapping" where "flapping" is the noun, and the nounal "a blind," which yields both the liminal sense of wind through a window and the very Merrillian pun on "a shade." "Oak" is density itself, enduring, hard, and brave, the stuff of coffins and of Charon's boat; it likewise yields by complement and metaleptic association to the impenetrability of "Black water," the waters of oblivion, "black" linked with "blind," and all with the sense that these are at once emblems, or "omens," and that there is "Nothing [that] requires you to make sense of them." Meaning persists in Hades, but it is a backward reflection from the living world. "Shiver," "shore," and "Gazing" each bespeak another liminality, neither accustomed nor numb, a visceral and urgent "vacillation" where the feeling is all that's left of either viscera or time, neither land nor water, neither blind nor understanding. And the "omens" naively published in underworld reveal a watery beginning blasted by fire, as they mix dawn and decimation to form an icon both of this timeless world and the telescoped history of living men.

The speaker views this scene as if it had been presented in a diorama in a cultural anthropology or natural history museum. The lake-people's remains, egg cup and "boat with feet," tell of refinements of necessity and of imagination—that which sustains this life and may carry us to the next. Merrill's speaker is impressed by the evocative power, the human "truth," of these relics, but oppressed by the divisive and hegemonic "fall into history" that the guide's narrative, and the museum itself, represents. The [spirit?] guide's "tale of godless hordes / Sweeping like clockwork over Switzerland" meant to incite "your very blood" to "tick out" blood-besotted "truths" and "traffic in strong prescriptions" such as "live" and "die," recalls the pendular flight of the phoenix, swinging from ardor to ashes, now played out on the stage of history and nations. History and politics would make "life or death" voluptuaries of us all. Their simplifying tales and homilies are so much more "blind flapping" as from mouths also blind.

In the preceding section, mention of Switzerland, the landlocked island of a "thousand years of peace" nonetheless beset with the "godless hordes" of history, serves as a geographic counter-image to Yeats's unspoken Ireland in the first stanza of "Sailing to Byzantium." As Yeats's Ireland is awash in nature and natural crises ("Whatever is begotten, born, and dies"), Merrill's Switzerland is awash in history.

Yeats has his "mackerel-crowded seas," Merrill his sweeping "godless hordes." Yeats's island is "caught in that sensuous music," Merrill's Switzerland is entranced by the "Voluptuous homilies" national history would teach us. This contrasting parallel between the two poems allows Merrill once again to subsume Yeats's argument into his own. It is not just the apocalyptic, phoenix vision of personal relations, art, afterlife, and politics that Merrill criticizes. Yeats's view of nature is also apocalyptic: it is a world of crisis that must be overcome through crisis and the consuming fires of art and imagination. In "answering" Ireland with Switzerland, Merrill extends his critique back to each term in Yeats's governing dichotomy: nature and the "artifice of eternity." Neither is granted the apocalyptic extremity found in Yeats.

Ultimately we see that neither ancient nor modern attempts to domesticate death or make sense of time offer more than "Voluptuous homilies." With so much that is suspect in our master myths, it might seem reasonable to discount them altogether, to "traffic" in the simple-mindedness of "strong prescriptions." But Merrill takes a different and characteristic tack, suggesting that something might be wrong, not with the myth, but with how we read it.

In choosing to write about his bird of fire, Merrill has taken on one of tradition's most apocalyptic myths, in which everything is a matter of life and death, and links it with other tales we tell to give us wishful, aesthetic or rationalizing distance from, *or identification with*, the ambiguous "simplicity of fire"—this impulse whether to stride or slip "out of nature" and into the purity of idea. Just as the poem's first vision of the phoenix is presented as a counter argument ("But often at nightfall . . . a giant jeweled bird / Comes cawing to the sill . . .), so now Merrill suggests another counter argument, one even more squarely aimed at the notions of agony and transcendence found in both of Yeats's Byzantium poems:

> But couldn't the point about the phoenix
> Be not agony or resurrection, rather
> A mortal lull that followed either . . . ?

Merrill's question does more than offer a counter-reading to the usual, apocalyptic reading of this "bird of fire." In answer to the extremities of time, the pendulum-like trap of what Yeats called "All those antinomies / Of night and day" ("Vacillation"), of life or death, or of Merrill's "ever fiercer / Flights between ardor and ashes," Merrill answers not with an impulse off the wheel of generation, some way of being "out of nature" and thus able to sing safely of "What is past, or passing, or to come."

In Merrill's view, this Yeatsian "ardor" both includes and denies the transcendent claims of Yeats's Condition of Fire, his "brand, or flaming breath," that the body calls death and the heart remorse (Vacillation I). "Ever fiercer / Flights between ardor and ashes" includes by the grandeur of its diction; it denies by the irony of its context: the real "ashes" that Yeats hardly mentions in all his talk of "flame." [In all Yeats's poetry "ash" or "ashes," in the sense of the aftermath of fire, occur but three times.] But in arguing that Merrill criticizes Yeats's impulse toward transcendence in these poems it is noteworthy to recall that Yeats took Plato and Plotinus to task in section III of "The Tower" for just this offense and then, in 1928, admitted to a certain amount of projection and scapegoating in his mockery: "When I wrote the lines about Plato and Plotinus I forgot that it is something in our own eyes that makes us see them as all transcendence" (Qtd. in Jeffares *Commentary* 258). In a similar way, Merrill misreads, or simplifies, Yeats in order to construct an external figure for "something in [his] own eyes" that is drawn to the claims of transcendence, simplicity, and unity. As we see in the shifting identities in Merrill's early fire poems, Yeats's "presence" serves a valued aspect of himself, but one he must also guard and argue against as he tries to build a poetry that is commensurate with both reality and truth, or "reality and justice" in Yeats's terms (*Vision* 25).

In contrast, Merrill insists on the time of in-between, on the "mortal lull" that may follow extremity.

> . . . A mortal lull that followed either,
> During which flames expired as they should,
> And dawn, discovering ashes not yet stirred,
> Buildings in rain, but set on rock,
> Beggar and sparrow entertaining one another,
> Showed me your face, for that moment neither
> Alive nor dead, but turned in sleep
> Away from whatever waited to be endured?

The series of images that Merrill uses to depict this "lull" reveals a startling richness of association and implicit activity that obliquely recalls the stream of images in the opening stanza of "Sailing to Byzantium." In both the end of Merrill's poem and the beginning of Yeats's we have lovers, birds, and buildings (or monuments); in one the fall of rain, in the other "salmon-falls"; in one the order of flames which "expired as they should," in the other the succession of "dying generations." Merrill's "Ashes not yet stirred" harkens back to fires that resemble the flame of "unageing intellect" whose monuments in Yeats's poem "all neglect." His "whatever waited to be endured" echoes (and inverts) Yeats's "Whatever is begotten, born, and dies." Yet, for all these glancing parallels and the similar flow of image after image, the tone of the two sections could not be more different. Where Yeats's lines suggest an ambivalent disgust that motivates the old man's flight, Merrill's present a welcome resignation, a willingness to stay and wait, in keeping with his general "critique." Whereas in "Sailing to Byzantium," Yeats argues for a journey and radical, flaming purgation to release the speaker from time, here Merrill suggests we might focus less on pyrotechnic extremes, which only *seem* to take us out of time, and focus more on our embeddedness in time, where for escape we may turn at most "in sleep / Away from whatever wait[s] to be endured."

Though I have emphasized the way Merrill's conclusion points to Yeats's opening, two elements of Merrill's conclusion do point to the end of Yeats's poem.

Merrill's "Beggar and sparrow entertaining one another" seems a parody of Yeats's "drowsy Emperor" and golden bird. Not only does Merrill's pairing invert Yeats's social hierarchy, and call into question Yeats's aristocratic values; Merrill's sparrow is expressly not his phoenix (or Yeats's bird of fire). As one of nature's least things, and not the work of sublime artifice or legend, the sparrow belongs with the mode of "mortal lull"; and the mutuality, the social interplay of "entertaining one another" even across the gap of species, not only mimes the interconnectedness of being in time, it serves as emblem for the best recompense embeddedness in time may offer. (In a similar way, Yeats's tableau, with its social and affective isolation—the radical disconnections between mechanical singer, its epic material, and trivial purpose, presents a haunting emblem of transcendent longing, while it also reflects the difficulties and dangers of thinking as if such transcendence of time and nature had been or could be achieved.)

The other Yeatsian element is the phrase, "neither / Alive nor dead." This phrase points to the condition of being "out of nature" that characterizes Yeats's golden bird. It contrasts with the matters of life and death that occupy Yeats's "dying generations" and Merrill's critique of what we might now call a pervasive "mistaken phoenix syndrome." It seems to point to a possible identification between Yeats's bird, and hence his understanding of "the Condition of Fire," and Merrill's sleeper. But as we will see this would be a mistake.

Clearly, with all its somber-seeming images, Merrill's poem does not offer Yeats's wanted exaltation at the end; but it does indicate a "dawn." Merrill's speaker draws assurance from the order of things. His "mortal lull" is where temporal and physical orders seem to hold, where "flames expired as they should." This "should" and the succeeding images suggest modes of moral, social, and cultural order, but without any stridency. Mention of "building in rain" recalls the blackened ruins of "four rows of stilts," which like all human building stand as an emblem for any creative enterprise as a kind of *poesis*, a "building again" to use Yeats's terms from "Lapis Lazuli." These wooden stilts, which earlier in the poem announced "a first trace of culture," were also importantly seen "at dawn." The depredations of time are not forgotten, but here Merrill chooses to show us buildings that, however beset by weather, are still "set on rock" and may for a time endure. "Beggar and sparrow entertaining one another" evokes social and natural orders but, problematically, also suggests that the social order is in some sense natural. "Entertaining" puts a Panglosian spin on what threatens to sound like bad Wordsworth.[4] But before this incipient sentimentality has time to register, Merrill delivers the verb phrase "Showed me your face," which rushes the reader away from the "environmental" images dawn has discovered and into the intersubjective drama that underlies the poem.

It is within the "mortal lull," and not while caught in the talons of phoenix-driven pyrotechnics, that the lover's face can be seen. That it appears "neither / Alive nor dead" is unsettling. It may suggest the superhuman "death-in life and life-in-death" of Yeats's Byzantium poems, the condition of being "out of nature" and beyond the reach of time, but I think these associations arise so closely only so that Merrill may make his concluding revisionary reading of the "condition of fire." The lover is not lifted out of time in appearing neither alive nor dead. This vision is expressly "for that moment" and deeply involved with anticipated future time. Even in the gesture of turning away, the lover responds to the pressure of "whatever waited to be endured." What might seem a transcendent condition, Merrill immediately naturalizes into "sleep." And although the phoenix's flames have expired "as they should," the scene is not devoid of light or flame.[5]

The seeing ("discovering") fire of the sun at dawn is the presiding image at the poem's end, and the speaker's gaze on his sleeping lover is a mirror of that image. Both sun and speaker look out on an anxious kind of sleep, as on "ashes not yet stirred." And as "dawn" is a particularly time-bound evocation of the master-fire of nature, as it looks forward but also trails evidence of the past night, so too does Merrill's speaker look both forward and back. Dawn's light is solar fire, the speaker's light is love. But it is love profoundly qualified by time, pity, and the common order that lets "all things pass away."[6]

To conclude, Yeats's poem takes the shape of a spiral. Its "social" setting at the end, with drowsy Emperor, lords, and ladies, recalls the mingled "societies" of the first stanza, but at a "higher" level. The bird's song of "What is past, or passing, or to come" recalls the first stanza's "Whatever is begotten, born, and dies," but at a higher level of generality. This structure is at once in keeping with and a qualification of the argument of Yeats's poem. But with this return to time, generation, and multiplicity, Yeats's poem begs the question of whether it succeeds in presenting a vision of "the condition of fire" where all is music and rest. Similarly, the structure of Merrill's poem reflects his argument. In keeping with the image of the phoenix as a pendulum, Merrill's poem moves from opening dissatisfaction (A: "If it were simply a matter of life or death"), to a death scene (B), to vision of the phoenix (C), and then swings back through a second death scene (B), to a second dissatisfaction (A: "If it were less that a matter of life or death"). But Merrill's repetitions are far from mechanical; each repetition argues a difference. Nor does "About the Phoenix" end where it began, a movement that would be too like the reading of the phoenix Merrill argues against, and too like the spiral of Yeats's poem. Instead by questioning "the point about the phoenix," the poem concludes by reaching back into its center to recall and reread the emblem of the bird and its flames. Thus, the structure of Merrill's argument may be mapped A B C B A C—a structure that resembles several characteristic stanza forms and which would seem to press for a sense of thematic as well as formal closure.

But other elements press back against the totalizing "finish" of claiming the last word. Just as the opening "But" points to a time and interaction before the poem, the concluding question and the presence of the lover as the specific addressee, link the poem to a specific, possible future response. Merrill's final question is rhetorical, or "closed," only in the sense that it admits but one answer: "yes, we could read the phoenix this way." But the force of Merrill's question, unlike Yeats's use of questions in "The Second Coming," "Leda and the Swan," "Among School Children" or "Vacillation I," is not to freeze the moment in a suspension of pointed indeterminacy; rather, Merrill's question sweeps the imagination into the events of time and anticipation of the future.

Thus, the accumulated sense of things happening overshadows the effect of the sentence as question. Indeed, the question is so easily assented to that it seems already answered long before we reach the unexpected reminder of the question mark. Merrill carefully sets this sweep of events and observations in the simple past. He does not employ a fictive present, as if the poem were meant to exist in an eternalizing present outside the rush of time. Instead, the accumulation of past events, combined with the final, opening gesture of the sentence's question mark, directs the poem toward the moment beyond the poem—perhaps Merrill's most eloquent answer to Yeats's longing for "the artifice of eternity" and his surest sign that he welcomes "Those dying generations– at their song." [7]

Appendix B
Merrill's Early Reading in Metaphysical and Psychological Topics

THE LIST THAT FOLLOWS IS PRIMARILY MEANT TO GIVE AN INDICATION OF Merrill's early interest in broad, systematic, imaginative, and theoretical efforts to understand the human psyche and its relation to art, language, history, and the cosmos. Merrill pursued by far the most massive excursus into these realms with his reading in the early 1950s of P. D. Ouspensky's *A New Model of the Universe*, *The Psychology of Man's Possible Evolution*, and *Tertium Organum: The Third Canon of Thought, A Key to the Enigmas of the World*. It is interesting that in his early reading of Krishnamurti and Ouspensky (the chief disciple of Gurdjieff), Merrill links two divergent branches of Theosophy, thus establishing an attenuated, though nonetheless clear, relation with the thought of Mme. Blavatsky, who also gave Yeats's interest in spiritualist and esoteric knowledge its earliest home. Merrill's Yeats studies included a volume of the Letters, Hone's biography, Yeats's *Essays and Introductions*, and Yeats's *Mythologies*, which collects much of the supernatural tales and spiritualist and esoteric writing, including *Per Amica Silentia Lunae*. Merrill's interest in the metaphysical and spiritual aspects of poetry also brought him to Elizabeth Sewell's *Orphic Voices: Poetry and Natural History*, as well as a number of studies of Dante, Blake, and Rilke. In the late 1940s and through the 50s, Merrill's reading also included studies of Buddhism, particularly Zen, by R. H. Blythe, Christmas Humphries, D. T. Suzuki, and Alan Watts. He read C. Sivaramurti's edition of the *Mahabalipuram* and Krishnamurti's *Commentaries on Living*; Martin Buber's *I and Thou* and Paul Tillich's *The New Being*, as well as a number of theological volumes by C. S. Lewis, William Schamoni's *The Face of the Saints* and E. V. Rieu's edition of *The Four Gospels*. Merrill also studied Robert Graves's *The Nazarene Gospels Restored* and *The White Goddess*, while pursuing his interest in myth and symbol through the anthropological studies of Ruth Benedict, Margaret Mead, Joseph Campbell, Maya Deren and Heinrich Zimmer, as well as such studies as Paul Schilder's *The Image and Appearance of the Human Body*, Susanne Langer's *Philosophy in a New Key: A Study in the Symbolism of Reason, Rite, and Art*, and Bachelard's essays on the imagination and elemental substances, *La Pyschanalyse du Feu* and *La Terre et Les Reveries du Repos*. These interests also inform his reading of Freud which included during this period the *Introductory Lectures of Psycho-Analysis*, *An Autobiographical Study*, *Totem and Taboo*, *Leonardo da Vinci: A Study in Psychosexuality*, and *Moses and Monotheism*. (Merrill did not begin reading Jung until the early 1970s with such volumes as *Four Archetypes*, *Introduction to a Science of Mythology*, *The Portable Jung*, and *Man and His Symbols*.) Merrill's "early" philosophical reading also included Kierkegaard (*Fear and Trembling*), Wittgenstein (*The Blue and Brown Notebooks* and Norman Malcolm's memoir), Emerson (a selection of the Journals), Berenson (*Aesthetics and History*), and, in response to the "dawning" atomic era, Cassirer (*Substance and Function and Einstein's Theory of Relativity*) as well as Kenneth Heuer's *The End of the World* and Laura Fermi's *The Atom in the Family*. Merrill also read and annotated Norman O. Brown's *Life Against Death: The Psychoanalytical Meaning of History* (as well as the later volume *Love's Body*), and Hans Jonas's *The Gnostic Religion*. (In the mid-1970s Merrill's reading of Giorgio de Santillana and Hertha von Dechend's massive study, *Hamlet's Mill: An Essay on Myth and the Frame of Time*, which provided images for "Verses for Urania," as Julian Jaynes' *The Origin of Consciousness in the Breakdown of the Bicameral Mind* contributed significant ideas and images for *Mirabell*.)

Appendix C
Manuscript Variations in *Mirabell* and *Scripts*

VARIATIONS IN UPPER-CASE "DICTATED" MATERIAL BETWEEN THE PUBLISHED poem and manuscript versions sent to J. D. McClatchy and Alfred Corn while Merrill was working on *Mirabell* are numerous enough to show the weight of Merrill's shaping hand. Most involve clarifications. A few suggest fundamental reconsideration. The most impressive of these is signaled by a change in nomenclature for Mirabell's highest power. What is given in the published poem as the "SOURCE OF LIGHT" or "S/O/L" was earlier conceived as a much darker, more Nietzschean or more Foucauldian "CENTER OF POWER" or "C/O/P" (S. 251). "CENTER OF POWER" may have served well enough in most contexts, but the disciplinary connotations of "C/O/P" let surface a line of thinking that rests uncomfortably with Merrill's more conventionally paradisal imagery. (The page numbers given below indicate the approximate location passages would have had in the published volume.)

Some of the variations entail cutting material that seemed, perhaps, too rough-from-the-board or extraneous, such as: "WHEN OUR RACE FELL GOD B GRASPD / THE BASIC GENE STRUCTURE & KEPT IT IN AIR TO SETTLE / & ENGENDER AT RANDOM MORE OF THIS LATER SO THESE / CREATURES IN FORM MOST CLOSELY RESEMBLING THE IMAGINED / CENTAUR RULED" (S. 167 "Atlantis 2") or, concerning the niceties of bat-angel breeding, "HALF OUR NUMBERS HAD EGG SACS & HALF HAD INSULATED / RADIUM VESICLES WHICH FERTILIZED THEN FED THE EGGS" (S. 170, "4.3"). Others show the poet enriching his text. Where Maria, in the published text, asks, "IS IT MES ENFANTS A TAPESTRY OF BEASTS / AROIUND WHICH THE LADY OF THE LOOKING GLASS?" in manuscript her question reads more simply and more determinately, "IS IT MES ENFANTS A MORALITY PLAY?" (S. 171). In another variation, based on Lewis Thomas's *The Lives of a Cell*, Merrill not only tightens the writing but also adds new material based on his reading about quarks. The manuscript version reads:

197

> THE CELL IS OUR WORLD   THE ATOM IS ITS 1ST
> UNIT & THE UNIVERSAL UNIT THE MOLECULE
> THE GREENHOUSE IS A CELL MULTIPLE & MANAGEABLE
> ALL MATTER IS THERE4 PARFT OF THE CELL IF WE THINK (M)
> OF THE MICROSSCOPE UNDER THE EYE OF GOD B WE SEE
> ON THE SLIDE CALLD EARTH THE LITTLE SCALE OF OUR LIVES.

The published version is also careful to change that final inclusive "OUR LIVES" to the less problematic second person:

> THE ATOM IS OUR UNIT   THE WHOLE GREENHOUSE
> IS BUT A CELL COMPLES BUT MANAGEABLE   ALL MATTER
> THERE4 IS PART OF THAT CELL   IF AS WE PRESUME GOD B'S
> EYE PEERS DOWN THRU HIS MICROSCOPE AT THE SWIMMING PLANETS
> U ON THE SLIDE CALLED EARTH MAY GUESS AT THE SCALE OF YR LIVES:
> LESS THAN THOSE LEAST PARTICLES THAT IN ISOLATION DIE
> EACH WITH ITS OWN STRANGENESS & COLOR & CHARM A PRICELESS
> IF EXPENDABLE FORCE IN MEANING'S OWN GROWING MOLECULE (S. 210)

Merrill has acknowledged feeling "a perfect magpie" in adopting Alfred Corn's joke about "E—Ephraim—equaling any emcee squared" ("Interview with McClatchy" 66), but the interview does not show, as McClatchy and Corn's typescript does, Merrill penciling in the addition in other-worldly caps, with "Thank you, A[lfred]." in parentheses.

Some material is added as a means of building anticipation and establishing, in the reader's mind, a sense of fulfillment when what is predicted comes to pass; one such instance is the passage: "BUT THE GREAT / MIRACLE IS THE REINCARNATION OF TE GODS. THIS / WE WILL LET OUR MASTERS REVEAL." (S. 225). Another set of variations reveals how making Mirabell's last lessons serve as a kind of convalescence was layered in at a later date. In section "7.7," the lines starting "THE WORST IS BEHIND US . . . " and continuing to "AN (M) ORDERLY IN WHITE" were added (S. 233-34), as were the variations, "Helps just to dramatize our "convalescence"? and "DIVINE CONCEPT RADIATING / HEALTH TO THE POOR INVALID PARTICULAR. . . " (S. 252) and this insertion: "THERE! BY NOW IN IMAGINATION / OUR PATIENT IS FAR AWAY HIS TV GLOWS TILL ALL HOURS / HIS CHART IS NORMAL" (S. 254).

Speaking with Fred Bornhauser, Merrill talks about how the words of Apollo or the Archangel Michael "which *we* put into his mouth, become part of the vast system whereby the universe reveals itself to us" (58), and we are reminded of the lines in "Matinees," in which "a voice . . . in the speech of birds" says: "My father having tampered with your mouth, / From now on, metal, music, myth / Will seem to taint its words." (Where in "Matinees" this father seemed to refer to Yeats, here Merrill has himself covertly assumed the doctor's role.) Occasionally, in doctoring his instructor's voices, Merrill shows this principle in action, putting words from his mouth into theirs. In manuscript, it is JM who briefly relates that Pope Innocent VI served as the basis for the Faust legend; whereas, in the published version, 741 elaborates the story to some length (S. 130-31). Again, in Book 7, the lines that WHA speaks ("MY DEAR IS THAT THE POINT? ISN'T IT RATHER / THAT THEY TOGETHER WERE THE FIRST LAB SOUL?") were 'originally' JM's (S. 225). What Merrill calls the "showiest" example of "where I presume to pass 'my own words' off as a message from the other world . . . is Wystan's evocation of the manor house [*Mirabell*, 9.1]. It came welling up from me one afternoon, instead of from the Board. I never again felt so 'possessed'" (Polito "Conversation" 11).

Other passages are simply cut, perhaps for offering too much clarity or too soon. Mary Jackson tells JM early on (0.6) "YOUR THOUGHTS CREATE US FOR EACH OTHER DURING THESE TALKS," this coming well before Bezelbob's "WE ARE YOU YOU ARE WE EACH OTHERS DREAM" (S. 117), which in manuscript read less cryptically, "I AM U U ARE ME WE ARE THE DREAM." In 2.7 Merrill trades the news that "There are some thousand orphans seven years / Old—in China, Russia, the U. S.— / Who, grown, will tidy up the world-wide mess: / WARDS OF THE ANGELS" for supposition about the likes of "those thirty-six 'Just / Men of the Jews" (S. 142-43). The published poem tells us "TAT YOUR VERY SPIRIT LIVES / IN OUR RED CELLS" (S. 212), which sounds clear until we wonder whose "RED CELLS"? The manuscript gives us a slightly more corporeally coherent version: "IN THE VERY WISDOM / OF THE RED CELLS THAT WE USE IS YOUR SPIRIT." Merrill also edits out the greater personal clarity of the manuscript's discussion of JM's poetic relationship to Hans Lodeizen. The published poem tells us, "I wrote my 'Dedication'— / Entered, intersected by his death. / & HIS TALENTS HE NOW FEELS A GROWING PART OF YR WORK" (S. 221). Previously this read:

> Yes, I see now. It is what *I* felt
> Writing that "Dedication"—entered by,
> Nourished by his dying . . .
> & TALENTS ALL ONE And Orion?
>   HL'S ROMANTICISM SAW THE STARS
> AS ETERNAL   U SEE THE WORK
> And now, is he aware of being used?
>   HE KNOWS THE WORK GOES ON

Such clarity may lift the veil too far.

Merrill tells us that in April of 1979 he was "mulling over cuts and changes" he had in mind for *Scripts* (and that he received Michael's enthusiastic go-ahead: "CHNGE! / REVISE, RISE, SHINE!") ("From the Cutting Room Floor") and that "in *Mirabell* the problem was to cut and cut and cut, without leaving out anything crucial [whereas] with *Scripts*, the transcripts, by and large, simply became the text, or that part of it in small caps" (Polito "Conversation" 11). Given its considerably greater length, it is impressive how little apparent "doctoring" that volume's otherworldly material reveals. Evidence from J. D. McClatchy's typescript shows that most textual *variations* occur in Merrill's lower-case "commentary." Upper-case material is added or cut, but not apparently "reworked." Interesting material cut from the poem includes elaboration on Nabokov's exclusion from the "salon" (412-13, 425), camp passages featuring Luca [David Kalstone's patron (419)], and occasional peaks at "COMING ATTRACTIONS" (371). More revealing material dropped from the poem concerns such matters as Merrill's Christianity ["were we Christians? / For we were, once" (426)], Ephraim's numeric formula and role as guide and "Our glowing Eros" (423), how "'MAKING SENSE OF IT' WAS FROM THE START / MAKING A LANGUAGE" (414), and Maria's characterization of the last years of life and a soul's lot in heaven:

> WE BRACE
> OURSELVES FOR THE LAST DECADE OR SO ON EARTH,
> WISE UP, LEARN SOMETHING, & TOO SOON BLINK OUT
> YET THE MOMENTUM GOES ON   WS [Wallace Stevens?] STILL "WORKS"
> SO DOES MAYA   DAILY THE WHOLE LOT
> (MAMAN TOO, WEEDING IN HER SUNNY PLOT)
> GO ON ATTAINING THAT BRIEF RAPTURE OF
> THE THING DONE WELL AS IF A MORTAL RACE
> CONTINUED AGAINST TIME. SO THAT LAST GRACE
> GIVEN ON EARTH, TO BE THE BEST WE WERE,
> IS STILL OURS HERE IN HEAVEN   (371)

Notes

NOTES TO THE INTRODUCTION

[1] In quoting from interviews gathered in *Recitative*, Merrill's volume of collected prose, it is important to realize that Merrill is fully in control of his responses—fragments, shifts of topic, and all—since, in almost all cases, Merrill gave his replies in writing. His editor, J. D. McClatchy, wryly comments, "The illusion of spontaneous conversation is after all attainable at the writing-desk" (*Recitative* xi). Merrill's interest in kinds of control that give the illusion of spontaneity is an abiding concern and one of the first lessons he may have taken from Yeats, who in "Adam's Curse" acknowledges, "A line will take us hours maybe / Yet if it does not seem a moment's thought, / Our stitching and unstitching has been naught." With this in mind, it is interesting to note that Merrill concludes his 1968 interview with John Boatwright and Enrique Ucelay DaCal, students at Hotchkiss and Bard by saying: "I want full control over my own product" (39), a desire that will largely shape Merrill's conceptions of a largely voluntary species of poetic influence.

[2] For significant correspondences between poems by Merrill and Yeats before "The Book of Ephraim" see Steven Yenser's review of *Braving the Elements: Poetry*, 1973, 122:3, 163–168. Richard Sáez also counts Merrill as one of the few masterful successors to Yeats's symbolism in an early 1974 essay (Sáez 55). After *Sandover*, Harold Bloom lists a number of similarities between Merrill and Yeats: "Merrill, like Yeats, is both an occultist and an erotic poet, and again like Yeats he is a curious kind of religious poet . . . " (Bloom *Merrill* 1); and Leslie Brisman notes some other general stylistic and thematic correspondences between earlier Merrill poems and the "Yeatsian esthetic" before he asserts that "Yeats's spirit hovers over the entire enterprise of *The Changing Light of Sandover*" (Brisman 190–91). In a note to his 1987 *The Consuming Myth*, Stephen Yenser maintains that Yeats has been an "influential presence in Merrill's work at least since *Nights and Days*" and that "Yeats figures especially often in *The Fire Screen*" (348). In the "Afterward" to his 1994 *A Reader's Guide*, Robert Polito provides a substantial discussion focusing on the Yeats/Merrill relation in *The Changing Light at Sandover* (256–262). Andrea Mariani presented a perceptive article (in Italian) on Merrill's Yeatsian mask in the 1993 article, "Yeats in Merrill: maschera e figura." And, most recently,

Steven Matthews devotes six pages to the Yeats/Merrill relation in his omnibus study, *Yeats as Precursor: Readings in Irish, British and American Poetry*. Matthews sees *Sandover* as "the logical extension of Merrill's preoccupation with the Byzantium poems" and concludes, "Merrill's remains perhaps the most complex of the engagements which American poetry has made with Yeats since his death" (179, 181). The particular value of Matthew's study, apart from the range of poets he addresses, is the clarity and resourcefulness of his opening chapter on "Yeats: Influence, Traditions and the Problematics of reading."

³ Hugh Kenner notes that "Sailing to Byzantium" is itself "a transformation wrought on two Odes of Keats, about a bird not born for death and about a Grecian artifice of eternity" (164). In light of this relation, Merrill's deflection of attention from Yeats on to Keats may be a way of marking a recycling economy of influence: Yeats's transformations of Keats become Merrill's transformation of Yeats reflected back onto his precursor, Keats. The displacement from Yeats to Keats may also have a more biographical source—as well as the Merrillian argument from spelling and puns, in which the common appetite featured in both names betrays their "hidden wish" (*Recitative* 111). As we shall see, in Merrill's dedicatory poem to *The Black Swan*, Keats also serves as a sort of "screen memory" for Yeats and for Merrill's mentor and lover, Kimon Friar. In a similar vein, we shall also see that Merrill deflects attention onto Stevens and away from Yeats in discussing his early poem "Medusa" and that he also chooses not to include "More Enterprise" in his 1982 collection, *From the First Nine*, and later excludes "Flying from Byzantium" from his 1992 *Selected Poems*, these being his only two poems which directly evoke Yeats's poems in their titles.

⁴ Yeats famously offers: his "curse on plays / That have to be set up in fifty ways, / On the day's war with every knave and dolt, / Theatre business, management of men . . ." ("The Fascination for What's Difficult"). To which Merrill seems to reply with this prose paraphrase: "What I really hated about working in the theater was the demand on your time—conferences, explaining your lines to actors, making yourself available for rewrites, and all that" ("James Merrill at Home" 26).

⁵ Asked whether he is "interested in enriching the myth-starved culture" which he sees around him, Merrill responds: "I certainly feel it is myth starved. I am first of all enriching myself with some of these attitudes and possibilities and if other people are hungry for them, fine" ("James Merrill at Home" 32). If contemporary individuals feel hungry for myth, it is fitting that our spiritual counterparts feel the opposite. We recall that Yeats's spirit-voices would chide him when he had not sufficiently furnished his mind with the "concrete expressions" of history and biography: "We are starved," they would say (*Vision* 12).

⁶ In the Sandover books, the character representing Merrill's long-time partner, David Jackson, appears as "DJ" and Merrill as "JM."

⁷ Throughout this study, I refer to the four parts of Merrill's *The Changing Light at Sandover* with the single names "Ephraim," *Mirabell, Scripts*, and "Coda," and to the volume as a whole as *Sandover*, abbreviated in citations as "S." Communications from the other world made via the Ouija Board are given throughout in the board's capital letters.

⁸ In a more general discussion of Merrill's "refusal to grant authority to literary predecessors," Piotr Gwiazda comments:

> When 'The Book of Ephraim" was first published in Divine Comedies (1976), many readers, noticing its grounding in the occult, took it for a poetic descendant of *A Vision*. The subsequent installments laid these comparisons to rest, even though Yeats remained a palpable presence in the trilogy until its very end, without ever

attaining the prominence of Auden or enjoying the kind of authority that "Ephraim" might have lead us to expect. (426)

In contrast to this view, part of what my study hopes to show is that comparsions between *Sandover* and *A Vision* do indeed remain fruitful throughout Merrill's poem, but that Merrill deliberately works to deflect attention from such comparisons, in part by making any facile sense of similarity immediately suspect. I will also contend that, particularly given the role of Yeats in Merrill's other poetry early and late, such deflections, displacements, and seeming reductions of Yeats's authority as operate in *Sandover* are but a further sign of how important Yeats is to Merrill's occult epic.

[9] For further discussion of the ways in which Bloom's theory of poetic influence relates to Yeats in Merrill's poetry, see the Coda in Chapter Four of this study.

[10] See Chapters 4 and 5 in Bloom's *Yeats*.

[11] In his 1997 preface to *The Anxiety of Influence*, Bloom asserts, "I never meant by 'the anxiety of influence' a Freudian Oedipal rivalry, despite a rhetorical flourish or two" and that "influence-anxiety does not so much concern the forerunner but rather . . . that the anxiety of influence *comes out of* a complex act of strong misreading, a creative interpretation that I call 'poetic misprision'" (xxii, xxiii, emphasis in original). And yet Bloom continues to evoke "the agonistic misprision performed upon powerful forerunners by only the most gifted of their successors" (xxiv) and takes pains to describe the seemingly very Oedipal struggle Shakespeare undertook to emancipate himself from the image of Marlowe (xliii), who was "primarily a personal image of the dramatist's power over the audience" (xxiv). Following Bloom's practice, this study focuses on Merrill's own on going and "complex act of strong[ly] misreading" Yeats. But it supports these readings, in part, by undertaking to illuminate the psychodynamic associations that link Merrill's relationships with his parents and with Kimon Friar to the poetry and personality of W. B. Yeats. Bloom would not authorize these excursions into biography, although they often serve to underscore the particular textual relationships that most interest him.

NOTES TO CHAPTER ONE

[1] The poems in question include the "Theory of Vision" poems, "The Green Eye," "The Cosmological Eye," and "Perspectives of the Lonesome Eye."

[2] Harold Bloom comments that "all poets, weak or strong, agree in denying any share in the anxiety of influence, . . . even as they more and more strongly manifest [such anxieties] in their poems"; "more than ever," Bloom insists, "[contemporary poets] tell continuous lies, particularly about their relations to one another, and most consistently about their relations to their precursors" (*Map* 10, 162). Given what we shall see of his considerably vexed relationship with Yeats's poetry, Merrill's sunny remarks about influence provide an excellent example of what Bloom has observed about modern poets in general.

[3] "I began writing in imitation of him [Freddy Buechner]. By the following year we were reading each other's work avidly, lovingly, enviously" ("Interview" *Lawrentian* 9). "My classmate Frederick Buechner wrote his poem first. In a flash I thought: I can do that too! And away we went" (*Recitative* 5). "I wrote my poems out of envy of my friend Freddy Buechner. . . . This soon became a habit, and before long I worked up to a poem a day" (Ibid. 40).

[4] In "Choosing Our Fathers: Gender and Identity in Whitman, Ashbery and Richard Howard," David Bergman argues that gay poets, because they do not fully identify with their fathers, are freer to choose their poetic fathers. Ashbery and Howard, for example, find "in

Whitman, not a Father who must be rejected in the Oedipal drama (as Pound, for instance, enacted), but a companion whose hand can be grasped" (400). Merrill consciously follows this pattern in his relation with W. H. Auden and his congenial accounts of poetic influence. But, as we shall see, Yeats calls up deeper and more pressing anxieties.

⁵ Maria is also, Merrill tells us in his memoir, "the closest I'll ever get to having a Muse. There is no one saner or more sympathetic, more in love with overtones, quicker to register anything said or left unsaid" (*Different* 230–31). She and Elizabeth Bishop most fulfilled his quest for "'the right woman,' someone my spirit could aspire to resemble or . . . to whose turn of mind and way with emotion I felt attuned" (Ibid. 141).

⁶ In the Finale of *Scripts* Wystan and Maria are dressed as if for their wedding (he in cutaway, she in "WHITE SARI WITH ORANGEBLOSSOMS" (S. 515), and JM presides at what is at once the shattering violence of their death and their re-birth:

> JM WILL TAKE THIS MARBLE
> STYLUS & GIVING US TH BENEFIT
> OF A WELL AIMED WORD, SEND OUR IMAGINED SELVES
> FALLING IN SHARDS THRU THE ETERNAL WATERS
> . . . & INTO THE GOLDEN BOUGH
> OF MYTH ON INTO LIFE D'ACCORD? (S. 516)

By virtue of this ceremony, JM becomes the young god, "risen," who releases Pegasus (the flight of his own best poetry) and hears the proud, lonely call of his father-God, God B (S. 517). Thus, this conclusion to *Scripts* is at once a grand evocation of the power of the poetic imagination and a highly charged and ambivalent fantasy about both overcoming and establishing oneself as the source and receptacle of parental power.

⁷ This evocation of his mother's needlework at the beginning of Merrill's poetic career bears an uncanny relation to the scene in Yeats's "Cuchulain Comforted," written at the end of his. There, one spectral figure bids the dead hero join them in taking up needle and thread to sew his own shroud. Yeats underscores that this spiritual making is a shared endeavor: "and all we do / All must together do." In the final section of "The Forms of Death," Merrill suggests the deadly costs of his mother's smothering aestheticism, no matter how sociable or shared. There, "A woman while I slept stood by my bed / And with a needle and gold thread began / To stitch with gold each agony of my skin / . . . Gold like a jaundice spread / Until I changed into a tapestry, / . . . a gold nonchalance of doom." The "shaped and polished and begemmed" achievement of Merrill's early poetry, "the world becoming art," would continue to attract him ["What happened is becoming literature. . . . The world will have put on a thin gold mask" ("For Proust")]; but, after his early work with Kimon Friar, Merrill grew more anxious to find a "living voice" with the power to spark dialogue and evoke response that was at once conventional and visionary (*Different* 6, 18). As we shall see, it is Yeats who most consistently offers Merrill the ambivalent attractions of both his mother's aestheticism and his father's unsettling power.

⁸ For instances in *Sandover* where Merrill, perhaps following Bloom, explicitly makes the Primal Scene a stage performance ("PART OF A MASTERMASQUE") and Scene of Instruction and Interpretation ("Scene: The schoolroom, once the nursery") in which the principles of Resistance and Innocence, Creation and Idea are first interrogated, see S. 297, 319–24.

⁹ Bloom mentions the link between poets, influence, and the imagery of stars, saying "Poets tend to think of themselves as stars because their deepest desire is to be an influence, rather than to be influenced" (*Map* 12). Bloom also recognizes that an imagined freedom, or

"illusion of freedom," is what sponsors the self-begetting ambition of both poet and poem (*Anxiety* 96); he discusses the "catastrophe of poetic incarnation" as a species of divination that involves tropes both of foretelling and of becoming a god by foretelling and quotes Mircea Eliade to emphasize the compelling link between questions of origin and "the mystery of 'creation'" (*Map* 19, 47).

[10] "Marsyas" is one such poem:

> I used to write in the café sometimes:
> Poems on menus, read all over town
> Or talked out before ever written down.
> One day a girl brought in his latest book.
> I opened it—stiff rhythms, gorgeous rhymes—
> And made a face. Then crash! my cup upset.
> Of twenty upward looks mine only met
> His, that gold archaic lion's look
>
> Wherein I saw my wiry person skinned
> Of every skill it labored to acquire
> And heard the plucked nerve's elemental twang.
> They found me dangling where his golden wind
> Inflicted so much music on the lyre
> That no one could have told you what he sang.

Here the rival poetry is characterized in just the sort of terms (reminiscent of Elinor Wylie), "stiff rhythms, gorgeous rhymes," that Merrill has criticized in his own work. An Oedipal reading has the rival poet (the poetic father) in full command of the feminine artifice of rhythm and rhyme. But, to the younger poet, the father's claims are stifling (his rhythms "stiff"). The younger poet makes a face in protest. In the ensuing contest, although the rival poet is triumphant and the café writer transformed into merely his rival's plucked instrument (surely as anxious a figure for male poetic influence as one could want), the poem itself announces a different result: "gorgeous rhymes" are caught in "fluent speech and vehement gesture." Merrill has given "living voice" to poetry's "feminine" attributes so that, in intimate contest with the father, the son has had his wish.

[11] "Amherst Days" was published in 1986, in *For James Merrill, A Birthday Tribute*, a festschrift edited by J. D. McClatchy honoring Merrill on his sixtieth birthday.

[12] 741 tells JM and DJ, "DANTE'S STRENGTH & THAT OF HIS TIME WAS FIERCE CREDULITY / ALL POSSIBLE GOOD & EVIL WRESTLING . . . DREAM, FACT & EXPERIENCE WERE ONE" (S. 132–33). Later, criticizing the considerable incoherence of *Sandover*, Robert Morse remarks, "Everything in Dante knew its place" (S. 256). Friar presents many of the same ideas in his essay "Myth and Metaphysics" appended to *Modern Poetry*:

> Dante was freed by the belief of his society and the genius of Aquinas from any necessity of diverting his genius into the creation of critical or philosophical systems, and could therefore use and transform given symbols and systems of his culture into the concrete embodiment of a poem, the *Divine Comedy*, within whose aesthetic structure he could create his own world yet make it the unique but multiple blossom of medieval vision. In no poem before or since have aesthetic and ethical orders been so identical, have quantitative and qualitative rhythms been so simultaneously orchestrated. (423)

[Yeats too comments on the "public certainty that sufficed for Dante and St. Thomas" (*Vision* 289).]

In an 1987 interview published in "State of the Arts," the house journal of the Connecticut Commission on the Arts, Merrill acknowledges Friar in a rare appreciative sentence: "Before I graduated I'd read—thanks to a teacher, Kimon Friar, who helped me immensely with the poems I was writing—all the modern poetry that, in those days, never appeared in the curriculum: Yeats, Stevens, Dylan Thomas, Pound, as well as lesser figures" ("James Merrill on Poetry" 5).

[13] About the period of working with Friar and the difficulty of beginning to write for himself, Merrill comments: "Where I felt more at a loss was during the yeas after *First Poems* appeared. . . . I wasted a great deal of time trying to make the transition between school discipline, where you are told what to write and when to hand it in, to the discipline which you imposed on yourself" ("Exploring" 416). In 1991 when the interview took place, a reader might imagine "school discipline" meant advanced poetry writing classes at Amherst, instead of the much more personal and exacting discipline of Friar's tutorials. In another highly telescoped account of these years Merrill writes:

> [At Amherst] Kimon Friar put before me the living poets and gave the nine-day wonders that shot up like beanstalks from this richest of mulches their first and only detailed criticism. Many hands made light work. Four years after graduation my *First Poems* had appeared. I was living alone and unhappy in Rome and going to a psychiatrist for writer's block. (*Recitative* 6)

The rapidity with which Merrill moves from the suggestive, but not too revealing "many hands" making light work to "alone," "unhappy," and "writer's block" itself suggests how fraught this period of moving apart from Friar influence was for Merrill.

[14] The "Yeatsian" qualities that Brisman identifies as being antithetical to Merrill—qualities of detachment, coldness, carelessness with history and other people's lives, a willingness to "Let all things pass away," a conservative elitism and fondness for tradition (195–98)—are all qualities that Merrill also acknowledges as his own, even as he struggles with them. Thus it is little wonder that, from early in his career, Merrill should treat Yeats as his Daimon, his Jungian Shadow, and as Caliban to Auden's Ariel.

[15] The references here are to Yeats's "A Coat," to Yeats's enthusiasm for ice and the "cold eye" (see Yeats's *Essays* 522–23), and to his guiding metaphors of the dance and gyre. See also the reader's first sight of Orestes: "He was walking away from the town. It stretched on either side of him like a robe, its hues of white and stone hanging down to the still harbor" (2).

[16] The undated notebook entry concludes: "Meanwhile it emerges ever more vividly that we ourselves have all along been contriving that tragic fate: extinction is nothing if not man-made."

[17] This passage points forward quite explicitly to the project of *A Different Person*, in which Merrill recounts his relationship with Friar without "benefit" of this naive, heterosexual mask. The passage's last question and response, even in their defensiveness, also provide an uncanny anticipation of Merrill's later more confident inscription in Friar's copy of *Sandover*: "who'd have thought? *You* would"; they also underscore how much "the person I am today," Merrill's earlier self, needed both Friar's confidence in him and his skepticism about Friar to become the "different person," the masterful poet he became.

[18] It is appropriate that Merrill assumes the mask of a character in several crucial ways very different from himself, in part because of his own reticence about his homosexuality at

this point, but also because the mask is chosen to help in his project of active independence. As Yeats asserts:

> If we cannot imagine ourselves as different from what we are, and try to assume that second self, we cannot impose a discipline upon ourselves though we may accept one from others. Active virtue, as distinguished from the passive acceptance of a code, is therefore theatrical, consciously dramatic, the wearing of a mask. . . . (*Per Amica* 334)

And in another context:

> I think that all happiness depends on the energy to assume the mask of some other self. . . . We put on a grotesque or solemn painted face to hide us from the terrors of judgment, . . . where one loses the infinite pain of self-realization. Perhaps all the sins and energies of the world are but its flight from an infinite blinding beam" (qtd. in Jeffares *Commentary* 197).

The Mask is both a defensive and a creative strategy. After all, Merrill has never been one to deny himself the theatrical satisfactions of arranging "for one's / Own chills and fever, passions and betrayals, / Chiefly in order to make song of them" ("Matinees"). But in this second passage, Yeats underscores the defensive, almost self-deceptive, nature of the Mask, which we see dramatized in the *Diblos* writer's moment of self-realization, "Blind I go" (34). The question whether Orson, or "Our Son," is queer, also mirrors Merrill's anxiety during his affair with Friar about whether his parents knew that he was gay and provides another instance of what I call the "prismatic" sense of self-awareness in the novel.

[19] The dancing is explicitly sexual from the first: "The very hissing is sexual . . . and so commends itself to the dancer as a tiny linguistic feature related to mustache & phallus, one more fine feather of virility—" (70). The writer shows us two dancers, Kosta "with legs wrapped about O's waist, head fallen back, shoulders still undulating. The two pairs of arms outstretched, the 2 moustached heads oppositely inclined—something was there of Narcissus & his image, something of the Jack of Clubs" (70–71). Then it is Sandy's turn to join his brother, first being suspended from Orestes' waist ["It ends all too soon" (72)] and then taking on Orestes himself: "I cannot! Sandy has opened his mouth to cry—the blood pounding beneath his sunburn—he cannot—yet within seconds it appears that he can; he can, he can. Power & joy fill him. His eyes fill. He can dance under his brother's weight" (72).

[20] Yeats explains, "I think it was Heraclitus who said: the Daimon is our destiny. When I think of life as struggle with the Daimon who would ever set us to the hardest work among those not impossible, I understand why there is a deep enmity between a man and his destiny. . . . I am persuaded that the Daimon delivers and deceives us. . . . Then my imagination runs from Daimon to sweetheart . . . and that it may be 'sexual love,' which is founded upon 'spiritual hate,' is an image of the warfare of man and Daimon; and I even wonder if there may not be some secret communion, some whispering in the dark between Daimon and sweetheart" (*Per Amica* 336).

[21] The Daimon, who according to Yeats may also be "an illustrious dead man," such as Yeats for Merrill, "comes not as like to like but seeking its own opposite, for man and Daimon feed the hunger in one another's hearts. . . . [Man and Daimon] are but knit together when the man has found a mask whose lineaments permit the expression of all the man lacks, and it may be dreads . . ." (*Per Amica* 335). As we shall see, it is part of Merrill's poetic strategy to heighten the opposition between his own poetic Mask (his chosen and cultivated style) and

the Yeatsian Daimon that has chosen him. The "active virtue" of this strategy is that it provides the dramatic and formal impetus that helps get poems written. The point for Merrill may be "to *sound* personal" in his poems, but this is usually a consciously dramatic strategy, "the wearing of a mask" (*Per Amica* 334). Merrill makes a Yeatsian point, about both life and art, when he remarks: "Freedom to be oneself is all very well; the greater freedom is not to be oneself" (*Different* 129). For Merrill as for Yeats, opposition, or "RESISTANCE," is the generative power not only of "physical reality" (*Vision* 69; S. 453) but of man's sanity and "ALL GOOD DISCOURSE" (S. 306, 414; see also 202). As Merrill will admit later in *Sandover*, maintaining even the "weak signs" of skepticism and resistance is crucial to the formal integrity of his poem (S. 138, see also "Interview with Bornhauser" 53).

[22] Friar also allies Medusa with the destructive beauty Yeats (through the Mask of Owen Aherne) proclaims was "'brought into the world to destroy nations, and finally life itself, by sowing everywhere unlimited desires, like torches thrown into a burning city'" ("Medusa-Mask" 3).

[23] In 1937, after the publication of the second edition of *A Vision*, Yeats wrote to Edmund Dulac, "I do not know what my book will be to others—nothing perhaps. To me it means *a last act of defense against the chaos of the world*, & I hope for ten years to write out of my renewed security" (qtd. in Ellmann 291, emphasis added). In *A Vision*, too, Yeats writes, "A civilization is a struggle to keep self-control, and in this it is like some great tragic person . . ." (268).

[24] Merrill's young writer in *Diblos* makes a similar point, "how little I cared for him [Orestes/Friar], how much for the idea of him" (145). Merrill casts himself as an ironic Prospero ("Then I will (figuratively) drown my book") and frustrated Yeats "still on this island playing with them [his real friends and relations] in effigy, loving the effigies alone, masks behind which lay all too frequently a mind [his own] foreign to them" (133).

[25] Friar's phrase suggests the Yeatsian value of "repose" and how the "geometry" of his system would help him hold "in a single thought reality and justice" (*Vision* 25).

[26] Merrill's phrase for this "living dereliction" is "our lives somehow without our living" ("Medusa"). This Yeatsian False Mask of "Dispersal" (see *Vision* 140, 142) represents a very real fear for the young writer as it did for Yeats throughout his life. But Merrill will turn it into one of his most characteristic poetic strengths in his mature poetry; see my discussion of Dispersal in the first section of the Coda to Chapter Four, Yeats's Merrill.

[27] In Merrill's 1968 interview with Ashley Brown, Merrill makes these remarks about his early poem "Medusa":

> I wrote it over not long ago, I can't think why. It's a poem without content, really. I wrote so easily in those days. The stanza is one of Elinor Wylie's. But you are right in mentioning Stevens. You remember the passage about the stone mask in the *Notes*. I must have had that in mind, the image, I mean, as distinct from Steven's glorious sound effects. I thought of poems as visual artifacts back then. (42).

First, it is significant that, despite his disclaimer, Merrill chooses to revise "Medusa" late in 1967 or early 1968, one of the times during which he and David Jackson resumed their contact with Ephraim (S. 55). As we shall see, it is also during this period that Merrill was writing poems for what would be his most Yeats-saturated volume, *The Fire Screen*, and when he may have returned to his reading of *A Vision*. It is also telling that nowhere in Merrill's interview does he acknowledge Friar's role in the early poem; he gives no sense that Friar set both topic and form and no indication that the poem might be more than a "visual artifact."

Although Merrill's reference to Stevens is not ingenuous (given lines such as "No splashings to arrest / The formal face whose change is meaningless, / Since all is change"), it is nonetheless misleading. There is no "stone mask" in Stevens' *Notes Toward a Supreme Fiction*, only "One sole face . . . / Eye without lid, mind without any dream" and "a bird // Of stone" ("Change" VI). Nor does "Medusa" seem "a poem without content." It is a poem about the status of a relationship: "And turning each to the other we declared / Our lives were failing like a bleeding bird," and a poem with a strong argument against Yeats's "artifice of eternity": "for still in the still heart / Of time the snakes will writhe, the stone lips part."

Both in these and in similar remarks about "Willowware Cup" (see the Introduction), Merrill purposefully leads his questioners away from connections between Friar, Yeats, and his poems. There are a number of reasons why Merrill might have preferred to mention Stevens rather than Friar in his 1968 interview, including Stevens' prestige and Merrill's strained relations with Friar at this time. But there seems to be little reason to evade mention of Yeats in 1982 (the date of the remarks about "Willowware Cup"), when *Sandover* is complete and readers are already comparing the poem to Yeats's *A Vision*—no reason, except perhaps to avoid encouraging such comparisons. As this study progresses, it should become clear why Merrill would choose to "swerve" away from Yeats in his public remarks as well as in his poetry.

[28] Yeats is represented in the poem by allusions to "The Statues," "The Gyres," the imperishable birds and much of the music of the Byzantium poems. We also hear echoes of "Phases of the Moon" (lines 110 and following), "The Second Coming" in "blank eyes gazing past suns of no return" and the air of apocalypse where "stone lips part," and perhaps "Adam's Curse" for the "domestic" setting, aesthetic themes, chilling tone, and the typical conclusion blending "guileful melody" with an image of suspended violence.

[29] Freud's reading of Michelangelo's statue explains the ambiguity of Moses's posture as a record of distinct "emotional strata." Moses "desires to act, to spring up and take vengeance . . . but he has overcome the temptation," and is rendered as though frozen in the posture of his ambivalence, wrath and pain mingling with contempt (33). Merrill achieves a similar monumental ambiguity in his "*quivering* swords" and "*think* to kill" (emphasis added). In contrast, Friar's Perseus is all singleness of effect.

[30] For an indication of Merrill's early reading in Freud, see appendix B.

[31] For a helpful overview of the Medusa-myth in classical sources and later literary and psychological treatment, see Judith Suther's "The Gorgon Medusa" and Tobin Siebers's *The Mirror of Medusa*. Jerome McGann's "The Beauty of the Medusa: A Study in Romantic Literary Iconology" focuses on uses of the figure of Medusa in Shelley, Pater, Swinburne, and Morris to show that the Romantic Medusa, far from merely reflecting Romantic fascination with corruption, serves as a symbolic means of questioning and representing the fundamental relations between life and death. More recent feminist readings of the myth are discussed in Susan Bowers's "Medusa and the Female Gaze," Joan Coldwell's "The Beauty of the Medusa: Twentieth Century," and "Tsu-Chung Su's "The Monstrous Other: Freud, Irigaray, Cixous, & the Mask of Medusa."

[32] Siebers's discussion of Romantic versions of the myth of Narcissus in which "Narcissus personifies the idea of the artist in the act of self-discovery and creation" is also pertinent to Merrill's poem and his relationship with Friar (75–77). In this passage, Siebers argues that Romantic narcissism ultimately operates "as a means of self-torture and self-exile, and to create those all-important feelings of artistic suffering and superiority" (77).

³³ Merrill returned to "Medusa" and "wrote it over" late in 1967 or early '68 ("Interview with Brown" 42). This is a period in which Merrill seems particularly interested in coming to terms with both Yeats and Friar. See my discussion of the sudden richness of Yeatsian allusion in poems written for *The Fire Screen*, and of "Hourglass " (*Yellow Pages*) in Chapter Two.

³⁴ In *A Different Person*, Merrill provides an account of "those long-ago weeks" in the spring of 1950 when he first visited Kimon Friar in Greece and upon which he based much of *The (Diblos) Notebook*. Here too Merrill takes care to link Friar and the Medusa:

> Above the door into the Medusa, as Kimon had named the cottage where I would be staying with him, hung an ominous assemblage, a large grinning head made of hardware and jetsam. Thus Kimon, bent over work under her petrifying eye, could see himself as a latter-day Perseus, saved by the mirror-shield of Art. (22–23)

³⁵ The Other in *Diblos* is Orestes, Orson, O. all of whom are Friar, all of whom are also frustratingly Merrill: "*I* was 'Orestes.' They—whoever 'they' were—kept mostly beyond my reach" (133).

³⁶ See in particular "Accumulations of the Sea" (especially section IV, published only in *The Black Swan*), "The Drowning Poet," and "The Forms of Death."

³⁷ As Tobin Siebers states about narcissism generally: "The moment of self-recognition, therefore, is not a recognition at all. It is the moment of the greatest blindness" (84).

³⁸ For Merrill "*my* Byron" is the Byron of *Beppo* and *Don Juan*, rather than *Childe Harold's Pilgrimage*. "Witty exuberance," rather than melancholic or stormy introspection, is the hallmark of Merrill's Byronic and anti-Yeatsian persona (McClatchy "Lost" 305). In the early 1970s, J. D. McClatchy reports, Merrill typed a stanza from *Beppo* "that he imagined at the time described a person he might grow to resemble" ("Braving" 52):

> Then he was faithful, too, as well as amorous,
>   . . .
> His heart was one of those which most enamour us,
> Wax to receive and marble to retain:
> He was a lover of the good old school,
> Who still become more constant as they cool.

³⁹ In both novel and poem, the writer's decisive Persean strikes also represent a violent disciplinary reaction against the "impossible" desires and demands of the myth's would-be father-figures—a reaction against what Lacan would call the "voice of the father," and what Merrill's young writer calls Orson/Friar's "familiar 'teacher's' voice—the voice that says, 'I understand these things far better than you'" (141).

⁴⁰ *The Black Swan and Other Poems* (Athens: Icaros, 1946) was printed by M. Myrtidis in October 1946, in an edition limited to 100 numbered copies (Hall 6).

⁴¹ For a sample of Merrill's long-standing "imaginary argument" with his mother about his homosexuality, see *A Different Person* 231–32.

⁴² "The Forms of Death" has been published twice, once in *Accent* (8:2, Winter '48, pp. 94–96) and again in *TEN STUDENT POEMS: A Selection of Poetry Composed by Students in English 23–24, Advanced Composition, at Amherst College, 1944–1951*, Amherst, Massachusetts: Amherst College, ca. 1951. This "disowned" poem (also missing from the *Collected Poems*), together with "The Drowning Poet" and "Accumulations of the Sea," places Merrill where Harold Bloom says poets tend to incarnate, "by the side of ocean, at least in vision" (*Map* 13). Bloom, following Freud, figures Ocean as the primal mother of poets who

"mothers what is antithetical to her, the makers who fear (rightly) to accept her and [yet] never cease to move toward her" (Ibid. 15). Bloom also suggests the model of the poet "who fails of strength, and who wishes to return to the Waters of Night" where the danger is one of drowning (Ibid. 14) and asserts that "poets whose sexual natures manifest unusual complexity—Byron, Beddoes, Darley, Whitman, Swinburne, Hart Crane—rarely get very far away from the ocean of incarnation" (Ibid. 13). Leaving aside for now the wholly unexamined sexist [and heterosexist] assumptions of such formulations, in these poems Merrill does struggle to assert a poetic vocation that will acknowledge but not succumb to oceanic and maternal forces of oblivion. He may also draw on Proust's attention to identities between *mer* and *mère* and his fascination for *les méduses*: "Ne sont-elles pas, avec le velours transparent de leurs pètales, commes les mauves orchidées de la mer?" [Aren't they, with the transparent velvet of their petals, like the mauve orchids of the sea?] (*Recherche* III, 28; qtd. in Viti 62–63). In a similar vein, psychiatrist Albert Rothenberg discusses of the genesis of Merrill's "In Monument Valley" over a number of revisions, showing Merrill's at first unconscious intention in designating his poetic horse (Pegasus?) as a "mare" or "mère" in a poem that grew out of dreams whose wish was both to enjoy the support of and to achieve independence from the mother (15–29).

[43] After Friar's Medusa essay and Merrill's poem, the image of the desiccated jellyfish "medusa" itself suggests both the wreck of Merrill's relation with Friar and the effect, the "dry serpent horror," of his mother's hostility to their affair.

[44] This "ageless woman of the world" (S. 92) shares Merrill's mother's passion for needlework, quite literally for "cruel-work" in this chilling passage. When we next meet this "needlewoman" and her "crewel-work" in "Mornings in a New House," more than twenty years later, most of the present resentment has dissipated, although in the end the speaker takes remarkable pleasure in imagining his mother as a girl pricking her finger at her work:

> . . . once more, deep indoors, blood's drawn,
> The tiny needlewoman cries,
> And to some faintest creaking shut of eyes
> His pleasure and the doll's are one.

See my discussion of this poem in Chapter Two and of Merrill's mother's stitchery as an early pattern for his art, above, fn 7.

[45] Helen Vendler writes, "To write in a posthumous voice means to make the supreme imaginative act of imagining oneself dead" (qtd. in Ramazani 135). If the self-elegy is indeed "the supreme imaginative act," it is as such a trope for poetic mastery. In "Forms of Death," we see the barely twenty-one year old poet (over)reaching for the master's strongest magic: imagining his death operates at once as an index of his introjected anger toward his mother and his despair over her strength; but it also signals his determination to claim an answering, compensatory strength: the poet's ability to imagine the unimaginable and thus survive. For an excellent discussion of the self-elegy in Yeats and its Romantic tradition, see Jahan Ramazani's *Yeats and the Poetry of Death*, especially pp. 134–42 and 147–49.

[46] "Catastrophe" is how Merrill characterizes this love that is "always about to fail" in "Perspectives of the Lonesome Eye." Harold Bloom too asserts that catastrophe is "the central element in poetic incarnation" (*Map* 10), and trying to assure his poetic incarnation without Friar is exactly what Merrill sees as his most important challenge at this point.

[47] Compare Milton's use of King in *Lycidas* and, even more, Wordsworth's use of Coleridge (as the authorizing and fondly "departed" addressee) in *The Prelude*.

⁴⁸ Merrill's wry "if they ever do" does more than suggest that some poets never fully gain control of their language. It also implies that language persists in "using" even, and perhaps especially, the most accomplished poets for its own ends.

⁴⁹ Decades later, Merrill comments "in the long run I'd rather have what I write remind people of Pope or Yeats or Byron." He names these poets in particular just after remarking: "There's always a lurking air of pastiche that, consciously or unconsciously, gets into your diction. That doesn't bother me, does it you? No voice is as individual as the poet would like to think" ("Interview with McClatchy" 80). In another context Merrill adds, "The allusion of which the poet is unaware is more subtle, more enriching in the long run. That's when you really bring 'another poem into your own.'" He concludes by asking, "Is it what we mean by Tradition?"—evoking in a word the full weight of Eliot's authority ("Interview with White" 193–4).

⁵⁰ For early poems showing Merrill's interest in Proust's themes and methods see: "The Black Swan," "River Poem," "Willow," and "The House." "Foliage of Vision" gives an early hint of how Merrill emphasizes the primacy of Dante's paradisiacal vision. Here Merrill speaks of "Dante's ascent in hell / To greet with a cleansed gaze the petaled spheres," thus giving the pilgrim far more than Dante does at this point, who withholds such vision until the climax of *Paradiso*. For echoes of Keats see much of *First Poems*, but especially poems such as "Entrance from Sleep," "Procession," and "Foliage of Vision." For Donne, see especially "Transfigured Bird," part 2. Note the Miltonic notes struck in "The House": "May stumbling on a sunken boundary stone // The loss of deed and structure apprehend. / And we who homeless toward such houses wend / May find we have dwelt elsewhere. . . ." Steven's eye and language informs both "Accumulations of the Sea" and "Cloud Country." Note too, in "Medusa," the inflections of Stevens and Auden housed within an Elinor Wylie stanza that Merrill points to in his interview with Ashley Brown (42). Rilke, Auden, and Yeats, each adds his note and spot of characteristic color to "The Peacock," and Merrill writes of T. S. Eliot being "very much on the scene" in his youth. He recalls, "from [Eliot's] work came a sense of live menace and fascination: you felt that any rash expository impulse might cause it to strike back like a rattlesnake" ("Prefaces" 209).

⁵¹ Rachel Hadas, writing about Merrill's early poems, notes that "A cautionary irony hangs about the love of beauty either in or out of nature" in "Transfigured Bird" and continues, "'Sailing to Byzantium' is undoubtedly waiting in the wings" of this poem ("Early" 181).

⁵² Merrill's opening tercet begins the poem in the spirit of William Blake's symbology. "That day the eggshell of appearance split" echoes Blake's "Mundane Shell" delimiting the human world of appearance and separating it from the fires of the Divine Essence (*Milton* plate 34, Raine 114). "And weak of its own translucence" describes both the frailty of fallen human consciousness and the permeating intimations of a divine light beyond. The line continues that the eggshell "lay in the dew," where "dew" is the neo-Platonic symbol of the precipitating envelope of matter "which is attracted to generating souls" (Raine 103). To personify this soul and complete the Blakean tableau, Merrill's third line supplies the "child fond of natural things," here also Blake's fond or naive Innocent who may be so taken with the world of nature and natural appearance that he claims to have "discovered it." The last tercet of this section presents Merrill's modulation of bardic voice speaking out of Experience. The shell (in the original version) is something for the child "to find and fancy it was gay," "fancy" for Blake lacks the insight of true imagination. Merrill's revision of this line points even more strongly to the child's misreading of the shell; it is something "to take home, and for years

mislay," giving us not just the sense of "misplace," as in "misunderstand," but the punning intimations of "misattribute," "misconceive," even "mis-sing."

53 Merrill's use of Dante's terza rima in "Transfigured Bird" not only points to Merrill's reverence for Dante's technical mastery, but also helps underscore the metaphysical and narrative heritage of the form in the poem's meditations on naive, imaginative, and story-besotted seeing, on the pain and occlusions of earthly vision, on the terrors of an indifferent God and Nature, and on the prospect of waking into the dusk (and perhaps the promise of stars).

54 Poems by Yeats that strike notes similar to Merrill's "The Parrot" include "The Mask," "The Statues," all the dance poems, including "The Double Vision of Michael Robartes," and "Sweet Dancer," "The Spur," and the Crazy Jane poems, especially "Crazy Jane Grown Old Looks at the Dancers."

55 Yeats asks for poems "as cold / And passionate as the dawn" and famously remarks, "all that is personal soon rots; it must be packed in ice or salt"—particularly the "ancient salt" of the traditional stanza ("The Fisherman," *Essays* 522). Yeats's "cold and rook delighting heaven" has the power to leave him, like the shards of Merrill's bowl, "Riddled with light"; to the end, he commands, "Cast a cold eye / On life, on death" ("The Cold Heaven," "Under Ben Bulben").

56 For all that this and other details of the revision move the poem increasingly away from broken domestic particularities to general, indeed Horatian and Platonic, themes of "harmony from dissonance" and love's daemonic power, Merrill is careful to keep the domestic particular in view. The second stanza opens with a question about the heart, "Did also the heart shatter when it slipped?" as if to balance the grandeur of the "fledgling rainbow" that concludes the previous stanza. In the third stanza, the crucial phrase "inside us" welds what might otherwise seem overly portentous and abstract to the immediately personal. Memory of Robert Frost's 1923 poem, "Fire and Ice," in which Frost evokes the fire of the speaker's desire and ice of his hatred as analogs to the forces that will end the world, also helps braid the domestic and personal into the apocalyptic. Even simple mention of the word "bowl," in this lofty context, helps recall us to the domestic realm, especially given a reader's melodramatic, but I think inescapable, interest in possible narratives behind the breakage. Thus, by the time we hear the poem's answer, "Love does that," we are already well caught up in the play of intimate and cosmic perspectives (at the end, "Eye-beam and ingle spark," and "space, / Timeless and concentric") which is the very business of love to mediate, and which has been a leading concern in Yeats's poems throughout his career.

57 For example, in revision Merrill transforms the original Stevensian tones of "The Cosmological Eye" to these ringingly Yeatsian final lines:

Henceforth it is his pride no sooner to

Frame in a sense the blood-and-thunder Sea
(Its egg acrawl with noon deflecting summary)
Than flash! horizons made of yes and no
Tilt him beyond all telling—empty shell,
Dropped feather, footprint drained of sky. How shall
We know him, then? By the light of his blue eye.   (*From the First Nine*)

It is hard to imagine these lines without "Leda and the Swan," the Byzantium poems, the "Heaven blazing into the head" of "Lapis Lazuli," and the cosmic eggs and noons and contending primary and antithetical "tinctures" of Yeats's vision system. What is particularly telling is that Merrill should decide to heighten the poem's Yeatsian resonance shortly after completing *Sandover*, his most profoundly Yeats-inflected project.

Merrill's early "series on the eye and vision," as Kimon Friar terms it, includes the three poems published by *Poetry* (67: 6, 293–301, March '46), "The Green Eye," "The Cosmological Eye," and "Perspectives of the Lonesome Eye." "The Flint Eye," Wreath for the Warm-Eyed," and "Foliage of Vision" complete the series. As Friar states, the relative lack of Yeatsian engagement in these poems may simply reflect that were written "on [Merrill's] own inspiration and initiative" [and after reading Stevens' *Notes Toward a Supreme Fiction*] ("Amherst"; *Recitative* 117).

58 In using this language of incorruptibility and Euclidean form, Merrill comes very close to Yeats's "artifice of eternity" and "mouth that has no moisture and no breath." But in this poem, he "swerves" from Yeats's emphasis on the transcendent workings and "pure products" of imagination, the "male" realm of *poesis*. Instead, Merrill insists on the priority of his *prima mater* of rock, mind, language, before any use was made. She is a self-contained event; her head was "built in a blossoming / That recognize[s] no facile season." In *Sandover* she will be the triune muse Psyche/Chaos/Nature; here part of her Shiva aspect, "whether to keep / Them or destroy," falls to her "gardener," while she watches.

59 *The Oxford Book of Modern Verse*, ed. W. B. Yeats, New York, Oxford University Press, 1936 p 1.

60 The poem comes too early to be disguised "protest" against either "confessional" or "beat" practices of poetic nakedness, but it is not too early to implicate William Carlos Williams and his followers. Merrill later comments, "there is very little I care about in [Williams work], perhaps just the famous simple snippets that one wouldn't have thought were poems at all" ("James Merrill at Home" 24).

61 "Parable" serves as an excellent example of Bloom's first revisionary ratio, Clinamen, in which "the later poet swerves away from the precursor, by so reading the parent-poem as to execute a *clinamen* . . . [which is] the corrective movement of his own poem . . ." (*Anxiety* 14).

62 Among the poems Merrill wrote that winter are: "Hotel de L'Univers et Portugal," "Who Guessed Amiss the Riddle of the Sphinx," "The Octopus," "The Lovers," and "Fire Poem." All were later published in *Poetry* (78:324–9, July '51) and collected in *The Country of a Thousand Years of Peace* (1958).

63 In *A Vision*, Yeats pauses to wonder, "can even a visionary of today wandering among the mosaics at Ravenne or in Sicily fail to recognize some one image seen under his closed eyelids?"—so suffused with "supernatural splendour" were "these walls with their little glimmering cubes of blue and green and gold." (280–81). For other brief accounts of Yeats's Italian visit, see also Hone 219 and Jeffares *Yeats* 157–58.

64 At this point of Merrill's second birth as a poet, Merrill quotes Herbert, "Childhood is health," and then affirms about Ravenna, "and here is mine, along with Christianity's [childhood]" (*Different* 199). Where Merrill stresses the sense of empowering joy that accompanies his "glistening," advent into poetic vision, Bloom takes a longer, more pessimistic view of the same scene:

> What we see in the ephebe is the incarnation of the poetical character, the second birth into supposed imagination that fails to displace the first birth into nature, but fails only because desire fails when confronted by so antithetical a quest [the maturing poet's quest "for fire, when he seeks to burn through every context that the pre-

cursors created or themselves accepted" in his effort to attain his own originality] (*Map* 17).

Merrill's joy does modulate very soon into Bloomian anxiety marked by just this sort of "quest for fire" as we shall see in "Fire Poem," a poem written within the year.

⁶⁵ This passage borrows phrases from an "unsatisfactory poem" about Ravenna and "a versified account of the mosaics, lifted from a letter to Freddy" (*Different* 252). According to the memoir, Ravenna was to serve as the "safer vantage of time and space," the achieved perspective after the daring oceanic immersion (251). What the finished play shows is that Merrill later decided to split this role; Ravenna is a destination, achieved only metaphorically by Charles at the end in a moment of Gnosis; Venice is the present vantage of the play—Venice, which will be Merrill's counterpart to Yeats's Byzantium in *Sandover*. Merrill's plot sees its way to a rebirth; in Dr Detre's retelling, "a healthy and goodhearted man . . . is hauled from the sea" (*Different* 253). This rebirth-as-rescue echoes what Bloom sees as the tendency of poets "to incarnate by the side of ocean" (*Map* 13 ff.) and contrasts significantly with the highly ambivalent, Friar-era, poems of poetic incarnation, "Accumulations of the Sea," "The Drowning Poet," and the uncollected "The Forms of Death." In these earlier poems "To drown was the perfection of technique" ("The Drowning Poet") and to be a poet is never to emerge fully from Bloom's "Ocean, the matter of Night, the original Lilith or 'feast that famished'" (Op. cit.).

⁶⁶ In *A Different Person*, Merrill recalls Freddy Buechner's present of the Ouija board as Christmas present (625), while in his interview with J. D. McClatchy, Merrill remembers receiving it as a birthday present ("Interview with McClatchy" 66).

⁶⁷ *Poetry* 78:324–29.

⁶⁸ "The Charioteer of Delphi" ends by evoking the "fire and fury" of the passions, while "The Dunes" concludes with the more Yeatsian: "Up rose a burning couple far away. / Absolute innocence, fiery, mild." "The Charioteer of Delphi" first appeared in the British magazine, *Mandrake,* in 1952, although some lines for the poem appear in notebook entries as early as July 1950 (Hall 8). "The Dunes" was first published in *The Quarterly Review of Literature* 9.4 (1958): 238–39. Mona Van Duyn, in her 1959 review of *The Country of a Thousand Years of Peace*, comments on a similar cluster of "fire poems" ("The Phoenix," "Fire Poem," and "Charioteer") but sees only that "passion appears as a fire that consumes form, form as a drug that deadens feeling," missing the ambivalent complexity of Merrill's internal quarrel with Yeats (200).

⁶⁹ Merrill sometimes casts his own poetic adolescence in terms quite contrary to the advice he offers others. In his 1987 foreword to Julie Agoos's *Above the Land,* Merrill writes, "Until the forms of life are clearly felt, the forms of art will mean little" (ix). But about his own early practice Merrill writes:

> Because I didn't know what I felt, it seemed to me that what was obscurely said had a kind of resonance that charmed me and led me . . . [to try] deliberately to create a surface of such impenetrability and, at the same time, such beauty that it wouldn't yield up a meaning easily, if at all. . . . My point is that one needn't have any idea what one feels when one starts to write a poem. The poem is, in a way, an act of self-purification. The clarity you may arrive at is unforeseeable. . . . The feeling, too, can surface at the end. (*Recitative* 8)

However much truth there is in the generative, self-illuminating, self-purifying powers of composition, it seems clear, especially after Merrill's similar account of writing "Medusa," that Merrill casts himself as a naive aesthete, innocent of experience and life, in part to deflect scrutiny of the emotional and experiential basis of his poetry, and that strategies of deliberate obscurity, as well as offering a mode of personal discovery, also serve as a means of deliberate withholding. Thus, Merrill avoids a good deal of unwanted light by casting these poems as unconscious aesthetic play.

70 For an examination of Merrill's antithetical use of Yeats's "Sailing to Byzantium" in "About the Phoenix," see appendix A.

71 I have not found any concrete evidence of his having read *Per Amica Silentia Lunae* before 1959, the copyright date of Merrill's copy of *Mythologies*, but think it likely that he read it, or selected excerpts, as part of Friar's classes or on his recommendation. In the "Preface to the Appendix" of his 1951 critical anthology, *Modern Poetry*, Friar explains that his appendix, "Myth and Metaphysics: An Introduction to Modern Poetry," derives from his "many years of lecturing in colleges, universities and at The Poetry Center in New York City." It seems likely that the material Friar offers here is much the same as what he presented to Merrill at Amherst. Friar's remarks on Yeats lean heavily on *A Vision* ("knowledge of it is necessary for the full understanding of [Yeats's] later poetry") and on the same passages I refer to from *Per Amica Silentia Lunae*, giving particular prominence to the Condition of Fire in his discussion of the Byzantium poems (546, 552–53, 555). Friar's selections and discussion focus on poems written in the last twenty years of Yeats's life. Although they should not be taken to reflect the limits of Friar's teaching [Friar had wanted to include "many more [poems] of Yeats" in his anthology but was prevented by the publisher (*Modern Poetry* x).], they do bespeak the enthusiasm that Merrill noted for Yeats's spiritualism and personal mythology (*Different* 27).

72 This redoubled and hence "flashing" brightness recalls the visionary final stanza of "Kubla Kahn." This "eye" is also singularly detached from the speaker, as if the speaker watched both eye and fire engaged in their mutual mirror-play of brightening. The singular "eye" suggests Merrill's interest in the aesthetic objective of taking a god's-eye-view, a casting of his "Cosmological Eye," on whatever follows. It also suggests a scene of voyeurism that is given a certain masochistic relish by the following line, "Upon our knees, held by a leash of light." The ambivalent ambition of this "eye" is one of several features that link "Fire Poem" to Merrill's "*A View* of the Burning" (emphasis added).

73 Merrill's lines also echo an earlier passage in *Per Amica:* "He only can create the greatest imaginable beauty who has endured all imaginable pangs, for only when we have seen and foreseen what we dread shall we be rewarded by that dazzling, unforeseen, wing-footed wanderer. We could not find him if he were not in some sense of our being, and yet of our being but as water with fire, a noise with silence. He is of all things not impossible the most difficult, for that only which comes easily can never be a portion of our being.... *I shall find the dark grow luminous, the void fruitful* when I understand I have nothing, that the ringers in the tower have appointed for the hymen of the soul a passing bell" (332, emphasis added). I will return to this text in discussing Merrill's "A View of the Burning."

74 The demiurge in Platonic and Gnostic terminology denotes the deity that creates the material world, in this sense the form-giver, the personification of the creative process.

75 The opening stanza of Yeats's "Coole and Ballylee" provides what we may take as the paradigmatic example of this "naturalized" emblematic method. See Paul De Man's "Image and Emblem in Yeats" from *The Rhetoric of Romanticism*, especially pages 157, 165–66,

185–86, 195. Though this structure is most pronounced in Merrill's most Yeatsian middle stanza, it also pervades more subtly the first and last.

⁷⁶ Compare particularly with Yeats's third stanza of "Sailing to Byzantium":

> O sages standing in God's holy fire
> As in the gold mosaic of a wall,
> Come from the holy fire, perne in a gyre,
> And be the singing-masters of my soul.
> Consume my heart away; sick with desire
> And fastened to a dying animal
> It knows not what it is; and gather me
> Into the artifice of eternity.

Note especially the phrase "perne in a gyre." Yeats likely chose the variant spelling "perne" for "pirn" to allow the allusion to a kind of hawk as well as the winding motion as of thread onto a spool (or "pirn"), but the meaning that Kimon Friar emphasizes in his notes to this poem, and that Merrill may have remembered in composing these lines, is "to change"—"after Dr. Perne, Master of Peterhouse, Cambridge, 1554–80, who changed his opinions adroitly" (*Modern Poetry* 555). "Change" is certainly Merrill's emphasis as well. Yeats's winding or swirling motion is subsumed in Merrill's "storm," but Merrill keeps both "change" and the bird. Similarly, there is no direct appeal to "Come" or "Consume" or "gather" in Merrill's language, but an appeal or call to join the "shelter" of the fire is implicit and motivates the child's action in the next stanza. Where Yeats has "sages standing in God's holy fire," Merrill has the "rare bird bedded in the heart of harm"; but in terms of placement in the sentence, Merrill's "rare bird" is also closely linked to Yeats's "artifice of eternity," especially with the rhyming echo of "gather me" in "changing be." Merrill's "rare bird" points back to himself [see Yenser on the identity of *rara avis* and the Poet (*Myth* 38)] just as Yeats's golden bird is also a figure for the poet. Merrill's line may also echo Stevens' "A voluminous master folded in his fire" (*Notes Toward a Supreme Fiction* "It Must Be Abstract" I, 9)—from a poem Merrill found particularly revelatory and which in this opening section may also be a critique and warning about the temptations of a Yeatsian ideal ("Interview with McClatchy" 75; *Different* 14).

⁷⁷ Merrill remarks: "A protest *poem* would be one written against a poem of a different kind, one that reflected a different tradition. Wordsworth against Pope, Byron against Wordsworth" ("On 'Yánnina" 22).

⁷⁸ Compare "Vacillation" VII:

> *The Soul.* Seek out reality, leave things that seem.
> *The Heart.* What, be a singer born and lack a theme?
> *The Soul.* Isaiah's coal, what more can man desire?
> *The Heart.* Struck dumb in the simplicity of fire!
> *The Soul.* Look on that fire, salvation walks within.
> *The Heart.* What theme had Homer but original sin?

⁷⁹ Besides "Vacillation," I allude here to "Sailing to Byzantium" and "Lapis Lazuli" as representing Yeats's "simplest" and "Byzantium" his more tormented faith in images.

⁸⁰ See "The Black Swan," "The Green Eye," "Transfigured Bird," "A Vision of the Garden," "Scenes of Childhood," "The World and the Child," "The Broken Home,"

"Matinees," The School Play." Even Merrill's kidnap fantasy, "Days of 1935," reflects this Wordsworthian theme.

[81] Although I think Yeats is the primary influence being addressed in these fire poems, other sources surely figure in the background. Merrill would have been very familiar with Rilke's *Sonnets to Orpheus*, particularly sonnet II.12, which begins "Wolle die Wandlung. O sei für die Flamme begeistert, / drin sich ein Ding dir entzieht, das mit Verwandlungen prunkt." [Want change. O be enraptured with flame, within which a thing eludes you that is splendid with transformations.] While in Paris in the spring of 1951, Merrill also read Gaston Bachelard's *La Psychanalyse du Feu*, which draws on Jung, Frazer, Novalis and numerous seventeenth and eighteenth century sources to discuss the psychodynamics of fire and fire imagery (what Merrill calls "Bachelard's elemental, unpeopled reveries" (*Different* 69). Particularly pertinent to Merrill are Bachelard's notions of the "Prometheus complex" [which is "the Oedipus complex of the life of the intellect" and refers to "all those tendencies which impel us *to know* as much as our fathers, more than our fathers, as much as our teachers, more than our teachers" (12)—Merrill recalls feeling about his father as early as 1945, "One day I might even be his equal" (*Different* 150)] and the "Empedocles complex" [in which "the love and respect for fire" are united with " the instinct for living and the instinct for dying" (16)].

[82] Yeats, of course, was particularly well acquainted with alchemical, Hermetic, and Kabbalistic traditions from his long association with the "Hermetic Students of the Golden Dawn." For a study focusing on Yeats's involvement in these traditions, see Kathleen Raine's *Yeats the Initiate*, a book Merrill also owned. For discussion of Merrill's uses of the Hermetic and alchemical traditions see especially Evan Lansing Smith, "The Hermetic Tradition in James Merrill's *The Changing Light at Sandover*" and Timothy Materer's "Death and Alchemical Transformation in James Merrill's *The Changing Light at Sandover*" and "The Error of His Ways: James Merrill and the Fall into Myth." As well as his reading in Jung and Yeats, Merrill's would have gained some acquaintance with alchemical texts and principles from his reading of the central chapters of Bachelard's *La Psychanalyse du Feu*.

[83] "The Untiring Ones," *Mythologies*, 78. Also see the penultimate line of Yeats's "The Man who dreamed of Faeryland" for God burning Nature with a kiss, and the penultimate line of "He tells of Perfect Beauty" for God burning time.

[84] The conceit of hands as lovers also figures in Merrill's poem "The Lovers," but here the hands are not the speaker's or an angry man's but God's hands, God the good husbandman and supreme creator; and the dominant element is not fire but water, the tone not ambivalent or arch but lucent and full of wonder. "The Lovers," like "A View of the Burning" was also collected in *The Country of a Thousand Years of Peace*, but first published in 1951, in the same issue of *Poetry* as "Fire Poem," which features yet another important set of hands.

[85] Merrill's laughing flame at the end of this poem is a distinct, and perhaps "camp," variation on Yeatsian "gaiety" and has none of the weight of those who "but laugh in tragic joy" ("Gyres"). Merrill's "hilarity" emphasizes levity over elevation, but also captures the childlike delight and wonder of watching a flame. For further discussion of Merrill's camp sensibility, see Robert K. Martin's brief chapter on Merrill in *The Homosexual Tradition in American Poetry*, David Lehman's "Elemental Bravery" (40–41) and Robert von Hallberg's "James Merrill: 'Revealing By Obscuring.'" (Von Hallberg's critical appraisal of Merrill's camp "detachment" is rebutted in Lee Zimmerman's "Against Apocalypse: Politics and James Merrill's *The Changing Light at Sandover*.)

[86] Merrill returns to images of masturbation, sexual punishment, and self-punishment periodically throughout his work. There is the self-castration scene in *The Seraglio* (165–66),

scenes of masturbation and beating in *The (Diblos) Notebook* (9, 144–45) and the more complex images of masturbation and justice in *Sandover* (49). For further discussion of the thematic connections between poetry and masturbation, see Chapter Two.

[87] For a discussion of the poetic importance Merrill's sense of "unrealized possibilities," see the Prelude to this chapter. Elizabeth Bishop also understood that "What one seems to want in art, in experiencing it, is the same thing that is necessary for its creation, a self-forgetful, perfectly useless concentration," and her phrase may have a bearing on Merrill's "Useless to say" (Kalstone *Temperaments* 15). This ironic paean to the "useless" which points to a higher, more fruitful utility also anticipates much of the argument for "usefulness" in Sandover (see especially S. 59, 198) and *A Different Person* where we hear "what one wants in this world is not so much to 'live' as to . . . *be* lived, to be used by life for its own purposes. What has one to give but oneself?" (237).

[88] "Care," of course, means more than "sympathy," and I knowingly flatten Merrill's language here to stress its most immediate and benign sense. "Care" and "care for" also evoke notions of concern, worry, desire, choice, and preference in these lines. I would also call attention here to the speaker's almost comic, and certainly compulsive, repetition of the indefinite pronoun, "one." This semantic surplus relays an anxiety at the heart of the poem: the problem of speaking as a *single* self that has been part of its rhetorical drama as well.

[89] The juiciness of "succulence" is not entirely denotative. All the connotations of consummate sensual gratification, particularly oral and olfactory, and hence sexual, come into play here. Thematics of anger and desire, and anger at desire, which run throughout the poem, effectively burn down to two live words: "incensed, a succulence." At the level of mere sound too, which the neighbor rhyme with "incensed" helps stimulate, "succulence" evokes "sucking," "succor," and perhaps most closely "succubus"—all of which play well in this context.

[90] See Bloom's remarks about the initiatory "dialectics of accommodation and assimilation" in the early phases of the poetic Scene of Instruction (*Map* 51–54). Note too that the "harm" Merrill depicts in both poems, as being fundamental to the power of the precursor poet's fiery influence, is also a central issue in his own ambivalent masculinity. "It might be worth considering," Merrill remembers, his psychiatrist, Dr Detre, advising, "that this masculine self you crave is available within you, only you have not accepted the power to harm that goes with it." Merrill replies, "Must one do harm in order to be a man?" To which Detre responds, "You seem to have received that impression" (*Different* 220). Part of what both repels and attracts Merrill to Yeats so powerfully is the older poet's hyper-masculine persona. As Jahan Ramazani notes, Yeats typically presents a "self" that is "emphatically male, the poet suppressing what he represents as his femininity to win a hard, cold, masculine identity" (141), a stance that Merrill is bound to find almost aggressively self-limiting for all its compensatory claims to poetic power.

NOTES TO CHAPTER TWO

[1] Merrill's first encounters at the board without David Jackson came early in 1953, either after Christmas or after his birthday in March, the stories differing as to which occasion prompted Frederick Buechner's gift ("Interview with McClatchy"; *Different* 265). The date given for Merrill and Jackson's first attempt at the board is August 23, 1955 (Jackson "Lending" 301). We know that Merrill had some prior introduction to *A Vision* through Kimon Friar (and C. M. Bowra's *The Heritage of Symbolism*, which Merrill had as a text at

Amherst). Friar summarizes Yeats's linked psychological, historical, and metaphysical systems in considerable detail in his anthology notes on Yeats (431–32, 546–60), and Bowra discusses Yeats's symbology and spiritualism in relation to the theory and practice of Symons, Mallarmé and Valéry (180–218).

[2] On an "aesthetic ideology" and role of Yeats, see Mutlu Konuk Blasing's valuable introduction and her remarks on this phrase of Yeats's (*Politics* 2–21, 118). For a discussion of Yeats's understanding of "justice" as "an aesthetically gratifying wholeness," see Bloom's *Yeats* (276).

[3] For a list of some of Merrill's reading in matters of metaphysical interest see Appendix B.

[4] The interview comes at the end of the video version of Merrill's *Voices from Sandover*.

[5] This passing fellatio joke is typical of the camp tone that pervades Sandover and marks its self-consciously "queer" ambition to employ a gay life as the context for a sustained and "unified philosophical poem," as Merrill himself characterize the work in an unpublished letter (Dr. Chung).

[6] Merrill's phrases are from "Yánnina," one of his own Byzantium poems. He would have read Yeats's lesson in "Per Amica Silentia Lunae" (332).

[7] In Merrill's second-hand copy (of the Macmillan first edition) the previous owner's underlining and marginal notes in pencil are quite distinct from Merrill's notes in pen and a sharper, harder leaded pencil. There are two other "notes" in Merrill's copy of *A Vision* that point to passages relevant to his project in *Sandover*, and particularly the *Mirabell's Books of Number*. Both point to passages in Yeats's most explicitly Vision-based poem, "The Phases of the Moon." One is a check mark pointing to Aherne's brief lines on page 62 and the other is a line bracketing the last italicized quatrain of the poem. I will discuss both in my section on Yeats's role in *Mirabell*.

[8] As the speaker in "Voices from the Other World" declares, "Indeed, we have grown nonchalant / Toward the other world." In keeping with this theme of nonchalance, Leslie Brisman finds Merrill "toying with" his relation to Yeats and with what will be the poetic "machinery" of the larger enterprise of *Sandover* in this early Ouija board poem (191).

[9] Henry Sloss argues that "Voices from the Other World" and the subsequent account of the period 1955–57 in "The Book of Ephraim" (particularly sections B-L) portray Merrill's "unregenerate" determination to take the voices "clamoring overhead" simply for the "comfort, thrills and chills" they might provide. Sloss characterizes this attitude as determined "bravery" in the face of a call to "commitment." For him, "Ephraim" becomes above all a tale of conversion from nonchalance to commitment, from bravery to "the courage necessary to take on the other world" and its full significance (103–05).

[10] Meno (from *The Seraglio*), Eros (from the lost novel), and Ephraim (from "The Book of Ephraim") all share a similar biography. All three are former slaves and Hellenes, geographically and culturally mediating between East and West, Christianity, Judaism, and pagan religions. Meno and Ephraim were Roman slaves (with shared connections to sensuality, wealth, power, forbidden love, and violent death). Eros was a slave of Ptolemy, but not merely a "slave of intellect," he was also taught to feel (S. 47). Meno and Ephraim both come from a "broken home," their fathers lured away from their mothers' beds by Christianity. All three are also more than slaves; they challenge and threaten as well as offering wit, companionship, and revelations of the after-life. Meno and Ephraim describe a nine-staged system of reincarnation and the relation of patron to representative. Both are saddled with a feeble representative to care for, and both are contrasted with idiot voices and voices from the flames (such

Notes to Chapter Two 221

as those reported in "Voices from the Other World"). Meno and Ephraim also enjoyed a previous life at court at Versailles, and both retain their attractive young bodies, appearing of "the age at which it first seems credible to die" (S.16). All three are voyeurs and gain compensatory satisfactions from their relations on this side of the board. More could be said about the associations of their names and their relationship as personae for Merrill [from Meno's "Me, no." to the identity of Michael and Ephraim, yielding "M/E" (S. 551)], but these details should suffice to show their close identity.

11 "The whole right half / Of my face refuses to move."

12 Compare with "Vacillation": "And he that Attis' image hangs between / That staring fury and the blind lush leaf / May know not what he knows, but knows not grief" and "It seemed, so great my happiness, / That I was blessèd and could bless," or with these lines from the 1925 version of *A Vision*:

> He who attains Unity of Being is . . . no longer bitter, he may even love tragedy like those 'who love the gods and withstand them'; such men are able to bring all that happens, as well as all that they desire, into an emotional or intellectual synthesis and so to possess not the Vision of Good only but that of Evil. (qtd. in Croft 63).

13 See my discussion of Merrill's concern about the "losing" Strato to Ephraim at the end of Chapter Two, Interlude: Returning to Yeats's *A Vision*.

14 Francis is in many ways similar to the Gilbert character in Merrill's first play, *The Bait*. About Gilbert Merrill has commented that he represents "that fussy, expendable person I felt in recurrent danger of aging into" and that he "embodied aspects of myself I shrank from facing directly, like my cruelty and flightiness" (*Different* 252, 256).

15 In the summer of 1958 Merrill and David Jackson took a trip to Santa Fe and were very impressed with the spiritual power of the landscape. Some of Merrill's impressions find their way into section J of "The Book of Ephraim" as well as into "Words for the Familiar Spirit" and, later, a number of poems in *Braving the Elements*.

16 Thus, "Words for the Familiar Spirit," by retaining key images from "The Gyres" and from "The Second Coming" but using them to oppose and extend Yeats's meaning, serves as an example of Harold Bloom's second revisionary ratio, Tessera (Bloom *Anxiety* 14). Merrill returns to this image of "the quetzal floating up and up" at the climax of his 1971 fiction, "Peru: The Landscape Game." There the mythic bird emerges: "Broken out through spray, this fantastic thing, green fire in a soap bubble, wings slowly beating, in spirals up up up— / Utters in Quechua a single cry: / I am QUETZAL. I will never die" and gives us a fuller picture of what it meant to "endure . . . the quetzal floating up and up" in the earlier poem (*Recitative* 198).

17 See also S. 173, 260, 296.

18 Steven Matthews begins his remarks about Merrill's relationship with Yeats by discussing Merrill's devotion to "poems of habitation," in which the house is both a metaphor for the poetry (its rooms being so many stanzas) and a metonymy for the intimate, emotionally complex, inherited or self-made space in which poetry is made, reminding the reader that "the reviver of the tradition of houses as poetic spaces in twentieth-century poetry was, of course, Yeats" (224n71).

19 Merrill returns to this question of the soul's relation to the body in the prose passage attributed to his friend, Germaine Nahman, in "The Thousand and Second Night." She writes, "The soul, which in infancy could not be told from the body, came with age to resemble *a body one no longer had*, whose transports went far beyond what passes, now, for sensa-

tion" (emphasis in original). For Steven Yenser's discussion of this passage, in which he explains Nahman's sense that "to regain that original sensual experience [of infancy] would be to regain the unity of body and soul," see *The Consuming Myth*, pages 130 and 132–33.

[20] Yeats calls the fourth state of "The Soul in Judgment": "Marriage or the Beatitude" (*Vision* 232). He first explained it as "the momentary union of the Spirit and the Celestial Body with the Ghostly Self" (*Vision*, 1925, p. 235, qtd. in Croft 83–84). This state grants a "Vision of our own Celestial Body as that body will be when all cycles end" and bespeaks a union of "the unique image" with "all concrete universal quality and idea"(Ibid.). Later, Yeats's instructors make more explicit use of the Christian basis for his imagery, explaining that "'The Celestial Body is the Divine Cloak leant to all [in "A Tenancy" it is that lease-hold on the "little sun" risen in his throat, the internalization of the "source of light" or S/O/L], it falls away at the consummation [as the "light dies and the bell rings"] and Christ is revealed" [in Merrillian terms light's "leaner veteran will rise to face" an incarnate glory "gowned in changing / Flushes"](*Vision* 232). A covert Christology Yeats would also recognize continues in Merrill's poem. The gifts of the three visitors echo the gifts of the Magi (as the March afternoon of the poem also recalls Merrill's birth-month) and a possible pun on "host" makes the speaker a figure for Christ's resurrected body and Christ's sacrificial hospitality that others might dwell, if not "in his father's house," at least in the past his father authorized and paid for: "If I am host at last / It is of little more than my own past. / May others be at home in it."

[21] In Merrill's second stanza, the lines:

> A yellow pencil in midair
> Kept sketching unfamiliar numerals,
> The 9 and 6 forming a stereoscope
> Through which to seize the Real
> Old Fashioned Winter of my landlord's phrase . . .

—present a startling image of Merrill's own habitual "automatic writing." But such "doodling" is never wholly innocent. The image points back to Merrill's poem "The Doodler" in which God meditates on His habitual creations, and in which God and the poet are brought provocatively close together. The 9 and 6 also point forward to the double lenses (like Yeats's double cones) that bring reality into focus in *Mirabell* (S. 112, 174). And, linked as "69," these numerals also recall the symbol for Cancer which rules the quadrant of the Heart in Yeats's Great Wheel (*Vision* 81) and, between lives, is the sign for the Marriage, the fourth of the six stages of death in which the soul achieves "complete equilibrium . . . [and] good and evil vanish into the whole" (*Vision* 232). The numerals also recall the sexual posture which most closely mimes both Yeats's interpenetrating cones, his chief symbol for historical reality, and the Ouroboros, Yeats's "self-sown, self-begotten shape" ("Colonus' Praise") and the alchemical symbol of eternal processes, renewal, and psychic continuity, linked to the double natures of Mercurius and the hermaphrodite (Oxford English Dictionary, 2d edition).

[22] This passage also anticipates the Yeatsian conclusion of section 'R' in "Ephraim" and its "deep shriek" (S. 65).

[23] In an earlier, 1967, interview Merrill notes: "'An Urban Convalescence' is in the form of an Introduction and Allegro. In between comes a trill (on the word 'cold'), an organ point (following 'self-knowledge'); then the rhymes, the quatrains begin, in 4/4 time, as it were" ("Interview with Sheehan" 29). This passage also suggests that the difficult first section ended with the break after "eyes astream with cold" and that it was the musical idea of creating a

more formal second section that gave him the hint for the self-conscious "trill" and "organ point" of the following two lines. Merrill gives another account of his difficulty completing the poem fourteen years after the Brown interview in his Paris Review interview with J. D. McClatchy. Merrill writes: "I had the same problem with 'An Urban Convalescence' before writing those concluding quatrains. It broke off at the lowest point.... But then something affirmative had to be made out of it" (77). What's remarkable about this retelling, with Merrill's written responses and presumable access to the poem, is that Merrill misquotes a line, giving "heavy" for "massive," and that he marks the "lowest point" of the poem as "The heavy volume of the world / Closes again." That "closes again," with its intimations of cyclical time and a possible future reopening of the world's book, hardly seems the lowest point of the poem given the "gospels of ugliness and waste," the shrieking and tears and broken syntax which follow. But if Merrill's later account correctly places the point of "break down," we are left with the spectacle of Merrill in a sense manufacturing the poem's Yeatsian crisis in order to heighten the contrast with its formal conclusion. This bit of "artifice" then may help account for the uncharacteristic stridency and self-inflation of "Upon that book I swear...." On the other hand, this account may intentionally draw our attention away from the actual "lowest point"—that "shrieking to be faced / Full into"—so redolent of Yeatsian gesture and image.

24 I owe considerable debt in this discussion to Mutlu Konuk Blasing's account of "Urban Convalescence," particularly her reading of the "huge crane" in reference to Robert Graves, and matters of temporality and "transpersonal autobiography" (*Politics* 161–68).

25 Writing about "Merrill's Yeats," Leslie Brisman shows how in "Willowware Cup" Merrill writes against Yeats's "Lapis Lazuli" and in so doing writes against tendencies to fetishize aesthetic production (193), against "Yeats-as-poetic-father, and against the detachment of Yeats's Chinamen" (194). Furthermore, against the "ancient," stony wisdom of aesthetic detachment, Merrill poses the "warm and clear" (or "throbbing, intricate") importance of the affections (197). More generally, Brisman argues that: "In certain ways, Yeats represents for Merrill not only a number of specific literary debts but a vision of an old self that much of Merrill's verse is concerned to refashion and transcend" (190) and that "Yeats's spirit hovers over the entire enterprise of *The Changing Light at Sandover*" (191). He does not specify the characteristics of that "old self" and gives only glancing attention to Yeats's role in *Sandover*, but in both claims clearly suggests two lines of inquiry for the present study.

26 It is surely no accident that "Violent Pastoral" opens with "a thunderhead's / Blue marble," just as "Willowware Cup" closes with "thunderhead blue." In both, it is manifestly Yeats's thunder that Merrill, as Promethean poet, works to steal. See my discussions of this motif in "Ephraim" and *Scripts* in Chapter Three, sections I and III.

27 Merrill's overstruck "Orestes" bears an uncanny (and not merely typographic) resemblance to Lacan's concept of the "barred subject," represented by the "$." For both Freud and Lacan the "true subject" was this "subject barred from consciousness," that is "the Other subject in the subject's division from himself" (Wilden 181, 165, 267). See also Lacan, *Ecrits* 292–324.

28 Merrill comments in an interview with Fred Bornhauser: "A line kept recurring as I wrote my little Greek novel—'the sun and moon together in the sky.' I meant that I was drawn to both sides of things: masculine and feminine, rational and fanciful, passionate and ironic" (61). For Yeats the sun and the moon are always together contending for the character of the embodied soul, except at Phase 1 and Phase 15 when first the sun and then the moon "consumes" the other tincture. Merrill does not specify the ideal balance between these

forces; whereas, Yeats favors those phases clustering around Phase 15. But for both the goal is the same: to achieve in ourselves a "form created by passion to unite us to ourselves" (*Vision* 82).

[29] This passage, a prose "revision" of Merrill's "Swimming by Night" from the 1962 volume, *Water Street*, gives the first intimation of just how closely Merrill's unnamed narrator is associated with his own self-as-writer. [The paragraph even opens saying, "What one *can* use is the poetry of the night . . . " (9)]. Where the poem presents "a gradual body / Half remembered, astral with phosphor," the *Diblos* passage gives: "To swim then: one's limbs, stippled with phosphorescence, bringing to mind—to my mind—ectoplasm." The poem's "genie chilling bids you limp / Heavily over stones to bed" becomes the "genie conjured . . . merges at last into the dark chilled bulk of its master's body stumbling over stones to sleep." The poem offers the night universe as "your master's robe"; whereas, in *Diblos* the "master" is the swimming subject. The *Diblos* passage also suggests more explicitly occult and masturbatory overtones linking it to both the magic and ambivalent self-pleasuring that characterizes the scene of writing.

[30] See in "The Thousand and Second Night," the opening stanzas of "Carnivals" and the "cold man" in "Mornings in a New House."

[31] Stephen Yenser's reading of this poem (and these lines) is invaluable. Yenser explains that Merrill uses Yeats's lines ironically because "For Merrill, Istanbul has been a place not of unification but divisions." He continues that Merrill "leaves the holy city, which has proved closer to Eliot's "Unreal City, " for the worldly one" of Athens (*Myth* 128). Yenser's discussion continues to show the ways in which Merrill recasts Eliot's *The Waste Land* in this poem and how Merrill uses Yeats as an antithetical resource throughout.

[32] Of course Yeats too wrote from a divided self, through the voices of contrasting personae, perfecting strategies of vacillation. Merrill builds on these precedents and extends them into a poetic explicitly antithetical to Yeats's "simplification through intensity." For further discussion of Merrill's use of Dispersal, see the first section of the Coda to Chapter Four, Yeats's Merrill.

[33] The quotations are from "Crazy Jane Talks with the Bishop" and "Crazy Jane on the Day of Judgment."

[34] We note that even when writing against Yeats in this fashion, Merrill avails himself of two of the older poet's chief figures, the transcendent yet embodied dancer and the fated daimonic mask. Kalstone further suggests that, in this section, Merrill strikes a further Yeatsian note with his "'sumptuous farewells to flesh'" ("Merrill" 148).

[35] See the similar moment in "Vacillation IV":

> While on the shop and street I gazed
> My body of a sudden blazed;
> And twenty minutes more or less
> It seemed, so great my happiness,
> That I was blessèd and could bless.

[36] In his discussion of the "Carnivals" section of "The Thousand and Second Night," Stephen Yenser calls attention to the onanistic overtones of Merrill's celebratory "Love. Warmth. Fist of sunlight at last / Pounding emphatic on the gulf. / High wails / From your white ship" and cogently discusses the relations in Merrill's poem between masturbation and writing, body, soul, maker, and muse, citing Derrida's treatment of the same themes in *Of Grammatology* (*Myth* 133). ("Stripping the blubber from my catch [or 'crotch'], I lit / the oil-

soaked wick, then could not see by it. / Mornings, a black film lay upon the desk"). Yenser highlights other sexual/textual play in the poem when he calls attention to Merrill's ironic use of "carnival," which "comes from roots meaning literally 'to raise flesh.'" He explains: "At the end of Carnival, the meat is raised and removed from the table to comply with the strictures of Lent, but in 'The Thousand and Second Night' meat is first of all raised in one way and another to one set of lips and another . . . [foreshadowing] the fellatio and the fornication in 'Postcards from Hamburg, Circa 1912'" (*Myth* 131).

[37] Yenser characterizes this fourth section of the poem as "the one section whose existence we would not specifically sense the need of if it were not there. Once there, it is indispensable"(*Myth* 122).

[38] Yenser opens his discussion of "The Thousand and Second Night" with this passage from Sheehan's interview and points out that "An 'air of irrelevance' is not irrelevance," that to *seem* casual is part of Merrill's goal (*Myth* 120). His discussion also helpfully draws attention to Donald Sutherland's description of "the *gallant* style" as a way of characterizing the Merrill's achievement in this poem: such verse "can handle a wandering narrative line, varying or interrupting it with passages of description, reflection, or lyric exclamation, which count in verse as varieties of movement . . . so that the events never crystallize into fact or conclusion on their own, nor into objectivity" (qtd. in *Myth* 121).

[39] Jeff Westover argues that Yeats's theory of the poetic mask, as described in *Per Amica Silentia Lunae*, offers a particularly pertinent way of understanding the necessary difficulty of Merrill's poem (303, 315) and demonstrates the many ways in which Merrill's poem "plays with Yeats's view of the mask by dramatizing the process of its formation and assumption" (308). What Westover's article does not argue, as I would, is that Merrill wrote with prior knowledge of Yeats's theory of the mask and that he might have had lessons from *Per Amica* in mind in composing "From the Cupola."

[40] "From the Cupola" is a dialogue not only of self and soul (James and Psyche, two characters named in the poem), but also includes Psyche's senses "shrill and ominous," her "flesh and blood" sisters, Gertrude and Alice (voices of mundane cynicism, fear, and appetite), and her "correspondent" and "projection," Eros, the angel who flees and the animal within.

Merrill's poem may also draw on Yeats's "To Dorothy Wellesley," which also seems to conflate elements of the Eros and Psyche story: the occult night, the sense of reaching for what can't be touched, the animal "sunk in sleep," the woman waiting a Daimonic visitation, the posture of the "Proud Furies each with her torch on high." Perhaps remembering these Furies, Merrill has Psyche face "a small troop of furies" after her dream encounter with Eros, whose "tear-streaked muzzle" she later recalls.

[41] See also "Interview with Bornhauser" 54 and "James Merrill at Home" 31 for further remarks about why Merrill did not feel free to make use of the Ouija board material.

[42] The phrase is from Merrill's 1963 poem "We Walk in Woods" which concerns the difficulties (if not the joys) of being a poet, a subject, he tells Donald Sheehan, "I've tried to resist" (32). The poem is particularly notable for the vehemence of its concern about issues of influence and identity:

We Walk In Woods

Of our own words
Our fathers planted the strangler vine,
Perspectives, glooms of meaning.

> The taproot enfolds
> Earth's heart and ours.
> A topmost verbiage whispers
> *Not only silence is golden.*
>
> Nevertheless on dreams
> Of the ringing ax,
> Shudder and crash,
> Light streaming in.
>
> Whose speech am I
> And what is being said
> When, tightlipped and barehanded,
> I make a silence, briefly? [emphasis in the original]

[43] See, for example, WHA's remarks, "OUR PULSES QUICKENED / MY DEAR BY THE ELECTRICAL 4 FLASHES / OF YR POEM" (S. 267).

[44] In "Days of 1971" Merrill's concluding sonnet begins: "Strato, each year's poem / Says, goodbye to you," and by 1970, in "Strato in Plaster," we have the clear sense that Merrill's affair with Strato has run its course. (A postcard of an Apollo recalls "Strato as he used to be.") Judging from the poetry ("Days of 1964," "To My Greek," "Last Words," and "Another August") and Merrill's comment, "Strato's qualities / All are virtues back in '64" (S. 50), the height of the affair seems to have extended from 1964 to 1968. Likewise, the notion, expressed in his annotation that Merrill feels he is failing to assert himself with S[trato], suggests that he wrote it later rather than earlier in this period. In Merrill's quest for "consuming passions" (S. 50) he may well have returned to Yeats's *A Vision* for a better understanding of "the erotic mask / Worn the world over by illusion / To weddings of itself and simple need" ("Days of 1964"), especially given Yeats's suggestion of "some secret communion, some whispering in the dark between Daimon and sweetheart" in "Anima Hominis" (*Per Amica* 336).

[45] See the introduction and the prelude to Chapter Two for discussion of this evasion.

[46] Writing about the Dreaming Back, Yeats explains: "Every event so dreamed is the expression of some knot, some concentration of feeling separating off a period of time, *or portion of being*, from the being as a whole and the life as a whole, and the dream is as it were a smoothing out *or an unwinding*" (qtd. in Croft 81, emphasis added). Here is the passage in question:

> Behind a door marked DANGER
> (This is a dream I have about my friend)
>
> Swaddlings of his whole civilization,
> Prayers, accounts, long priceless scroll,
>
> Whip, hawk, prow, queen, down to some last
> Lost comedy, all that fine writing
>
> Rigid with rains and suns,
> Are being gingerly unwound.

This is certainly, as Yeats would say, "history grown symbolic, the biography changed into a myth" (qtd. in Croft 117) and shows the same meshing of history, myth, and individual psychology that animates Yeats's system of winding and unwinding, interpenetrating gyres.

[47] See my discussion of "perpetual possibility" and fulfilling "unrealized possibilities" in the Prelude to Chapter One.

[48] "More Enterprise" also inverts the usual form of Yeats's characteristic ottava rima stanza, starting rather than ending with a rhyming couplet. This formal "upending" in it self serves as a signal of Merrill's interest in making a pointedly contrasting use of the older poet. (See the opening of Chapter Four for a brief discussion of Helen Vendler's remarks on Yeats's Ottava Rima.) I give Merrill's poem in its entirety:

> A sideways flicker, half headshake of doubt—
> Meaning, confusingly, assent—fills out
> The scant wardrobe of gesture I still use.
> It clings by habit now. The old strait swank
> I came in struts the town in local heirs.
> Koula's nephew has the suit she shrank,
> Andreas coveted my Roman shoes. . . .
> Into the grave I'll wear that Yes of theirs.

[49] About such writing "against" Merrill explains: "A protest *poem* would be one written against a poem of a different kind, one that reflected a different tradition. Wordsworth against Pope, Byron against Wordsworth" (Kalstone "The Poet" 45).

[50] For further discussion of the photographic image and its relation to Yeats's "artifice of eternity," see the conclusion of Chapter Three, section I, Yeats in "Ephraim."

[51] Eric Selinger also discusses the Yeatsian self-interrogation implicit in Merrill's "Flying from Byzantium." He finds parallels between Merrill's last section and the conclusion of Yeats's "The Circus Animals' Desertion" and also points to "Last Words" "as a sort of coda" for the preceding poem in which "part of the self suffers identifications and ecstasies while another sighs that 'There's nothing I don't know / Or shall not know again, / Over and over again'" and argues that in this poem Merrill "revises yet a third poem from Yeats," turning "Mohini Chatterjee" into "a poem of reductive repetition" (44–46, 65)—missing, I think, the terrible joy of Yeatsian affirmation. See especially "A Dialogue of Self and Soul II" and "The Gyres."

[52] See Helen Vendler's discussion in *Yeats's Vision and the Later Plays* 67–69.

[53] Merrill "quotes" here from "some Lives of Obscure Listeners."

[54] In Yeatsian terms, we are shaped by the masks, the "images of good and evil," that we see and come to love; "They had a relation to what one knew and yet were an extension of one's knowledge" (*Per Amica* 325, 345). As Mask, that "'form created by passion to unite us to ourselves,'" great performers in certain roles operate as an "object of desire or ideal of the good" recalling "moments of exaltation in [our] past lives" and drawing us toward a fuller unity of self (*Vision* 82, 83; pages Merrill marked in his copy of *A Vision*). Merrill shows this shaping relation in the poem's sixth sonnet:

> When Jan Kiepura sang His Handsomeness
> Of Mantua those high airs light as lust
> Attuned one's bare throat to the dagger-thrust.

> Living for them would have been death no less.
>
> Or Lehmann's Marschallin!—heartbreak so shrewd,
> So ostrich-plumed, one ached to disengage
> Oneself from a last love, at center stage,
> The beloved's dazed gratitude.
>
> What havoc certain Saturday afternoons
> Wrought upon a bright young person's morals
> I now leave to the public to condemn.
>
> The point thereafter was to arrange for one's
> Own chills and fever, passions and betrayals,
> Chiefly in order to make song of them.

[55] (*Zarathustra* 238); for a detailed account of Nietzsche's influence on Yeats, see Otto Bohlmann, *Yeats and Nietzsche*.

[56] See my discussion of Merrill's mother as his problematic "needlewoman" in the Prelude to Chapter One.

[57] See Yeats's discussion in the eleventh section of "The Soul in Judgment" (*Vision* 237–39).

[58] Poems such as "In Monument Valley," "Another April," "Banks of a Stream Where Creatures Bathe," "Under Mars," "In Nine Sleep Valley," "The Black Mesa," and "Under Libra: Weights and Measures."

[59] Also noted by Yenser (*Myth* 185) and Mariani ("Yeats" 97).

[60] For an excellent discussion of these features of the poem see Yenser (*Myth* 193–94).

[61] Barbara Croft points to these proud words in Yeats's 1925 dedication to *A Vision*: "I am the first to substitute for Biblical or mythological figures, historical movements and actual men and women," and comments: "The substitution of historical figures for mythological ones is ingenious, for it both makes Yeats's system modern (in a way that Blake's and Dante's no longer seem to be) and revives the sense of reality mythology once had" (32). For both poets, History and Reality (personal, epochal or scientific) furnish the rational and material authority out of which Myth and Metaphor craft meaning (s) and emotional appeal (also aesthetic and ethical).

[62] See references to the novel's waterfall in sections "N," "T," and "X" in "The Book of Ephraim" (S. 49, 70, 84) and further waterfall references in *Sandover* (59, 117, 192, 426, 472, 517). At one point in *A Vision*, Yeats considers but rejects the waterfall as an emblem of the "irrational bitterness" of life and love: life is "no orderly descent from level to level, no waterfall but a whirlpool, a gyre" (40). In contrast, Merrill takes up the waterfall as his ambivalent image of immanent transcendence.

[63] Of course Yeats too trades on the symbolic riches of falling or moving water. But Yeats's waters, even at their most emblematic, lack the full sublimity of Merrill's waterfalls. "What's water but the generated soul?" Yeats asks in "Coole and Ballylee, 1931." "Adam's Curse gives us "time's water's" and "Love and Death" these early lines:

> Behold the flashing waters,
> A cloven, dancing jet,
> . . .

> Go ask the springing flowers,
> And the flowing air above,
> What are the twin-born waters,
> And they'll answer Death and Love

[64] Robert Polito makes a similar point when he writes: "Any possible salvation in *Sandover*, moreover, far from transpiring in an idealized, timeless present, remains embedded in the ongoing temporal cavalcade" (*Guide* 259).

[65] For two scenes of this forgetting, see *A Vision* (233) and "All Soul's Night," Yeats's epilogue to *A Vision*, where the soul "is whirled about / . . .

> Until it plunge into the sun;
> And there, free and yet fast,
> Being both Chance and Choice
> Forget[s] its broken toys
> And sinks into its own delight at last.

[66] In this, Merrill's and Yeats's thinking are most close. Helen Vendler gathers a useful compendium of characteristics of the Daimon in her study *Yeats's Vision and the Later Plays* (152).

[67] JM revisits this image in *Scripts*, where he suggests that the purpose of being born is to "feed the earthward flow / Of Paradise . . . [t]hat final waterfall / Ephraim first mentioned" (S. 426). In manuscript Merrill was even more forthcoming. In answer to DJ's question, "Why were we born?" JM replies: "If nothing else, the waterfall / They promised us we'd be two bright drops in— / Our energies translated, not destroyed, / By Paradise, when it comes."

[68] In "Chimes for Yahya" it is the "ringing" and "ringing" of an iron triangle that "drown[s] out" the children's' Christmas verses, Merrill's version of Yeats's "Turning and turning," the falconer not being able to hear, and the "drown[ing]" of a "ceremony of innocence" (those children's verses). The anarchy loosed in Merrill's poem is the children themselves, "All day children will be prowling loose," and "full of passionate intensity," they are "Eager to tell, tell, tell, what the angel said." It is Christmas tomorrow; thus, "Surely the Second Coming is at hand," and, as in Yeats, no sooner "are those words out" but Merrill provides images as if out of *Spiritus Mundi*: "Black figures from a crèche, part king / Part shepherd and part donkey, stamp and steam"—not unlike Yeats's "shape with lion body and the head of a man." "Thirty years pass" is Merrill's parodic reduction of Yeats's "twenty centuries of stony sleep." Yeats's "nightmare" becomes Merrill's "despair" and "sufferings." There are no "slow thighs" in Merrill's poem or waiting for birth "its hour come round at last"; instead, "'These mountain women *will* give birth / Under one's roof. They will wait until their labor's / So far advanced we've no way to prepare—.'" "Chimes for Yahya" builds suspense about its nativity, "what rough beast" indeed, until "Into her credulous / Outstretched arms laid—*not* a wriggling white / Puppy! Horrors twinkled through the brain." The eighth section of the poem offers something of a reprise of many of these elements, concluding with a falcon-like image: "It might as well be pleasure I rise in." Other Yeatsian notes include a perfectly Yeatsian fourfold composite portrait: "Lover, warrior, invalid, and sage, / Amused, unenvious of one another, / Meet in your face," as well as a two-line reduction of "Sailing to Byzantium" in which the speaker wants to spend "One lifetime there as a divinity / Student niched in shallowest faience" [here "divinity / Student" apply captures, inverts, and deflates Yeats's "be the singing masters of my soul. / . . . and gather me / Into the artifice of eternity"].

NOTES TO CHAPTER THREE

¹ Merrill kept one copy of Yeats's *Essays* at his home in Stonington and one at the house in Athens, one of very few books kept in duplicate this way. The copy I refer to is the one Merrill used in Athens. The copy Merrill kept in his bedroom in Stonington does not have any marginal notes. Although I believe Merrill's date on the title page, 1971, tells when he first acquired and read the book, there are indications that he may have returned to it a number of times over the years. For the most part, Merrill's annotations consist of underlining and marginal checks or lineation, so it is impossible to say for certain when these marks were made.

² X. J. Kennedy in his 1973 review of *Braving the Elements* remarks that Merrill's "mastery of forms, whether new or old, keeps his self-revelatory poems (and some of them are painful) from the worst lapses of recent poets of the confessional school. Merrill never sprawls, never flails about, never strikes postures. Intuitively he knows that, as Yeats once pointed out, in poetry 'all that is personal soon rots; it must be packed in ice or salt'" (102). Kennedy is right to make the connection, but this annotation shows that Merrill's "intuitive" knowledge was considerably reinforced by his reading. Indeed, this line was sufficiently significant for Merrill that he opens the last paragraph of his 1987 preface to the reissued edition of *The Seraglio*, with this paraphrase of Yeats's line: "The personal rots away, Yeats tells us, unless packed in ice or salt" (*Collected Novels* 631).

³ "In Memory of Major Robert Gregory" is one of the few poems Merrill marked both in the table of contents and within the body of the poem itself in his copy of Yeats's *Collected Poems* (New York: Macmillan, 1942). For the reader of *Sandover*, Yeats's opening stanzas, where he entertains thoughts of his dead friends, touches a number of Merrillian chords. Particularly striking is Merrill's literalizing of Yeats's aristocratic phrase "that discourtesy of death" (line 48), so that in the salon or seminar room of *Sandover* every courtesy is extended to help the newly dead over their shock. As in Yeats's poem, "Always we'd have the new friend meet the old / And we are hurt if either friend seem cold" (lines 9–10). Yeats's ultimate glorification of Major Gregory's early death, "What made us dream that he could comb grey hair," is not a theme that Merrill pursues in *Sandover* (though youthful suicide haunts some of the work of his late-teens and early twenties). Rather, Merrill again literalizes Yeats's metaphor, "others may consume / The entire combustible world in one small room / As though dried straw" (lines 81–83), reliving in horror his own earlier death by fire as Simpson (S. 6, 8) and making an all-consuming, atomic fire the looming threat behind his whole poem (S. 56, 113, 127, 134, 139, 441).

⁴ In his 1982 interview with J. D. McClatchy, Merrill comments, "There were things I enjoyed enormously, like fishing." His explanation for this enjoyment, that it offers "something responding and resisting from deep, deep down" ("Interview with McClatchy" 73), also defines one of the primary motives for his writing and one of his principle ways of understanding his work at the Ouija board. A brief sampling of significant moments of metaphoric fishing include:

> Was anybody there? As when a pike
> Strikes, and the line singing writes in lakeflesh
> Highstrung runes, and reel spins and mind reels
> YES a new and urgent power YES
> Seized the cup.   (S. 6)

Notes to Chapter Three

> (Why not, deep down, admit we're hooked? I make
> These weak signs of resistance for form's sake,
> Testing the tautness of the line whereby
> We're drawn—tormented spangles, I now guess,
> The measure of our mounting shallowness—
> Willy-nilly toward some high and dry
> Ecstasy, a light we trust will neither
> Hurt nor kill but permeate its breather.
> One wants to have been thought worth fighting for,
> And not be thrown back, with a shrug, from shore.)   (S. 138)

> (Beneath my incredulity
>   All at once is flowing
> Joy, the flash of the unbaited hook—
> *Yes, yes, it fits, it's right, it had to be!*
> Intuition weightless and ongoing
>   Like stanzas in a book
> Or golden scales in the melodic brook—)   (S. 466)

> Gabr. O FATHER, TWIN STAR, BROTHERS, SISTER, HEAR THEM: THEY HAVE
>   MADE SENSE OF IT.
>   DID NOT OUR DEAR ONE REPORT 'AND WHAT A FISH!' (YOU, GOOD
>   YEATS, WERE THE ONE THAT GO AWAY)   (S. 478)

> [Nature, concluding her masque:]
> MICHAEL YOUR RAINBOW LINE, IT IS OUR WISH
> YOU REEL US IN LIKE FLOPPING FISH,
> BUT LET ME CRY A LAST RESOUNDING YES
> TOP MAN, MAN IN HIS BLESSEDNESS!   (S. 489)

See also works such as "The Cosmological Eye," "The Forms of Death," "Accumulations of the Sea," "The Pelican," "Periwinkles," *The Bait*, "The Octopus," "The Parrot Fish," "Swimming by Night," "Remora," and "Koi."

⁵ Two of Merrill's annotations seem primarily to point to particular images: "And move like wings of light on dark and stormy air" (73) and "poison dying out of the green things" (71)—this latter perhaps recalling Merrill's ambivalence for "green things": in *Sandover* Mirabell tells JM and DJ, "YET U BOTH RIGHTLY AVOID GREEN ROOMS . . . YR NATURES BEING WHAT THEY ARE SEEK GREEN OUTSIDE THEMSELVES" (S. 216); in this passage too Merrill recalls putting by the emerald his mother wanted to give him for his bride ("The Emerald"). Other notes point to certain bits of "wisdom" that caught Merrill's eye. In one, as Yeats quotes Shelley's notes to *Queen Mab* on the presumption of a "perfect identity between the moral and physical improvement of human species," Merrill picks out the notion that "wisdom is not compatible with disease." Shelley's sentence continues: "that, in the present state of the climates of the earth, health, in the true and comprehensive sense of the word, is out of reach of civilized man" (71). Merrill also underlines Yeats's comments on Shelley's knowledge of magic: "though I do not find anything to show that he gave it any deep study," a remark that Merrill might have been happy to see given his own comparative "shallowness" of study in Yeats's vision system and in the realms of magic and the occult (78). On the following page, Merrill underlines, "grow perhaps dizzy with the sudden conviction that our little memories

are but a part of some great Memory that renews the world and men's thoughts age after age, and that our thoughts are not, as we suppose, the deep, but a little foam upon the deep." [This passage shows a number of parallels to WHA's paean to language late in *Mirabell*, where language corresponds to Yeats's "great Memory" and the writer's words, thoughts, and very self are alike epiphenomena (S. 262).] Merrill also picks out the sentence, "And 'the looms of stone' are the symbols of the 'souls that descend into generation'" (83) and then the phrase, "shining not beyond their portals"—this in a context regarding the limits and great creative self-sufficiency of mind as existence, which Merrill takes up in numerous places, but in *Sandover* in particular (85). Finally, Merrill draws a line in the margin beside Yeats's scenario from Oscar Wilde: "Some old magical writer, I forget who, says if you wish to be melancholy hold in your left hand an image of the Moon made out of silver, and if you wish to be happy hold in your right hand an Image of the Sun made out of gold" (93). Here too Merrill's interest in such imagery surely predates but gathers particular emphasis in *Sandover*.

⁶ Judging by volumes in Merrill's libraries in Stonington, Athens, and New York, Merrill did not read Shelley as intently as he read Yeats. His working copies included a *Selected Poetry and Prose* (Holt, Reinhart and Winston, 1963) in Athens, and a 1962 Dell paperback *Poetry* and 1966 NAL *Selected Poetry and Prose*, also in paper, in Stonington. None are annotated.

⁷ For references to Nature's multi-faceted femininity in *Sandover*, see pages 67, 92, 156, 202, 229, 230–35, 313, 365, 407, 426, 489, 516–17.

⁸ Psyche/Nature/Chaos, *Sandover*'s triune goddess, and Gabriel are close allies in Merrill's cosmology. (For indications of Gabriel's close alliance with Nature, see *Sandover* 410–11, 416–17, and 492.)

⁹ The last passage Merrill indicates in his copy of Yeats's *Essays and Introductions* is also the last few sentences of the book. A line in the margin picks out: "—the poetic theme has always been present. I recall an Indian tale: certain men said to the greatest of the sages, 'Who are your Masters?' And he replied, 'The wind and the harlot, the virgin and the child, the lion and the eagle'" (530). Merrill might have answered in kind, "fire and the angel, the child and the lover, the tree and the waterfall." What he did say about the characters called-for in *Sandover* is that they should be "conventional stock figures / Afflicted to a minimal degree / With personality and past experience— / A witch, a hermit, innocent young lovers, / The kinds of being we recall from Grimm, / Jung, Verdi, and the commedia dell' arte" (S. 4).

Merrill's copy of the *Essays* held one other "bookmark" (a Greek airmail envelope, unaddressed) marking pages 154–155 of Yeats's "The Symbolism of Poetry." He made no marks on these pages, but they do contain material that seems likely to have caught Merrill's eye—the quotation from Goethe: "a poet needs all philosophy, but he must keep it out of his work" and Yeats's fervent reply that such denial "is not always necessary," arguing that "it has often been this philosophy, or this criticism, that has evoked [artists'] most startling inspiration, calling into outer life some portion of the divine life, or of the buried reality, which could alone extinguish in the emotions what their philosophy or their criticism would extinguish in their intellect" (154). Merrill may also have been struck by this sentence of Yeats's: "because the divine life wars upon our outer life, and must needs change its weapons and its movements as we change ours, inspiration has come to them in beautiful startling shapes" (155). What better rationale for the whole discipline and wonder of revelation via the Ouija board?

¹⁰ Shelley, who was directly important to Yeats and through Yeats and Elinor Wylie also significant to Merrill, reminds us that "all poets, like the co-operating thoughts of one great mind" are at work on the same great poem [*A Defense* 493]. Harold Bloom has, of course, made significant contributions to our thinking about the agonistic mechanisms that inform

this work of "co-operation." His Oedipal theories of poetic influence have particular relevance to the relation between Yeats and Merrill but ultimately prove inadequate to the complexity of that relation.

[11] Rajan's study of Romantic texts has particular relevance for postmodern poets such as Merrill (and for Yeats as the "last Romantic") and their relation to earlier Romantic sources and practices.

[12] From a letter to Stephen Spender, May 20, 1964, Kirchstetten, Austria, in the Berg Collection of the New York Public Library (Qtd. in Mendelson 206). Leslie Brisman makes a similar point when he says that "Yeats represents for Merrill . . . a vision of an old self that much of Merrill's verse is concerned to refashion and transcend" (189). But where Brisman speaks of a "vision of an old self" in a way which implies a good deal of already achieved psychic distance, I see Merrill's repeated contests with his "Yeatsian Daimon" as more immediate and an ongoing relationship, one that only begins to lose its haunting cast in Merrill's posthumous collection *A Scattering of Salts*.

[13] Robert Polito in the afterword to his *Reader's Guide to* The Changing Light at Sandover, comments that many of the passages that concern other poets "crackle with the high anxiety that Harold Bloom marks as the essence of all poetry relationships" (253). He speaks of Merrill inhabiting "the shells of his literary progenitors *only* to crack them open" (254, emphasis added) in the same spirit that he earlier remarks that through the "foster parents of Maria and Auden, Nature and God B, Merrill appears to have silenced the Oedipal horrors that agitated his strongest lyrics" (251). In neither case does Polito acknowledge that Oedipal and literary anxieties continue powerfully to animate and inform Sandover's chief themes and structures. The evidence he cites of struggle, displacement, and Merrill's need to "cherish and cast away" both sources of anxiety (256) is in itself a sign, not of progenitors surmounted or Oedipal horrors silenced, but of the enduring vitality of these forces. Polito gives five pages to his discussion of Merrill's "pressing back" against Yeats: two listing "correspondences" and "thematic analogs," the rest given to "Merrill's antisystematic dismantling of *A Vision*" and the ways in which Merrill's poem "at once releases and terminates" Yeats's theory of the mask (260). By this Polito means the way "Merrill nails down the corners of Yeats's rhetoric, dramatizing his transcripts instead of paraphrasing them, accepting poems instead of "metaphors for poetry" from his guides" (261). These points are certainly just, and Polito makes a number of other revealing and pertinent points in his discussion. But that Merrill "terminates" any Yeatsian contribution is not one. The claim makes sense only in so far as Merrill extends Yeats's thought and practice to serve his own characteristic ends. I gratefully draw on Polito's insights and examples in a number of places in what follows.

[14] In the Paris Review interview, J. D. McClatchy remarks to Merrill that "one of your strengths as a poet is to disarm your reader, often by including his possible objections." To which Merrill replies: "That might even be the placating gesture of a child who is inevitably going to disappoint his parents before he fulfills the expectation they haven't yet learned to have. I was always very good at seeming to accede to what my father or mother wanted of me—and then going ahead to do as I pleased" ("Interview with McClatchy" 77). If we substitute "readers" for "parents" (and "poet" for "child") in this statement, as context seems to authorize, we are presented with an instructive scenario. The poet/child disappoints because the reader/parent has not yet learned to have appropriate expectations. Thus, the poet/child instructs us in what we should expect, as he seems to accede to our (parental) wishes, or our objections, by nonetheless doing as he pleases. It is as though merely hearing our wishes or

objections acceded to is enough to free us for the moment to entertain what the poet/child would (also or rather) have us see.

¹⁵ This characterization, which will become a refrain, shows that Merrill probably recalled the terms of Yeats's "True Mask" (at Phase Seventeen) "Simplification through intensity" (*Vision* 140). Yeats's presence, spread in patches throughout *Sandover*, also seems to fulfill the terms of the "False Mask," "Dispersal," in a way that points up Merrill's anxious or "false" relationship with the older poet. There is something apt as well as perverse in Merrill's insisting on Yeats's simplifications. Neither *A Vision* nor Yeats's poetry is simple, but Yeats's passion for finding a system that will allow him "to hold *in a single thought* reality and justice" (emphasis added), his fusion of dramatic rhetoric with emblematic compression, his faith in the power of the symbol, and quest for "Unity of Being," all tend toward a kind of apparent simplicity and reflect the belief that art or revelation can in some way "fix" the sublime indeterminacies of history, psychology, and morality.

¹⁶ As well as the obvious affinities between "Ephraim" and *A Vision* are also such particular details as Yeats' introductory announcement addressed to Ezra Pound, "I send you the introduction of a book which will, when finished, proclaim a new divinity" (*Vision* 27) and Merrill's introductory announcement of his theme, "The incarnation and withdrawal of / A god" (S. 3). Yeats writes that "Much that has happened, much that has been said, suggest that the communicators are the personalities of a dream shared by my wife, by myself . . . " (*Vision* 23), just as Merrill's "ex-shrink" suggests that their communications at the board are JM and DJ's "folie à deux" (S. 30).

¹⁷ See "Interview with Vendler" 49; Merrill "Exploring" 417, 420.

¹⁸ The visual idiom here, of "see" and "observe," is misleading; but I lack the language for what is throughout a verbal (that is at once an oral and a textual) manifestation.

¹⁹ "This year's girl" may also be another guise for Merrill. After all, Merrill as much as Maya Deren worried about "Hair-roots white" (and dyed his hair and used make-up to the end). He too is known for "wit, affection" and, at times, "despair" (See "Chimes for Yahya") and could claim for himself "touches of tart and maiden, muse and wife." Stephen Yenser locates another instance when Maya and JM's identities seem to merge in the description of Maya's stroke and the pun on "eye" in "the other eye . . . " (*Myth* 231), and Robert Polito points specifically to JM's description of Maya's stroke (S. 63–64) as an instance of a more general pattern in which "JM . . . uncovers aspects of himself by observing friends and mentors" (*Guide* 237).

²⁰ In a context where coincidences may still be "NO ACCIDENT," it is interesting to recall that Yeats's *Per Amica Silentia Lunae*, the book Harold Bloom calls the "introduction to the visionary center" of Yeats's work, first had the working title of *An Alphabet* (Bloom *Yeats* 178) and that the fictional book that figures as the source of Michael Robartes' occult wisdom in *A Vision* is *Speculum Angelorum et Holmium* or "Mirror of the Angels and of Men" (*Vision* 38)—an apt anticipation not only of the cover design for the dust jacket of Merrill's *Divine Comedies* but also of the role and theme of the mirror throughout *Sandover*.

²¹ See Bloom *Figures* 9. A quatrain from Merrill's 1958 poem "The Doodler" helps reinforce this Bloomian reading of thunder. The speaker, it becomes clear in the poem, is God, addressing both a primitive and contemporary would-be artist:

> Like thunderheads one day in sultry foretaste
> Of flashes first envisioned *as your own*
> When, squat and breathless, you inscribe on stone
> Your names for me, my inkling of an artist—   (emphasis added)

Here thunderheads mark the anxious transaction whereby the poet/scribe appropriates for himself the divine "flash" of imaginative vision and naming. The poet is always almost a thief—but one who in his thievery or appropriative mis-taking gains reflective consciousness. "My inkling of an artist," as Merrill's divine speaker calls his poet, "more than image then, a rain, a river / Of prescience, you reflect and I rejoice!" Here, against the voice of Yeats's Rocky Face who looks on man and can "but laugh in tragic joy" and who knows but one word "Rejoice" ("The Gyres"), Merrill posits a childlike, somewhat compulsive divinity as his model of the artist, gay beyond the reach of tragic joy, who, when a page goes brittle or burns, simply begins again, delighted by his own facility, so that "Again / Emerge, O sunbursts, garlands, creatures, men, / Ever more lifelike out of the white void" ("The Doodler"). The poet's joy can, at best, only be a reflection of such gladness.

22 This "deep shriek" in the context of sport turned menacing also recalls Yeats's "Nineteen Hundred and Nineteen, IV," a passage Merrill marked in his 1942 edition of the *Collected Poems*: "We, who seven years ago / Talked of honour and of truth, / Shriek with pleasure if we show / The weasel's twist, the weasel's tooth."

23 And yet Yeats himself insists in an essay Merrill knew well: "Talk to me of originality and I will turn on you in a rage. I am a crowd, I am a lonely man, I am nothing" (*Essays* 522). This is also Keats's lesson, and, minus the so clearly self-dramatizing "I," is one of the chief lessons Merrill gives himself to learn in the course of *Sandover*: how to achieve the "Self-effacing balance," how to become "sufficiently / Imbued with otherness," how to manage "So many voices," including God B's rippling "O O O O O O O O O O" (S. 89, 301, 360). Part of what Yeats counsels in this essay when he says "all that is personal soon rots; it must be packed in ice or salt . . .[and] Ancient salt is best" (Ibid.) is take up by WHA when he chides JM:

> CAN YOU STILL BE BENT,
> AFTER OUR COURSE IN HOW TO SEE PAST LONE
> AUTONOMY TO POWERS BEHIND THE THRONE,
> ON DOING YR OWN THING: EACH TEENY BIT
> (PARDON MME) MADE PERSONAL AS SHIT? . . .
>   THINK OF WHAT A MINOR
> PART THE SELF PLAYS IN A WORK OF ART
> COMPARED TO THOSE GREAT GIVENS (S. 262).

24 Section "R" opens with the call to "Rewrite P" and casts a revisionary light upon the earlier section. The opening evocation of "P," "Powers of lightness, darkness, powers that be . . ." in this backward light carries now more the sense of a spell being cast, a conjuration. Perhaps it is as early as this that Yeats, the poet as magician starts to materialize. A kind of rough, Faustian magic (indiscriminate of light or dark) informs the first several lines of "P," and lines of occult relation with the later section, in retrospect, begin to show. The "thunder of clear skies," is it stolen? The "Pole the track star floats from like a banner," is it the not also the "track the pole star floats from," the azimuth, and hence "the star that marks the hidden pole"? Does "P's" record needle and "R's" sharpening "blade /On grindstone" recall complementary gyres—the one decelerating, the other "upwind[ing]"? And is not our dollar sign, "Where Snake and Tree of Paradise entwine," more a hermetic caduceus than a bacchic thyrsus? Merrill concludes section "P" lightly, with mercurial wit; but it is wit that meditates upon the sheer fire(bird) of apocalypse ("fire-sheer / Solar plume on plume") and the absolute azure of oblivion. These last meditations also take the form of and may well represent the first sonnet in the sequence of section "R."

²⁵ In this brief passage, Merrill, who wrote his Amherst honors thesis on *A la rechereche du temps perdu* and has repeatedly noted his debt to Proust, seems to have felt "sufficiently imbued" with Proust's "otherness" to essay this assumed quotation (*Recitative* xi, 78; "James Merrill at Home" 21).

²⁶ Stephen Yenser traces JM's links of identity with St. Theodore, whose column is this "'I' of stone," and Teddie the "Mrs. Smith" anecdote in section "Q" (*Myth* 232).

²⁷ Merrill is forever being drawn to, while at the same time insulating himself and the reader from, "the naked current [of the absolute] where it / Flows through field and *book*" (S. 84, emphasis added).

²⁸ The first two lines of each quatrain take their rhymes from the preceding two lines, so that Merrill's favored "ABBA" is both "torn" or cleft and strung across the stanza break, thus: AB //BACD//DCEF//FE. This *enchainement* binds the passage in quatrains to the preceding blank verse, while the shift to quatrains also announces a break from what has gone before. Even though each quatrain depends on what comes before it and enjambment across stanza breaks impel a forward momentum toward closure, the final couplet, though resolving one cleft quatrain, announces itself a fragment with a dash. The fragmentary, aggregating syntax also suggests a looseness of "conception" that the rigors of this stanza structure belie. Thus, in high-modernist fashion, form replicates the stresses of continuity and departure, movement and arrest that animate the quarrel of these passages.

²⁹ What may be the last faint echo of Yeats in "The Book of Ephraim" comes fittingly at the end of section "Y" where DJ (who is explicitly linked with Yeats throughout the rest of *Sandover*) helps JM see David's aging parents in terms particularly reminiscent of "Vacillation II":

> These two old people at each other's gnarled,
> Loveless mercy. Yet David now evokes
> Moments of broadest after-supper light
> Before talk show or moon walk, when at length
> The detergent and the atrocity
> Fight it out in silence, and he half blind
> And she half deaf, serenely holding hands
> Bask in the tinted conscience of their kind. (S. 88)

³⁰ In his memoir, *A Different Person*, Merrill remarks that Mirabell "had for one long summer at the Ouija Board sung to us 'of what is past, or passing, or to come'" (245). But this acknowledgment of Mirabell's Yeatsian mission does not establish the all-important matter of tone. In a manuscript passage dropped from *Scripts* [which would have come after Mirabell's "E V E N NUMBERS?" on page 429], JM characterizes Mirabell as "cunning" and tells him "you are the great / Genie we call on to de-escalate." Thus, Mirabell's paradoxical role, for all his "soaring" elaboration on Yeats's system as R-Lab, is one of parodic deflation. JM continues (in the manuscript), giving in four lines the metaphysical force of Mirabell's strategies of inversion and reduction:

> How long, how patiently you've fitted this
> Soaring, materializing edifice
> Back to the lucid atoms of the brain,
> Like a skyscraper in a drop of rain.

Although I think he takes too much at face value, Piotr Gwiazda gives a valuable account of Merrill's parodic deflation of Yeats and other poetic authorities in his "Views from the Rosebrick Manor: Poetic Authority in James Merrill's *The Changing Light at Sandover*."

[31] Harold Bloom also notes the "complex irony of the close of 'The Phases of the Moon,'" but argues that Aherne's laughter betrays a hollowness in the poem, rather than a moment of knowing self-mockery on Yeats's part. "The laughter of Aherne, at the expense of Yeats, is a hollowness, for the finder of mere images, the poet, never expects to find anything but endless cycle . . . and an absurd life" (*Yeats* 206). This reading distorts Yeats's faith in the power of images to suggest "the escape" (the Condition of Fire, the Thirteenth Cone) and to give meaning to life's "phantasmagoria."

[32] See Vendler *Yeats's Vision* 8, 26.

[33] As Yeats puts it, "These pairs of opposites whirl in contrary directions, *Will* and *Mask* from right to left, *Creative Mind* and *Body of Fate* like the hands of a clock, from left to right" (*Vision* 74).

[34] Robert Polito lists further "bird's-eye" adaptations in which "Merrill's spirit guides reproduce intricacies" from Yeats's *A Vision*: "The losses and dispersals that signify increase and elevation ['the stripping process'] are adumbrated in Phase 17. Self-discovery through self-forgetting ('the joy of self-surrender') is the burden of Phase 24. The description of the Receptive Man in Phase 23, especially Yeats's warm account of the dramatist Synge, underlies the bat-angel's praise of Merrill's openness and receptivity in the poignant "WE MET ON THIS FAIR FIELD" interlude in *Mirabell* [*Sandover* 257–56]" (*Guide* 258).

[35] For a succinct discussion of Yeats's race philosophy, his long standing commitment to eugenics, and the authoritarian bias to his theory of historical cycles and antinomies see Marjorie Howes's chapter on "The rule of the kindred" in her study, *Yeats's Nations*, pp. 160–185.

[36] Although he turns to his angels for hypothetical authority, and rhetorical "cover," Merrill's published remarks outside of *Sandover* appear at least as problematic as Yeats's in *On the Boiler*:

> But let's be serious for a moment. If our Angels are right, every leader—president or terrorist—is responsible for keeping his ranks thinned out. Good politics would therefore encourage death in one form or another—if not actual, organized bloodshed, then the legalization of abortion or, heaven forbid, the various chemical or technological atrocities. *Only this last* strikes me as truly immoral, perhaps because it's a threat that hadn't existed before my own lifetime.
>
> ("Interview with McClatchy" 72, emphasis added)

[37] Such "affiliation" should come as no surprise by this point. But what does startle are the instances in which Yeats seems to adopt Merrill's idiom. One example occurs when Yeats writes after finishing the proof sheets for *A Vision*, "I begin to see things double, doubled in history, world history, personal history. . . . Perhaps it makes every poet's life poignant, certainly every poet who has 'swallowed the formulas'" (*Letters* 887). Here Yeats's language sounds uncannily like JM musing after one of Mirabell's lessons. In this statement, we not only seem to hear Yeats indulging in a typically Merrillian pun and anticipating *Mirabell*'s general fondness for formulae and double-mindedness, but hear more specifically anticipations of JM's confession, "Fact is, I remain, like any atom, / Two minded" (S. 232); we also catch intimations of the arch comment already mentioned in which Merrill avows that he and Jackson, as "docile takers-in of seed," merely "swallow / [the formulas]" their bat voices dic-

tate (S. 154). If this is an example of Bloom's Apophrades, it operates with distinctively Merrillian wit. [Merrill was given a copy of Yeats's Letters by Claude Fredricks in 1954 and may have recalled this letter. Helen Vendler draws attention to the first part of this letter (to Dorothy Wellesley, May 4th, 1937) and Robert Polito makes the connection between Merrill and *Mirabell* (*Guide* 257).]

[38] The one major example of JM's approaching such a moment comes at "7.6," his "starstruck hymn to Mother N."

[39] "Mandala," S. 534. For more of Merrill's recuperative vision, see also the conclusions of "Fléche d'Or" and "Lost in Translation," also S. 186 and 376.

Yeats says that he turns to the Commedia dell' Arte when he wishes "for some general idea which will describe the Great Wheel as an individual life" (*Vision* 83), but in the heterosexualized interplay between Man and Daimon, Will and Mask, that colors the whole system an element of tragic disjunction prevails. Yeats's sense of the tragic is notably capacious, however, and sometimes seems only to exclude the banal: "All happy art seem to me that hollow image [of fulfilled desire], but when its lineaments express also the poverty or the exasperation that set its maker to the work, we call it tragic art" (*Per Amica* 329). By these lights, given the weight of Merrill's "exasperations," even the high comedy of *Sandover* might qualify as tragedy.

[40] Merrill acknowledges himself "a perfect magpie" when it comes to making use of chance or "found" contributions to his poem, which is very much in keeping with the both the active (appropriative) and the receptive strands of his remarks on poetic influence ("Interview with McClatchy" 66).

[41] I am indebted to Robert Polito for pointing out this parallel (*Guide* 236). What Polito does not discuss are the questions of identity that arise in this passage. The question that elicited 741's Yeatsian response concerned the identity of the spirit-voice: "Ah, you're developing a way with words. / In fact you sound like—maybe you *are* Ephraim?" With the board's cryptic answer, the issue of identity does not drop away; indeed the reply that follows JM's next question, about whether the spirit is "good—what *we* mean by the word," also points proleptically to Yeats in that it indicates both the blessing and painful discipline Yeats confers and suffers as the residing "energy that activates" DJ's hand (217): "What if D put his hand down on the board now? / IT WD BE BLEST / KISSD HE IS OUR PEN WE HURT HIM TO GET HIS ATTENTION" (S. 117).

[42] 40070 [perhaps the same representative of the OO who dictated to Yeats (S. 424)] discloses how, through a kind of receptive sympathy, "cloning," or influence, also happens within (and not just between) lives: "CLOSE YR EYES THINKING YOU SINK INTO OUR THOUGHTS A FORM OF / CLONING YR DC CAME IN THIS WAY THRU OUR INFLUENCE" (S. 121). 40070 supplies the link between the Scribe who "sits by" JM in "Ephraim, section 'U,'" and "AN UNBROKEN CHAIN" of scribes who have similarly taken dictation from the OO. Turning back to section "U," we see how quickly JM's "anxiety of influence" issues in discipline and punishment aimed covertly at Yeats. JM has just been told, "A SCRIBE SITS BY YOU CONSTANTLY THESE DAYS / DOING WHAT HE MUST TO INTERWEAVE / YOUR LINES WITH MEANINGS YOU CANNOT CONCEIVE," and JM responds heatedly, "Parts of this, in other words—a rotten / Thing to insinuate—have been ghostwritten?" (S. 72). Shortly afterwards comes the first disciplinary assault on DJ's Hand. Thus, if Yeats is the Scribe who "sits by" JM throughout these sessions [being the energy in DJ's hand "that activates / These very messages" (S.217)] Yeats is also, with DJ, the one in the poem who suffers both belittlement and pain. This violence against the precursor poet may be another "revisionary ratio" to add to the six Bloom presents in *Anxiety*.

Notes to Chapter Three

(See also page 424 where JM asks, as if naively, "But does Yeats suffer *now?*") For further discussion of how such violence relates to Bloom's account of influence, see the second section of the coda to Chapter Four, "Merrill's Bloom."

43 "but all that is personal soon rots; it must be *packed in ice or salt"* (Merrill's emphasis). See the prelude to this chapter.

44 On these topics, Merrill tells J. D. McClatchy that "No voice is as individual as the poet would like to think" and that he had "early on" begun to "understand the relativity, even the reversibility, of truths" ("Interview with McClatchy" 80).

45 This "exchange with Wystan is largely contrived" Merrill tells McClatchy in 1982 ("Interview with McClatchy" 64).

46 For an overview of significant manuscript variations in *Mirabell* and *Scripts*, see Appendix C.

47 In *Scripts* Merrill makes explicit this identification of Mirabell with "Juno's bird" (S 298). Yeats's context for this cry in *A Vision* is more apocalyptic, but not irrelevant, given the revelations at hand in *Sandover*. The "scream of Juno's peacock" here attends that moment in a civilization, when the struggle for self-control surrenders to the irrational and revelation (*Vision* 268).

48 Timothy Materer's "Death and Alchemical Transformation in James Merrill's *The Changing Light at Sandover*" provides an insightful reading into the alchemical basis of this and related passages in *Sandover*. Materer focuses on the Jungian parallels to Merrill's hermeticism, but notes several of the Yeatsian echoes as well. He gives a Yeatsian as well as alchemical rationale for why "the nonhuman member of the seminar should be a peacock" (90), notes the Yeatsian images of music and dance in the first stanza (92), and the parallel to Yeats's "Vacillation VII" in Merrill's third stanza. Materer does not pursue Merrill's reading of Yeats's "Rosa Alchemica" as a possible source for some of Merrill's alchemical understanding and does not argue that Merrill was acquainted with Jung's alchemical writings.

49 The rhyme between "snores" and Hugo's "Oracular sophomores" helps undermine any positive equivalence between Milton's wonders and Yeatsian "immense conceit." JM trivializes the importance of knowing about spiritual sources, lumping together the inspiration stories of Milton, Hugo, and Yeats as "The things one knows. And cheerfully ignores." But he does not take the strong Nietzschean position and claim the creative necessity of such forgetting.

50 This section, 4.7, opens with references to Blake and closes with the Miltonic "Deck with green boughs the ways of God to man" (S. 179), which in manuscript reads even more directly "Multiply the ways of God to man."

51 As a reflection of what Harold Bloom considers Yeats's bondage to "the idols of determinism" (*Yeats* 436), "No Accident" also threatens the poetic freedom and vitality of considerable stretches of this part of the poem. "No Accident" and all it represents in *Sandover* corresponds to what Bloom calls the "Covering Cherub," that "demon of continuity" whose "baleful charm . . . reduces a world of differences into a grayishness of uniformity" (*Anxiety* 39). In the recuperative movement of *Scripts*, the authority of this "law" is consequently undermined and qualified by the higher imaginative voices of the poem. (See S. 411, 476, 495.)

52 The "Soul in Judgment" chapter in *A Vision* details the six stages the soul or Spirit "lives through" in the indefinite period between death and birth; in it, Yeats, like Mirabell, concludes with the paired image of dance that also is the ultimate gyre, Yeats's Thirteenth

Cone, which is "like some great dancer . . . dancing some primitive dance and conscious of his or her own life and of the dance" (*Vision* 240).

⁵³ Note the sense that Yeats is as responsible for Mirabell as he is for his bird of gold enameling and that Merrill, by making Yeats's a *talking* bird rather than one that sings, reaches back to reshape or correct the older poet's image. Note too that what both birds talk or sing about remains "Time! The forbidden, the forgotten theme—" (S. 438) or more explicitly, mortality: what is past, or passing, or to come.

⁵⁴ With *Scripts*, the characters that multiplied along with the "DESIMPLIFYING" of *Mirabell* more and more reveal themselves to be aspects of fewer, more basic identities, until Michael reveals that he was Ephraim, or the "M/E" of Merrill himself and, in the Coda, JM alone remains to tell his tale. The whole epic, cosmogonic fabric folds itself inside the story of the Broken Home once more—a radical simplification indeed (S. 557). As usual, Merrill chastises Yeats for the very impulses he admires (however ambivalently) and hopes to emulate (however indirectly or idiosyncratically).

⁵⁵ As Harold Bloom puts it, "Every poem we know begins as an encounter *between poems*. I am aware that poets and their readers prefer to believe otherwise, but acts, persons, and places, if they are to be handled by poems at all, must themselves be treated first as though they were already poems, or parts of poems. Contact, in a poem, means contact with another poem, even if that poem is called a deed, person, place or thing" (*Map* 70).

⁵⁶ Yenser continues:

> What is the point, this [second] stanza asks, in escaping an ordinary, uninspired, unaspiring life if one is going to lose oneself in sterile artifice? As JM's imagination removes him anew from the natural world, *à la* Yeats, that world becomes more attractive—and less easily distinguished from the poetic one. "Once out of nature," rather like Dante in the *Paradiso*, XXVII, he envisions Earth as though from a satellite, with the different climatic zones alternating "by 'turns' as in a music hall" (*Myth* 276–77).

⁵⁷ Merrill's eight-line stanza, which doubles his favorite quatrain form, may also point back to Yeats's use of ottava rima, and thus be another instance of revising a Yeatsian construct in order to establish what is "eminently me." For further discussion of Yeats's use of ottava rima, see Helen Vendler's article "Yeats's Ottava Rima."

⁵⁸ The contrast between Yeats's apocalyptic unicorn, harbinger of the destruction preceding the new age, and Merrill's Uni, docile and affectionate survivor of the earth's first apocalypse, presents one revealing gauge of the shift in tone in this book. George Melchiori presents Yeats's unicorn as "a scourge from above which will bring renewal, through ruin" (Qtd. in Bloom *Yeats* 145) and Septimus in Yeats's *The Player Queen* announces "the end of the Christian Era, the coming of a New Dispensation, that of the New Adam, that of the Unicorn. . . . Man is nothing till he is united to an image. Now the Unicorn is both an image and beast; that is why he alone can be the new Adam" (*Eleven Plays* 99, 102). The best introduction to Uni in *Sandover* is the section "A New Friend" (378–82). In *Sandover*, Merrill's New Adam (S. 508) is the Alpha Man (S. 308, 455–56, 483):

> A CREATURE MUCH LIKE DARLING MAN, YET
> PHYSICALLY MORE ADAPTABLE.
> HIS IMMORTALITY WILL CONSIST OF PROLONGATION, IN THE
> BEGINNING PHASE, UNTIL HIS IDEAL IS REACHED IN NUMBER.

THEN TIME WILL STOP
AND LONG FRUITFUL SPACES BE GIVEN HIM TO LEARN THROUGH
   SONG AND POETRY
OF HIS OLD HELPLESS FEELINGS & WEARY PAST (S. 512).

About this passage Merrill later comments: "Well, toward the end of *Scripts*, when we have that little session called "glimpses of the future, "there is a kind of science-fiction cartoon of a different kind of human being" ("Exploring" 428).

⁵⁹ Cotzias argues for the place of vision, the voice of "Juno's Bird," in science and relates how, after a moment of such vision, he woke "*Knowing* that what had reached me was the song / The Phoenix sings throughout eternity" (S. 298–99). An earlier version of this passage reveals more Yeatsian echoes, subdued in the published version. When Cotzias speaks defensively of his "visions" and how he hears "the same ice-cold but not unloving / Woman telling me the same sublime / Truths about the cosmic organism," it is hard not to be reminded of similar moments in Yeats, particularly the icy authority of his muse, Maude Gonne. Merrill's published version changes "visions" to "voices," drops the Yeatsian link with "ice," and subtly deflates the rhetoric of "sublime truths" to truths "too deep, too antilogical / Ever to grasp" (S. 299). Cotzias hears his "icy voice" once again and recognizes it as "MY PHOENIX!" when he is introduced to Urania, the cold and universal muse of Milton, Shelley, and, by her attributes, of Yeats as well (S. 400).

⁶⁰ In some sense Yeats anticipates this "correction," and not just in his "Crazy Jane phase." In "The Circus Animal's Desertion," Yeats famously acknowledges the limitations of his past aesthetic, listing "Vain gaiety, vain battle, vain repose, / [as] Themes of the embittered heart." But Leslie Brisman is correct that "Yeats never turned to the fund of what might be called 'sensual memory' . . . with anything like the regularity and liveliness of Merrill" (197), and Brisman is again correct when he suggests that Merrill writes against a decidedly simplified version of the older poet (Ibid.). Merrill's insistence on a sociable delight, a dance rather that a battle of opposites, may also operate as part of Merrill's suspicion of Harold Bloom's anxious theory of poetic influence, which I discuss at the conclusion of this study.

⁶¹ A good deal of the irony is certainly the part WHA finds himself playing in Merrill's most occult and Yeats-saturated poem. After all, it is Auden who declared that although "there is scarcely a lyric written today in which the influence of [Yeats's] style and rhythm is not detectable, one whole side of Yeats, the side summed up in the *Vision*, has left virtually no trace" ("Yeats as Example" 188). Auden's scorn for "such nonsense" makes Merrill's use of him all the more daring, and rhetorically effective.

⁶² For references to Blake, see S. 391, 407, 408, 410.

⁶³ Merrill had read Hans Jonas's *The Gnostic Religion* before discussing it with Bloom in 1977. They discussed Jonas (a personal friend of Bloom's), Gershom Scholem, and Carl Jung and other attendees at the Erato Conferences. Merrill also read Bloom's Gnostic rhapsody, *The Flight of Lucifer*, and wrote him to say he found it interesting but did not understand why all the characters should be so antipathetic. In contrast, Bloom characterizes *Sandover* as "sublimely cheerful" and says that the book is only in the loosest, broadest sense of the term more Gnostic than orthodox Christian (Conversations with Harold Bloom, February 5 and July 1, 1997).

⁶⁴ Maria's phrase recalls more than the cadence of Yeats's "mackerel-crowded" and "gong-tormented" seas; it engages Yeats's deep ambivalence about the power of images to serve as compelling "personifications," visions meant to be seen through, while also being in them-

selves "living and vivid" and resistant to conceptual reduction (*Per Amica* 346, see also "Byzantium" V).

⁶⁵ DJ specifies that canonical authors such as Goethe and Rilke are "mined out" to fuel their current *readers*, but this process surely applies to writers as well, since they are like to be among the most assiduous readers of all.

⁶⁶ According to notes on his typescript title page, Merrill considered several possible epigraphs from Rilke for *Scripts*, including lines from *Book of the Hours* and the first Duino Elegy. The first elegy opens with lines that are particularly apt:

> Who, if I cried out, would hear me among the angels'
> hierarchies? and even if one of them pressed me
> suddenly against his heart: I would be consumed
> in that overwhelming existence. For beauty is nothing
> but the beginning of terror, which we still are just able to endure,
> and we are so awed because it serenely disdains
> to annihilate us. Every angel is terrifying.
> (translated by Stephen Mitchell)

Merrill, describing his distrust of the power of beauty, comments similarly in his memoir: "beauty was terrifying, and only a very foolish moth expected any good to come from his affair with the flame" (*Different* 176). It is possible that something of Yeats's linkage of terror and beauty in the refrain "A terrible beauty is born." ("Easter, 1916") may be behind both Rilke and Merrill's lines. [Whether Rilke would have known Yeats's refrain or whether this line had any influence on the first elegy is hard to determine. Rilke reported interest in reading a volume of Yeats's *Stories and Essays* in the fall of 1916 and, to the end of his days, "showed himself fully aware of Yeats' importance" (Mason 112).]

⁶⁷ JM's "almost vatic" note is struck by his correctly guessing that the previous day's demonstration atomic explosion was an actual one (S. 462). We also remember Bloom's words about "a more Promethean phase where [the poet] quests for his own fire, which nevertheless must be stolen from his precursor" (*Figures* 9) and see how hard it is for Merrill to totally forego Yeats's terms and experiences when Gabriel tells him, "WE FIX UP A SYSTEM . . . WHEREBY THIS IS DONE: / SO THE SLEEPER'S DREAM, THE APPROACH THROUGH VISIONS, & MANY A CLEVER WAY TO BRING HIS DARLING WITHOUT TERROR . . . INTO [God B's] PRESENCE" (S. 463).

⁶⁸ Eventually even God B sanctions this Yeatsian, ideographic, method when he dictates: "YES to NO to A to Z to YES" and JM interprets in verse that echoes (and repeats) the symbol's shape:

> (Qincunz where ghosts of Five and Twelve perambulate)
>   The cup . . . crosses itself? Inscribes a stark
>   Twinbladed axe
>   Upon the block, sideways? Is it the mark
>   That cancels, or the letter-writer's kiss?
>   The X
>   Of the illiterate?
>   Fulcrum and consort to our willowy &?
>   The space of a slow breath indrawn
>   Simplicity itself, it waits and then goes on,
>   Taking us like children by the hand: (S. 493–94)

The passage is also notable for its echoes of the Bible and Fitzgerald's *Rubaiyat*, as well as Yeats's "simplicity." But perhaps most significantly, God B's gesture allies the divinity with the power of signs as well as words.

69 In manuscript this read: "Our lessons—from your viewpoint, Mr Yeats, / Do they bear out or contradict your own?" Thus, both poets in their now open "inner quarrel" want to hear who is right and who is wrong.

70 *A Vision* 25, 235, 236.

71 See S. 217, 324, 361, 424, 473, 478 and "DJ: A Conversation with David Jackson" 41.

72 Alison Lurie argues that David Jackson should have been given more credit for his contributions to *Sandover*. Her memoir, *Familiar Spirits: A Memoir of James Merrill and David Jackson*, without drawing attention to these scenes, alerts readers to take seriously DJ's fears and his being made to suffer for and by *Sandover*'s dictating voices, since they may indicate real costs he paid in terms of his own writing and in terms of his relationship with Merrill.

73 We might remember Merrill's nervous comment regarding Friar's influence on his early poems: "Many hands made light work" (*Recitative* 6).

74 The Arthur Orson character represents much the best of what Merrill sensed he would become without the balancing vocation of poetry (first seriously presented to him by Friar), a character of wit, refinement, and superficiality, for whom Merrill nonetheless has clear affection and respect, even as he notes his limitations: "Orestes' lectures were about serious things. Poetry, for Arthur, might be cleverness, mere icing on the cake; for Orestes it was a life. 'Believe me,' said his friend [Arthur], 'so is cleverness'" (*Diblos* 102).

75 Andrea Mariani calls attention to this "explicit allusion" in his helpful essay on "Dante's Language in Merrill's Trilogy" ("Polylinguism" 207).

76 The complete quatrain: "The friends that have I do wrong / When ever I remake a song, / Should know what issue is at stake: / It is myself that I remake." (*Variorum Edition* 778).

77 In discussing this passage, Leslie Brisman reads the pun as commenting more on Yeats than on Merrill's correction. He comments that "the final pun on *airloom* as both heirloom (preservative of the past) and air-loomed (ethereal) captures the high tension that was Yeats's own between the desire for transcendence and the all-too-human veneration of traditions and traditional things of this earth" (190–91). It is part of the resourcefulness of Merrill's punning regard for "English in the billiards sense" that either spin proves productive and apt.

78 For all the barely contained irony of this passage, Andrea Mariani finds in Auden's reply an "obvious" allusion to Statius's reverence for Virgil in the *Purgatorio* when the younger poet bends to embrace the older and is rebuffed: "Frate, / non far, ché tu se' ombra e ombra vedi." ("Brother, don't, what you see is a shade, as shade you are." XXI.131) but then replies:

> "Or puoi la quantitate
> comprender dell'amor ch'a te mi scala,
> quand' io dismento nostra vanitate,
> trattando l'ombre come cosa salda." (133–36)

(Now you can understand the quantity of love for you that scalds me, when I forget our emptiness and treat a shade like a solid thing.) (Qtd. in Mariani "Yeats" 91)

The allusion is certainly present (and serves archly to call attention to the problem of seeing and hearing, let alone touching, these "shady" manifestations of the alphabet); but in pointing to this passage in Dante as an instance of Merrill's (indirect) homage for the "life and work of the great predecessor" Yeats, Mariani misses the pathos of WHA's cutting irony (Ibid.). There would be no need for Merrill to insist that WHA's message, which is after all spelled out like any other, arrives "with the straightest of faces"—if sincerity were indeed expected. The superlative alone marks the passage as ironic. In another discussion of Auden's reply, Mariani insists that "the term 'Maitre,' even though in French, is enough to send the reader back immediately to this passage in Dante: 'Tu se' lo mio maestro e 'l mio autore . . .' [you are my master and my author], from *Inferno*, I, 85" ("Polylinguism" 205). A letter, dated May 20, 1964, Kirchstetten, Austria, to Stephen Spender, who had asked for a contribution to a book of essays on Yeats, gives a better indication of Auden's ambivalence toward the older poet—an ambivalence Merrill accentuates and Mariani chooses to overlook:

> I am incapable of saying a word about W. B. Yeats because, through no fault of his, he has become for me a symbol of my own devil of unauthenticity, of everything which I must try to eliminate from my own poetry, false emotions, inflated rhetoric, empty sonorities.
>
> No poem is ever quite true
> But a good one
> Makes us desire truth.
>
> His make me whore after lies. (Qtd. in Mendelson 206)

[79] Merrill's other notes on this same page in the typescript (corresponding to 489–90 in the published poem) show him very conscious of previous poets. He writes "Shakespeare" after "Minute glissandi such that ear of wheat / Must bend to listen—in one shimmer span / Modes of bliss never yet unthinkable to man" (and could as easily have mentioned Dryden or Coleridge). Opposite "MICHAEL YOUR RAINBOW LINE, IT IS OUR WISH / YOU REEL US IN LIKE FLOPPING FISH," he writes the initials "BE," referring to "The Book of Ephraim" (S. 6). He also underlines and divides "HERE ALONE / IN EMPTY SKY" writing "Pegasus" beside the line as if to underscore the particularly Mallarméan character of poetic inspiration.

[80] Merrill's interest in becoming "sufficiently imbued with otherness," particularly Yeatsian otherness, may be seen as a form of introjection, what Harold Bloom identifies as "a fantasy transposition of otherness to the self . . . [that] incorporates an object or instinct so as to defend against it (thus overcoming object-relationships)" (*Map* 102). Similarly, Merrill's (rather showy) campaign to effect Yeats's vanishing or erasure operates as a particularly heightened form of projection, in which Merrill not only "seeks to expel from the self everything that the self cannot bear to acknowledge as being his own" by attributing the prohibited qualities to Yeats (Ibid.), but defends against these qualities even more strongly by attributing them to an enfeebled or vanishing precursor.

[81] David Bergman, in seeking to explain the "egolessness of the gay male poet," argues that the poet undergoes an "erasure of self" because he is unable to fully identify with either his father or his mother—so that his subsequent work and personality are characterized by less emphatic and more complex and fluid "ego structures" (384–85). Although applicable to Merrill in broad outline, Bergman's too-easy distinction between straight and gay also leads to simple error. In contrast to Robert Lowell, for example, for whom "history is a mirror into which Lowell finds pieces of his ever more fragmented but omnipresent face, Merrill's mirror [*Sandover*] is a history taking him farther and farther from himself" (Ibid.). Such a charac-

terization of the poem ignores just how much *Sandover* and Merrill's work in general turns on, and returns to, Merrill's only mock-modest "ah, me" (S. 506).

We note too how in this passage Merrill uses Yeats's "Dance" and Dante's "Stars" to frame his persistent themes of "Gods" and "Time." As we shall see, *Sandover* ultimately concerns the imaginative "incarnation and withdrawal" of *all* gods, the poet included. Similarly, we shall see how the poem operates as a defense against "Time! The forbidden, the forgotten theme" (S. 438) by incorporating it ("harmlessly") into the poem's recycling structure.

[82] Andrea Mariani in discussing the trilogy as a whole notes that "Merrill's models are, precisely, 'Dantesque / Or Yeatsian systems'" ("Polylinguism" 199) Yet I would argue that the link with Dante is gratuitous and diversionary in this particular context.

[83] We remember that Merrill evokes Yeats's "Black out" from the same line in another anxious interplay between Auden and Yeats toward the very end of Scripts (S. 514–15).

[84] As Yeats quotes Blake, " There is a place at the bottom of the graves where contraries are equally true" (*Vision* 72). Both Merrill and Yeats also knew Oscar Wilde's formulation of a similar notion: "a Truth in art is that whose contradictory is also true" (Wilde 432).

[85] Dickinson's "certain slant of Light" is one of the touchstone phrases that runs throughout Sandover. Her admonition to tell the truth but "tell it Slant" echoes too throughout the book. Merrill's "birdsong" is the general property of all his precursor poets. It is only made slightly more Yeatsian by virtue of the gem-like artifice suggested by "sparkling bloom."

[86] This image also recalls Yeats's memory of his first sight of Maude Gonne, whose complexion appeared "luminous, like that of apple blossoms through which the light falls" (*Autobiography* 82). Yeats's image too has an element of unattainability (one of the persistent hallmarks of his relation with Maude Gonne) and it may have suggested itself to Merrill as an analog to his relations with predecessor poets and his muse. Merrill would have known of this passage from Hone's biography. My recourse to Bloomian language in discussing these passages follows more than the gracious hint Merrill offers when he gives "sparkling bloom" in the context of poetic blossoms placed anxiously "too high to pluck." In an earlier manuscript version of lines published on page 499, Merrill wrote "And Harold Bloom / Pleads for no more big speeches in small caps." I discuss the relationship between poet and critic in the final chapter of this study.

[87] Lynn Keller devotes two excellent chapters to the Merrill-Auden relationship in her study of contemporary American poetry and the modernist tradition, *Re-making it new*. In these chapters, Keller demonstrates the profound continuities and telling divergences between Auden and Merrill's poetics. Although Keller argues that "like Merrill, Auden felt the lure of lofty, earnest proclamations" and, by extension, that Merrill would share Auden's need "to purge Yeats' oracular voice from his writing" (196), she nowhere acknowledges the force of Merrill's engagement with Yeats, either directly [as in Merrill's allusion to "Sailing to Byzantium" in "Matinees" (235)] or indirectly through Auden.

[88] Nonetheless, for Steven Matthews, "the huge scope of the poem is unable to throw off the sense that it might be (*contra* notions of influence-as-contest such as Bloom's) 'TEXT TO WBY'S FOOTNOTE,' since Merrill's epic seems "a mere extension of the process of listening to the instructors whose words gave impulse to *A Vision*" (180).

[89] In these ways WHA provides Merrill another means of "swerving" away from Yeats in *Sandover*. Leslie Brisman thinks, "it is Auden more than anyone else who deflected Merrill from the grand and more Yeatsian enterprise of *The Book of Ephraim*" (198). But Merrill may have wanted to engineer just this effect, given his acquaintanceship with Bloom's theory of influence. Whether consciously or not Merrill's use of Auden "against" Yeats is analogous to

Coleridge's use of Cowper to defend against a flood of "Miltonic influx" (Bloom *Figures* 12). How fitting that Auden, who memorialized a Yeats more manageably minor or "silly like us" ("In Memory of W. B. Yeats"), should help perform the same work again at Merrill's behest.

⁹⁰ As Merrill's *Diblos* footnote puts it: "My Dialogue pits 2 dreams against each other, instead of living antagonists. Life, Art—they are words. It's on a lower level that the mongoose closes with the cobra. In a footnote. In the dust" (91).

⁹¹ In this passage, titled "About Maria," Robert Morse takes up the Yeatsian matter of "MOODS," "PERSONALITY," and, repeatedly, the "THINKING MIND." JM's intervening moments of interpretation and questioning further heighten the Yeatsian context: "This self, then, recomposing stroke by stroke / To blank the stars out, so that love is blind / Even *there*—," and "HER THINKING MIND / A mask?" (S. 527). This passage addresses something very like Yeats's "Faculties" and the "recomposing" process between lives and points out not only the composite nature of the soul and the strange resistance of personality to decay, but also Merrill's version of Yeats's "Unity of Being": "MM ALONE WAS TOTALLY HERSELF / MIND ONE WITH MATTER" (Ibid.).

⁹² How fitting that at this moment of imagining the attainment of his highest powers as a poet, Merrill echoes the recuperative turn of Wordsworth's "Ode: Intimations of Immortality from Reflections of Early Childhood," which Harold Bloom characterizes as "a dedication to the poet's higher powers" and "paradigm for the modern lyric" (*Map* 145, 95).

⁹³ As Merrill imagines Yeats snoring at the end of his poem, we remember George's earlier snores (S. 178). Now it is Merrill who is empowered by Yeats's sleep.

NOTES TO CHAPTER FOUR

¹ In her article on "Yeats and Ottava Rima," Helen Vendler asserts: "It is Yeats who establishes *ottava rima* as a viable modern stanza, fit for everything serious—valediction, ode, historical meditation" (27). Part of what Merrill achieves in this poem (and others such as "Yánnia," "Clearing the Title," "Tony: Ending the Life," "164 East 72nd Street," and "Self Portrait in Tyvek (TM) Windbreaker") is a further refurbishing of the *ottava rima* stanza to fit suit his need for mixing "everything serious" with the wry leaven of wit and the mundane.

² In Timothy Materer's formulation, "Santorini" "begins with an allusion to Yeats's 'Sailing to Byzantium' [and] ends with the theme of 'Lapis Lazuli' that all things rise and fall but fulfillment comes in creating them anew" (*Apocalypse* 138). This summary gives little hint of the poem's complex engagement with Yeats and unfortunately over-simplifies the ambiguity of Merrill's conclusion.

³ Yeats's prose draft for "Byzantium" reads in part:

> Subject for a poem. Death of a friend. . . . Describe Byzantium as it is in the system towards the end of the first Christian millennium. A walking mummy. Flames at the street corners where the soul is purified, birds of hammered gold singing in the golden trees. . . . (Qtd. in Jeffares *Commentary* 352)

⁴ I take it that Bloom would see in this passage a movement between allusion to Yeats's metaphors (night, limbo, spectral fires, the dead) and "an identifying with the past . . . by substituting late words for earlier words in an anterior trope" (*Map* 103, see also 93 and 105 on the process of Substitution).

⁵ Merrill puts "worst" in quotation marks, drawing attention (via Yeats' "The Second Coming") to his wart's "passionate intensity" and, more substantially, to the problematic mix-

ture of irresolute "best" and passionate "worst" within the self. In this glancing allusion to "The Second Coming," Merrill turns Yeats's social critique to psychological advantage. As we shall see, Merrill makes similar use of Yeats's poem in "Vol. XLIV, No. 3" in *A Scattering of Salts*.

⁶ The play is "The Image Maker" which follows immediately in *The Inner Room*.

⁷ Just as "Willowware Cup" offers a "queered" reading of particularly the last two stanzas of "Lapis Lazuli," so all of "A Room in the Heart of Things" responds, albeit much more loosely, to material largely in "Lapis Lazuli's" first three stanzas. The prominence Yeats gives to acting and the theater, to the immediate and distant incursions of history, and to the nexus of poets, timeless wisdom, and "gay" could not have failed to attract Merrill taking up a poem addressed to his new actor-lover.

⁸ Merrill's "twenty-six / Millennia, say" points directly to Yeats *A Vision* (and to either a good close reading of pages 202–204 –which seems unlikely– or to a good account of those pages). Merrill's archly colloquial "say" catches Yeats's point precisely: "But these twenty-six thousand years are but a norm, a convenient measure, much may shorten or lengthen the whole or some part of the whole" (*Vision* 202).

⁹ For more on the ratio of Daemonization and the characteristic irony of Clinamen see *A Map of Misreading*, 97, 99. Merrill's particular affinity for poems linking a concluding Daemonization with a pervasive Clinamen, is not one of the "variants and displacements" Bloom discusses, but it does satisfy his "principle of substitution, in which representations [ratios of Tessera, Daemonization, and Apophrades] and limitations [ratios of Clinamen, Kenosis, and Askesis] perpetually answer one another" (*Map* 105).

¹⁰ From its opening image of "features unseen embers and tongs once worried / bright as brass," recalling Yeats's "golden smithies of the Emperor!," "Arabian Night" puts an Oedipal spin on the Yeatsian thematics of Mask and Unity of Being. Here, Merrill contemplates how he has come to "resemble the antithetical self" of his father (*Per Amica* 333–34) in Yeats's words "turning from the mirror to meditation upon a mask" (a mask whose names become "Rime's Emir," "Father Time," and the Sultan "straight out of Baghdad"). As Yeats also suggests, this "meditation" upon the antithetical other is fundamental to both Merrill's creativity and his own self-fashioning. Merrill comments suggestively about this poem that it's "about being old enough to see one's own father's face in the mirror. Or maybe it's about the Tradition, personified as father and son" ("James Merrill: Education" 2). But (as we have seen) Merrill does not customarily speak of the poet's relation to Tradition in terms of rivalry, as he clearly does in this poem. [He only goes so far as to speak of the "individual pro and con from one generation to the next [as] rapid and automatic" ("Literary Tradition" 25)—and then amends this line in *Recitative* to read: "the pendulum of individual tone from one generation to the next keeps moving briskly" (9), as if even this much note of actual intergenerational contention needs to be abstracted into a systemic periodicity.] Given Merrill's palpable sense of Oedipal anxiety and competitiveness regarding his father and the depth and duration of anxious contention in his relationship with Yeats (not to mention the Yeatsian notes struck within this poem), I suggest that Yeats is the particular face of the Tradition that Merrill personifies in this poem.

¹¹ The intervening sections of the poem complete Bloom's six-part scheme, although not in the traditional order. Most interesting are the literal Kenosis or fragmentation of section 3 (in which words cut off from their context take on the metonymous aura of the things they name) and the two-part Askesis of section 5, which, while it restores the poem "lost" in section 3, underscores the inadequacy of metaphoric language, the language "our old poets knew

to make" (their "Harbor, palace, temple" are all at once "no further off" and as inaccessible as "infancy")—and section 6, which heightens the anxiety attendant on the limitations of language ("when aphasia skewered /The world upon a word") and points to the evasions inherent in what Jahan Ramazani terms "sublimations of mortality" (*Yeats* 5)].

[12] For the record, "Sailing to Byzantium" is not the only poem Merrill uses repeatedly to pattern his memoir. Variations on the last line of Frost's "The Road Not Taken" ("And that has made all the difference") also provide a frequent refrain. But it is Yeats's poem that Merrill uses most often to underscore crucial sets of experience and belief.

[13] For example, notice how an echo of the last line of "Among School Children" leads immediately into an image from "Vacillation" (particularly the tree "half all glittering flame and half all green"):

> . . . while belief and believer—why, just to breathe the words set up a green rustling in my mind. I'd been ravished to discover that (in English at least) "truth" and "tree" shared a single Indo-European rood. Truth, then, could be felt as a living organism, varying from time to time and place to place. Now a seedling among thousands, now a gaunt trunk crowned with fire, it grew and withered in natural cycles. . . . Any creative spirit truly a la page came most to life, I hoped, by the perpetual freshening of human language— (*Different* 261)

[14] Timothy Materer alerts us to the ways that the puppets in "The Image Maker" recall the scene of Yeats's "The Dolls" in which the created objects "revolt and assert their superiority to the merely human figure who created them" (*Apocalypse* 131). And, indeed, both Yeats's poem and Merrill's play dramatize the uncanny power of the creature to confront and appall the human creator.

[15] In *Per Amica Silentia Lunae,* Yeats tells us: "The poet finds and makes his mask in disappointment, the hero in defeat." He also describes the world as being "yet debonair," before it breaks the hero and breaks faith with the poet (337).

[16] The title, "Vol. XLIV, No. 3," itself sounds like it might be the latest edition of *Spiritus Mundi,* but "Volume 44, Number 3" may contain a much more pointed allusion to Yeats's poem. If Yeats's "The Second Coming" trades ironically on Christian expectations of Christ's rebirth heralding the last of days, the Merrill title may go Yeats one better by suggesting that Christ ("X") will (or will not) live ("LIV") a third time ("No. 3"). A fitting "Yes and No" apocalypse for this "new age." J. D. McClatchy points to this poem in particular as evidence that Merrill, in his final book, "has a nearly Yeatsian vigor in the face of the end" ("Braving" 59).

[17] In "More or Less," Merrill mocks the "myopic / Simplicity" of those enchanted by a latter-day, "breathing sphinx" and "Their sad knowhow, their fingertip control." The sphinx-like image in question is a holograph of Einstein, "Bespectacled, white-maned," but the confluence of sphinx, simplicity, knowledge and control evokes Yeats, and Merrill's critique of the older poet's vision, as well.

[18] Merrill returns to this image of the Christmas tree as a figure for his own liminal status, hovering between life and death in "Christmas Tree," a shaped-poem published posthumously in *Poetry* magazine's Merrill memorial issue (September 1995). Here the tree is not a sign of Merrill's disease or of cultural collapse ("another sack of Rome"); instead, the tree enables Merrill to speak out of the experience of his disease about the culture and love that has both felled and sustained him. In Yeats's terms this poem strives to offer a more objective

Notes to Chapter Four

or primary reply to the more subjective or antithetical stance taken in "Vol. XLIV," a Yes to that poem's No. I give only the lower "branches" and base of the poem:

> ... And in shadow behind me, a primitive IV
> To keep the show going. Yes, yes, what lay ahead
> Was clear: the stripping, the cold street, my chemicals
> Plowed back into the Earth for lives to come—
> No doubt a blessing, a harvest, but one that doesn't bear,
> Now or ever, dwelling upon. To have grown so thin.
> Needles and bone. The little boy's hands meeting
> About my spine. The mother's voice: *Holding up wonderfully!*
> No dread. No bitterness. The end beginning. Today's
> > Dusk room aglow
> > For the last time
> > With candlelight.
> > Faces love-lit,
> > Gifts underfoot.
> Still to be so poised, so
> Receptive. Still to recall, to praise.

In these lines, Merrill speaks movingly from within his own "stripping process." Part of the fine balance Merrill strikes here between "Yes, yes" and "No . . . No . . ." between "end" and "beginning," between sentimentality and wit, is the poise learned from Yeats's vacillation. Parts of Merrill's receptivity, his openness to memory, to blessing, and willingness to praise are likewise lessons learned from his older master. What is unlike anything in Yeats is the calm intensity of these lines, their willingness "to let the silence after each note sing" (S. 85), as opposed to Yeats's occasional fervent declarations of contentment, such as at the end of "A Dialogue for Self and Soul." What Merrill achieves is not "simplification through intensity" but the reverse, an intensity born out of a deliberate simplification of diction, syntax, and tone.

[19] Harold Bloom argues that similar moments in Coleridge's "Limbo" and "Ne Plus Ultra" "make us read Book II of *Paradise Lost* a little differently; they enable Coleridge to claim a corner of Milton's Chaos as his own" (*Figures* 15). Likewise, Merrill's "Vol. XLIV, No. 3" (as well as such poems as "Downward Look", "Upward Look," "Big Mirror Outdoors," "Alabaster," "Pyroxenes," and "Press Release") enables Merrill to claim a corner (the vacillating corner) of Yeats's apocalyptic expectation as his own.

[20] Harold Bloom might call this a "chilling touch of the great Yeats who is neither humane nor humanistic" (*Yeats* 441).

[21] See both Merrill's early poem "The Cosmological Eye" and its post-*Sandover* revision, "The Blue Eye" for the source of these images. I give the last lines of "The Blue Eye" in note 57 in Chapter One.

[22] I stress Yeats's "paternity" here; but it is also important to note that at least in his earliest reading of Yeats, the older poet may have seemed like a way to bring the worlds of both mother and father back together again, a theme as constant as their divorce throughout Merrill's poetry. Yeats was always a poet who offered both polish and potency, convention and prophesy, a living voice and a voice from beyond the grave.

[23] Auden is the usual model of avuncular or nonanxious influence. Yet even in Auden's case, Merrill shows a particular need to appropriate, revise, and constrain, to shape retrospec-

tively, rather than be shaped by, Auden's influence. The early poem, "Marsyas," may capture some of Merrill's initial anxious response to reading Auden: "that gold archaic lion's look // Wherein I saw my wiry person skinned / Of every skill it labored to acquire...." Here Merrill acknowledges both himself the "wiry person" or lyre upon which the precursor poet plays and how that knowledge threatens his "unmaking" as a poet. But the poem does not end before a final ambivalent turn: "They found me dangling where his golden wind / Inflicted so much music on the lyre / That no one could have told you what he sang." The precursor poet is granted his sign of divinity, a power beyond the power of words to tell. But, in being flayed and flooded by the precursor's "golden wind," in being made quite literally an instrument of influence, the young poet attains a heightened vocation: he moves from one who writes "Poems on menus, read all over town" (poet as a social phenomenon) to one who yields "so much music," which is the language of the gods.

[24] Robert Polito makes the point that Yeats tends to distinguish speakers only in terms of "*what* they say, the particular *knowledge* that they hold"; whereas, Merrill's speakers "act out" their differences in their diction (*Guide* 260–61). Helen Vendler likewise notes: "It is clear that [Yeats's] plays are dramatic neither in conception nor in end, but are rather devices within which to embody lyrics . . . and in fact one feels that Yeats would have preferred a single voice to speak all the way through, with the simplest indication of his changing personae" (*Yeats's Vision* 141).

[25] Merrill repeatedly invokes Mercury, god of thieves, in his efforts to make a redemptive or compensatory sense of "the life lived . . . the love spent." It is Mercury who delivers the alphabet at the end of *Scripts*, which Gabriel calls "THE NEW MATERIALS . . . FOR A NEW FAITH" (S. 446), and Mercury who animates the many mirrors in Merrill's poetry, who in Yeats's terms makes the mirror into a mask (*Per Amica* 334). Merrill sees his life "rinsed with mercury"; it is what allows "our life [to see] through that craze / Of its own creation / Into another life" (S. 42).

[26] Bloom asserts that "a poem is written to escape dying. Literally, poems are refusals of mortality" (*Map* 19).

[27] "As to Composition," JM remarks, "few had found /A cleaner use for power" (S. 82) and, in an interview, Merrill stresses the "innocence" of writing poetry as a deployment of power: "Hours go by and nobody's been harmed" ("James Merrill" Bolt 42). In this "cleaner" and "innocence" we hear something of Merrill's concern for the ethics of writing poetry.

[28] This is perhaps why Merrill is always at such pains to deny his intellectual accomplishments and interests: "In neither the world's poem nor the poem's world have I / Learned to think for myself, much" (S. 85); "Oh Lords, I find it hard to have / Ideas while busily transcribing yours. / Michael: 'THAT NOT SO INNOCENTLY SAID'" (S. 321); "I still shy away from ideas, at least on principle" ("James Merrill at Home" 28).

[29] Jefferson Humphries, in his 1988 article "The Voice within the Mirror: The Haunted Poetry of James Merrill," offers a similar characterization that likewise strikes notes of Yeatsian Dispersal: "Merrill has discovered and embraced loss, failure in love, not as event but as the essence of all events, the *logos* not only of poetry but of every human endeavor, thought"; he has seen that "the self is not a thing, not a mirror but what occurs between the mirrors. The self is misplaced, displaced, dispersed" (189).

[30] Here it is helpful to have one of Merrill's sources—Cavafy's note on Ruskin, which Merrill quotes in his 1975 appreciation "Unreal Citizen": "When we say 'Time' we mean ourselves. Most abstractions are simply our pseudonyms. It is superfluous to say 'Time is scytheless and toothless.' We know it. We are time" (Qtd. in *Recitative* 102):

[31] Bloom's books were widely reviewed in journals such as *Poetry, Times Literary Supplement, New Republic,* and the *New York Review of Books,* with Merrill's friend John Hollander, for example, contributing a substantial review of *The Anxiety of Influence* in the *New York Times Book Review.* (4 Mr. 1973: 27).

[32] Early in 1977, as Bloom recalls, Merrill called Bloom to ask about Yeats's *A Vision.* Merrill had not yet "attempted" Bloom's study of Yeats and Bloom recommended that he only read the chapters on *Per Amica Silentia Lunae* and *A Vision,* which he did. Bloom also recalls that Merrill was rather put off by Bloom's irreverence toward what he called Yeats's "spooks"; Bloom considers Merrill's "skepticism" a trope, staged for the benefit of the poem and not reflective of his own "crazy" belief in his voices. Bloom concluded our second interview by telling the story of his accosting Merrill at a Mory's dinner before a reading by Elizabeth Bishop. He "jovially" took Merrill to task for the "outrageous, tactless presumption—unprecedented in the history of poetry"—of Merrill writing Stevens and Auden poems from beyond the grave, thus subsuming them into his own achievement. Merrill was flattered, Bloom recalls, thanked him and "smiled broadly, evidently very pleased" (Conversations with Harold Bloom, February 5 and July 1, 1997).

[33] Bloom wrote Merrill, after receiving another manuscript passage from *Scripts,* that he hoped for no more long speeches in small caps. Merrill was apparently a bit stung and wrote back, Bloom recalls, feeling like "Ganymede dropped by Zeus" (Conversation with Harold Bloom, July 1, 1997).

[34] Bloom's jacket copy for *Divine Comedies,* taken from his review in the New Republic (Nov. 20, 1976), reads in part: "its apocalypse (a lesser word won't do) is a 100 page verse-tale, *The Book of Ephraim,* an occult splendor in which Merrill rivals Yeats' *A Vision,* Stevens' ghostly *The Owl in the Sarcophagus,* and even some of Proust." Toward the end of our second conversation, Bloom remarked that he never felt particularly close to Merrill, though Merrill was always charming and gracious and though they shared several close, mutual friends. These friends told him that Merrill maintained a certain distance because he was afraid of Bloom as a "terrific intellect" and scholar, though Bloom protested he had always been "jovial and benign" in person (Conversation with Harold Bloom, July 1, 1997).

[35] Bloom writes of "Freud's poem" not being severe enough (*Anxiety* 9) and famously proclaims, "There are no interpretations but only misinterpretations, and so all criticism is prose poetry" (Ibid. 95).

[36] See the discussion of the Venice section of "Ephraim" in Chapter Three.

[37] For Bloom's discussion of Clinamen, Kenosis, and Askesis as ratios of limitation, see *A Map of Misreading* 88, 98–99.

[38] Whatever pleasures Merrill may have enjoyed in "antithetically completing" this aspect of Bloom's model, something of Bloom's description of Tessera also seems to hover around the passage in which Merrill describes writing at his computer, in which "minimal bits of information . . . like the tesserae of a mosaic, flicker and reassemble before my eyes" (*Different* 202). Merrill continues:

> As best I can—here slubbing an image, there inverting a hypothesis—*I set about clothing the blindingly nude mind of my latest master.* Line after line wavers in and out of sense, transpositive, loose-ended, flimsy as gossamer, until a length of text is at last woven tightly enough to resist unmaking. Then only do I see what I had to say. (Ibid., emphasis added)

Here is Bloom:

Tessera, which is completion and antithesis; I take the word not from mosaic-making, where it is still used, but from the ancient mystery cults, where it meant a token of recognition.... A poet antithetically "completes" his precursor, by so reading the parent-poem as to retain its terms but to mean them in another sense....
(*Anxiety* 14)

[39] Under the aspect of Daemonization "the later poet opens himself to what he believes to be a power in the parent-poem that does not belong to the parent proper, but to a range of being [or in *Sandover*'s case "beings"] just beyond the precursor. He does this, in his poem, by so stationing its relation to the parent poem as to generalize away the uniqueness of the earlier work" (Bloom *Anxiety* 15). In *Sandover* we learn that Yeats's visionary poems and system are just some of the many "ghostwritten" communications in our literature.

[40] Bloom remarks that the "Romantic tradition ["which is of course *the* tradition of the last two centuries"] is *consciously late*, and Romantic literary psychology is therefore necessarily a *psychology of belatedness*" (*Map* 35). Thus, the goal of a strong poem is not so much one of contriving a kind of "earliness" as it is for the poet to make "of his own belatedness a strength rather than an affliction" (*Map* 80).

[41] For Bloom's discussion of the primacy of imaginative self-preservation as a motive for poetry, see *Map* 67.

[42] In *A Map of Misreading*, Bloom asserts that "greatness results from a refusal to separate origins from aims. The father is met in combat, and fought to at least a stand-off, if not quite a separate peace" (80).

[43] In this, Merrill vindicates the German Romantics' faith in "Witz" as an alchemical *menstruum universal* or universal solvent. Wit as "elegance, enjoyment, invention, ingenuity, and as the composition of figures and imagination" also effects in language the "fusion of philosophy, art, science, literature and society" (Nancy 259, 261). Novalis declared, "Witz is creative, it produces resemblances," and Friedrich Schlegel celebrated Witz in these fragments:

> Witz is the principle and the organ of universal philosophy . . . the science of all sciences perpetually mingling with each other and separating . . . [like Merrill's "quicksilver joke" that keeps "scissoring and mending" ("Yánnina").]
>
> Language is poetical, writing is philosophical, Witz links them to each other.
> (Qtd in Nancy 261–62)

[44] Of course there is place in the house of language for Satan's high Romantic agony, but it should not be mistaken for the whole mansion (or all of its loftiest galleries). Bloom, on the other hand, asserts that "modern poetry begins in two declarations of [Milton's] Satan: 'We know no time when we were not as now' and 'To be weak is miserable, doing or suffering'" (*Anxiety* 20) and proceeds to argue that Satan, "the hero as poet, finding what must suffice, while knowing that nothing can suffice," becomes the type for the belated, modern poet. See also *A Map of Misreading* 78.

[45] "THEY GAZED INTO ME WHO HAD / COME OUT OF ME, / GAZED WITH THE CURIOUS LOOK A CHILD GIVES TO ITS MOTHER," says the watery archangel Emmanuel, speaking out of a "gently rippling aquamarine light" (S. 325), and RM (Robert Morse) considering the even more pervasive light that greets the soul after death speculates: "BUT THIS LIGHT? HMM IT'S LIKE A STAR WE ENTER / TO FIND OURSELVES" (S. 499). *Sandover* is suffused with such "UNIVERSAL LUMINOSIT[IES]." They are, like heaven, "the surround of the living" (S. 59), and answer to the light in human eyes. At one point early in *Scripts*, Ephraim declares, "MY POOR

slave's vision overflows with love / around u both such joy such radiant light" and JM's dismissive reply ("If so, a joy not ours to feel, a light / We are the two contracted pupils of.") is immediately corrected by WHA in the same terms of gratitude and tenderness Sedgwick's voice reports: "yet for that focal darkness thank god b / my boys   it is yr precious sanity" (S. 305–06). In such exchanges, we see how *Sandover* functions as both model for and instruction in Sedgwick's "true and revelatory relationship[s]."

NOTES TO APPENDIX A

¹ Without mentioning Yeats's influence on this early poem, Lynn Keller rightly notes that Merrill's opening line also "seems a rejection of all Merrill's preceding work," especially in the tendency of his earlier poetry to devalue the normal fare of daily life in favor of a "high-flown" rhetoric derived from Yeatsian intensities or Stevensian "gaudiness" (195).

² This strategy of personal address heightens, or reanimates, the sense of the poem as part of an ongoing argument which was established with the opening "But. . . ."

³ For Merrill's elaboration on the apocalyptic significance of these opening images see Emmanuel's speech in the first lessons of *Scripts*:

> *The light, till now predominantly green,*
> *Pales to gently rippling aquamarine.*
> [The cup surges and ebbs like lapping water. <variant in typescript>]
> Emm. staked in my shallows, what? a fledgling of storks?
>   and from these slight supports they gazed into me who had
>   come out of me,
>   gazed with the curious look a child gives to its mother.
> JM.   People standing ankle-deep in water?
> Emm. poet, their long gone house: the lakedwellers who fished in me.
>   i was giving them suck. ah twin, those innocent nursery
>   days! out of the caves & back to mother's house
>   why? their cave innocence had received its first shocking
>   idea: fear of each other.
> DJ.   They moved to water as we did, that year,
>   To Stonington, away from the rat race.
>   Like us, they meant to civilize themselves.
> Emm. and to put distance between themselves.
>   & you would not say, Raphael, that their stilted rooms were
>   but another cave? i think not.
>   i think they were longing, while there was still time,
>   still a chance,to escape that fearful forward march.
>   back to our fishlife, innocent, calm & deep! they knew, ah
>   they knew!
>   yes, brothers, shades, my old lakedwellers, you knew, you know
>   the gritty history since then is only a wash away from innocence,
>   but such a wash! (S. 325–26)

⁴ The line "Beggar and sparrow entertaining one another" largely avoids sentimental overtones if this section is read as I am suggesting with Yeats's poem in mind. Without a Yeatsian context, the line seems dangerously sweet and ill considered.

⁵ Timothy Materer characterizes "About the Phoenix" as "Merrill's elegy for Hans Lodeizen" (*Apocalypse* 144). Lodeizen was a fellow poet and Merrill's Dutch friend whom he'd met while at Amherst and whom he visited at a Swiss sanatorium shortly before his friend's death (Merrill *Different* 46–52). Materer's identification of the occasion for the poem underscores the deeply personal turn of the poem's last three lines. In a telling parallel, especially since elegy and self-elegy are so closely allied, Yeats describes the occasion for "Byzantium" this way: "Subject for a poem. Death of a friend" (Qtd. in Jeffares *Commentary* 352), and his notes regarding "Sailing to Byzantium" offer the poem as a meditation on his own mortality and the "state of my soul" (Ibid. 253).

⁶ Looking at a sleeping figure becomes a recurring image in Merrill's poetry and always conveys the melancholy blend of distance and involvement, great value and the threat of loss, safety and vulnerability that characterizes this scene of "mortal lull." (See "The House," "The Bed," "Walking All Night," "Between Us," "From the Cupola," "Days of 1935," "Verse for Urania," "Peter," "David's Watercolor," *A Different Person* 203.) In these instances, Merrill may be said to take Yeats's "intense visions of sleep," not in the intended sense of visionary dreams that give him access to "the fire that makes all simple," but as an intensive observation of a (beloved) person asleep. Yeats says that, "in those brief intense visions of sleep, I have something about me that, though it makes me love, is more like innocence" (*Per Amica* 365). Merrill's gaze on a sleeping person also evokes love, but it comes out of something much more akin to loss of innocence, a recognition that little in truth is simple or endures (except perhaps idea or sensation that something waits to be endured).

⁷ Both "Sailing to Byzantium" and "About the Phoenix" employ the present tense through most of their length. In the end, Yeats shifts to a future conditional and Merrill to the simple past. Yeats's present tense modulates from indicative to imperative mood in the third stanza, while Merrill's swings back and forth between an indicative present of direct address, the present subjunctive, and the projective present of dream, prophesy, or atemporal vision. This last makes up the bulk of Merrill's poem, from "One night" to "Voluptuous homilies," the section that presents and melds the ancient myth of the underworld to the modern myth of progressive history. Each of these uses of present time is linked to different problems, but the present tense of direct discourse is by far the least thematically problematic. Indeed, "tempered" as it is by the past tense of the last stanza, this time frame serves Merrill's argument well. That he is very conscious of the effect of different tenses is obvious enough from his poetry; this concern is supported by remarks Merrill makes in his 1972 interview with David Kalstone: "For me a "hot" tense like that [first-person present active indicative] can't be handled for very long without cool pasts and futures to temper it. Or some complexity of syntax, or a modulation into the conditional—*something*. An imperative, even an auxiliary verb, can do wonders. Otherwise, you get this addictive, self-centered immediacy, harder to break oneself of than cigarettes" ("Poet" 21).

Works Cited

Auden, W. H. "Yeats as an Example." *Kenyon Review* 10 (1948): 187–195.
Bergman, David. "Choosing Our Fathers: Gender and Identity in Whitman, Ashbery and Richard Howard." *American Literary History* 1.2 (1989): 383–403.
Bachelard, Gaston. *The Psychoanalysis of Fire*. Trans. Alan C. M. Ross. Boston: Beacon Press, 1964.
Blake, William. *Blake's Poetry and Designs. A Norton Critical Edition*. New York: W. W. Norton & Company, 1979.
Blasing, Mutlu Konuk. *Politics and Form in Postmodern Poetry: O'Hara, Bishop, Ashbery, and Merrill. Cambridge Studies in American Literature and Culture*. New York: Cambridge University Press, 1995.
Bloom, Harold. *The Anxiety of Influence: A Theory of Poetry*. New York: Oxford University Press, 1997.
———. *Figures of Capable Imagination*. New York: The Seabury Press, 1976.
———, ed. *James Merrill*. Modern Critical Views. New York: Chelsea House, 1985.
———. *A Map of Misreading*. New York: Oxford University Press, 1975.
———. "On Poetry." *New Republic* 175 (1976): 20–24.
———. "On Poetry." *New Republic* 177 (1977): 24–6.
———. Personal interviews. 5 February and 1 July 1997.
———. *Yeats*. New York: Oxford University Press, 1972.
Bohlmann, Otto. *Yeats and Nietzsche: An Exploration of Major Nietzschean Echoes in the Writings of William Butler Yeats*. Totowa, New Jersey: Barns & Noble, 1982.
Bowers, Susan R. "Medusa and the Female Gaze." *NWSA Journal* 2.2 (1990): 217–35.
Bowra, C. W. *The Heritage of Symbolism*. London: Macmillan & Co., 1943.

Brisman, Leslie. "Merrill's Yeats." Bloom, *James Merrill* 189–198.
Cixous, Hélène. "The Laugh of the Medusa." *Signs: Journal of Women in Culture and Society* 1.4 (1976): 875–93.
Coldwell, Joan. "The Beauty of The Medusa: Twentieth Century." *English Studies in Canada* 11.4 (1985): 422–37.
Croft, Barbara L. *"Stylistic Arrangements": A Study of William Butler Yeats's A Vision.* Lewisburg: Bucknell University Press, 1987.
de Man, Paul. *The Rhetoric of Romanticism.* New York: Columbia University Press, 1984.
Ellmann, Richard. *Yeats: the Man and the Mask.* New York: E. P. Dutton, 1948.
Freud, Sigmund. "Group Psychology and the Analysis of the Ego." *The Standard Edition of the Complete Psychological Works of Sigmund Freud.* Ed. James Strachey. London: The Hogarth Press, 1955. 18: 69–143.
———. "Medusa's Head." *The Standard Edition of the Complete Psychological Works* 18: 273–74.
———. "The Moses of Michelangelo." *On Creativity and the Unconscious: Papers on the Psychology of Art, Literature, Love, Religion.* Ed. Benjamin Nelson. New York: Harper & Row, 1958. 11–41.
Friar, Kimon. "Amherst Days." *For James Merrill A Birthday Tribute.* Ed. J. D. McClatchy. New York: Jordan Davies, 1986.
———. "Medusa-Mask." *Medusa* 1.1 (1946): 1–7.
Friar, Kimon, and John Malcolm Brinnin, Eds. *Modern Poetry: American and British.* New York: Appleton-Century-Crofts, Inc., 1951.
Frost, Robert. *Complete Poems of Robert Frost.* New York: H. Holt, 1959.
Gwiazda, Piotr. "Views from the Rosebrick Manor: Poetic Authority in James Merrill's *The Changing Light at Sandover.*" *Texas Studies in Literature and Language* 43:4 (2001): 418–39.
Hadas, Rachel. "James Merrill's Early Work: A Revaluation." *Kenyon Review* 20.2 (1998): 177–184.
Hall, Holly. *James Merrill, Poet.* St. Louis: Washington University Libraries, 1985.
Harrigan, Anthony. "Two Neo-Romantics." *Poetry* 78 (1952): 233–36.
Hartman, Geoffrey H. *Beyond Formalism: Literary Essays 1958–1970.* New Haven: Yale University Press, 1970.
Hecht, Anthony. "Poetry Chronicle." *Hudson Review* 19 (1966): 331–32.
Hollander, John, "The Anxiety of Influence." *New York Times Book Review* 4 March 1975: 23.
Hone, Joseph. *W. B. Yeats: 1865–1939.* 2nd. ed. London: Macmillan, 1962.
Howard, Richard. "James Merrill." *Alone With America: Essays on the Art of Poetry in the United States since 1950.* New York: Atheneum, 1980.
Howes, Marjorie. *Yeats's Nations: Gender, Class, and Irishness.* Cambridge: Cambridge University Press, 1996.
Humphries, Jefferson. "The Voice Within the Mirror: The Haunted Poetry of James Merrill." *Boundary 2* 15–16.3–1 (1988): 173–94.

Jackson, David. "DJ: A Conversation with David Jackson." With J. D. McClatchy. *Shenandoah* 30.4 (1979): 25–44.

———. "Lending a Hand." Lehman, *James Merrill* 298–305.

Jeffares, A. Norman. *A Commentary on the Collected Poems of W. B. Yeats*. Stanford: Stanford University Press, 1968.

———. *W. B. Yeats: A New Biography*. London: Hutchison, 1988.

Kalstone, David. *Five Temperaments*. New York: Oxford University Press, 1977.

———. "Merrill." *Partisan Review* 34 (1967): 146–50.

———. "The Poet: Private." *Saturday Review* 55.49 (1972): 42–45.

Keller, Lynn. *Re-making It New: Contemporary American Poetry and the Modernist Tradition*. New York: Cambridge University Press, 1987

Kennedy, X. J. "Translations form the American." *Atlantic Monthly* 231.3 (1973): 101–03.

Kenner, Hugh. *The Pound Era*. Berkeley: University of California Press, 1971.

Kuusisto, Stephen, Ed. *The Poet's Notebook: Excerpts from the Notebooks of Contemporary American Poets*. New York,: W. W. Norton & Co., 1997.

Labrie, Ross. *James Merrill. Twayne's United States Authors Series*. Boston: Twayne Publishers, 1982.

Lacan, Jacques. *Écrits: A Selection*. Trans. Alan Sheridan. New York: W. W. Norton & Company, 1977.

Lehman, David. "Elemental Bravery: The Unity of James Merrill's Poetry." Lehman, *James Merrill* 23–60.

Lehman, David and Charles Berger, eds. *James Merrill: Essays in Criticism*. Ithaca: Cornell University Press, 1983.

Lurie, Alison. *Familiar Spirits: A Memoir of James Merrill and David Jackson*. Viking Penguin, 2001.

Mariani, Andrea. "From Polylinguism to Metalinguism: Dante's Language in Merrill's Trilogy." *Critical Essays on James Merrill*. Ed. Guy Rotella. New York: G. K. Hall & Co., 1984. 190–214.

———. "Yeats in Merrill: maschera e figura." *Yeats oggi: studi e ricerche*. Ed. Carla de Petris. Rome: Terza universitá degli studi de Roma, Depatemento di litterature comparate, 1993. 89–105.

Martin, Robert K. *The Homosexual Tradition in American Poetry*. Austin: University of Texas, 1979.

Mason, Eudo. *Rilke, Europe, and the English-Speaking World*. London: Cambridge University Press, 1961.

Materer, Timothy. "Death and Alchemical Transformation in James Merrill's *The Changing Light at Sandover*." *Contemporary Literature* 29.1 (1988): 82–104.

———. "The Error of His Ways: James Merrill and the Fall into Myth." *American Poetry* 7.3 (1990): 64–86.

———. *James Merrill's Apocalypse*. Ithaca: Cornell University Press, 2000.

Matthews, Steven. *Yeats as Precursor: Readings in Irish, British, and American Poetry*. London: Macmillan Press LTD, 2000.

McClatchy, J. D. "Braving the Elements." *The New Yorker* March 27, 1995: 49–61.
———. "James Merrill's Inner Room." *Raritan* 19.1 (1999): 1–22.
———. "Lost Paradises." *Parnassus* 5.1 (1976): 305–20.
———. Personal interview. 8 October 1995.
McGann, Jerome J. "The Beauty of the Medusa: A Study in Romantic Literary Iconology." *Studies in Romanticism* 11.1 (1972): 3–25.
Mendelson, Edward. *Early Auden*. New York: The Viking Press, 1981.
Merrill, James. Afterword. *The (Diblos) Notebook*. New York: Antheneum, 1994.
———. Annotation in Yeats's *Essays and Introductions*. 1971.
———. Annotations in Yeats's *A Vision*. 1955.
———. "The Bait." *Artists' Theatre (Four Plays)*. Ed. Herbert Machiz. New York: Grove Press, 1960. 79–124.
———. *The Black Swan and Other Poems*. Athens: Icaros, 1946.
———. "*The Changing Light at Sandover:* A Conversation with James Merrill." Robert Polito. *Pequod* 39.1 (1990): 10–13.
———. *The Changing Light at Sandover, Including the Whole of The Book of Ephraim, Mirabell's Books of Number, Scripts for the Pageant and a New Coda, The Higher Keys*. New York: Antheneum, 1982.
———. *Collected Poems*. Eds. J. D. McClatchy and Stephen Yenser. New York: Knopf, 2001.
———. *Collected Novels and Plays*. Eds. J. D. McClatchy and Stepen Yenser. New York: Knopf, 2002.
———. "A Conversation with James Merrill." Jean Lunn. *Sandscript* .6 (1982): 2–23.
———. *The (Diblos) Notebook*. New York: Antheneum, 1965.
———. *A Different Person: A Memoir*. New York: Alfred A. Knopf, 1993.
———. "Exploring *The Changing Light at Sandover:* An Interview with James Merrill." With C. A. Buckley. *Twentieth Century Literature* 38.4 (1992): 415–35.
———. *From the First Nine: Poems 1946–1976*. New York: Antheneum, 1982.
———. "The Forms of Death." *Accent: a quarterly review of literature* 8.2 (1948): 94–96.
———. Foreword. *Above the Land*. By Julie Agoos. New Haven: Yale University Press, 1987. ix-xii.
———. "Interview." *The Lawrentian* Autumn 1991: 9–10.
———. "An Interview with John Boatwright and Enrique Ucelay DaCal." *Recitative* 37–39.
———. "An Interview with Fred Bornhauser." *Recitative* 53–61.
———. "An Interview with Ashley Brown." *Recitative* 40–48.
———. "An Interview with J. D. McClatchy." *Recitative* 62–86.
———. "An Interview with Donald Sheehan." *Recitative* 24–36.
———. "An Interview with Helen Vendler." *Recitative* 49–52.

———. "An Interview with James Merrill." With Heather White. *Ploughshares* 21.4 (1995): 190–95.

———. "James Merrill [an interview]." With Thomas Bolt. *BOMB* 36. Summer (1991): 38–42.

———. "James Merrill at Home: An Interview." With Ross Labrie. *Arizona Quarterly* 38.1 (1982): 19–36.

———. "James Merrill: Education of the Poet." *Envoy* 51 (1988): 1–5.

———. "James Merrill on Poetry: An Interview." With Jordan Pecile. *State of the Arts, a Publication of the Connecticut Commission of the Arts* 23 (1987): 4–7, 22.

———. *James Merrill: Voices from Sandover*. Princeton, New Jersey: Films for the Humanities, Inc., 1991.

———. Letter to Dr. Chung. 1 May 1983. James Merrill Papers. Washington University Library, St. Louis.

———. "Prefaces: Five Poets on Poems by T. S. Eliot." *The Yale Review* 78.2 (1989): 209–10.

———. *Recitative: Prose by James Merrill*. Ed. J. D. McClatchy. San Francisco: North Point Press, 1986.

———. *The Seraglio*. New York: Knopf, 1957.

———. *Voices from Sandover*. N.p.: n.p., 1980.

———. "On 'Yánnina': An Interview with David Kalstone." *Recitative* 14–23.

Merrill, James, et. al. "On Literary Tradition: A Symposium." *Shenandoah* 33.3 (1982): 25–28.

Merrill, James and David Jackson. "The Plato Club." *Paris Review* 34.122 (1992): 14–84.

Molesworth, Charles. "Promethean Narcissism." *Partisan Review* 51.1 (1984): 155–58.

Nancy, Jean-Luc. "Menstrum Universale." *The Birth to Presence*. Stanford, California: Stanford University Press, 1993. 248–65.

Nietzsche, Friedrich. *Thus Spoke Zarathustra*. Baltimore, Maryland: Penguin Books, 1961.

"Ouroboros." The Oxford English Dictionary. 2nd ed. 1989.

Polito, Robert. *A Reader's Guide to James Merrill's The Changing Light at Sandover*. Ann Arbor: University of Michigan Press, 1994.

Raine, Kathleen. *Yeats the Initiate*. Montrath: The Dolmen Press, 1986.

Rajan, Tilottama. *The Supplement of Reading: Figures of Understanding in Romantic Theory and Practice*. Ithaca, NY: Cornell University Press, 1990.

Ramazani, Jahan. *Yeats and the Poetry of Death: Elegy, Self-Elegy, and the Sublime*. New Haven: Yale University Press, 1990.

Rilke, Rainer Maria. *Selected Poetry of Rainer Maria Rilke*. Trans. Stephen Mitchell. New York: Random House, 1982.

Rothenberg, Albert. *The Emerging Goddess: The Creative Process in Art, Science, and Other Fields*. Chicago: University of Chicago Press, 1979.

Sáez, Richard. "James Merrill's Oedipal Fire." Bloom, *James Merrill* 35–56.
Said, Edward W. "The Poet as Oedipus: *A Map of Misreading.*" *New York Times Book Review* 13 April 1975: 23.
Sedgwick, Eve Kosofsky. *A Dialogue on Love.* Boston: Beacon Press, 1999.
Selinger, Eric Murphy. "James Merrill's Masks of Eros, Masques of Love." *Contemporary Literature* 35.1 (1994): 30–65.
Shelley, Percy Bysshe. *Shelley's Poetry and Prose. A Norton Critical Edition.* New York: W. W. Norton & Company, 1977.
Siebers, Tobin. *The Mirror of Medusa.* Berkeley: University of California Press, 1983.
Sloss, Henry. "James Merrill's *The Book of Ephraim.*" *Shenandoah* 27 & 28.4 &1 (1976): 63–91, 83–110.
Smith, Evans Lansing. "The Hermetic Tradition in James Merrill's *The Changing Light at Sandover.*" *Cauda Pavonis: Studies in Hermeticism* 15.1 (1996): 7–12.
Spiegelman, Willard. *The Didactic Muse.* Princeton: Princeton University Press, 1989.
Stade, George. "Romantic Anxiety." *Partisan Review* 40.3 (1973): 494–500.
Stevens, Wallace. *Wallace Stevens: Collected Poetry and Prose.* New York: Library of America, 1997.
Su, Tsu-Chung. "The Monstrous Other: Freud, Irigaray, Cixous, & the Mask of Medusa." *Studies in Language and Literature* 7 (1996): 113–33.
Suther, Judith D. "The Gorgon Medusa." *Mythical and Fabulous Creatures: A Source Book and Research Guide.* Ed. Malcom South. New York: Greenwood Press, 1987. 163–178.
Van Duyn, Mona. "Sunbursts, Garlands, Creatures, Men." *Poetry* 94 (1959): 199–202.
Vendler, Helen. "James Merrill." Bloom, *James Merrill* 69–93.
———. "Yeats and *Ottava Rima.*" *Yeats Annual* 11 (1995): 26–44.
———. *Yeats's Vision and the Later Plays.* Cambridge, Massachusetts: Harvard University Press, 1963.
Viti, Elizabeth Richardson. "Marcel and the Medusa: the Narrator's Obsfucated Homosexuality in *À la recherche du temps perdu.*" *Dalhousie French Studies* 26 (1994): 61–68.
von Hallberg, Robert. "James Merrill: 'Revealing By Obscuring.'" *Contemporary Literature* 21.4 (1980): 549–571.
Westover, Jeff. "Eros and Psyche: The View *FROM THE CUPOLA.*" *Classical and Modern Literature* 18.4 (1998): 303–28.
Wilde, Oscar. *The Artist as Critic: Critical Writings of Oscar Wilde.* New York: Random House, 1968.
Wilden, Anthony. *The Language of the Self.* Baltimore: Johns Hopkins Press, 1968.
Wordsworth, William. *Selected Poems.* New York: Penguin Books, 1994.
Yeats, William Butler. *The Autobiography of William Butler Yeats.* New York: Collier Books, 1924.

———. *The Collected Poems of W. B. Yeats: A New Edition.* New York: Collier Books, 1989.
———. *Eleven Plays of William Butler Yeats.* New York: Collier Books, 1964.
———. *Essays and Introductions.* New York: Collier Books, 1961.
———, ed. *The Oxford Book of Modern Verse: 1892–1935.* New York: Oxford University Press, 1936.
———. "Per Amica Silentia Lunae." *Mythologies.* New York: Collier Books, 1917. 319–369.
———. *The Letters of W. B. Yeats.* New York: Macmillan, 1955.
———. *Mythologies.* New York: Collier Books, 1959.
———. *The Variorum Editon of the Poems of W. B. Yeats.* New York: The Macmillan Company, 1968.
———. *A Vision [A Reissue With the Author's Final Revisions].* New York: The Macmillan Company, 1961.
Yenser, Stephen. *The Consuming Myth: The Work of James Merrill.* Cambridge, Massachusetts: Harvard University Press, 1987.
———. "Feux D'Artifice." *Poetry* (1973): 163–68.
Young, Timothy G., comp. *A Catalog of Books in James Merrill's Libraries.* N.p.: n.p., 1995.
Zimmer, Heinrich. *The King and the Corpse: Tales of the Soul's Conquest of Evil.* New York: Pantheon Books, 1948.
Zimmerman, Lee. "Against Apocalypse: Politics and James Merrill's *The Changing Light at Sandover.*" *Contemporary Literature* 30.3 (1989): 370–386.

Index

alchemy 45, 62, 126–27, 132, 168, 218 n.82, 222 n.21, 239 n.48; *see also* Mercury
absolute, the 55, 95, 144, 160, 171, 174; *see also* sublime
artifice xiv, 20, 22, 27, 28, 34–35, 47, 61–62, 65, 74, 76, 79, 90, 93–94, 97, 99–100, 102, 113, 115–16, 118, 122, 135, 148, 149, 157, 165, 167, 194, 214 n.58, 240 n.56; *see also* technique
Auden, W. H. as an influence, xvii, 4, 5, 8, 17, 19, 46, 136, 168, 170, 176, 182, 203 n.8, 204 n.4, 206 n.14, 212 n.50, 245 n.67, 249 n.23; in *Sandover*, 4, 8–9, 10, 75, 107, 122–23, 126, 127, 128, 129, 133, 134, 137, 138–39, 141, 146, 149, 150, 151, 152, 153, 181, 182, 226 n.43, 233 n.13, 235 n.23, 239 n.45, 241 n. 61, 243 n.77, 243–44 n.78, 245 n.69, 251 n.45, 252–53 n.45; on Yeats, 110, 132, 134, 146, 241 n.61

Bachelard, Gaston 196, 218 n.81,82
belief, questions of xv, 51–54, 76–77, 83, 88, 92, 122, 207 n.21, 251 n.32; *see also* occult
Bergman, David 203 n.4, 244 n.81
Bishop, Elizabeth 4, 8, 182, 204 n.5, 219 n.87, 251 n.52

Blake, William xiv, xii, 35, 43, 54, 93, 127, 136–37, 151, 156, 212 n.52, 245 n.84
Blasing, Mutlu Konuk 220 n.2, 223 n.24
Bloom, Harold in *Sandover*, 177–81, 245 n.89; on Merrill, 201 n. 2, 241 n.63, 245 n.86, 251 n.32–34; on poetic influence, xvi-xvii, 5–6, 8–9, 13, 21, 170, 172, 176, 203 n.11, 2, 204 n.9, 210 n.42, 211 n.46, 214 n.64, 232 n.10, 240 n.55, 245 n.89, 246 n.90, 247 n.9, 249 n.19, 250 n.26, 251 n.35, 252 n.39, 40, 41, 44; on Yeats, 52, 168, 172, 234 n.20, 237 n.31, 239 n.51, 249 n.20; theories applied to Merrill's writing, 37, 40, 49, 94, 111, 129, 159, 160, 163, 164, 168, 171, 176–77, 181–83, 185, 204 n.8, 214 n.61, 215 n.65, 221 n.16, 237–38 n.37, 238 n.42, 242 n.67, 244 n.80, 246 n.4, 247 n.11, 252 n.38
Bowra, C. W. 219–20 n.1
Bravery, *see* nonchalance
Brisman, Leslie xiv, 19, 54, 56, 65, 112, 133, 134, 201 n.38, 206 n.14, 220 n.8, 223 n.25, 241 n.60, 243 n.77, 245 n.89
Byron, George Gordon 27, 32, 70, 79, 156, 170, 210 n.38, 211 n.42, 212 n.49
Byzantium 16, 73, 74, 100, 115–16, 142,

147, 148, 149, 160, 215 n.63; *see also* Istanbul, Ravenna, Rio de Janiero, Venice

Cavafy, C. P. 5, 182, 250 n.30
cloning 6, 7, 92, 130, 238 n.42; *see also* influence, poetic
condition of fire, xviii, 20 40–45, 48–49, 60, 67, 85, 97, 99–102, 127, 142, 149, 166, 185, 190, 192–93, 216 n.71, 237 n.31; *for Merrill's response, see* waterfall; *see also* sublime
Crane, Hart 17, 18, 27, 38, 210–211 n.42
Croft, Barbara L. 228 n.61

daimon 20, 21, 66, 69, 73, 83, 102, 129, 153, 154, 170, 206 n.14, 207 n. 20, 21, 226 n.44, 229 n.66, 233 n.12, 238 n.39; *see also* mask
Dante xiv, 5–6, 10, 17, 18, 19, 32, 33, 35, 63, 71, 91, 163, 177, 182, 205–206 n.12, 212 n.50, 213 n.53; in *Sandover*, 120, 136, 138, 139, 140, 144, 145, 151, 240 n.56, 243–44 n.78, 245 n.82
de Man, Paul 217 n.75
Demogorgon, as Gabriel 108
Deren, Maya 17, 19, 83–84, 113, 114, 115, 147–48, 149, 234 n.19
Dickinson, Emily 114, 151, 245 n.85
discipline and disciplinary violence 19, 23, 27, 38, 43–44, 47, 68, 69–71, 95, 102, 123, 124, 130, 137, 138–39, 143, 144–45, 148–49, 165, 173, 179, 206 n.18, 210 n.39, 238 n.41, 42, 243 n.72
dispersal (Yeats's False Mask) 57, 75, 172–74, 176, 208 n.26, 234 n.15, 250 n.29; *see also* intensity, mask, simplification
DJ *see* Jackson, David
double-mindedness 3, 12, 49, 52–54, 56, 58, 88, 122, 127, 136, 139, 141, 145, 165, 176, 237 n.37; *see also* belief, dispersal, vacillation
dramatization 41–44, 49, 70, 73, 90, 122, 123, 153, 161, 165, 167, 170, 177, 179, 206 n.18, 207 n.21, 225 n.39, 233 n.13, 235 n.25, 250 n.24; *see*

also mask
Dreaming Back *see* Yeats's *A Vision*

Eliot, T. S., 8, 13, 32, 35, 71, 75, 79, 212 n.49, 224 n.31; in *Sandover*, 116, 128, 129, 130
Ellmann, Richard, 122, 208 n.23

fathers, poetic xvi-xvii, 16, 19, 37, 82, 85, 86, 91–92, 94, 160, 165, 170, 172, 180–82, 203 n.4, 11, 205 n.10, 210 n.39, 218 n.81, 224 n.25, 225 n.42, 233 n.33,34, 245 n.81, 247 n.30, 249 n.22; *see also* influence, paternal *and* influence, poetic
Freud, Sigmund 13, 24–26, 49, 92, 196, 223 n.27
Friar, Kimon "Amherst Days" 17–19; and Merrill, 9, 16–31, 38, 39, 68–69, 70, 71, 72, 95–96, 137, 143, 153, 164, 170, 202 n.3, 203 n.11, 205 n.12, 13, 17, 208 n.27, 210 n.33, 34, 35, 39, 211 n.46, 216 n.71, 243 n.73, 74; "Medusa-Mask" 22–23, 24, 25, 208 n.22, 209 n.29; on Yeats, 18, 216 n.71, 217 n.76, 219 n.1
Frost, Robert 16, 213 n.56, 248 n.12

Gnosticism 36, 41, 137, 216 n.17, 241 n.63
Goethe, Johann Wolfgang v. 137, 138, 232 n.9
Gwiazda, Piotr 202 n.8, 236–37 n.30

Hadas, Rachel 212 n.51
Harrigan, Anthony 30
Hartman, Geoffrey H. 65
Hecht, Anthony 74, 78
homosexuality 9, 10, 15, 19, 21, 29, 47, 60, 88, 134, 162, 203 n.4, 206 n.18, 210 n.41, 218, n.85, 220 n.5, 244 n.81, 247 n.7
Hone, Joseph 214 n.63, 245 n.86
Howard, Richard 87
Howes, Marjorie 237 n.35
Hugo, Victor xiv, 127, 239 n.49
Humphries, Jefferson 250 n.29

Index

influence, maternal 3–4, 8–10, 11, 14, 19, 28–30, 91, 94–95, 204 n.7, 210 n.41, 42, 211 n.43, 44, 45, 233 n.14, 244 n.81, 249 n.22; *see also* muse, maternal

influence, paternal 3–4, 8–10, 11–14, 15, 91, 135, 164; *see also* fathers, poetic

influence, poetic 4–19, 29–31, 32–33, 35, 170–71, 176–77, 181–83, 202 n.3, 218 n.81, 249 n.23; in *Sandover* 9–11, 129–30 178–80, 238 n.42; Merrill's accounts of 4–11, 13–14, 38–39, 181, 203 n.2, 4, 225 n.42, 238 n.40; *see also* Bloom, Harold; Friar, Kimon; **precursor poets**; Yeats, W. B.

innocence 40, 41, 44, 45, 72, 93–94, 122–23, 132, 150, 157, 174, 187, 208 n.8, 212 n.52, 215 n.69, 250 n.27, 28, 254 n.6

intensity 44, 45, 71, 75, 79, 86, 110, 114, 127, 135, 165–66, 170–72, 174–76, 224 n.32, 234 n.15, 148 n.18, *see also* simplification

Istanbul 73–74 224 n.31; *see also* Byzantium, Ravenna, Rio de Janiero, Venice

Jackson, David xv, 19, 39, 51, 63, 83, 84, 98, 197, 143, 153, 219 n.1, 221 n.15, 243 n.72; and punishment, 130, 138–39, 179, 238 n.41, 42; in *Sandover*, xv, 54, 130–21, 123, 128–30, 133, 137–39, 142–43, 144–45, 150, 151, 179, 234 n. 26, 236 n.29; *see also* discipline

Jeffares, A. Norman 59, 214 n.63

JM *see* Merrill, James

Jung, Carl 101, 196, 218 n.82, 232 n.9, 241 n.63

Kalstone, David 76, 219 n.87, 224 n.34, 254 n.7

Keats, John xiv, 18, 20, 30–31, 32, 33, 35, 63, 85, 95, 152, 202 n.3, 212 n.50, 235 n.23

Keller, Lynn 245 n.87, 253 n.1

Kennedy, X. J. 230 n.2

Kenner, Hugh 202 n.3

Lacan, Jacques 210 n.39
Lehman, David 129, 218 n.85
Lodeizen, Hans 254 n.5
Lowell, Robert 12,17, 107, 108, 244 n.81
Lurie, Alison 243 n.72

Mallarmé, Stéphane 5, 118, 169, 176, 244 n.76

Mariani, Andrea 144, 201 n.2, 243–44 n.78, 245 n.82

Martin, Robert K. 218 n.85

mask xiv, 2, 20, 21, 33, 55, 60, 62, 66–67, 69, 73, 76, 79, 80, 86, 88, 95, 113, 115, 120, 161, 165, 170, 173–74, 176, 201 n.2, 206 n.18, 207 n.21, 208 n.22, 24, 26, 27, 225 n.39, 227 n.54, 233 n.13, 234 n.15, 237 n.33, 238 n.39, 246 n.91, 247 n.10, 248 n.15, 250 n.25; *see also* daimon, dispersal, dramatization

masturbation, and writing 47, 72, 78, 218 n.86, 224 n.29, 36

Materer, Timothy 218 n.82, 239 n.48, 246 n.2, 248 n.14, 254 n.5

Matthews, Steven 201–202 n.2, 221 n.18, 245 n.88

McClatchy, J. D. 3, 14, 40, 85, 102–103, 128, 201 n.1, 210 n.38, 248 n.16

Medusa 22–28, 29, 209 n.31, 210 n.33, 211 n.43; *see also* Merrill's "Medusa"

Mercury, also Hermes 45, 132, 162, 250 n.25

Merrill, Charles E. *see* influence, paternal *and* fathers, poetic

Merrill, Helen Ingram *see* influence, maternal *and* muse, maternal

Merrill, James and Harold Bloom 177–80, 241 n.63, 245n, 86, 251 n.32–34; and Kimon Friar 9, 16–31, 38, 39, 95–96, 202 n.3, 203 n.11, 206 n.13, 17, 210 n.34, 35, 39, 211 n.46, 216 n.71; and father 3–4, 8–10, 11–14, 15, 91, 135, 164; and mother 3–4, 8–10, 11, 14, 19, 28–30, 91, 94–95, 204 n.7, 210 n.41, 42, 211 n.43, 44, 45, 233 n.14; on poetic influence 4–11, 13–14, 38–39, 181, 203 n.2, 4, 225 n.42, 238 n.40; in *Sandover* xv, 9,

111–15, 117, 120–21, 123–33, 134, 139–46, 149–50, 151–55, 171, 179; *see also* homosexuality, Ouija board, Ravenna, Yeats; works:
"About the Phoenix" 40, 44, 118, 176, 185–94, 254 n.5, 7
"After the Fire" 85, 97
annotations in Yeats's *Essays and Introductions* 105–109
annotations in Yeats' *A Vision* 51–55, 83–84
"Arabian Night" 14, 164, 247 n.10
The Bait 39, 54, 221 n.14
"The Broken Bowl" 22, 28, 34–35, 176
"The Broken Home" 4, 8, 12–13, 14, 60, 62, 67, 217 n.80, 240 n.54
The Changing Light at Sandover xiv-xv, xvii, xviii, 17, 18–19, 35, 54, 83, 84, 92, 99, 100–101, 106–154, 155, 174, 177–81, 202 n.8, 204 n.8, 205 n.12, 213 n.58, 219 n.07, 220 n.5, 7, 9, 10, 230 n.3, 231 n.5, 232 n.7, 8, 234 n.15, 235 n.23, 238 n.39, 239 n.48, 240 n.58, 252 n.39, 45; manuscript variations 126, 128–29, 136, 139, 140, 146, 149, 153, 178, 197–200, 229 n.67, 236 n.30, 239 n.46, 50, 242 n.66, 243 n.69, 244 n.79, 245 n.86, 251 n.33, 253 n.3
"Charles on Fire" 60, 67
"Childlessness" 60, 61, 177
"Chimes for Yahya" 85, 102–103, 229 n.68, 234 n.19
"Christmas Tree" 248 n.18
"Clearing the Title" 143, 155–56, 246 n.1
"The Cosmological Eye" 169, 213 n.57
"Days of 1964" 60, 226 n.44
"Days of 1971" 226 n.44
"Days of 1935" 217 n.80, 254 n.6
The (Diblos) Notebook 8, 19, 20–22, 26–28, 60, 68–73, 96, 143, 152, 207 n.18, 208 n.24, 210 n.34, 35, 224 n.29, 243 n.74, 246 n.90
A Different Person: A Memoir 4, 7, 9, 10, 11, 15, 16, 17, 19, 28, 30, 32, 38–39, 73–74, 106, 153, 164, 177,

204 n.7, 206 n.17, 207 n.21, 210 n.34, 41, 214 n.64, 215 n.65, 66, 218 n.81, 219 n.87, 90, 220 n.1, 221 n.14, 236 n.30, 242 n.66, 248 n.13 251 n.38
"The Doodler" 222 n.21, 234 n.21
"Dreams about Clothes" 62, 98
"The Fire Poem" 40–44, 49, 110, 166, 171, 176, 214 n.62, 215 n.68, 216 n.72
"The Flint Eye" 36, 213 n.57
"Flying from Byzantium" 85, 86, 88–90, 91, 96, 177, 202 n.3, 227 n.51
"For Proust" 60, 66, 80, 204 n.7
"The Forms of Death" 29–30, 31, 51, 204 n.7, 210 n.42, 211 n.45, 215 n.65
"The Friend of the Fourth Decade" 85, 86–87
"From the Cupola" 60, 73, 75, 79–82, 97, 177, 225 n.39, 40, 254 n.6
"Home Fires" 166, 181
"Hourglass" 95–96
"The House" 212 n.50, 254 n.6
"The Image Maker" 165, 248 n.14
"Keats on board ship for what we shall call Rome" 30–31, 95
"Last Words" 85, 86, 90–91, 226 n.44, 227 n.51
Letter to Dr. Chung, 220 n.5
"Little Fanfare for Felix Magowan" 61
"Log" 85, 97, 177
"Lorelei" 85, 86
"Losing the Marbles" 163–64, 177, 181
"Lost in Translation" 102
"Marsyas" 176, 205 n.10, 249 n.23
"Matinees" 7, 72, 85, 86, 91–94, 145
"McKane's Falls" 97, 99–102, 177
"Medusa" 18 22, 23–24, 25–26, 27, 28, 176, 202 n.3, 208 n.26, 27, 210 n.33, 212 n.50, 215 n.69
"Monday Morning" 161
"More Enterprise" 85, 86, 87, 88, 177, 202 n.3, 227 n.48
"Mornings in a New House" 94–95, 211 n.44
"Parable" (in "Four Little Poems") 36–37, 214 n.63

"The Parrot" 33–34, 213 n.54
"The Prism" 60, 66
"Prose of Departure" 7, 183
"Rescue" 166
"A Room at the Heart of Things" 55, 161–63, 177, 247 n.7
"Santorini: Stopping the Leak" 10, 156–61, 177, 181, 246 n.2
"Self Portrait in Tyvek™ Windbreaker" 166, 181, 246 n.1
The Seraglio 8, 39, 57–58, 81, 83, 218 n.86, 220 n.10, 230 n.2
"Swimming by Night" 62, 135, 224 n.29
"Table Talk" 66
" A Tenancy" 60, 62–63, 83, 177, 182, 222 n.20
"The Thousand and Second Night" 73–79, 80, 81, 82, 88, 176, 177, 221 n.19, 224 n.36, 225 n.37, 38
"Transfigured Bird" 33, 176, 212 n.50, 51, 213 n.53
"Upward Look" 27, 155, 168, 181
"Urban Convalescence" 60, 63, 64–65, 168, 172, 176, 222 n.23, 223 n.24
"A View of the Burning" 40, 43, 44–49, 171, 218 n.84
"Violent Pastoral" 60, 67–68, 73, 134, 177, 223 n.26
"A Vision of the Garden" 173
"Voices from the Other World" 54–55, 56–57, 113, 220 n.9
"Vol. XLIV, No. 3" 167–68, 248 n.16, 249 n.19
"Watching the Dance" 59–60
"We Walk in Woods" 82, 225 n.42
"Words for the Familiar Spirit" 58–60, 221 n.15, 16
Milton, John, xv, xvi, 13, 17, 32, 127, 211n, 240n, 241 n, 249 n, 252 n.44
MM *see* Mitsotaki, Maria
muse, maternal 9, 11, 14
mother, *see* influence, maternal *and* muse, maternal
Mitsotáki, Maria 4, 8, 9, 10, 11, 107, 126, 137, 138, 139, 140, 150, 151, 171, 172, 178, 181, 204 n.5, 6, 233 n.13, 241 n.64, 246 n.91

Mouflouzelis, Strato 58, 83, 84, 131, 226 n.44
mythopoesis xv, xvii, 17, 20, 23, 25, 71, 80, 109, 111, 116, 188, 190, 202 n.5, 228 n.46

Nancy, Jena-Luc 252 n.43
Nietzsche, Friedrich 66, 93, 167, 228 n.55, 239 n. 49
nonchalance xvii, 39, 55, 56–58, 59–60, 62, 67, 73, 79, 82, 85, 97, 98, 112, 127, 155, 167, 220 n.8, 9

occult, the xv, xvii, xviii, 17, 19, 51–54, 55, 56–60, 64, 67, 81, 83, 86, 94, 98–101, 107–109, 116, 120–23, 124, 138, 143, 177, 179, 183, 201 n.2, 202 n.5, 8, 219 n.1, 220 n.10, 224 n.29, 231 n.5, 238 n.41, 243 n.72, 251,n.32, 34; *see also* belief
otherness 147, 159, 172, 235 n.23, 236 n.25, 244 n.80; *see also* dispersal
Ouija board xv, 4, 10, 20, 39, 51, 56–60, 81, 82, 83, 85, 86, 97, 99, 108, 110–11, 128, 132, 137, 139, 143, 183, 215 n.66, 219 n.1, 230 n.4, 232 n.9, 236 n.30, 234 n.16

parody xvii, 40, 65, 69, 80, 85, 89–90, 102–103, 110, 111, 115, 118–21, 124–26, 127–28, 132, 134, 139, 141, 144–45, 147–49, 158, 160, 165, 176, 179, 180–81, 192, 229 n.68, 236 n.30
Pater, Walter 22, 36, 103, 115, 127, 147
Phase One, Phase Fifteen *see* Yeats's *A Vision*
Polito, Robert 115, 147, 148, 201n, 229n, 233n, 237n, 238n, 250n
Pope, Alexander 5, 32, 114, 151, 170, 212n, 217n
possibility, poetic 13, 47, 87, 170
Pound, Ezra 12, 17, 32, 71, 129, 141, 204n, 234n
power, poetic 134, 165, 171–72, 181, 204 n.6, 250 n.27; voice of 170–72, 174–76
precursor poets *see* Auden, Bishop, Blake, Byron, Cavafy, Crane, Dante, Eliot,

Goethe, Keats, Mallarmé, Milton, Pater, Pope, Proust, Rilke, Stevens
Proust, Marcel 4,5, 6, 7, 8, 32, 65, 66, 92, 95, 115, 116, 138, 150, 151, 152, 177, 182, 210–11 n.42, 212 n.50, 236 n.25, 251 n.34; *see also* Merrill's "For Proust"
punishment, *see* discipline
Prometheus 40, 113, 140, 141, 162, 170, 218 n.81, 223 n.26, 242 n.67

quarrelling, self- xv, xvii-xviii, 19, 31, 70, 73, 74, 82, 105, 110, 115, 118, 132, 133, 134, 139, 141, 142, 148, 149, 152, 155, 170, 172, 243 n.69

Raine, Kathleen 212 n.52, 218 n.82
Rajan, Tilottama 109, 233 n.31
Ramazani, Jahan 211 n.45, 219 n.90, 247–48 n.11
Ravenna xviii, 38–40, 73–74, 214 n.64, 215 n.65; *see also* Byzantium, Istanbul, Rio de Janeiro, Venice
receptivity 5, 6–7, 8, 9, 124, 172–73, 237 n.34, 238 n.40, 42, 248 n.18
resistance 12, 22, 24, 136, 137, 180, 183, 204 n.8, 207 n.21
Rilke, Rainer Maria 5, 15, 16, 17, 32, 136, 138, 156, 170, 176, 182, 212 n.50, 218 n.81, 242 n.65
Rio de Janeiro 76; *see also* Byzantium, Istanbul, Ravenna, Venice
romanticism 52, 65, 66, 76, 93–94, 117, 147, 172, 175, 209 n.32, 233 n.11, 252 n.40, 44
Rothenberg, Albert 210–11 n.42

Sáez, Richard 152
Said, Edward W. xvi
scene, of instruction 14–15, 41, 49, 148, 204 n.8, 219 n.90; **primal** scene 11–14, 49, 157–58, 204 n.8
Sedgwick, Eve Kosofsky 182, 252–53 n.45
Selinger, Eric Murphy 227 n.51
Shelley, Percy Bysshe xv, 45, 107, 108, 120, 141, 231n, 232 n.6, 241n
Siebers, Tobin 209 n.31, 32, 210 n.37
simplification 42, 45, 48, 71, 73, 86, 110, 120, 126, 127–28, 129–30, 135, 141, 149,156, 165, 169, 172, 174, 176, 185, 186, 187, 189, 190, 191, 224 n.32, 234 n.15, 240 n.54, 241 n.60, 242 n.68, 248 n.17, 18; *see also* intensity
Sloss, Henry 54, 98, 220 n.9
Smith, Evan Lansing 218 n.82
Soul in Judgment *see* Yeats's *A Vision*
Spiegelman, Willard 154
spiritualism, *see* occult
Stade, George 6
Stevens, Wallace 5, 8, 17, 18, 32, 79, 101, 137, 138, 170, 176, 202 n.3, 206 n.4, 208–209 n.27, 212 n.50, 213–14 n.57, 217 n.76, 251 n.32, 34
Strato, *see* Mouflouzelis, Strato
sublime, the 163, 175, 234 n.35; *see also* absolute, condition of fire, waterfall

technique, as formal discipline 18, 21, 42, 65, 105–106–136, 157, 165, 172, 215 n.65; *see also* artifice
thunder, in Merrill's poetry 112–14, 117, 118, 134, 166, 179, 223 n.26, 235 n.21, 24

Unity of Being *see* Yeats's *A Vision*

vacillation 2, 16, 24, 43, 49, 58, 59, 74, 79, 86, 89, 93, 115, 122, 130, 160, 162, 166, 167, 170 171–72, 189, 224 n.32; *see also* dispersal, double-mindedness
Van Duyn, Mona 215 n.68
Vendler, Helen 4, 127, 146, 211 n.45, 229 n.66, 237–38 n.37, 240 n.57, 246 n.1
Venice 115–17, 147, 179, 215 n.65
von Hallberg, Robert 218 n.85

waterfalls, in Merrill's poetry 99–103, 228 n.62, 229 n.67; *see also* absolute, condition of fire, sublime
Westover Jeff, 225 n.39
WBY *see* Yeats, W. B.
WHA *see* Auden, W. H.
Wilde, Oscar 231–32 n.5, 245 n.84
Williams, William Carlos 12, 118, 214

Index

n.60
Whitman, Walt 113, 142, 210–11 n.42
wit 9, 32, 57, 60, 64, 65, 71–72, 103, 106, 113, 133, 137, 155, 156, 163, 165, 167, 181, 220 n.10, 234 n.19, 235 n.24, 243 n.74, 252 n.43
Wordsworth, William xvi, 13, 43, 152, 170, 192, 211 n.47, 217 n.77, 246 n.92
Wylie, Elinor xii, 5, 6, 15, 17, 38, 170, 171, 205 n.10, 208 n.27, 212 n.50, 232 n.30

Yeats, William Butler xii–xvi, xvii–xviii, 176–77, 183; in Merrill's early poetry 32–49, 185–94; in Merrill's poetry (1957–76) 56–82, 85–103; in post-*Sandover* writing 155–69; in *Sandover* 110–54, 178–81; works:
"Adam's Curse" 93, 121, 122, 136, 163, 201 n.1, 209 n.28, 229 n.63
"All Soul's Night" 229.65
"Byzantium" 45, 49, 67, 68, 70, 75, 85, 87, 97, 102, 113, 114, 115–18, 130, 135, 148, 158, 159, 160, 161, 163, 190, 246 n.3, 254 n.5
"The Circus Animals' Desertion" 28, 33, 34, 43, 61, 62, 64, 72–73, 76, 85, 86, 88, 124, 153, 156, 166, 167, 227 n.51, 241 n.60
"A Coat" 7, 37, 61, 86, 87–88, 98, 156
"The Cold Heaven" 213 n.55
"Coole and Ballylee, 1931" 216 n.75
"Crazy Jane and Jack the Journeyman" 150
"Crazy Jane on the Day of Judgment" 76
"Crazy Jane Talks with the Bishop" 34, 35, 76, 162
"Cuchulain Comforted" 34, 85, 114, 182, 204 n.7
"A Dialogue of Self and Soul" 76, 77, 78, 85, 92, 100, 112, 113, 114, 164, 179
"Easter, 1916" 62, 68, 242 n.66
Essays and Introductions 151, 152, 230 n.1, 232 n.9, 235 n.23; Merrill's reading of 105–109
"The Fascination of What's Difficult"
202 n.4
"The Fisherman" 56, 64, 75, 213 n.55
"The Gyres" 29, 36, 59, 85, 209 n.28, 218 n.85, 221 n.36, 234 n.21
"Her Vision in the Wood" 114
"In Memory of Eva Gore-Booth and Con Markievicz" 45
"In Memory of Major Robert Gregory" 106, 230 n.3
"Lapis Lazuli" xiv, 36, 48, 67, 70, 85, 98, 113, 114, 124, 134, 142, 150, 151, 153, 161, 162, 163, 192, 213 n.57, 223 n.25, 246 n.2, 247 n.7
"Leda and the Swan" 35, 60, 68, 97, 213 n.57
"Love and Death" 228.63
"Man and the Echo" 43,36, 64, 114
"Meditations in Time of Civil War" 20, 85, 93, 126, 163
"Men Improve with the Years" 33
"News for the Delphic Oracle" 34
"Nineteen Hundred and Nineteen" 163, 235 n.22
"Pardon, old fathers, if you still remain" 61
Per Amica Silentia Lunae 20 21, 22, 31, 40–45, 48, 54, 58, 60, 64, 66, 72, 100, 109, 110, 124, 137, 139, 156, 161, 170, 186, 206 n.18, 207 n.20, 21, 216 n.71, 73, 225 n.39, 226 n.44, 227 n.54, 234 n.20, 238 n.39, 241 n.64, 247 n.10, 248 n.15, 250 n.25, 251 n.32, 254 n.6
"The Phases of the Moon" 18, 85, 118–20, 209 n.28, 220 n.7, 237 n.31
"A Prayer for My Daughter" 93, 122, 132, 157
"Sailing to Byzantium" 16, 22, 31, 33, 34, 39, 40, 42, 43, 45, 47, 49, 62, 65, 67, 73, 74, 76, 85, 88, 89, 90, 91, 92, 39, 94, 97, 99, 100, 101, 102, 113, 114, 115–18, 126, 130, 131, 134–35, 148, 149, 156, 157, 158, 161, 171, 172, 185–94, 202 n.3, 217 n.76, 229 n.68, 236 n.29, 240 n.86, 246 n.2, 254 n.5
"The Second Coming" 35, 59, 68, 69, 73, 85, 102, 103, 112, 114, 122,

124, 142, 148, 149, 162, 167–68, 194, 209 n.28, 221 n.16, 229 n.68, 246 n.5, 248 n.16
"The Statues" 22, 34, 75, 163
"Under Ben Bulben" 64, 133, 206 n.15, 213 n.55,
"Vacillation" 44, 45, 48, 62, 63, 72, 76, 77, 80, 91, 95, 100, 113, 114, 122, 126, 131, 149, 156, 158, 162, 163, 190, 194, 217 n.78, 79, 221 n.12, 224 n.35, 236 n.29, 239 n.48, 248 n.13
A Vision 5, 7, 71, 87, 94, 100, 108, 156, 161, 162, 179, 191, 202 n.5, 6, 205 n.12, 207 n.21, 208 n. 23,25, 214 n.63, 221 n.21, 222 n.20, 21, 223 n.28, 227 n.54, 228 n.61, 62, 229 n.65, 234 n.16, 237 n.33, 238 n.39, 239 n.47, 52, 245 n.84, 247 n.8; Dreaming Back 87, 96, 131, 132, 226 n.46; and Kimon Friar 18, 216 n.71; in *Sandover* xv, 110, 111, 118–21, 123, 124, 125, 127, 131, 132, 137, 139, 141, 148, 152; Merrill's reading of 51–55, 83–84, 208 n.27, 219 n.1, 229 n.7, 226 n.44, 251 n.32; Phase One 120, 124–25, 137, 223 n.28; Phase Fifteen 54, 55, 120, 126, 137, 161, 223 n.28; Soul in Judgment 128, 131, 222 n.20, 228 n.57, 239 n.52; Unity of Being 20, 21, 57, 66, 71, 126, 131, 221 n.12, 234 n.15, 246 n.91; *see* condition of fire, dispersal, mask

Yenser, Stephen 66, 72, 80, 85, 87, 91, 98, 130, 131, 156, 201 n.2, 217 n.76, 221–22 n.19, 224 n.31, 224–25 n.36, 225 n.37, 38, 228 n.59, 60, 234 n.19, 236 n.26, 240 n.56
YES & NO *see* double-mindedness, vaccillation

Zimmer, Heinrich 165, 176
Zimmerman, Lee 218 n.85

Copyright Acknowledgments

All selections from the work of W. B. Yeats reprinted with the permission of Scribner, an imprint of Simon & Schuster Adult Publishing Group, from THE COLLECTED WORKS OF W. B. YEATS, VOLUME 1: THE POEMS, REVISED, edited by Richard J. Finneran. (New York: Scribner, 1997.) Selections from "All Soul's Night," "Leda and the Swan," "Meditations in Time of Civil War," "Nineteen Hundred and Nineteen," and "Sailing to Byzantium" Copyright © 1928 by The Macmillan Company; copyright renewed © 1956 by Georgie Yeats. Selections from "Easter, 1916," A Prayer for My Daughter," and "The Second Coming" Copyright © 1924 by the Macmillan Company; copyright renewed © 1952 by Bertha Georgie Yeats. Selections from "Byzantium," "Coole and Ballylee, 1931," "Crazy Jane and Jack the Journeyman," "Crazy Jane on the Day of Judgement," "Crazy Jane Talks with the Bishop," "A Dialogue of Self and Soul," "Her Vision in the Wood," "In Memory of Eva Gore-Booth and Con Markievicz," and "Vacillation" Copyright © 1933 by The Macmillan Company; copyright renewed © 1961 by Bertha Georgie Yeats. Selections from "The Circus Animals' Desertion," "Cuchulain Comforted," "The Gyres," "Lapis Lazuli," "Man and the Echo," "News for the Delphic Oracle," "Statues," and "Under Ben Bulben" Copyright © 1940 by Georgie Yeats; copyright renewed © 1968 by Bertha Georgie Yeats, Michael Butler Yeats, and Anne Yeats.

Quotations from ESSAYS AND INTRODUCTIONS reprinted with the permission of Scribner, an imprint of Simon & Schuster Adult Publishing Group. Copyright © 1961 by Mrs. W. B. Yeats.

Quotations from AUTOBIOGRAPHY OF WILLIAM BUTLER YEATS reprinted with the permission of Scribner, an imprint of Simon & Schuster Adult Publishing Group. Copyright © 1924 by The Macmillan Company; copyright renewed © 1952 by Bertha Georgie Yeats.

Quotations from A VISION reprinted with the permission of Scribner, an imprint of Simon & Schuster Adult Publishing Group. Copyright © 1937 by W. B. Yeats; copyright renewed © 1965 by Bertha Georgie Yeats and Anne Yeats.

Quotations from MYTHOLOGIES reprinted with the permission of Scribner, an imprint of Simon & Schuster Adult Publishing Group. Copyright © 1959 by Mrs. W. B. Yeats.

All selections from the work of James Merrill appear by permission of Alred A. Knopf, a division of Random House, Inc. Poems from THE CHANGING LIGHT AT SANDOVER © 1980, 1982 by James Merrill. Selections from A DIFFERENT PERSON © 1993 by James Merrill. Poems from COLLECTED POEMS © 2001 by the Literary Estate of James Merrill at Washington University.

Quotations from the first "Duino Elegy," from the *Selected Poetry of Rainer Maria Rilke*, trans. Stephen Mitchell, reprinted with the permission of Alfred A. Knopf, a division of Random House, Inc. Copyright © 1982.

Quotations from *Recitative: Prose by James Merrill* are copyrighted by The Literary Estate of James Merrill at Washington University and used by permission of the Literary Executors.

For Product Safety Concerns and Information please contact our EU representative GPSR@taylorandfrancis.com
Taylor & Francis Verlag GmbH, Kaufingerstraße 24, 80331 München, Germany

www.ingramcontent.com/pod-product-compliance
Lightning Source LLC
Chambersburg PA
CBHW070302010526
44108CB00039B/1467